Nikolai Klyuev

Northwestern University Press
Studies in Russian Literature and Theory

Nikolai Klyuev

TIME AND TEXT, PLACE AND POET

Michael Makin

NORTHWESTERN UNIVERSITY PRESS/EVANSTON, ILLINOIS

Northwestern University Press
www.nupress.northwestern.edu

Printed in the United States of America

ISBN 978-0-8101-3483-6

The Library of Congress has cataloged the original, hardcover edition as follows:

Makin, Michael.
Nikolai Klyuev : time and text, place and poet / Michael Makin.
p. cm. — (Studies in Russian literature and theory)
Includes bibliographical references and index.
ISBN 978-0-8101-2657-2 (cloth : alk. paper)
1. Kli͡uev, Nikolaĭ Alekseevich. I. Title. II. Series: Studies in Russian literature and theory.
PG3476.K544Z76 2010
891.713—dc22

2009040434

To my wife, Alina

Contents

Preface

I first became interested in Nikolai Klyuev while working on Marina Tsvetaeva. Searching for points of contrast and comparison for her folkloric *poemy*, I read Bazanov's article on Klyuev's narrative poem *Pogorel'shchina*, and then that work itself (both are discussed in the following pages). I was fascinated, at times mesmerized, by Klyuev's language and by the story told in *Pogorel'shchina.* I was also intrigued to see that Bazanov had published in the Soviet Union a scholarly article on a poem which itself had not, at that time (1979), been published there. Reading through *Sochineniya* (the two-volume edition of Klyuev published in Munich in 1969, which was for many years the most complete and reliable edition of his poetry and prose) and then looking at the glasnost-era publications of the poet, I was even more fascinated by his poetry, by his story, and by the story of his texts (the three things which form the core of this book). I began to work on him, first casually, and then more seriously. Reading Klyuev, even as provisionally and hesitantly as I have often read him, is a serious challenge, perhaps a task for a lifetime (especially, it must be confessed, for a non-native speaker). My desk and the floor of my study have often been covered in piles of books more varied in character than is usually the case, even with the most demanding of Russian authors. Many dictionaries and atlases, books on and from the Old Belief, guides to the folk arts of the Russian north, collections of medieval literature, architectural and artistic compendia, and encyclopedias of popular beliefs have demanded space in my study alongside philological volumes and collected works.

This book is the result of that reading, of my fascination and my struggles with Nikolai Klyuev. It aims to look at Klyuev as both a "philological" and a "culturological" (to use the Russian terms) phenomenon, and aspires to be of interest not only to readers of literature, but also to anyone engaged in the study of modern Russian culture. I hope that it will help to introduce Klyuev and his work to the English-speaking reader, while also using the example of the poet to discuss some of the most intriguing cultural problems and paradoxes of Russian culture, as they appeared in the later decades of Russian modernism, in the early decades of Soviet power, and again in the late and post-Soviet years. In other words, I have tried to write a book which describes and analyzes Klyuev's poetry and the cultural phenomenon of the poet himself, while also pursuing a number of general thematic lines.

My own research, Russian scholarship on Klyuev, and, in recent years, the Russian Internet have taken me repeatedly, if "virtually," to distant corners of Russian culture, and to distant corners of Russia itself. And Klyuev has also taken me physically to many parts of Russia. My Klyuev travels began in 1994, when I spent six weeks in Russia, and had the great good fortune to meet several of the leading Klyuev scholars, all of whom were gracious with their time and advice—Sergei Subbotin from the Institute of World Literature, Lyudmila Kiseleva from Kiev University, Konstantin Azadovsky and the late Aleksandr Mikhailov from Pushkin House, Elena Markova from the Petrozavodsk Russian Academy of Sciences Center—and also to meet the equally welcoming and generous Vitalii Shentalinsky, who had discovered and published (from the archives of the KGB) Klyuev's *Pesn' o Velikoi Materi,* long thought irretrievably lost. Moreover, I had the great good fortune to be invited to the annual *Klyuevskie chteniya* (Klyuev readings) in Vytegra, the town in the center of Klyuev's home region. That and my subsequent visits to Vytegra shaped greatly my thoughts on the poet and his place in Russian culture. As well as regular travels to Moscow and St. Petersburg, my visits to Kargopol' (Archangel oblast), Kirov-Vyatka, Sovetsk (formerly Kukarka, Kirov oblast), and Tomsk have been especially enlightening, although many other Klyuev topoi remain on my wish list.

This book could not possibly have been written without the help of the scholars I mention above—each of them has been very helpful and supportive—but I should particularly like to thank Sergei Subbotin, who has generously given of his time and patiently listened to my ignorant questions on many occasions. Others who have helped me a great deal include Lyudmila Yatskevich and her team at Vologda University (especially Sergei Smol'nikov and Svetlana Golovkina); Vladimir Semibratov from Kirov-Vyatka; Aleksei Kazakov from Chelyabinsk; Vasilii Firsov from Petrozavodsk; Valerii Domansky from Tomsk University; Boris Sokolovsky, director of the Audio Archives at the State Literary Museum, Moscow; and Gordon McVay from the University of Bristol. Lev Pichurin was my guide in Tomsk. I am especially grateful to Tamara Makarova, director of the Vytegra Museum, who has welcomed me to her hometown on numerous occasions, and gone out of her way to help me in all of my, sometimes eccentric, pursuits. For me, as for so many other *klyuevedy,* the trip to Vytegra is rewarding and exciting largely because of what she has achieved over many years and against the odds in what has become my *vtoraya rodina* (second homeland). The *klyuevedy* themselves are a very special group, and I am proud to be a bit-player in the ongoing story of the exploration of the Klyuev continent beside such distinguished and warm-hearted colleagues.

Many other colleagues, friends, and associates have helped me in my research. Among them I should especially like to thank Viktor and Tamara Zakharov, Mikhail Aizenberg, Elena Krasnoshchekova, Eugenia Gori, and Vadim Besprozvany, all of whom provided me with very helpful, often otherwise inaccessible, materials.

The staff of the Russian State Library and the Russian State Archive of Literature and the Arts, both in Moscow, provided vital assistance, and I am especially grateful to the director of the latter, Tat'yana Goryaeva, for the archive's assistance in my work on Klyuev's verse collection *L'vinyi khleb* in 2003.

My research has been supported by the Center for Russian and East European Studies and by the Department of Slavic Languages and Literatures at the University of Michigan, and by a short-term research grant from the International Research and Exchanges Board. Successive chairs of my department have allowed me to abandon my students for ten days in October to attend the *Klyuevskie chteniya;* Professor David Potter, erstwhile director of the Alice Lloyd Hall Scholars Program at the University of Michigan, provided generous research funding in return for a little teaching, and his support also helped me attend the annual Klyuev meetings. Conferences and seminars at the University of Michigan have provided a vital arena for me to try out my ideas on Klyuev, and I have also been fortunate enough to present papers on him at very helpful conferences at Ohio State University and at the University of Exeter, as well as at the *Klyuevskie chteniya* in Vytegra. The comments and encouragement I have received from these various venues have been of great importance in sustaining my pursuit of the keys to Klyuev.

I am more grateful than I can say to all the people listed above, and to many others, unnamed but essential not only in the joyful business of researching but also in the painful business of writing and, after great struggles, completing this book. What virtues the book may have are in large part because of the support I received; its flaws are, of course, entirely my own responsibility.

On the practical side, I also thank my parents-in-law, Oleg and Nina Ryabkov, who have greeted me, housed me, fed me, helped me make trains and planes, and ensured that no visit to Moscow, however brief, was ever dull. The late Viktoriya Vasil'evna Ryabkova, my father-in-law's mother, also made great contributions, not least at the stove, and I am most grateful for her time, efforts, and companionship. Equally generous with their time, their cars, their apartment, and their ability to arrange for me complex travel at short notice have been my sister-in-law and brother-in-law Viktoriya and

Sergei Nevodnichii. The late Marina Grigor'eva and her husband Anton Shtolyakov were many times generous hosts on their island of peace in Nemchinovka, and provided seemingly endless logistic assistance and advice. In St. Petersburg (and in Lemovzha) I was many times the guest of Vasilii and Natal'ya Morozov, whose friendship, generosity, and practical support made my visits to the northern capital one of the greatest pleasures among the many brought by travel in Russia. Vasilii has always been ready to abandon his own work in order to help me with mine, and the leisure time we spent together in town and country has provided some of the happiest moments of each trip. His willingness to accompany me, on several occasions, from St. Petersburg to Vytegra has not only provided me with the best traveling companion one could hope for, but has also enabled me to travel in the comfort of a private car (Vasilii's) along roads where those restricted to public transport encounter considerable discomfort. My generous friends German Krassil'shchikov and Svetlana Nikitina also worked hard to ensure that no trip to St. Petersburg was dull, and German also added most welcome companionship to one Vytegra trip. Vladimir and Nina Semibratov were genial hosts, and Vladimir was another engaging traveling companion as we made our way along the Vyatka River where Klyuev "waited out" several summers (see chapter 2). In Vologda I have been welcomed with warmth and hospitality on several occasions by Professor Yatskevich, her colleagues, and her family, and by the staff of the Vologda Oblast Library. In Bristol, Professor Neil and Maggie Cornwell opened their house to me on a flying visit, and I thank them too. Fedor and Tat'yana Kostitsyn were wonderful hosts during three rewarding days spent in Koshtugi, and our driver Valentin Sychev was a patient and helpful guide (whom I thank for my first sighting of a bear in the wild—*posol ot medvedya* indeed). Veniamin Tampio has been a tireless guide and kind friend on several of my recent visits to the Vytegra area.

Small parts of my commentary on Klyuev and prophecy first appeared in my article "Nikolai Kliuev—Prophet of Loss," *Slavic and East European Journal,* volume 49, number 4 (2005). Small parts of my discussions of the polemics around Klyuev's identity first appeared in my article "Whose Kliuev, Who Is Kliuev? Polemics of Identity and Poetry," *Slavonic and East European Review,* volume 85, number 2 (April 2007). I am grateful to these journals for permission to reproduce passages from those articles in this book.

I owe a special debt to one person, without whom I could not have undertaken the research nor managed the writing of this book—my wife Alina, who has been a constant source of support and guidance, who believed in this project and its author when less committed readers might have wavered, who has been an invaluable collaborator on several Klyuev projects, and who has also repeatedly taken on such mundane tasks as teaching for me while I make my visits to Olonia, reading and commenting on my work, helping me with my and Klyuev's Russian, editing the work I have presented and published in Russian, and last, but by no means least, looking after our three sons, Gordon, Neil, and Nigel (two became three while I worked on this book), when their father had abandoned them for Klyuev. To her I dedicate this book.

Note to the Reader

Russian is transliterated in this book according to British Standard 2979:1958, without diacritical marks. I find this system, and not only for patriotic reasons, the most efficient at telling the Russophone reader what the Russian is, while giving the non-Russophone reader some chance of pronouncing the words. An exception is made for proper names familiar in an established form (thus "Mandelstam," for example), and for all last names that end in *skii;* they become *sky,* as in "Mayakovsky" and "Azadovsky." References are provided in endnotes, with works cited fully on first appearance and subsequently in short form (details may be checked again in the bibliography). There are three exceptions: Klyuev's verse, whenever possible, is quoted from *Serdtse edinoroga* (*Heart of the Unicorn*), edited by Viktor Garnin, with an introduction by Aleksandr Mikhailov (St. Petersburg, 1999), and when necessary from *Sochineniya* (*Works*), two volumes, edited by Gleb Struve and Boris Filippov (Munich, 1969); Klyuev's prose and letters are quoted, wherever possible, from *Slovesnoe drevo* (*Tree of Words*), edited by Viktor Garnin, with an introduction by Aleksandr Mikhailov (St. Petersburg, 2003). These references are given in the text of the book within parentheses (often at the end of the translations of titles): to *Serdtse edinoroga* simply as a "page number, preceded by a comma" (for example, 160); to *Sochineniya,* in the form "volume number, colon, page number" (for example, 1:481); and to *Slovesnoe drevo* in the form "*Sd,* page number" (for example, *Sd* 310). Prose is quoted within the text in translation, with the Russian original provided in notes only where the clarification of specific points seems necessary. Verse is quoted in Russian, with a translation into very unpoetic English (titles and page references appear the first time a poem is cited). In my Tsvetaeva book I attempted something metrical when translating; the results were mixed, and they would have been worse for Klyuev. I plead that readers who struggle with the Russian of Klyuev's verse use my translations only as a rough, prosaic, and certainly imperfect guide to the originals, and not as an attempt to render in English the complex magic of his best lines.

Nikolai Klyuev

Introduction

Nikolai Klyuev (1884–1937) is a remarkable figure, in many ways unique in the history of Russian literature. Especially striking are the evident contradictions of his life and work: an autodidact of peasant background, he was also a full-fledged Russian modernist; a defender of archaic cultural values, he was also the author of homoerotic poetry and of works in which his own homosexuality was quite openly stated; his poetry is often strange and difficult, to many even rebarbative, yet it repeatedly claims to represent a popular, folk point of view. At the same time, and despite all the qualities that make both him and his poetry so striking and unusual, he and his work also tell stories that are very typical in twentieth-century Russia. Klyuev's career and posthumous story follow a familiar path for the period. He was a widely acknowledged poet in the 1910s; anticipating positive change, he greeted the Bolshevik coup with initial, if eccentric, enthusiasm, but then he became persona non grata and was exiled from the literary world, at first figuratively, then literally; aspects of his literary stance and thematics that might initially have been seen as literary projections for high modernism were to become matters of life and death in high Stalinism, and the state's persecutions concluded with his execution in 1937. After the Second World War, his poetry seeped across borders—first to the West for publication, then back into the Soviet Union for secret consumption by a few; finally, in the glasnost period he "returned" in full, when the texts previously only published abroad were joined in the pages of Russian journals by new discoveries from secret archives. As a result of this process, there is no "natural" chronology in the publication and reception of much of his work; the fragmentation and evident fracturing of his verse, which contributes to its difficulty, is both an integral feature of his own poetics and a fact of the material life of texts, manuscripts, archives, and publications. Every item in the trajectories of Klyuev's life and work finds analogues in the lives and stories of many twentieth-century Russian authors and texts, and exemplifies key features specific to Russian culture in the period.

The following pages attempt to elucidate both the ways in which

Klyuev is unique, strange, and intriguing, and the ways in which what is said about him can be understood as typical and representative in the context of the history of modern Russian letters in general. Even the most apparently unusual aspects of Klyuev—the literary realization of his sexuality, his treatment of many forms of Russian popular religion, his elusive, multiple cultural identities—can be read as expressive of features typical of Russian culture at certain moments in the last hundred or so years. And even the most typical elements in Klyuev's story—the path his verse takes toward long narrative form, the path the poet himself takes, or rather, along which he is taken, to execution—contain a great deal that is unique. Moreover, Klyuev, a poet from the "people," was to a considerable degree shaped by the ideas of the turn-of-the-century Russian intelligentsia about the people, although he consistently—and with full justification—emphasized the distance between himself and the typical representatives of that intelligentsia (to which, as a mature author, notwithstanding all qualifications, he nevertheless belonged). In these paradoxical combinations will be found some of the keys not only to Klyuev but also—and here is an ambitious claim which the following chapters will attempt robustly to support—to Klyuev's country and its ever-fascinating, ever-perplexing cultural history.

But it is also a primary assumption of this book that Klyuev is a poet who can fully justify his demands on the reader's time because of the immanent qualities of his verse. This—perhaps rather old-fashioned—assumption is what has driven the attempts to elucidate his poetics and thematics, especially in chapters on individual works. In other words, this book, like most studies of foreign authors on whom relatively little has been written for the Anglophone reader, will argue that Klyuev should be more widely read, even by those for whom his native language is not theirs, and not just because he is an interesting cultural figure but also because he wrote outstanding works.

The conceptual act of reading Klyuev will never be easy—much of his poetry is, to put it in the simplest terms, "very hard," and many readers are unwilling to make the effort required. This study attempts to encourage such an effort and to suggest that there are rewards for it. Fortunately, the physical act of reading Klyuev is now a great deal easier than it was a couple of decades ago; as the following pages will explain, recent scholarly editions of Klyuev's poetry, prose, and correspondence have brought together the work of many specialists who, since the mid-1980s, have made his literary legacy available in the pages of Russia's learned and literary journals. Scholarship about Klyuev has also flourished, as will be seen. Many individual scholars, and at least two groups of specialists, both working outside of the metropolitan centers of Russian culture, have made major contributions to the study of Klyuev, and abundant reference will be made to their work in the following chapters. A key marker of the growth of Klyuev studies in Russia has been the publication of several important collections of scholarly materials—mostly based on the proceedings of conferences.[1] The ever-expanding modern scholarship on Klyuev has its own story to tell, and, as will be shown, that story, too, is revealing of the fault lines of Russian culture and intellectual life today. However, for all the publications of recent years, making the poet notionally more accessible to the reader—whether "general" or professional—Klyuev remains, at best, on the periphery of the acknowledged Russian literary canon. This study attempts to explain why, while also aspiring to bring his life and work into greater focus for readers who are not familiar with the specialist work devoted to him.

Chapter 1 provides a detailed examination of Klyuev's life, as it can be documented, as the poet presented it, and as it has been discussed and disputed in the contentious ideological arenas where the poet was and continues to be the object of polemics. Klyuev's multiple claimed and disputed identities are fundamental to an understanding of the poet's creative projects, of the paradoxical situations in which he found himself, and of the ideological fault lines which express key elements in Russian cultural history of the twentieth century. First he was a beginner-author from the people; then he was a figure uniquely authorized to speak of the people's secret world—in both cases, to be understood in contrast to the intelligentsia, which cultivated particular images of the people, but was very remote from it. After that, he was briefly a peasant advocate of Bolshevism, and then that movement's critic and enemy—and in these later hypostases, the cultivation, begun in his first years of literary adulthood, of a popular identity tied to ancient Russia and to religious faith took on quite different meaning from its original connotations, which had been derived from the social and artistic preoccupations of the early twentieth century. Long after his death, the appropriation of his life story to politico-cultural programs by some and the wholesale rejection of his claimed identities by others continued, accompanied by assumptions that are very revealing about Russia and, especially, about how Russia imagines itself. The second chapter attempts a summary of the interrelations between material and conceptual texts, both in the general context of twentieth-century Russia and in the specific case of Klyuev, and surveys his poetry in its complex and pivotal relationship to and expression of concepts of time and place. Place, in particular, is a crucial but very elusive category in Klyuev's poetry and in his life-text: ideas of the "north" and the "village" dominate his work, and he is often presented in brief surveys largely in terms of these two categories, yet both can be revealed, upon careful examination of his work, to be surprisingly abstract or disconcertingly mobile, while the actual places of Klyuev's biography can seem largely elided. Approaching Klyuev's oeuvre through its relationship to time and place also enables the exploration of many other key aspects of his poetry, while emphasizing how important has been the shaping and misshaping context of historical location. Moreover, radical transformations of place, and especially of conceptions of place, and the repeated reimaginings of Russia's chronology have fundamentally shaped and misshaped Russian culture in the last hundred years. Thus, Klyuev's engagement with these concepts provides access to two of the primary vectors of Russian cultural history.

With reference to the general observations of chapter 2, Klyuev's poetics are analyzed in detail in the final four chapters of this work, with particular attention paid, in successive chapters, to works representative of, respectively, the poet's early lyric collections, his prose, his late, uncollected lyrics, and his narrative poetry. First to be examined is the poet's second collection, *Bratskie pesni* (*Fraternal Songs*) of 1912, which promotes a striking program of religious, political, cultural, and sexual action (chapter 3). Chapter 4 looks at his diverse and very unusual prose, especially his fascinating "mytho-autobiography" "Gagar'ya sud'bina" ("The Loon's Fate"), which describes both the emergence of the poet's sexual identity and the construction of his place in the cultural matrix of Russian modernism. Chapter 5 examines his complex late poetry, produced in "pre-Gutenberg" conditions, and only recently published in full, with a detailed reading of the cycle "Razrukha" ("Destruction"). Chapter 6 addresses his *poemy* (long, narrative poems), especially the long-lost magnum opus *Pesn' o Velikoi Materi* (*Hymn of the Great Mother*), published for the first time only in 1991, after its discovery in the Moscow archive of the KGB. Of these four exemplary texts, only *Bratskie pesni* appeared in his lifetime (in multiple versions), while the other three, products of the Soviet period and unpublished until long after Klyuev's death, display additional textual problems that exemplify the encounter of late Russian modernism with the Soviet literary environment. The works are examined in the chronological order of their composition ("Razrukha" and *Pesn' o Velikoi Materi* are approximate contemporaries), so that they also provide a series of narrative windows on Klyuev's career.

Bratskie pesni, his second lyric collection, has many of the general characteristics of the *sbornik* (poetry collection) of the modernist period, including relative thematic and chronological unity, while also displaying some of the problems of instability which are especially typical of the material and conceptual textuality of Klyuev's poetry. *Bratskie pesni* is, moreover, a very important landmark in the exploration and statement of the poet's cultural and sexual identity, and very revealing both of Klyuev's approach to Russian popular religion and of the general preoccupation with that phenomenon, characteristic of Russian culture in the early decades of the twentieth century. "Gagar'ya sud'bina" is Klyuev's longest autobiographical text, constructing for the poet an elaborate, mythologized persona which is to be understood in relation to both his origins and the time of the work's composition—the early 1920s. Recorded by Klyuev's friend and amanuensis, Nikolai Arkhipov, it is characterized both by "orality" and by elaborate literary gestures, while its very form is predicated on the special circumstances of literary production in the Soviet period. The distance between the time and circumstances of composition and the time and circumstances of publication is also instrumental in the scholarly reception of this work, as is the case with both "Razrukha" and *Pesn' o Velikoi Materi.* These last two works, as products of the "pre-Gutenberg" period of Klyuev's career, show many of the textual instabilities and uncertainties characteristic of works produced in such circumstances. They are also key markers of the (at times provocative) maintenance and elaboration of Klyuev's poetic and cultural identity in the Stalinist period, while their history and fate as physical texts are illustrative not only of that period but also of the period of their discovery and publication.

A basic interpretive principle informs the following chapters—that the mutable versions of Klyuev's life, as told by himself and presented by others, are not only analogous to the mutabilities and instabilities of his texts, but also share common sources in the literary environment of the period and in the specifics of Klyuev's own situation. Equally important is the contention that the circumstances which shaped and misshaped his life and the posthumous treatment of that life had a crucial impact on both the creation and the reading and rereading of his verse. In other words, Klyuev, as an author of the early decades of the twentieth century, read again at the beginning of the next, is very much a figure of both times, and as such is both typical of and exceptional in a country that, with its tendencies to binary divisions, has encouraged opposite images of itself and of its authors. Klyuev, it turns out, is often "both A and B," just as his poetry often both asserts and denies, or simultaneously claims artistic cohesion and dismantles itself before the reader's very eyes.

For that reason, the following chapters attempt to combine "philological" and "culturological" approaches (to use the Russian terms). That is to say, the reader is invited to look at Klyuev's work in terms of its literary characteristics, origins, and effects, broadly understood (language, metrics, form, sources and models, communicative strategies, and so on), while also considering both the poet and his work as part of a broader narrative of Russian cultural history in and beyond the twentieth century. The axes of uniqueness and typicality are used (or are implied) to present Klyuev and his work, while the notion that Klyuev is both a poet of his own lifetime and of the period that began with his cultural "return" underpins the exploration of the history of his writing.

It is hoped that this study will not only succeed in combining the two approaches outlined above but will also enable the reader to find in Klyuev's work at least some of the qualities that have enthralled and challenged the author of this book. It is impossible to ignore this last task when writing in English about Klyuev, since, to date, the Anglophone world has been largely silent on the poet.[2] Any book on such an author must, of necessity, introduce, survey, and argue for the merit of the topic. Since Klyuev is, while much discussed and even contested in some circles of Russian literary scholarship, a poet relatively little read and probably even less liked by Russia's broad readership of modern poetry, the task of arguing for his merits before a readership assumed to consist primarily of native Anglophones is particularly demanding. To appreciate his poetry, the reader must move away from the poetic principles embodied in much of the most admired verse of Russian modernism (without forgetting that Klyuev remains very much a poet of that period). Intertextuality, compression, poetry as "riddle," and metrical innovation are not key features of his work, although there is plenty of abstruse reference, dramatic semantic and formal disjuncture, and striking sound texture. In fact, Klyuev's poetry sometimes seems hallucinatory, spellbinding, and even prophetic, recalling discursive models that are rather remote from those assumed in the oeuvre of many other major poets of the period (and remote, too, from those that can be assumed for other poets linked to the culture of the Russian village).

This study is predicated in part on the assertion that Klyuev's poetry richly rewards the reader who is willing to make the—sometimes not inconsiderable—effort to get to grips with it, approaching it with a sense of the specifics of its context and willing to accept its deviations from the canonical forms and canonical works of the period. The following pages show the results of such efforts, often time-consuming, sometimes frustrating, but certainly never dull. It is hoped that the reader will find the patience to follow those results, and, in so doing, will find in Klyuev and his work both cultural paradigms and unique achievements.

Chapter One

Lives of the Poet: Klyuev's Life, as Lived, Imagined, Re-created, and Disputed

THERE ARE MANY WAYS to tell a life story, but the most satisfactory lives often begin or are begun with death. Death brings with it the need and the possibility to tell the story from the end to the beginning—funeral eulogies and obituaries provide ample evidence of that need, while scandalous biographies of the famous, when recently deceased, make frequent use of the possibility. It seems that death inspires confidence that a life can be told in full—or at least that, of the transitory patterns a living person creates or into which a person can be fitted during the business of being alive, many can finally be excluded in favor of one or more dominant and recurrent patterns. Death is also, of course, convenient in guaranteeing the absence of the subject, who might take issue with the patterns identified by others. Although it is an illusion that death has indeed set life in its final and irrevocable pattern—even the lives of most of us, *unremarkable* people, change pattern time and time again after death as they are reviewed, retold, rethought—at the very least, death provides a moment of certainty and finality in the story. For most citizens of "developed" countries, even during exceptional periods such as wartime, death also has a mundane social clarity. The material evidence—the presence of the deceased, and the accompanying documentation, which sets in motion the familiar social and religious rituals—assures one of the private and public facts of death, and reinforces the need to begin the retracing of a life story. Although less ritualized, the moment of birth is given equally reassuring clarity by the mechanisms of modern, secular society—hospitals, nurses, doctors, birth certificates, birth announcements. In a word, most people in the "first world" today can be proved to have been born at a particular time and in a particular place, and can or will be attested to have died with equal clarity of geography and chronology.

Russia, as is so often the case with such generalizations, is something of an exception. Still predominantly a peasant country in the early twentieth century, and several times in that century the site of overwhelming and often violent change, Russian experience often defies the personal certainties of life and, especially, death that are usually accessible in other parts of modern Europe or North America, and very often in other parts of the world. This is especially true of the millions of victims of the Soviet period who disappeared into the Stalinist Gulag or perished during the Second World War. In many instances, all trace of them was lost; in other cases, people turned out not to have died at all, yet they returned home to find the circumstances of their own personal lives changed beyond recognition in their absence (spouses had begun new lives; children they hardly knew had grown up quite independently of them, and so on). And this is but one of the most dramatic examples of the ways in which constructing an *ordinary, unremarkable* life in twentieth-century Russia involved uncertainties largely alien to many otherwise culturally comparable countries. Equally familiar and shocking to any observer of that country are the uncertainties associated with many of the key moments between birth and death, moments which have the familiarity and illusion of organic patterning elsewhere: housing, family, career, to name three of the most vivid examples.

But even in Russia, where these matters are more problematic, death brings both the need and the possibility to clarify the course of an individual's life. And this is especially true in the case of those whose lives have been far from ordinary. The writers of Soviet Russia had, when alive, the privileges and strains of intense attention from their readers and from the state; when dead, they often (and, as the century wore on, increasingly) received the equally intense attention of scholars and other authors devoted to the project of creating some kind of certainty out of the multiple uncertainties and lacunae which comprised the known life stories of so many. Yet notwithstanding such attention, the end point from which such investigations are typically begun could remain elusive. Only the death of the Soviet Union itself rendered possible the discovery of the truth about the deaths of many of the country's most prominent victims. Finally, it was possible to discover how, where, when, and, with some qualifications, why famous people arrested during the purges had actually died. And with that discovery begins a new retracing of the lives themselves, informed by a confidence that the starting point for the narrative has been found in the final point of that which is to be narrated. And since this fate—disappearance into the machinery of repression—was shared with so many otherwise *unremarkable* people, the new retracing of the lives of the famous victims took on a special urgency and import. The story of their living and dying stood for the silent millions.

With those for whom living a life is a *remarkable* project, indeed, a *textual project,* the posthumous telling of life stories has a particular force and difficulty; that is, in the case of remarkable people who not only live by self-consciously inscribing and reinscribing themselves into cultural texts, but also simultaneously create literal texts—*literary texts.* These are people who themselves write and make texts of themselves; who, as it were, write their selves. Men and women of letters have had a special prominence in the culture and history of modern Russia, and have often lived their lives on multiple levels of self-consciousness and with a heightened sense of being in a public arena, not least—however paradoxical it may seem—when their access to any kind of "normal" contact with a reading public has been denied. Even among the famous, their lives are special.

Manipulation of individual experience is, of course, especially inherent in lyric poetry, with its tendency to foreground and privilege a speaking "I," and with a large part of its core thematics drawn from areas of intensely personal living. Throughout Europe, lyric poetry especially, although by no means only in the Romantic age, also provided particular opportunities for a heightened combination of life-text and text-life. The Russian examples of literary, above all poetic, lives are especially compelling, and have even greater force in the post-Romantic age.[1] While the textualization of life in general has long been part of the practice of Russian poets, it has, in the specific context of twentieth-century Russia, gained new and usually tragic meaning. The dramatizing and self-dramatizing lives of many members of the Russian poetic pantheon require no rehearsal here. The twentieth-century heirs of Pushkin, Lermontov, and other Romantic-era poet-martyrs—Gumilev, Tsvetaeva, Mandelstam, and many others—have been revered in the special cult of the poet as a figure combining personal and social testimony in a tragic setting: prophet, but also martyr. Hence, while Russia re-creates the lives of all its favored writers—especially its *recently dead writers*—with meticulous, antiquarian care, it reserves an especial piety for the poets, above all the martyred poets, as any reader of biographical scholarship or visitor to literary museums in Russia will confirm.

Even to readers abroad those same lives of the poets contribute much to the prestige and appeal of modern Russian letters. Whereas, in the Anglophone world, poetry has, since the Romantic age, occupied an ever smaller place in the cultural environment (reduced in the United States to the specialist university classroom for the most part), English-speaking readers continue to buy books about Russsian poets—mostly about their lives—and to speak with some awe of the pantheon of modern martyrs: Mandelstam, Tsvetaeva; with reservations, Mayakovsky and Esenin; with qualifications to the concept of martyrdom, Akhmatova and Pasternak; and a good many others. Similarly, ritual gestures in the direction of Russian poets are commonly made by English-speaking men and women of letters. Although Russian prose of the twentieth century is read in the Anglophone world far less than its nineteenth-century counterpart, and Russian poetry of any period is read in translation with understandable difficulty and frustration, the *lives* of the poets are read with some enthusiasm and with a confidence that here is the true assertion of the sacred in modern culture: the poet-witness whose martyrdom assured greatness.

Thus the death of the poet carries special weight, has often been anticipated in verse by the poet himself or herself, may even have been the work of the poet himself or herself, or, in the twentieth century, may have been the occasion of actual rather than metaphorical or romantic martyrdom in the cause of poetry. And the death of the poet-martyr has an especially powerful cultural charge. For that reason, the processes by which was clarified the nature of the death of Tsvetaeva, a suicide but still, for many, a martyr, or, perhaps even more tellingly, the incarcerated Mandelstam, seemed to represent far more than the satisfactory conclusion of biographical detective work.

The birth of the poet, whether literal or figurative, also occupies a place of special importance in the life-text. Although not quite as significant as the death and clearly less transformed by twentieth-century barbarities, it is, as the final point reached when narrating the way back from that death, for some a subject of mythmaking and piety. But in literal and mundane terms, the births of most twentieth-century Russian writers have been unproblematic in their documentation and hence their narration, although the "birth of a poet" as a theme has remained complex (and problematic).

In many ways the life—the lives—of Nikolai Klyuev could fit the models and patterns that are part of the classic twentieth-century Russian poet's life: testimony, prophecy, martyrdom, all recorded by Klyuev himself in a unique poetic voice; persecution from the state (a sine qua non), preceding and accompanying the martyrdom; contemporaneous with the persecution, struggles to "come to terms" with the state, attempts at compromise, and then resistance, largely in isolation; a very self-conscious making and remaking of the poetic and autobiographical self, often with an eye to the circumstances already listed; and a series of very patterned autobiographical texts in prose and verse. Much of the posthumous treatment of Klyuev confirms that his story is indeed a classic poet's life: the hagiographical element in some of the writing about him; an antiquarian preoccupation with the recovery of many details of his biography; the elision of other aspects of his work and life in some scholarly and literary treatments of him; the strong sense of semimystical rebirth that has accompanied the recovery of his works in his homeland. Yet Klyuev is also a highly problematic figure in these and so many other ways. Problematic in life, in death, in verse, in prose, in life-text, text-life, and even in the life and afterlife of his literal (literary) texts.

It was asserted earlier that confidently told lives can begin only with death. Yet even here, there can be little confidence in the case of Klyuev. He was one of the many victims of the Stalinist purges: arrested in 1934, he was exiled to Siberia. For many years nothing more was known for certain. A characteristic death myth held sway: he had died "on the way back to European Russia, at a railway station," and with him had perished a suitcase of manuscripts. The story has been traced back to a former companion of Klyuev, with whom the poet corresponded from exile. It appeared in print for the first time in the posthumously published memoirs of the critic Ivanov-Razumnik, who had known Klyuev and advocated his work since the 1910s.[2] These memoirs were published abroad in 1951, and were used by other writers in the West. They could not, of course, be quoted directly in the Soviet Union when limited and cautious discussion of Klyuev resumed, but they were widely used as an unnamed source, giving the legend considerable support.[3] Other stories of Klyuev's death persisted—he had died in prison in Tomsk, for example.[4] The legends and the history of their dissemination are, of course, both highly characteristic of the cultural puzzles and mazes of the later Soviet period.

Finally, in the 1980s and 1990s, it became possible to discover some details of the fate of many of the victims of the purges, and to clear away the myths, official and folkloric, that were a recurrent feature of biographies of the purged. Many of Klyuev's letters from exile were published; the files compiled by the NKVD were found and some were made public; and a few witnesses to his last years were discovered. It is now known that after three years of Siberian exile in harsh (but by no means unusual) conditions, Klyuev was arrested, interrogated, and condemned to death as a monarchist plotter (*sic*). It is known that he was shot. But, in a quirk which characterizes the many paradoxes and puzzles of his life, the date of his death remains unknown. Klyuev was executed between the twenty-third and the twenty-fifth of October 1937, as recorded on the last page of his Siberian NKVD file. The hour is unknown, and the signature of the officer confirming the execution is illegible. No place of burial will ever be found.[5]

Thus Klyuev's death has been forever obscured by the very mechanisms of the state against which he spoke out in verse and prose. Those mechanisms are now comprehensible as historical forces, in part through the individual recorded testimony of survivors and through the records left behind by the state's loyal mechanics. The victims could, of course, leave no record of their own, and if the record kept by their executioners is incomplete, then final times and places will never be known. So, even in the post-Soviet era, and even with access, albeit unpredictable, to the vast documentation of repression maintained by the Stalinist state, there is no precise end point from which to retrace the pattern of Klyuev's life.

Working back, uncertainly, to the beginning of his life, the would-be biographer finds a striking symmetry. When and where Klyuev was born remain to this day less than completely clear. While the uncertainty around the precise date of his death is purely a product of the mass scale of the repressions to which he and so many others fell victim, the question of his birth is hard to answer for other, equally eloquent, reasons. He himself provided various years and dates for his birth, and many older sources place a question mark beside the years 1886 or 1887, drawing on Klyuev's own commentaries and narratives (some of which were themselves restricted to archives until recently). It seemed that the first author of the post-Stalinist period to work on Klyuev—the Petrozavodsk *kraeved* (local historian) Gruntov—had clarified the issue, obtaining an extract from the register of births stating that he was born in the township of Koshtugi (village not noted) on October 10, 1884.[6] Klyuev's own relatively consistent reduction of his age and manipulation of his birthday thus became two of many such maneuvers in his subsequent mythologizing of himself, and the long uncertainty simply a function of the geographically remote and socially lowly nature of his birth. However, while recent years have clarified somewhat the nature of his death, they have also cast further doubt on his birth. One Petrozavodsk author has pointed to a series of inconsistencies in the evidence, and further emphasizes what is, in fact, the single most significant fact about Klyuev's origin, explaining but not dissipating so much of the confusion: almost everything that he came from and grew up around has been lost or destroyed, leaving very little trace behind.[7] Even the identity of the church of his baptism is open to question. And while most recent sources will speak confidently of the poet's birthplace as "Koshtugi," it should be pointed out that in the late nineteenth century this designated an extensive complex of small villages, while, in the twenty-first century, it designates a smaller and more scattered community, within which no trace of a Klyuev family home has yet been found. Thus, while most scholars would probably agree that the poet was born in 1884 and baptized in Koshtugi, it is very unlikely that we will ever know *where exactly* the poet was born. The relationship of the physical geography of Klyuev's home region, both in his time and now, to a reading of the poet and his life is a matter of considerable importance, and is explored at greater length in chapter 2.

Klyuev's own most significant statement on his birth comes in the opening lines of his "Gagar'ya sud'bina" ("The Loon's Fate"; discussed as part of the poet's "created lives" in this chapter and again in chapter 4) but does nothing to illuminate the documentary questions. Indeed, its very self-consciously literary, almost playful, quality warns against assuming the statement's transparency (a "pagan" baptism, but in anticipation of the priest and linked to a Christian feast day, as if to reiterate the classic "double faith" with which the Russian village is so often endowed by observers; birth associated with bread-making—a key motif and symbol of creativity for the poet; and the almost incantatory reiteration of the root for the word "birth": *Ya* ***rodilsya*** . . . *Mamen'ka-**roditel'** **rodila*** . . . ***rozhaya*** *tebya* . . . *kak tebya* ***rodila***—five times in three sentences):

I was born—and cried fiercely, and in case I die before the priest arrive, old Solomonida baptized me in the wooden vat for making sourdough bread.

But when it was that my birth mother gave birth to me—she could not remember. She used to say, "When I was giving birth I got so cold, just like at an ice hole at Epiphany; I don't recall how I gave you birth." (*Sd* 31)[8]

The symmetry in the problems of birth and death is surely striking. The specific physical places of Klyuev's exile have been razed; the record of his execution is imperfect; his mortal remains are lost forever. And no document establishes with certainty the place and date of his birth; almost nothing is left of the place where he was born, and little of the everyday culture into which he was born. And while these facts make Klyuev's life something of an exception in the literary martyrologion of modern Russia, they also make it powerfully representative of the story of Russian culture in the last century—one of many paradoxes essential to an understanding of the poet.

Chronology and geography are uncertain in the birth and death of many people in very many countries, of course, even today. And many Russian peasants of the last century must have entered and left this world in such a manner. But that these circumstances are shared by the poet Klyuev is itself telling. That they may be seen as articulating the very things which Klyuev lived by—in myth or in the everyday—is what makes them remarkable.

Thus the beginning and the end of any life of Klyuev must be told with greater qualifications than would be expected for most European, even Russian, artists of his generation. And much of what comes between is also uncertain, for many of the conceptual landmarks one might expect to see have been razed with as much finality as the physical spaces he inhabited.

Often, clarification of a writer's life comes from the meticulous comparison of the author's own assertions and mythological constructions with prosaic material from other sources. Such comparison is possible with Klyuev, but frequently the poet's own constructed lives of himself are no more extravagant than the memoirs and accounts of others, while the evident drama of his known and attested life speaks for itself.

In order to clarify—or, perhaps, fruitfully to complicate—these lives of the poet, it must be understood that even while the material out of which posthumous lives are built has been accumulated, several partially separate narratives of Klyuev's life have retained greater independence than is usually the case, even with the most elusive of posthumous subjects. The first is the attested life—a matter of documentary records. As has already been seen, at crucial moments this is very thin, although the scholarly collation and commentary of letters, memoirs, and other documents has now shed a great deal of light on many aspects of Klyuev's factual biography. The second is the life told by the poet himself. This is very rich at times, silent at others, and always elusive. The third is the life told (or judged) by others—not so much a mass of partially intersecting commentaries out of which some generalized narrative may be drawn, but rather two sets of polar opposites, powerfully attracting and repelling.

By far the most significant biography of Klyuev based upon the known documentary sources is Konstantin Azadovsky's *Nikolai Klyuev: Put' poeta* (*Nikolai Klyuev: The Poet's Path,* 1990), modified and expanded somewhat in his *Zhizn' Nikolaya Klyueva: Dokumental'noe povestvovanie* (*The Life of Nikolai Klyuev: A Documentary Narrative,* 2002). Azadovsky is one of the most assiduous, meticulous, and sophisticated Klyuev scholars, and his books provide a very effective chronological account of Klyuev's life, drawing on many archival materials, some of which have been published by Azadovsky himself. Although his point of view may be challenged in some places, his books provide by far the best starting point for any reader of Russian who wishes to uncover the "poet's path," and are among the major sources for the information presented in the following pages. Sergei Subbotin, another major Klyuev scholar, whose archival research has led to many excellent publications, and Ivan Kostin provide a very informative, although brief, biographical sketch in the introduction to Subbotin's edition of Klyuev's poetry, *Pesnoslov* (*Hymn Book,* 1990).[9] As will be seen below, Azadovsky and Subbotin have disagreed publicly on several significant aspects of Klyuev's life. Aleksandr Mikhailov's essay "Nikolai Klyuev i mir ego poezii" ("Nikolai Klyuev and the World of His Poetry"), the introductory article to the fullest edition of Klyuev's poetry to date, *Serdtse edinoroga* (*Heart of the Unicorn,* 1999), provides another fine, if also brief, approach to questions of the poet's biography (7–74). The essays of Filippov in the two major Western editions of Klyuev, especially his expanded "Nikolai Klyuev: Materialy dlya biografii" ("Nikolai Klyuev: Materials for a Biography," 1:5–182), while long overtaken by the publication of new materials, should also be mentioned as perceptive commentaries which have greatly influenced views of the poet in his homeland as well as abroad.[10] While not a comprehensive treatment of the poet's life, Lev Karokhin's 2002 book on Esenin and Klyuev also provides a great deal of testimony on many important episodes.[11]

The documentary story of Klyuev's life, in rudimentary outline, is as follows. He was probably born (and certainly baptized) in the village of Koshtugi, near the southern end of Lake Onega, and to the southwest of the small town of Vytegra, in 1884. Koshtugi is some sixty-five kilometers distant from Vytegra, and lies south of the main road from Vytegra to St. Petersburg as it runs near the southern edge of Lake Onega. The Koshtugi parish was divided, in the nineteenth century, between the Olonian and St. Petersburg *gubernii* ("provinces," equivalent to modern oblasts). Early in his life the future poet moved to the village (*derevnya*) of Zhelvachevo (sometimes Zhelvacheva), northeast of Vytegra. It lies east of the road from Vytegra to Pudozh, as that road runs north from Vytegra, near the eastern shore of Lake Onega. In the late nineteenth centuries, these places—both the villages and the town—although distant from urban centers, enjoyed reasonable prosperity. The villages were beside or near rivers (Zhelvachevo is bounded by the Andoma; Koshtugi surrounds the meeting of the Megra and Kimreka), and the areas were quite populous. Zhelvachevo, although itself small, adjoined a much larger village (Makachevo, the *selo* [large village] of which the *derevnya* of Zhelvachevo now forms a part); some houses in the area were large and richly adorned, and there were churches both of brick and of wood serving the several villages nearby. Vytegra was on a major canal system (the Mariinsky) and enjoyed a high level of literacy. The town had adequate schools, fine merchant houses, and was dominated by a large cathedral. This part of northern Russia had relatively few landowners from the nobility—in the later nineteenth century it was the merchant class that was dominant here—and the north, as a whole, had not known serfdom; both of these facts are important for understanding not only Klyuev's own background, but also his presentation of the north in his work, and the general construction of the north in Russian culture at the time.

One hundred years later, however, these places are all less prosperous and the villages appear in terminal decline. In Zhelvachevo, by the year 2000, only two houses seemed to be occupied year-round (the other remaining houses were either derelict or used only as summer cottages). In the colder months, the village shows virtually no signs of life. The Koshtugi church where Klyuev most probably was baptized was abandoned for many years, and, although reconsecrated in the 1990s, is now barely standing; the other village church disappeared long ago, while the churches, winter and summer, in the churchyard in Makachevo where Klyuev's parents are buried were in ruins in the 1990s and have now collapsed completely (the destruction of the larger, brick "winter" church was ensured when it was blown up during an antireligion campaign in the early 1960s). A cross stands on the presumed burial site of Klyuev's mother, but even this cannot be documented. Vytegra continues to draw some prosperity from its place on the northern canal system, but suffers from all of the economic and social deprivations which make the citizens of twenty-first-century St. Petersburg and Moscow shudder—perhaps excessively—before the word *provintsiya* (the provinces), and invest the notions of small-town and village life with negative connotations far beyond the familiar complaints of late-nineteenth-century literary and actual denizens of *uezdnye goroda* (local centers) and distant villages. In order to aspire to even a partial understanding of what Klyuev was, did, and now stands for, it is essential to realize that the physical world from which he came has all but disappeared, that its intellectual or imaginative reconstruction is very difficult and contentious, and that the remains of that world are now, by most standards, more impoverished, remote, and inaccessible than they were one hundred years ago.[12]

At the time of Klyuev's birth, his father, Aleksei Timofeevich Klyuev (1842–1918), was a village police constable, having earlier completed fifteen years of military service; subsequently he became the landlord of a government liquor store in Zhelvachevo and lived in the house of which the store formed a small part. Where that house once stood a memorial plaque and bench were installed in the 1990s. The house itself was moved to Makachevo in the second half of the twentieth century, served for a time as a school building, and then stood empty for many years. In the summer of 2003 it came back into use—hosting the village's modest library and temporarily replacing the "house of culture," recently destroyed by fire. A plaque on it commemorates the poet's inhabitation of it.

Little is known for certain about Klyuev's mother Praskov'ya Dmitrievna (1851–1913), although she is a prominent figure in his verse from the time of her death, which provoked intense and prolonged grief in the poet. If Klyuev's later image of her is to be taken literally, then she was a spiritually sophisticated woman, linked to the Old Belief. Certainly, the villages where Klyuev grew up had significant Old Believer affiliations up to the end of the nineteenth century, and he must have seen at least something of the old faith as a child; that his mother was herself an Old Believer has yet to be confirmed. According to Gruntov, who was able to interview many local people who remembered the poet and his family, Klyuev spent part of his childhood in Vytegra, where his father owned a house, and he studied in the town's schools.[13] He probably spent one year at the Petrozavodsk school for medical assistants (feldshers), but left because of ill health.[14] While the family was legally registered as members of the peasantry, they probably never engaged in peasant farming as their primary means of support—another fact of significance for an understanding of subsequent disputes over the literary-social identity of the poet.

In the first years of the twentieth century Klyuev began to write verse, appearing in print for the first time in 1904 in a collection which sponsored young writers "from the people." Predictably, his early verse seems derivative and often unremarkable. Both the "peasant poets" of the nineteenth century and Nekrasov and his followers have been mentioned by scholars looking at this very earliest work.[15] Klyuev probably visited St. Petersburg around this time, and it has been suggested that he sought temporary work in the capital.[16] He also began to take part in political activities, which attracted the attention of the authorities, and his poetry around the period of the 1905 Revolution is strongly marked by images of political martyrdom and even revolutionary fervor. He spent part of 1906 under arrest for distributing revolutionary pamphlets. A copy of Marx's *Capital* was confiscated from him. A police report, written in a manner which seems self-parodic but which no doubt reflects quite unself-consciously the literacy of its author, speaks of the poet's activities at this time. For example, Klyuev and his father are asserted to have accused the local land captain (*zemskii nachal'nik*) of the misappropriation of funds:

> In the month of November, when the land captain in the Makachevo township was giving out alms to the poorest wives of reservists of the lower ranks, provided by the charity of Her Highness Mariya Fedorovna, Nikolai Klyuev and his father Aleksei told those wives who had not received any alms that the money intended for them, he, the land captain, had taken for himself and divided with the village elder and the clerk. This is based on the evidence of the village midwife Maikova, who, as she abides on the upper floor above the Klyuevs' accommodation and above the liquor store, heard this conversation the Klyuevs had through the floor, as it is of a single layer and everything people say there when they speak without caution [*ne stesnyayas'*] can be heard, and a week later the midwife once again heard through the floor the wife of the liquor store landlord Klyuev and his daughter talking with women, she assumes with soldiers' wives, advising them to go to town and ask the land captain for money, and if he refused, to smash the windows in his apartment and send a petition to Her Highness.[17]

In 1908 Klyuev was himself called up for military service, which he appears to have refused to fulfill on grounds of principle. After a prolonged examination, he was judged medically unsuitable and released. Shortly before this aborted military service, he had initiated a correspondence with Aleksandr Blok, the greatest of the symbolist poets. Klyuev's letters have been preserved and were published in full in 1987 by Azadovsky, who produced a revised and expanded edition in 2003.[18] Klyuev wrote mostly from the village of Zhelvachevo; Blok from the capital city of St. Petersburg. Klyuev wrote as a novice poet to Blok as an acknowledged master, but he also wrote as a self-conscious voice of the people to the gentleman Blok. Klyuev had caught precisely the right moment to enchant Blok, and the correspondence with the older poet, which continued intensively for some four years, and intermittently for nearly one and a half decades, is one of the more remarkable items in the documentary record of Klyuev's life. (Blok's letters to Klyuev have been lost.)

Although, as has been noted, Klyuev had published verse before 1907, it was his epistolary acquaintance with Blok which facilitated his emergence as a significant new figure on the literary scene. Klyuev became associated with editors and authors interested in the social and religious qualities of the Russian *narod* (literally "people," but in this period almost synonymous with "peasantry"), and was soon widely published. For several years he was an especial favorite of a group called the Golgotha Christians, who called for practical spiritual renewal in this world (thereby blending religious and social programs). The leader of the Golgotha Christians was Iona Brikhnichev, a defrocked priest, who promoted Klyuev very actively in the group's publications, and wrote an early biographical article on the poet.[19] Klyuev's works of this period sometimes reflected the religious and social interests of Brikhnichev's group, and of those left-leaning members of the Russian intelligentsia who looked to the peasantry for inspiration (and for criticism). They were also strongly marked by his reading of the Russian symbolists.

Throughout this rise to relative fame he resided in the village of Zhelvachevo, at his parents' house, while also spending time in St. Petersburg. His first collection of poetry, *Sosen perezvon* (*Peal of the Pines*), is dated 1912, although it appears to have been published at the very end of 1911. The symbolist poet Valerii Bryusov, whom Klyuev knew and with whom he corresponded in the early 1910s, wrote the preface. The collection was greeted warmly, and established his reputation as a major new voice. Klyuev became a familiar and fairly significant figure on the literary scene, and his work was welcomed and published in major journals. The years 1912 and 1913 saw the publication of five more volumes: two versions of a collection called *Bratskie pesni* (*Fraternal Songs*), two of *Lesnye byli* (*Forest Tales*), and a second edition of *Sosen perezvon.*[20] *Bratskie pesni* and *Lesnye byli* marked Klyuev's move away from his early manner, often conventionally lyric or derivative (of the symbolists), toward a more original manner, sometimes drawing on folklore, or rendering stylizations of folk motifs. *Bratskie pesni* is also marked by "sectarian" features—he imitates, appropriates, and manipulates the aesthetics and thematics of the culture of Russian religious sects (including the *khlysty* or flagellants, and the *skoptsy* or castrati). But *Bratskie pesni* also owes much to the program and interests of the Golgotha Christians. In *Lesnye byli,* as in subsequent works, Klyuev draws on features of the peasant world and its culture to elaborate a poetic universe predicated upon a mythologization of life in the countryside. Although this poetic universe is gradually transformed, complicated, and even fractured, some of the most salient features of *Lesnye byli* are to remain significant throughout his oeuvre—for example, the marked combination of conventional Christian motifs with "pagan" and folkloric elements in order to render the peasant worldview (a combination expressed so clearly and self-consciously in the account of his birth quoted earlier). Already evident and soon to be more prominent is the potent mixture of social, religious, and sexual motifs in some of his most striking verse.

For a time Klyuev was close to the acmeists, becoming a more or less established Petersburg literary figure, and spending much of his time in the city. By now other poets from the Russian peasantry were emerging, and Klyuev was soon recognized as the doyen of what were to be called the *novo-krest'yanskie poety* (new-peasant poets—a term coined by the critic L'vov-Rogachevsky). In 1913 he began to correspond with a young Aleksandr Shiryaevets, soon to be identified as one such poet. Associations with the others (Sergei Esenin, Sergei Klychkov, Petr Oreshin) were formed in the next few years. As Klyuev's literary career progressed and his reputation grew, he gave readings in Petersburg and lived among the major figures in contemporary literature and publishing. He also traveled to Moscow. Nonetheless, his home remained the Olonian villages where his family resided, and he now maintained a metaphorical as well as physical distance between himself and the urban and urbane writers whose support had been important to him at the beginning of his career (Blok, Bryusov, and others). The death of his mother in 1913 seems to have had a profound impact on the poet; she was to feature prominently, often in highly mythologized form, in his mature lyric and narrative verse, and his autobiographical prose also emphasizes her importance in shaping the poet's cultural world. In 1915 Klyuev met the young Esenin, soon to be the most famous "new-peasant poet," with whom he had already corresponded, and for a time the two were closely associated. The debutant poet was, at this time, much under Klyuev's influence. Both poets shared the general patriotic mood provoked by the outbreak of the First World War, and some of Klyuev's poems of the time are frankly militaristic—surprisingly so for a poet who not so many years before seems to have refused military service. His collection *Mirskie dumy* (*Secular Meditations*) of 1916 contains much of his patriotic work, as well as poems which sustain the manner of *Lesnye byli.* It should be noted, however, that the former, although colored by certain chauvinistic sentiments evidently inspired by the outbreak of war, is nowhere near as narrowly patriotic as commentators, writing in Russia during the Soviet period, would have had their readers (who had no easy access to these poems) believe.[21]

Klyuev spent a large part of the First World War in Petrograd—as the capital was now called—participating in the activities of the literary elite, and gaining new supporters (and new enemies). He visited Tsarskoe Selo, where he had helped to install Sergei Esenin as an orderly in a military hospital (thus saving him from service at the front), and the two poets enjoyed considerable popularity in socially prestigious circles, some of them associated with the imperial family. In 1916 Klyuev twice toured Russia with the folk singer Plevitskaya, visiting and reading in a series of major provincial centers, including Vitebsk, Orel, Penza, Orenburg, Baku, Tiflis, Vladikavkaz, Stavropol', Rostov-on-Don, Nizhnii Novgorod, Vladimir, and Tver'.

Despite his recent imperial patriotism, the Soviet-era clichés of the sort "greeted the Revolution with unqualified enthusiasm" may be applied to Klyuev's reactions to the events of 1917, which he—like other "peasant" authors—seems to have seen as the harbinger of a long-awaited remaking of Russia along the lines of vaguely imagined rural utopias. It is thus no surprise to find such clichés frequently in Soviet-period accounts of Klyuev.[22] The February Revolution found him in Petrograd, but by the time of the Bolshevik coup he was living in his father's house in the village of Rubtsovo, on the Andoma, a few kilometers downriver from Zhelvachevo. In 1918, after his father's death, he moved to Vytegra, and in that year he became a member of the Bolshevik Party. But even his revolutionary hymns of this period sound notes of alarm for the destruction of ancient and popular Russian culture, while his celebrations of the new Soviet power and its leadership are often eccentric and paradoxical—for example, casting the new social order in terms drawn from the culture and history of Russia's Old Believers.

Klyuev spent the first six years of Soviet power mostly in Olonia, for a time taking an active part in the cultural and political life of Vytegra, and appearing frequently in the local press. Although he lost some contact with his literary confrères in the big cities, his own artistic development continued rapidly. His *Mednyi kit* (*The Copper Whale;* dated 1919; a photo-reprint was published in 1990) collected much of his work of the later 1910s, including some of his postrevolutionary works. The two-volume *Pesnoslov* (*Hymn Book,* also 1919) brought together all of what the poet himself regarded as his major work to date, including, in the second volume, a considerable number of previously unpublished works. As late as 1999 this collection remained the largest and fullest collection of his work published in Russia. In it the early lyricism and the subsequent folkloric stylizations encounter quite different poetic forms and themes, including not only his ecstatic revolutionary songs but also his equally ecstatic, neo-erotic poems, some of them elaborating themes and concepts drawn from peasant sectarianism and first explored in *Bratskie pesni.* Most striking of these is his series of poems related to the *skoptsy.* Here, perhaps more clearly than anywhere else in his poetry, homoerotic notes are struck. By now, moreover, the religio-apocalyptic tone which marked his revolutionary verse was also being applied to his treatment of urbanization, and, increasingly, Sovietization, often in combination with sinister prophecy. Another striking feature of the newer work in *Pesnoslov* is the universalization of what had been, in the poetry of *Lesnye byli,* a largely local, or at least national, myth: the mystic culture of the Russian peasantry is now explicitly linked to "exotic" cultures, especially of the East. This syncretism has a counterpart in a recurrent lyric solipsism, which sometimes leads the poet to claim transcendent status for himself, his biography, and oeuvre.

In the immediate postrevolutionary period Klyuev was associated with the short-lived but intriguing Scythian grouping, headed by Ivanov-Razumnik (Razumnik Vasil'evich Ivanov), which also included Andrei Bely, Aleksei Remizov, and other prominent writers enthralled by the notion that Russia's messianic mission was about to be realized. Klyuev's works appeared in their two published almanacs *Skify* (*Scythians*) and in two small collections of his verse, *Izbyanye pesni* (*Songs of the Izba*) and *Pesn' Solntsenostsa: Zemlya i zhelezo* (*Hymn of the Sunbearer: Land and Iron*), which were published in Berlin by the Scythian publishing house in 1920. Here again clearly sounds Klyuev's mythologization of the peasant universe, this time around a series of key images and figures: *izba* (peasant hut), *kovriga* (a round rye loaf, the baking of which is for Klyuev the culmination of the rituals and routines of the peasant world and the rural life cycle), popular semi-pagan saints, and so on. The same year saw the publication in Vytegra of the collection *Neuvyadaemyi tsvet* (*Unfading Flower*), consisting of twenty-three of the poet's folk stylizations. The original edition is by far the rarest major item in Klyuev's bibliography; the Chelyabinsk reprint of 1995 was a most welcome addition to the growing number of such Klyuev reprints.

Klyuev's Lenin cycle, published as a separate volume in 1923 (with reprints in 1924) makes clear how idiosyncratic was his interpretation of the Bolshevik coup: Lenin is cast as an inheritor of the Old Believer traditions of social and religious steadfastness in opposition to the establishment and in fidelity to a passionate and mystical faith. This view of Lenin, while politically eccentric, is typical of Klyuev's poetic treatments of contemporary events, which he often colored with religious and mystical images and concepts. Another major element in his thematics by this time, although evident as early as *Lesnye byli,* was the opposition of urban and rural culture, in which the latter was depicted as the victim of the former's morally and socially degrading industrialization. During this period Klyuev also wrote articles for the local press and gave speeches calling for the preservation of the delicate but rich culture of the north.

In 1922 his collection *L'vinyi khleb* (*Lion's Bread*) was published in Moscow. Although it contains some relatively optimistic works, many poems sound the apocalyptic note first heard in his immediate postrevolutionary work and especially characteristic of many of his later treatments of the fate of Russia and its culture. Other poems expressly polemicize with literary or political dogmas of the new regime and its culture. In the same year his first two *poemy* (long poems) were published in separate editions: *Mat'-Subbota* (*Mother Sabbath,* 640–49) and *Chetvertyi Rim* (*Fourth Rome,* 635–40). These *poemy,* like many of his shorter works of the period, create a rural microcosm of balanced and cyclical life in which popular religious elements are combined with certain natural and agricultural features, and with markedly Oriental motifs, to produce a highly idiosyncratic, notionally peasant cosmos. In particular, details of rural northern Russia are often blended with aspects of the Islamic world to produce a strange, supposedly universal mysticism explicitly based on the culture of the Russian peasant, and implicitly asserted as a special quality of Klyuev's own verse. Many of Klyuev's works from his postrevolutionary years in Vytegra are, it may be argued, among his best, and as a lyric collection, *L'vinyi khleb* is without doubt a culminating point in his career.

Gradually—and in retrospect, not surprisingly—Vytegra became a less welcoming environment: some of the local intellectuals whose company Klyuev once kept departed, and the regional party organizations seem to have tired of Klyuev's personal (although by no means unique) interpretation of contemporary politics. He was publicly criticized for combining party membership with attending church, and although his reported defense was eloquent and characteristically sophisticated, even sophistical, he was expelled from the party in 1920.[23] In 1922 he was attacked by Trotsky in an article first published in *Pravda,* and then republished in a Petrozavodsk paper. Trotsky's criticism (reiterated verbatim in his *Literature and Revolution* of 1924) marked a significant growth in official hostility toward the poet and provided the material out of which grew, later in the decade, the image of Klyuev the "kulak poet."[24] After an arrest in 1923 he left Vytegra for Petrograd, returning, as far as is known, only once (in 1924 to retrieve his possessions). In the former capital he settled on Bol'shaya Morskaya Street (later in the Soviet period, Herzen Street), one of the principal streets of the city, in a small apartment attached to the elegant *osobnyak* (town house) which had formerly belonged to the Meshchersky princes—number 45. There he lived until 1931, establishing a sort of Old Russian domestic world (in this most unlikely of settings—an apartment attached to a grand house in the center of what had been imperial St. Petersburg, Peter the Great's Enlightenment statement of Russia's reorientation toward the West) by furnishing the apartment with native antique and folk items.

The end of Klyuev's Vytegra period and his early years in Petrograd/Leningrad seem to have been entirely without poetry: in *Serdtse edinoroga* there are no poems dated 1923 or 1924; the first poem of 1925, "Ne budu pisat' ot serdtsa" ("I will not write from the heart," 522–23), is dated "30th July." After Klyuev's move to Petrograd and the publication of the Lenin volumes, only one more book was published during his life: *Izba i pole* (*Peasant House and Field;* Leningrad, 1928; reprinted Murmansk, 2003). His poetry came to reflect more and more despair at the fate of the country, its literature, and especially its peasantry (depicted as the bearer of the unique values which separated Russia from the rest of the world, but also tying the country to other national cultures across all political, cultural, and linguistic barriers). Meanwhile Klyuev—like so many other literary figures of his generation—became increasingly isolated and unwelcome in the pages of Russian literary journals. With the rise of the Stalinist notion of the kulak (literally "fist"; in fact, the more or less entrepreneurial and prosperous peasant, supposedly providing the main opposition to plans for the collectivization of Soviet agriculture and the transformation of the Russian countryside into a site of neo-industrial productivity), the new-peasant poets were an easy and appropriate target for literary ideologues, and Klyuev was treated with special hostility. His *poema* of 1926 mourning the suicide Esenin, *Plach o Sergee Esenine* (*Lament for Sergei Esenin,* 653–62), was followed into print a year later by *Derevnya* (*The Village,* 663–70), in which the loss of the Klyuev cosmos was treated apocalyptically. The publication of this *poema* in a Soviet journal—itself a rather surprising fact—guaranteed Klyuev's status henceforth as literary persona non grata.

Much of Klyuev's literary path and fate in these years conforms more or less to the familiar paradigm of the persecuted author under Stalinism. He made several attempts to write frankly propagandistic works, sometimes with results which, were it not for the circumstances of composition, might be described as intriguing. Meanwhile, he also wrote poetry of a quite different nature, of which the *poema Pogorel'shchina* (*Burnt Ruins,* 670–95; written at the end of the 1920s, it was not published until 1954 in the West, and 1987 in Russia) makes perhaps the most dramatic statement of apocalyptic disaster for Russia. Acute professional problems were, as is familiar in this paradigm, accompanied by equally pressing material concerns, as Klyuev, whose health was beginning to fail, became obliged to rely on subventions from literary organizations and even perhaps on begging for his subsistence. But not all of Klyuev's painful difficulties with Soviet power fit the general paradigm.

At this point in the chronology it is essential to address another element in Klyuev's story, unspoken but assumed heretofore: his homosexuality. There is ample reason to assume homosexual liaisons in the poet's biography before he settled in St. Petersburg in the 1920s: one may speculate on the nature of his relations with a number of his poetic addressees; his apparently close friendships in Vytegra in the immediate postrevolutionary years surely included love affairs; and his relations with Esenin at the height of their association in 1915 and 1916 have been the subject of much speculation. Documentary materials, however, are relatively scarce, as might be expected. Among early sources, a 1914 letter to the then novice poet Aleksandr Shiryaevets, living in Turkestan, contains odd and contradictory remarks on homosexuality:

> If I were putting together literary surveys, I would have written the following about Russian society: "Klyuev was in Petersburg [*Piter*].—Russian society

> almost licked him all over, but twenty-four hours later Russian society became disappointed in the poetic gifts of this son of the soil, for sons of the soil are unable to drive off to the bathhouse with soft gentlemen and do not see transformation of the flesh in pederasty. . . .
>
> . . . I have heard that in your neck of the woods the Sarts manage fine without schoolmistresses, using for love boys whom they deliberately keep in teahouses and inns. You might try this out—like the Sarts . . . Only definitely write me about the results [. . .]. (*Sd* 219, 220; final ellipsis indicates editorial cut in publications)[25]

And a postcard, possibly from 1920, addressed to the Simbirsk "peasant" author Nikolai Il'in, opens with the remark: "I, sinner that I am, would not refuse a brown-skinned boy with the eyes of a savage" (1:203).[26] The apparent scarcity of early documentation of Klyuev's homosexuality, it might be suspected, is partly because in Russia scholars working on archival materials and writers of literary biographies continued until very recently to treat with some caution issues of sexuality, and especially homosexuality, as the cut in the (1993) publication of the letter to Shiryaevets seems to illustrate. These and other reasons for such elisions will be explored below.

As the postcard cited above suggests might be the case, Klyuev's homosexuality is more evident, both in his poetry and in accounts of his life, by the 1920s. In 1928 Klyuev met the great love of his life, Anatolii Yar-Kravchenko, a young artist, who was seventeen at the time of their acquaintance, and was then known simply as Anatolii Kravchenko. It was Klyuev who suggested the name change, and it was under that name that he would become a very famous and successful "official" artist in later years. Yar-Kravchenko remained Klyuev's companion during the poet's final years in Leningrad, and was the addressee of many affectionate letters after Klyuev moved to Moscow; Yar-Kravchenko's marriage, in 1933, was a huge blow.

Some of Klyuev's poetry and prose as early as the late 1910s is also marked by frank homoeroticism, most notably in the section "Dolina edinoroga" ("Valley of the Unicorn") in *Pesnoslov.* Here are to be found, in addition to the poems proposing his aesthetic program, drawn from the natural and peasant worlds of the north, and his literary polemics in the poetry addressed to Esenin or preoccupied with self-definition, some of his most striking "sectarian" lyrics, in which the erotic mysteries seem to be mostly homosexual: for example, "Gromovye, vladychnye shagi" ("Thunderous, masterful steps," 323), "Dva yunoshi ko mne prishli" ("Two young men came to me," 324–25), "Budet brachnaya noch', sovershenie tain" ("There will be a wedding night, the completion of mysteries," 351), and "O skopchestvo—venets, zolotoglavyi grad" ("O castrati sect—the crown, the gold-headed city," 333). Later, in his lyric poetry of the early 1930s, much of it addressed to Anatolii

Yar-Kravchenko, a more personal and less mythologized, romantic, homosexual love is much in evidence. Among examples are "Pis'mo khudozhniku Anatoliyu Yaru" (1932; "Letter to the Artist Anatolii Yar," 579–83); "Sredi tsvetov kupave tsvest'" ("Among the flowers must flower the water lily"), "Pod pyat'desyat p'yanee rozy" ("At almost fifty, drunker than a rose"), and the other poems of the cycle "O chem shumyat sedye kedry" (1930–32; "What the Gray Cedars Talk of," 551–70), also addressed to Yar-Kravchenko. It need hardly be said that the combination with homosexuality of apparently archaizing literary and ideological interests was not only yet another indicator of Klyuev's paradoxical nature but also a potential source of extreme personal danger in Stalinist Russia—as the last years and the death of the poet would prove.

Klyuev's homosexuality ill suits many of the agendas which the poet has been used to promote, and seems still, if not a taboo subject, at least an inconvenience to many of his Russian readers and students. Yet it was surely one of the most powerful wellsprings of his art, and it surely contributed to the particularly elusive, contradictory, and mutable nature of the mature poet and his work.

Following his move to Petrograd in 1923, Klyuev visited Moscow a number of times, and he spent summers near Poltava, then in Saratov, and finally, from 1929 until 1932, near Vyatka (Kirov), on the Vyatka River, the last location appearing in some of his late poetry.[27] Despite the increasing hostility of published attacks, Klyuev continued to write, and his summers on the Vyatka—with Yar-Kravchenko—were especially productive. In fact, the early 1930s saw a revival of his lyric productivity, with the writing of a series of long lyric poems in a manner evidently developed from the lyrics of the 1920s, which had shed many of the ornamental features characteristic of the poetry of the later 1910s. Instead, they display more conventional language and metrical structure, at times a heightened rhetoric, but the same insistence on the priority of the natural world as a source of spiritual and artistic life. He was, however, rarely published after the mid-1920s (the appearance of *Izba i pole* in 1928 being a late and misleading indicator of grounds for optimism).

Much of his later oeuvre was first published abroad in the 1950s and 1960s and published in Russia only in the late 1980s and early 1990s. The period of glasnost in the Soviet Union also saw the discovery and publication of previously unknown works. Among the most significant of all of these posthumous publications was that of a draft of his longest work, *Pesn' o Velikoi Materi* (*Hymn of the Great Mother*), long thought to have been lost, but in fact carefully preserved in Klyuev's personal file held by the KGB in Moscow. In this work, dated 1929–34, the mythological and narrative preoccupations of the earlier *poemy* are continued and elaborated (this is his longest work by far—some 4,000 lines) in a treatment of an imagined and generalized northern world, based around the shore of the White Sea, one of the great centers of the Old Belief. However, other features (for example, at times a playful, even humorous narrative; and historical reflections on the fate of the imperial family) make *Pesn'* a quite distinct work, unique in Klyuev's oeuvre.

At the end of the 1920s Klyuev ceased to be a full-time resident of Leningrad (as the city was now called), moving first temporarily and then permanently to Moscow—a move replicated by a number of authors, probably in the hope of finding a slightly less hostile environment. From 1932 until 1934 he lived at 12, Granatnyi Lane (later in the Soviet period, Shchusev Street). In 1933 he prepared a new collection, containing lyrics written in the early 1930s, many of them associated with Anatolii Yar-Kravchenko. Not surprisingly, this small collection of thirty-three poems (entitled *O chem shumyat sedye kedry,* after the cycle which formed its core) was not published.[28] His health continued to decline. In 1934 he was arrrested and exiled to the Tomsk area. Until quite recently virtually nothing was known of his arrest, exile, and death, but now access to KGB archives and the publication of his correspondence and writings in exile have made this last period of his life relatively transparent.

Although Klyuev's perceived hostility to Soviet power and his "anti-Soviet" works were long thought to have been the cause of his arrest, it had also been suggested that the immediate cause was his homosexuality (tolerated in the 1920s, but subsequently persecuted, and the object of new legislation in 1934). The party functionary and editor Ivan Gronsky claimed that it was his denunciation of the poet's sexual orientation that led to the poet's arrest. Gronsky's information about Klyuev's sexuality came from his brother-in-law, the young poet Pavel Vasil'ev.[29] Klyuev's Moscow dossier indicates that, during interrogation, he criticized the destruction of Russian peasant culture under Bolshevik rule, and he defended his own poems in which that destruction was noted and lamented (especially works such as the late cycle "Razrukha" ["Destruction"], 624–31).[30] In these remarks during interrogation he showed remarkable strength of will and considerable courage (however, the dossier should not be read as a verbatim transcript of interrogation—in all likelihood it was one of many examples of that strange literary collaboration between interrogator and victim). The dossier also confirms that Klyuev was, indeed, convicted under *two* statutes—he was exiled both for political reasons and for his homosexuality, although Shentalinsky, in his publications from that dossier, chose not to provide details of that second charge (confirmation of Klyuev's arrest on *two* charges can be found in more recent publications from the Tomsk dossier, and in Azadovsky's *second* version of his biography).[31]

In exile Klyuev lived first in the settlement of Kolpashevo, near Narym in Siberia. His pleas to friends in Moscow and to officialdom (contained in his late correspondence, published in the 1980s) seem to have facilitated his removal to the somewhat greater comfort of Tomsk, although he continued to live in very bleak conditions.[32] In Siberia he composed his final works, of which two are known and have now been published: the *poema* entitled *Kreml'* (*Kremlin,* 1934), in which the poet denies his earlier self, praises "red Moscow," and asks for clemency; and what seems to be his very last work, the lyric "Est' dve strany, odna — Bol'nitsa" (1937; "There are two countries—one the Hospital," 631–32).[33] In the latter he anticipates his own demise as *pevets olonetskoi izby* (singer of the Olonia peasant house) and remarks in extremis of his sustained love for rural Russia.

Klyuev was arrested twice in Tomsk, the second arrest coming on June 5, 1937. At that time he was charged with participating in an anti-Soviet monarchist plot. (Such a charge, in Tomsk, at the height of the Stalinist repressions, itself indicates the grotesque unreality of the narratives into which Stalin's victims were forced—and is, moreover, clearly modeled on purges of the intelligentsia already undertaken in the capitals: persecution by template.) After interrogation he was convicted and executed "between the twenty-third and the twenty-fifth of October 1937."[34] Plaques were later installed on two of his places of residence in Tomsk, including the house from which he was taken during his final arrest (but, sadly, that house was demolished in 2007: the city of Tomsk remains ambivalent about the memorialization of those exiled or executed there during Stalinism, while property developers are more sanguine about building than preserving). However, his place of burial—presumably a mass grave—is unknown.

Such, then, is the outline of the documented life of Klyuev, an outline which is far clearer now than before the period of glasnost began in the Soviet Union. During and after that period a great deal of material became widely available, and some very significant discoveries were made—the latter most strikingly in the archives of the machinery of Stalinist repression. It is probable that almost all of the extant poetry and prose has now been published. The story told in a very brief sketch in the preceding pages speaks largely for itself. The path from the provinces to the capitals, and from derivative imitation of the preceding generation of writers to original and powerful literary statement of one's own is familiar among major Russian writers. The persecution and repression of Klyuev are also examples of an all-too-familiar pattern in Soviet cultural history. Klyuev's failed attempts to come to an accommodation with a culturally alien and hostile power were repeated by many. Even the emergence from the countryside of a voice articulating a point of view which may be regarded as grounded in peasant and patriarchal Russian culture is a paradigm encountered in the careers of other, for the most part doomed, "new-peasant" authors. Yet Klyuev's story remains striking, even when all the similarities with others are recalled. His northern location (to be examined below); his early entry into Petersburg's "decadent" literature; his diverse poetic output, changing so much over time; his homosexuality—these and many other elements make his story unique, and perhaps even uniquely engrossing. But to return to the starting point for this narrative, his story is also remarkably elusive at many points. This fact becomes especially clear when the documentary story is set beside the stories Klyuev told of himself, and the stories others told of him.

It is no surprise to find that what Klyuev said and wrote about himself differs somewhat from what may be constructed out of documentary records. While such differences must exist in every case and may be an essential feature of any artist's self-conscious presentation of his artistic and personal identity, the degree of divergence between Klyuev's documented and claimed lives, and the persistent uncertainty over the status of many possible events in those lives, are striking and telling. Equally striking, as discussion of the "disputed life" (below) will show, is the polarity of responses and the variety of credibility provoked to this day by some aspects of Klyuev's autobiographies. Many aspects of those various autobiographies (some are contained in his prose texts, others—more fragile constructions for the would-be biographer, to be sure—are drawn from his poetry, and yet others are attested in memoirs and recollections of the poet) are quite startling in their claims. Among the more dramatic features of Klyuev's own stories which to date have found neither confirmation nor contravention elsewhere are the following: Klyuev was a descendant of the archpriest Avvakum, the great leader of the early schismatics in the seventeenth century, and author of some of the finest prose of the period; Klyuev spent considerable time as a youth at the famous monastery on the Solovetsky Islands in the White Sea, wearing the fetters of an ascetic there; the young Klyuev journeyed secretly to the Caucasus as an emissary of a northern religious cult; Klyuev traveled extensively, not only in Russia but also beyond; Klyuev was an intimate acquaintance of the imperial favorite Grigorii Rasputin.

For some readers, many, if not all, of these unsubstantiated claims remain absolutely credible; for others they are willful misrepresentations, or part of a disingenuous artistic pose. In order to understand not only how such claimed details of his life can remain to this day open to diverse interpretation but also to understand why the claims and their interpretation are so important and so problematic, it is worthwhile to examine again and more broadly *where* Klyuev *came from.*

Two preliminary points must be borne in mind. First of all, as has already been shown, Klyuev was born and brought up in an area remote in every sense from the urban centers of early twentieth-century Russia (although, perhaps, comparably less remote then than now). Second, Klyuev was a member of a social milieu which was not the object of detailed bureaucratic recording (except when its members fell foul of the organs of state security). Thus, Klyuev himself is bound to be the only source for some information about his early life. But a third point is more telling: remote and, in some ways, "backward" though Klyuev's native world was in the eyes of educated Russian society at the time of his emergence as a poet, it was also subject to considerable attention, even to fascination, and to a degree of cultural and political mythologization from that same educated society. Moreover, not only had the Russian peasantry in general been, for the intelligentsia, the object of a cult of the *narod* for some time—mythologized as the genuinely Russian part of society, untouched by Western perversions and maintaining its unique forms of life and belief, many of them admirably communal—but the north of Russia had become an especially favored locus of this cult. The north appealed in part simply because it was indeed remote and was not being developed as fast as other parts of the country, but it also had a more specific appeal, based on special historical circumstances. Among other things, it will be recalled that there had been no serfdom in the north (hence the peasantry was supposed to be less worn down by institutions imposed from above); the Tatars had not reached the north (hence the northern Russians could be seen as more "Russian" than those in the central and southern parts of the country—although to say this is to forget, as many were wont, the presence of very large numbers of non-Russian native peoples in the area); and, most significant of all for the early twentieth century, the north was the abode of many long-established communities of Old Believers and sectarians—those groupings which had broken away from the established Orthodox Church to live in separate, secretive, and often very conservative social units, following their own blend of official and often heretical religious doctrine and practice. Last, but by no means least (especially for Klyuev's late autobiographies), there was a powerful prototype for the autochthonous, autodidact intellectual of the Russian north in the figure of Mikhail Lomonosov, who was himself, according to early biographies, briefly associated with schismatics in the north before coming south to make his name—a topic explored in relationship to *Pesn' o Velikoi Materi* in chapter 6.

The north was immensely appealing to Russian writers and thinkers in the second half of the nineteenth century and at the beginning of the twentieth, as is testified by such diverse representatives of this interest as the ethnographer Sergei Maksimov (*God na severe* [*A Year in the North*], 1859, subsequent editions 1864, 1874, 1890, also in collected works, 1908); the poet Konstantin Sluchevsky's *Po severu Rossii: Puteshestvie ikh imperatorskikh Vysochestv Velikogo Knyazya Vladimira Aleksandrovicha i Velikoi*

Knyagini Marii Pavlovny v 1884 i 1885 godakh (*Through the North of Russia: The Journey of Their Imperial Highnesses the Grand Prince Vladimir Aleksandrovich and the Grand Princess Mariya Pavlovna in 1884 and 1885*, 1886); and the young Mikhail Prishvin's travel works, such as *V krayu nepuganykh ptits: Ocherki vygovskogo kraya* (*In the Land of Unfrightened Birds: Sketches of the Vyg Region*, 1908). There are also many direct parallels to Klyuev in the northern interests of his mentors, associates, and literary confrères—from the poet and intellectual leader Aleksandr Dobrolyubov to the artist Boris Grigor'ev, from Nadezhda Bryusova, sister of the poet Valerii Bryusov, to Mikhail Kuzmin.

Russian intellectuals had been attracted to the Old Believers since at least the time of Dostoevsky. The schismatics seemed to preserve many features of Old Russia (i.e., without Petrine and post-Petrine "European" dilutions)—they were visibly archaic in their dress, audibly archaic in their speech, and evidently archaic in many aspects of their daily lives. They provided an interesting and paradoxical model of Russia by being simultaneously very loyal to a specific national identity and very hostile to many institutions proper to the country as a whole (central and peripheral at the same time). Although conservative in religious belief and social mores, the Old Believers were widely seen as a source or potential source of political, even revolutionary activism, not least because of their powerfully apocalyptic myths and expectations. Where Old Belief faded into more extravagant sectarianism (the *khlysty* and the *skoptsy*—and it sometimes seems that little distinction is made by outsiders between such sects and the Old Belief as a whole), symbolist-era Russia constructed an appealing model of erotic, even sadomasochistic mysticism. And lastly, the Old Belief might be especially attractive for an author of Klyuev's background and interests because it was, simultaneously, truly *popular* and distinctly *intellectual*—the Old Belief was a learned and sophisticated culture, flourishing among the *narod*. Mel'nikov-Pechersky and many others—some sympathetic, some institutionally hostile (Mel'nikov-Pechersky managed to be both)—had made the world of the Old Belief more or less accessible to readers of the late nineteenth century, although it remained a tantalizingly proximate but closed world. Mel'nikov-Pechersky had also helped to do the same for Russian sectarianism, which had become the object of intense public interest by the early years of the twentieth century.

In short, Klyuev could be and was associated in many ways with a world that was both distant and very actual to the literary and social agenda of the first two decades of the twentieth century. The extent to which he belonged to that world, or the various versions of it we see in his autobiographies, and the extent to which he belonged to that world as imagined by educated, liberal Russia (and these are two different issues) are highly charged questions, not only for Klyuev's own time but also for the present. And the view from the present is further complicated, of course, by the fact that in the late 1920s the problem of the poet's identity was resolved, at least for the duration—and for the forced conclusion—of his own life when he was unilaterally declared a kulak and an enemy of the new state.

If Klyuev's biography were to be told—as it often has been, and still is sometimes—with ample reference to his own, unsubstantiated, autobiographical claims, it would sound roughly as follows (the general points are summarized here, although many autobiographical texts have unique features). Emerging from a culture which was so settled and archaic that it resembled medieval Novgorod, Klyuev was a peasant autodidact, brought up on ancient Old Believer books and on legends told to him by his talented mother, who was familiar with the culture and beliefs of the schism. On his mother's side he was descended from the archpriest Avvakum, who was revered by his maternal grandfather, a devoted and prosperous Old Believer. His paternal grandfather had made a living as a popular entertainer, traveling the countryside with a trained bear—at least until the authorities outlawed the practice. Attracted both to sectarianism and to the elemental rebelliousness of the peasantry (especially the schismatic, northern peasantry), Klyuev himself traveled widely as a young man, acting as a messenger between exotic sects in Transcaucasia and his own home area. At the same time, he had experience of native asceticism, having spent considerable time in the Solovetsky Monastery as a youth. His poetry, eschewing the manner and thematics of contemporary educated poets, spoke for the people from whom he himself was issued, and drew extensively on their worldview, to the extent of elaborating the hidden Orientalism and universalism in the culture and daily life of the northern peasant. He was persecuted and several times imprisoned as a young man. When he came to St. Petersburg, he was uncomfortable in the company of writers from the intelligentsia but was a natural companion for other peasant poets, most notably for his younger brother-in-song, Sergei Esenin, whose self-destructive path was struck when he abandoned Klyuev for the seductive but ultimately fatal charms of the city and its culture. Often prophetic in voice and behavior, Klyuev had anticipated the fate of the imperial family. He had also been close to the last and most mysterious intimate of that family, Grigorii Rasputin.

In addition to these narratives, other features of Klyuev the man and the poet should be borne in mind whenever his created lives are examined. First, Klyuev was by all accounts a remarkable reader of his own and of others' poetry, and there is ample documentary testimony of the powerful impression he created when reading, whether on stage or in a private setting. In other words, Klyuev was a great performer. Indeed, while radically different portraits of Klyuev emerge from various memoirs, there is one fact which provokes no dispute: Klyuev was an enthralling reader of his own works.[35] This talent, and his interest in the theater, foreground what some call his *akterstvo* (acting; acting ability) or his ability to put on a mask. Second, Klyuev was a passionate autodidact. As early as a letter to Blok of 1912, the reader will observe an interest in Old Russian culture (see his comments on Daniil Zatochnik; *Sd* 200). By his maturity, Klyuev had acquired a broad knowledge of many aspects of pre-Petrine and Old Believer Russia—evident in his frequent allusions to favorite figures such as the schismatic leader and author Andrei Denisov, or the sixth-century Byzantine hymn-writer St. Romanus the Melodist. This cultural knowledge clearly shaped his mature notion of Russian culture as a whole, and of his place in it, as did his knowledge of Russian folklore, which he also seems to have studied with some interest, if not with a scholarly approach. It should, however, be added that his studies were by no means limited to Old Russian and Byzantine materials—his eclecticism led him to interests in Western cultures too. Third, the mature Klyuev was not only a passionate autodidact but also a passionate collector, and he surrounded himself both in Leningrad and later in Moscow and even in Siberia with artifacts and books which reflected his interests and his image of himself and of Russian culture. Many memoirists speak of the powerful impression created by the objects among which he lived in Leningrad and in Moscow (although they may disagree about the meaning of this collection). The inventory of his personal property taken by the NKVD at the time of his arrest in 1934 makes clear that even after years of poverty, the collection was considerable (*Sd* 414–16).[36] Each of these aspects of his activities and character contributes, besides the autobiographies he wrote or told, to the created lives examined here, and also provides a context within which to understand those lives.

The autobiographical texts themselves, although from the 1920s and 1930s, mostly provide details, as will be evident from the summary above, of his early life and his emergence as a poet, and are related to earlier statements made in letters, or quoted by others, although there is at least one record from the late 1920s of a narrative of more or less contemporary events in the same style as his stories of his youth: he claimed, in conversation with Viktor Manuilov, according to the latter's memoirs, that he had visited remote and secret Old Believer communities north of Lake Pechora in the summer of 1927 (no documentary evidence supports this claim, whereas it is known that he spent part of the summer of that year in a village near Pskov).[37] Of course, his life in the 1920s, largely spent in Leningrad, is more clearly attested than his early years, and is evidently more mundane (and was even, as Klyuev's own commentaries on it suggest, distressingly impoverished later in the decade). However, it should not be forgotten that it was here that Klyuev very actively constructed that striking private material environment (which provoked varying reactions from those who encountered him and which is also open to interrogation in terms of its "authenticity"): meticulously collecting Old Russian artifacts, as noted, he turned his Leningrad accommodation into a "cell" with exclusively traditional furnishings, and he sometimes dressed in traditional peasant clothes. In other words, the material world he routinely inhabited in Leningrad corresponded to the textual past he provided for himself in these autobiographies, and both were in striking contrast to the Petrine and Soviet urban setting within which he (re)constructed his persona.

Only two of Klyuev's prose autobiographies were published during his own lifetime. A half-page autobiography, recorded in 1922, appeared in a volume of "peasant and proletarian" poets in 1925; a year later the journal *Panorama* published a seven-paragraph text (*Sd* 43, 46–47). Two longer autobiographies, "Praottsy" (1924; "Forefathers," *Sd* 44–45) and "Gagar'ya sud'bina" (*Sd* 31–42), were published in full in 1987 and 1993 respectively, having been quoted extensively in earlier treatments of Klyuev. Other short autobiographical notes published posthumously include texts of 1919, 1923, and (as tentatively dated) about 1930 (*Sd* 29–31, 42–43, 47). In addition to these texts, there is a significant corpus of remarks and stories noted down by Klyuev's friend and intimate Nikolai Arkhipov, of which eighty-five items are published in *Slovesnoe drevo* (*Sd* 51–76).[38]

Those autobiographical statements, all made after the Bolshevik coup, not only should be seen in the context of the cultural preoccupations with the north, the Old Belief, and other such issues as outlined above but also should be set beside the many short autobiographies produced, often for collections, by Russian authors in the early Soviet years. Such autobiographies, which can be very intriguing, although often formulaic, frequently seem intended to remake the early or earlier life of the author into an acceptable Soviet paradigm. During the Soviet period, these autobiographical statements became part and parcel of the insertion of all Soviet citizens into bureaucratic structures, and were often "sanitized," or reconfigured as the official context demanded.[39] Klyuev's works, published and especially unpublished in his lifetime, draw on quite different models (including, most obviously, hagiography—especially popular versions of saints' lives—and folklore), but certainly invite comparison and contrast with the politically sanitized products of other writers of the period. In other words, Klyuev might be seen as producing a provocative mirror image of the politically "safe" autobiographies which others provided—or invented—for themselves.

As indicated above, the creation of the autobiography began long before the 1920s. Indeed, it began even before Klyuev had the opportunity to encounter much of the society preoccupied with the color and the magic, autochthonous charm of the north. The very first statement of this kind—

provocative, open to dispute, perhaps self-consciously re-creative of the author's life—might be said to come in the opening words of his very first letter to Aleksandr Blok, of 1907:

> I, the peasant Nikolai Klyuev, am writing to you to request that you read my poems and, if they are fit to print, make an effort to place them in a journal. Be so kind as not to refuse. Our village is remote, far from the town, and even there I have no friends who are close to literature. (*Sd* 164)

The tone—a mixture of supplication and insistence—is characteristic of the entire correspondence, but it is the simple but problematic parenthesis "the *peasant* Nikolai Klyuev" which gives pause. Klyuev was indeed legally registered as a peasant, but it is almost certain that he never worked the land for a living, and the documentary record suggests that by 1907 he certainly must have been at least as far from the basic preoccupations of the average Zhelvachevo peasant as that "remote" village was from the town. In any case, one of the most important features of Klyuev's correspondence with Blok is the former's repeated insistence on the social distinctions which determine the nature of their relationship: Klyuev is a peasant; Blok is a gentleman (and to be rebuked for it, in the eyes of both poets). That distinction provides one of the abiding, if often implied, features of Klyuev's created lives. Self-consciously Klyuev speaks from a point of view with which few educated readers could have personal familiarity, and speaks on behalf of an entire class. Both Klyuev's early political affiliation with the All-Russian Peasant Union and his emergence as a "peasant poet" in the context suggested earlier contributed, no doubt, to the marked tendency in his poetry to speak "for the people": a poem of 1910 is entitled "Golos iz naroda" ("Voice from the People," 125–26); while the opening line of a famous 1918 lyric declares "Ya posvyashchennyi ot naroda" ("I bear the people's consecration," 391–92).

But as Klyuev came into contact with the Golgotha Christians and more widely with the Petersburg literary world, his role and image as a poet from and of the people became more clearly defined (or, as some would see it, self-consciously elaborated). Azadovsky traces in the preface to his publication of "Gagar'ya sud'bina" the emergence of what he calls the "myth of Klyuev." Some of Azadovsky's points are discussed as the "disputed poet" is addressed later in this chapter, while his outline of the emergence of Klyuev's created biography from the formative self-identifications of the Blok correspondence to the autobiographies of the 1920s may be fruitfully reviewed here. Klyuev's letters are of some significance in this process, but the most important documents are the articles on Klyuev for which material had evidently been provided by the poet himself. The naïf Iona Brikhnichev, defrocked priest and leader of the Golgotha Christians, made one of the first significant contributions with his "Severnoe siyanie" ("Northern Lights," 1912).[40] In exalted tones he praises Klyuev (so exalted that the editors of the newspaper which published the article felt obliged to append a note distancing themselves from Brikhnichev's unquestioning praise for the young poet's humility, simplicity, and tolerance), comparing him, among many others, to Lomonosov and even to St. Francis of Assisi, and noting that "the poet is especially gentle with animals." The biographical information, however, is limited, and is all from Klyuev himself. We are informed that Klyuev is from a small, impoverished village where the inhabitants are distinguished largely by their ignorance (they cut down the only tree to make things "smooth"). Klyuev himself is barely understood by his fellow-villagers or even by his parents (who prefer their other son, whose successes are more evident in worldly matters), but the poet is kind and indulgent to those around him. Only one of the striking details from the created autobiographies appears here: Klyuev's earlier residence at the Solovetsky Monastery:

> While still young, tender, and innocent, the poet came as a novice to the Solovetsky Monastery, where he spent several years. What he tolerated among the coarse, hopelessly coarse and depraved Solovetsky monks—of that I will say nothing here. . . .
>
> I will say simply that his young soul could not stand the stifling atmosphere of the Monastery and he fled to the freedom of the meadows.

There is no evidence to corroborate the claim, subsequently repeated and developed many times in Klyuev's autobiographies, that he had spent time in the Solovetsky Monastery. But the far north (and it is worth noting that, remote as it may seem, the Vytegra area from which Klyuev came is not part of the *far* north), and, especially, the White Sea coast and its islands would become very important in Klyuev's later works: they are associated with the Old Belief, with the intransigence of popular resistance to authority (the siege of the monastery from 1668 to 1674), and with the idea of a special, magical ecology. It is not inconceivable that Klyuev never went there at all. But it is also quite possible that he did, at the very least, visit briefly the Solovetsky Monastery, and the appearance of the motif so early in Klyuev's published biographies supports this supposition. The Solovetsky episode, as related in Brikhnichev's article, is not colored with exotic asceticism as it will be in the following versions, but is closely, although somewhat obscurely and detrimentally, associated with Klyuev's homosexuality—the monastery is populated by "coarse and depraved" monks and is "stifling." This last feature of the poet's character is present, covertly or overtly, in many of the created lives, and some of the more exotic episodes in those lives detail sexual initiations or else appear intended to account for his sexuality. In general, of course, both the Old Belief and sectarianism were frequently associated in the popular imagination with sexual incontinence—as Andrei Bely's novel *Serebryannyi golub'* (*Silver Dove,* 1909) demonstrates—so the link between the monastery as an ancient, although long-conquered, center of the Old Belief and "depravity" may be grounded in a familiar stereotype. It should also be noted that, as Laura Engelstein states, sectarians entrusted to the care of the father superior of the monastery in the 1820s and 1830s were reported as homosexuals.[41] Since this report appeared in Mel'nikov's materials on sectarians, there is at least some documentation for the association "Solovetsky Monastery—alternative religion—alternative sexuality."

However, Klyuev's time in the Solovetsky Monastery sounds quite different by the time of the article which marked the beginning of the formation of a more complex created life, "Narodnyi zlatotsvet" (The People's Marigold," 1916; *zlatotsvet* is *Chrysanthemum segetum,* the corn marigold, but the Russian word literally means "gold flower"), by the literary historian Petr Sakulin.[42] For Azadovsky, this article and Ivanov-Razumnik's "Zemlya i zhelezo (Literaturnye otkliki)" ("Land and Iron [Literary Echoes]," also 1916) establish the image and reputation of Klyuev.[43] Sakulin's article, evidently based in part on conversations with the poet, states, among other things, that Klyuev went to the Solovetsky Islands at the age of sixteen and that, as a novice ascetic there, he wore nine-pound fetters. Here too first emerges the non-Orthodox image, as Klyuev had told Sakulin that his mother was from a long line of schismatics, and that members of his family had been among the self-immolants on Palei, the island where twice large numbers of Old Believers set fire to themselves and burned to death, rather than surrender to imperial authority (in 1687 and 1689). The image of Klyuev's family in this article is thus radically different from the portrait of primitive illiterates provided in Brikhnichev's article. Sakulin also emphasizes the remoteness of Klyuev's birthplace, remarking that it is five hundred versts (a verst—*versta*—is approximately one kilometer) from the nearest railway—a point Klyuev himself makes in correspondence, and which is repeated by a number of biographers, but which is somewhat misleading, given the proximity of his village to the northern canal system.[44] The Solovetsky motif henceforth recurs in his later autobiographical stories and is echoed in his prose piece "Krasnyi kon'" ("Red Steed," *Sd* 118–19) of 1919 and in his *poema* of 1926–28, *Solovki,* while the sectarian motifs are found in many poems and in some of the created life stories. The descriptions of church frescoes on the islands and of the reactions of visitors (including the author himself as a young man) to those frescoes in "Krasnyi kon'" are suggestive of the eyewitness (although not of an ascetic preoccupied with the mortification of the flesh). Among the memoirs attesting to the persistence of Klyuev's Solovetsky stories are those of Igor' Zapadalov, who relates what his parents heard from the poet in Leningrad in the 1920s, and of Nadezhda Khristoforova-Sadomova, who relays Klyuev's accounts to her in Moscow in 1932–33.[45]

The Solovetsky Islands motif also serves as a further reminder that Klyuev's autobiographies must be read not only in relation to general cultural and historical phenomena (the idea of the far north, the association of the islands with the Old Belief and popular resistance, and so on) but also beside the actual lives of contemporaries, which provide parallels and even, perhaps, models for Klyuev. In this case, it is the life of one of the first Russian "decadents," Aleksandr Dobrolyubov, who left St. Petersburg literary circles in 1898 to spend time in the Russian north, where he lived for a time in the Solovetsky Monastery, apparently preparing to become a monk.[46] Dobrolyubov, the Petersburg intellectual who turns to the north and the people, provides one of a number of such models, which Klyuev's autobiographies invert (the northern peasant follows the path of northern, popular religion before heading to the capital). Indeed, Klyuev's poetic address to Dobrolyubov, "Aleksandr Dobrolyubov — prechistaya svechen'ka" (1919–21; "Aleksandr Dobrolyubov—a pristine candle," 459–60) expressly articulates the relationship between addressee and popular, national identity, and implicitly the association between Dobrolyubov and Klyuev himself. However, to the models available from the lives of the intelligentsia must be added the popular counterweights: for example, by the early twentieth century, details of the lives, thought, and writings of Russian sectarians, especially the *skoptsy,* were widely available, and objects of much interest. The *Passion* of Kondratii Selivanov (*Strady Kondratiya Selivanova*), a founder figure of the sect, could, for example, be found in Vasilii Rozanov's collection *Apokalipsicheskaya sekta* (*Apocalyptic Sect,* 1914).[47] Some features of this and similar texts, and of the general cultural preoccupations of the sectarians (not to mention the preoccupations of educated Russian society *with the sectarians*), provide a useful context for reading Klyuev's autobiographies.

Turning now to the autobiographies themselves, the reader finds that the two modest texts published during the 1920s intersect, at points, with one another and with stories evidently composed and recorded but not published at that time. The shortest text, from 1925, begins with a characteristically provocative claim: "I am thirty-five. . . ." (Klyuev was probably forty-one). He continues:

> I was taught grammar, the composition of songs [*pesennyi sklad*], and all kinds of verbal wisdom by my late mother, whose memory I honor with tears, even unto death.
>
> My life has been like the journey of Batu [the thirteenth-century Tatar

> khan, whose invasion of Kievan Russia and destruction of Ryazan' is the subject of a famous medieval story]. It has run from Solovki to the blue mountains of China: and on it there have been many tears and secrets sealed. . . . My family tree is darkened at the roots in the time of Tsar Alexis, and curls with branches in the wonderful Stroganov writings, in the golden flame of miraculous fires and royal towers.
>
> My family tree goes back to the Passion of the Siege of the Solovetsky Monastery, to the self-immolants of Palei Island, to the unbending pillars of popular beauty from the Vyg community [one of the great Old Believer communities of the north]. (*Sd* 43)

It is characteristic that this highly stylized and self-consciously literary account, which has little in common with the standard brief autobiographical note, is nonetheless followed by an unremarkable enumeration of the poet's bibliography.

The second published autobiographical text, of 1926, is similar in manner, although it provides more details. Here it is the secular side of his ancestry which is described: the poet writes of his paternal grandfather, who made a solid living by taking a trained bear from village to village. The poet characterizes himself: "delicate-boned, white-skinned, soft hair. . . . My voice is pure and my words are measured. . . . I am not a drunkard or a smoker, but I am partial to sweet things" (*Sd* 46). The peripatetic motif is reiterated here: "My life has been like the journey of Batu: it has run from frozen Konevets—the steed's head—[an island on Lake Ladoga, with a monastery] to the purple bull of Shiva." But, as in the first text, the color and stylization are—and this is characteristic of the mature Klyuev—uneven. In a final paragraph he lists his favorite poets as "St. Romanus the Melodist, Verlaine, and King David"(!).

Many of these features are further elaborated in the autobiographies which Klyuev could not publish at the time. Of these, by far the most striking is "Gagar'ya sud'bina," which raises intriguing questions of genre and textuality, explored in chapter 4. Its story may be summarized as follows. Klyuev's birth was unusual and combined Christian and pagan elements (see the details of his "baptism" earlier in this chapter). He learned to read from ancient prayer books, saw visions as an adolescent, and had miraculous dreams after his beloved mother's death. Twice he lived on the Solovetsky Islands, and there he enjoyed the status of a respected and much-visited hermit and ascetic. But on the advice of an elder who came to see him and talked of Eastern religions, he turned to sectarianism and became a "Christ" (i.e., a flagellant). He spent two years as the psalmist of a sectarian "Vessel" (i.e., sectarian group) in Samara before escaping on the eve of the ritual castration planned for him. Then he went to the Caucasus, where he was taken captive by a band of swarthy youths, who took their pleasure of him by turns. His memories of his lover Ali, whose heart he broke when he left, remain fond to this day. Traveling all over Russia, he eventually came to Moscow and made the acquaintance of men of letters, but he disliked city life and educated company. He fled, via St. Petersburg (this is 1911–12), to his home region. There his mother foresaw and prepared for her death, which he continues to lament. None of his works is worth a single song of hers. As a youth, in the company of a group of castrati, he visited Tolstoy at Yasnaya Polyana. For refusing to serve in the military, Klyuev was imprisoned. In all he was imprisoned three times, on one occasion attracting the favors of the murderer Dubov. The guards, resenting his humility and silence, beat him mercilessly. During a pilgrimage in the far north, the young Klyuev encountered Grigorii Rasputin, whom he later visited on Gorokhovaya Street in St. Petersburg. Klyuev was taken to read his poetry before the empress. He also visited the empress's sister, Elizaveta Feodorovna, in Moscow. Such were the twists and turns of his life.

As must be evident from the summary, "Gagar'ya sud'bina" is highly episodic. It is also very stylized and combines, in characteristic manner, overt and hidden literary allusions (to the Bible, to Blok, and so on), folkloric turns of phrase, and highly poetic imagery. Elements of hagiography—literary and popular—are also to be found (for example, the youthful visions). Many of the episodes are echoed in his poetry: the Solovetsky Islands most obviously in *Solovki;* the Rasputin story in "Menya Rasputinym nazvali" (1918; "They called me Rasputin," 353–55) and in *Pesn' o Velikoi Materi;* and the story of his mother in the collection *Izbyanye pesni* and in *Pesn' o Velikoi Materi.*

Although some scholars remain convinced of the veracity of at least some episodes, it must be said that, on the whole, "Gagar'ya sud'bina" defies belief. Klyuev could not have spent as long as he claims either on the Solovetsky Islands or in a sectarian community. There is no evidence of an acquaintance with Rasputin, nor can the imperial favors he narrates be substantiated. Surely Klyuev was not sexually initiated by a band of swarthy lovers in the Caucasus? For Azadovsky, the story is one culminating point of the Klyuev myth, constructed by the poet as a response to the cultural climate of the day, from which he profited (see discussion of the "disputed poet" below). Yet this seems to be a somewhat reductive reading. First of all, the cultural climate of 1922, when the story was recorded, was no longer quite so clement. Second, there is a marked continuity between Klyuev's verse and these highly poetic prose texts—in thematics, language, imagery, discursive unevenness, and so on. And this continuity extends beyond the autobiographies into the realm of the poet's material existence (his dress, manner of speaking, domestic environment, and so on)—indicating something more substantial than or different from a literary "myth." Third, there is a recurrent and sometimes overt association between Klyuev's homosexuality and these constructed lives, which suggests that at least one key to his protean identities may lie in his sexuality.

A sober observer might add a fourth point: who on earth would take these autobiographies at face value? Indeed, there seems to be a gentle slippage from remarks on the "journey of Batu" from east to west and north to south (remarks which, contrary to the opinion of some readers, seem to invite interpetation as principally a commentary on Klyuev's cosmic poetics rather than his actual cultural tourism) to the elaborate description of episodes which seem evidently counterfactual. Yet the imagined sober observer would also have to confront the fact that many people did indeed take these claims literally and very seriously, and some still do. At the very least, many Russian commentators seem to believe either that these lives are a sly fabrication by a poet with an eye to what will appeal or are a direct narrative of the life of an indigenous seer and bard. Each side has evidence to support its point of view. Klyuev did have an eye for what would appeal, and these stories not only remain captivating but have become more enthralling over time. And Klyuev the bard and seer is easy to find—his use of the popular is obvious, and he was in many ways remarkably prophetic in his view of Russia. Yet a middle way, in which neither falsification nor substantiation is at issue, seems more sensible. Especially if the later versions of the created life are examined.

A short autobiographical note dated around 1930 reads:

> By birth I am a peasant from the northern coast. My forefathers are forever remembered for their defense of the ancient religion in the book *The Russian Vineyard.* I know Russia [Rus'] from the Karel people and Pinega to the sapphire mountains of the Chinese white waters. I have cried and I have pitied others many times in my life. I think of my verses only as the detritus of the mind [*sor myslennyi*]—my essence is not to be found in them. . . . For three whole years I have been pining [*toskuyu*] in the city for the paths of hares, the blue willows, my mother's miraculous loom.
>
> I learned, in my peasant house, from the fiery words of Avvakum the Archpriest, from Romanus the Melodist. (*Sd* 47)

As Azadovsky points out, the phrase *sor myslennyi* is a recurrent motif in these autobiographical texts—it appears in "Gagar'ya sud'bina" too. The phrase is a distortion of Paul in Philippians 3:8.[48] In passing, it should be noted that the phrase "For three whole years I have been pining in the city" might lead one to question the late dating of this text, but that date, given originally by Gordon McVay, the British scholar who published the text in *Sochineniya* (1:185–86), has been repeated in subsequent treatments. At any rate, compared with other autobiographies, the reiteration of themes and manner is striking, and if the date is correct, it confirms Klyuev's adherence to this version of himself, which is even more striking, given the open hostility with which precisely that aspect of him and his work was being treated by the end of the 1920s.

The singer Khristoforova-Sadomova, who, with her husband, accommodated Klyuev in Moscow in 1931–32, while the poet was completing the exchange of his Leningrad apartment for his permanent quarters in Moscow, provides further evidence that Klyuev not only adhered to his created lives in the ever more threatening atmosphere of the early 1930s but also expanded them. In her memoirs, written in 1967, and first published in full in 1992, she gives the following account of Klyuev's birth and youth.[49] His father was a wealthy fisherman from the White Sea coast. At around fifty years of age he married a local Old Believer girl, the seventeen-year-old Paraskeva (Praskov'ya). Shortly after Nikolai's birth, his father was crushed to death by icebergs. The future poet was brought up by his exceptionally devout mother, who turned the second floor of their prosperous house into a sort of chapel. At twelve, the young Klyuev was sent to the Solovetsky Islands, where he studied under the direction of an elder for two years. But he missed his mother so much that, instead of becoming a monk, he finally returned home, where he lived with his mother until her death at the age of thirty-seven (when he was eighteen). His mother's death was a terrible blow for the poet, although it was assuaged somewhat by her appearance to him in a vision, where she offered great comfort to her grieving son.

Several elements in this story echo other versions of his life (the image of his mother; his grief and his visions after her death), while the displacement of his homeland further north to the White Sea coast is consistent with his general preoccupation with the areas of the north not only most remote from urban Russia but also closely associated with the Old Belief.[50] Again, the echoes of the early life of Lomonosov (whose first official biography links his early education to contact with the Old Belief) are significant. Perhaps more important, however, is the fact that the geographical displacement of his birth in this story is in exact parallel with the geography of the magnum opus on which he was working at the time he told this story to Khristoforova-Sadomova—his *Pesn' o Velikoi Materi.* Again, poetic text and created life run in parallel (of course, given the distance between the acquaintance of memoirist with poet and the composition of the memoirs themselves, there is also the possibility that it is the memoirist who has run text into life).

These more elaborate created lives of the 1920s and 1930s must be seen in part as an aesthetic and even polemical response to the cultural and social transformation being wrought by Soviet power. They are also spiritual statements—made, let it be said, not without some courage. Their proximity to other aspects of Klyuev's activities also indicates that while, through their internal and mutual contradictions, they fracture any kind of putative wholeness in the poet's life and image, they also form part of an intriguing continuum of image, artist, and self. Historical circumstances also give earlier motifs, restated in the 1920s and 1930s, a quite different tenor. For example, the stories of Klyuev's Solovetsky Islands experiences, present from his very first projections of himself in the 1910s, take on a quite different meaning in the Soviet period, when the islands, previously the site of a famous monastery, had become the cradle of what would eventually be known as the Gulag. In other words, Klyuev's continued emphasis on and even expansion of his Solovetsky monasticism must now be read against the background provided by the conversion of the monastery into a prison camp, in an early example of Soviet barbarism.

Finally, if these stories are, in a sense, to be seen as provoked by the aggressive destructiveness of Soviet policies on religion, the village, and the peasantry, it must also be said that they are *facilitated* by those same policies. For the world from which Klyuev came was, by the 1930s, much more remote to the inhabitants of big-city Russia than it had been in the early years of the century. Russia was becoming an industrialized, urban country, and its urban population was becoming more and more isolated from the countryside (even though the majority of city-dwellers were descended from peasants, or had themselves been born in the country). Stalinism was dividing the country from the city yet more, even as it drove many peasants into the city to find work, or, at times, simply in order to survive. And in the years since the Second World War this divide, which in other industrialized countries has been bridged by mass communications, roads, and above all, mass automobile ownership, has in Russia become wider still—partly because of the absence of such bridging features. Moreover, since the beginning of collectivization, few peasants, once arrived in the big cities of Russia, have shown much inclination to return willingly to live permanently in the countryside (as was the case in the nineteenth century). At the same time, remnants of an archaic Russian peasant culture certainly remain active, if moribund and inaccessible to the urban dweller, whereas analogues in western Europe are nowadays to be found largely within the leisure and heritage industries—hence the image of popular peasant culture has especial power and tragic pathos in Russia today. For all the proximity of many urban Russians in generational terms to the peasantry, the closest most get to the life of the countryside is at the dacha (country cottage). A similar divide has been created in history—between the immediate pre-Soviet years and the present (a chronological divide of no more than a slightly above-average human life span): the social and intellectual history of early twentieth-century Russia appears far more remote, far more intangible, than is the equivalent in most other European countries. Consequently, not only must Klyuev's stories have been more appealing and credible to some listeners in the 1930s than might at first be suspected but, as will be suggested below, they have gained further appeal and credibility since then.

In order fully to understand the meaning and nature of Klyuev's life-creation, one further period of his biography must be considered—his exile. Even before his arrest in 1934, Klyuev had suffered years of deprivation and persecution, but they are not to be compared with his Siberian exile. His letters from Siberia often make for painful reading: he provides shocking details of his acute poverty, of the bleak conditions in which he is obliged to live, of his declining health, and of his own despair. In short, these are letters written in extremis (the primary addressees of published letters are the poet Sergei Klychkov, Klychkov's wife Varvara Gorbacheva, Khristoforova-Sadomova, and Klyuev's former companion Anatolii Yar-Kravchenko). Yet even in these letters, and in his everyday existence in exile, Klyuev retains many of the habits of his created lives. His letter to Klychkov announcing his arrival in Kolpashevo (Narym region; the letter is dated June 12, 1934) begins:

> My dear brother and poet, for the sake of my destiny as an artist, and for the sake of the monstrous woe, the abyss of misfortune, into which I am cast, hear me out without the struggles of vanity. I have been burnt on my *Pogorel'shchina* as once was burnt my ancestor Avvakum on the fire [at the stake] in Pustozersk. (*Sd* 313)

Such rhetoric (which, in a mixture characteristic of Klyuev's poetics in general, accompanies in these letters the most mundane and desperate of appeals—in plain language—for money, clothes, and support) is encountered throughout his late letters, notwithstanding the difficulty he evidently had even in obtaining writing paper or, after his paralysis, in actually writing at all. Equally striking is the association made with Avvakum, reiterating a favorite gesture of the autobiographical texts, and also found in the line "Gremel moi praded Avvakum" ("My ancestor Avvakum thundered") from "Gde rai finiftyanyi i Sirin" (1916–18; "Where lies the heaven of folk enamel and Sirin," 340–41). It is very telling that the transcript of Klyuev's Moscow interrogation records the same association.[51] Other parts of his late correspondence are equally revealing. For example, he provides different correspondents with two radically different accounts of his arrival in Tomsk. Immediately after his arrival, on October 12, 1934, he wrote to Gorbacheva:

> Dear Varvara Nikolaevna, it is a shame that I sent you a long letter, as I have been transferred to the city of Tomsk, they say it is clemency [*milost'*], but once again I am without a corner of my own and without a crust of bread.

> For a place to sleep, I knocked at the first door I came to: "For the love of Christ." The place turned out to be filled by a whole family, a mad son in the corner, he cannot control his bodily functions [*khodit pod sebya*], tormented. Oh Lord! What will become of me? Every drop of blood weeps. . . . Help with whatever you can. Farewell. (*Sd* 340)

On October 24, 1934, however, he described his first night in Tomsk to Khristoforova-Sadomova as follows:

> Right at the Feast of the Protection of the Holy Virgin I was transferred from Kolpashevo to the city of Tomsk, a thousand versts closer to Moscow. Such a transfer must be considered clemency and leniency, but, as I left the steamer on an unpleasant and cold morning, I found myself for the second time in my exile without a corner of my own and without a crust of bread. I set off despondently along the unbelievably dirty streets of Tomsk. Here and there I sat down, sometimes on a bench at some entrance, sometimes on some step or other. Wet through, hungry and cold, when it was already getting dark, I knocked at the first door of a crooked-sided old building in the remote outskirts of the city—hoping to be able to beg lodgings for the sake of Christ. To my astonishment, I was met by a pale, middle-aged man with curly hair and beard—and with the greeting, "Providence has sent us a guest! Come in, take your coat off, you must be tired." At these words, the man, with a smile, started taking off my coat, brought me a chair, knelt down and took off my boots, which were covered in thick mud. Then he brought me felt boots, bedding and a pillow, and quickly set up a place for me to sleep in a corner of the room. I thanked him, scarcely containing my tears, undressed and lay down—as the master of the house, without inquiring about anything, asked just one thing of me—to relax, lie down, and fall asleep. When I opened my eyes, it was already morning, a little samovar was boiling on the table, and there was black bread on a wooden plate. . . . Over tea the man told me the following: "There came to me a beautiful, stately woman in Old Believer attire, in a white head scarf worn down to her eyebrows: 'Take in my sufferer [*Primi k sebe moego stradal'tsa*],' she asked me, 'I will pay you for him,' and she offered me a gold coin." Dear Nadezhda Fedorovna, you must understand my tears and that condition, in which every drop of a man's blood weeps within him. She who gave me birth is watching over me [*moya roditel'nitsa uprezhdaet moi puti*]. (*Sd* 340–41)

Klyuev then describes another miraculous event which occurred in the home of his benefactor (an exiled church deacon): the unexpected discovery of a five-ruble golden coin hidden in a patch on his bag.

The difference between the two accounts is striking. One writer suggests that the second was written in an attempt to "comfort and calm" Klyuev's correspondent, but since his letters to Khristoforova-Sadomova are of an exceptionally confessional nature, and since all of Klyuev's correspondence from Siberia tends to emphasize rather than to elide his hardships, this explanation seems unlikely.[52] Rather, a comparison of the two pieces suggests that the immediate impressions of his arrival in Tomsk, as relayed to Gorbacheva, had undergone a transformation into a more appropriate form for a Klyuev narrative by the time of the letter to Khristoforova-Sadomova (written when the poet had already found permanent lodgings). It is quite possible that both accounts reflect aspects of Klyuev's actual experience that first day in Tomsk, but it is the second which belongs with his created lives. Equally noteworthy is another characteristic feature of Klyuev's writing—the verbatim and almost verbatim reiteration of lexicon in quite different (stylistic and tonal) contexts: "clemency"; "without a corner of my own and without a crust of bread"; "I knocked at the first door I came to: 'For the sake of Christ'" and "I knocked at the first door . . . to beg lodgings for the sake of Christ"; "Every drop of blood weeps" and "that condition, in which every drop of a man's blood weeps within him." These stylistic features, and the proximity of the second version to Klyuev's own intriguing and very literary dream narratives—told in the early 1930s to Khristoforova-Sadomova herself, among others (Klyuev certainly had a strong sense of his readership or audience, as, indeed, a comparison of the tone and manner of his letters from exile to different correspondents indicates very clearly)—suggest that even in the appalling conditions of his Siberian exile, an integrated artistic and personal life could be created and re-created by the poet.

Further evidence of such integration—and its cost—is provided by details in a letter of August 10, 1936, to Gorbacheva (*Sd* 379). Throughout his exile, Klyuev asked his correspondents to sell the potentially valuable artifacts and books which had been left in his Moscow apartment, and to send the proceeds to him to prevent his decline into total poverty. In an earlier letter he had described going out to beg at the market (to Gorbacheva, early December 1934; *Sd* 347). But in the letter of August 1936, written after he had been arrested and then released, having suffered a serious illness, he reveals the following: "I had a few rare books and old icons, obtained with effort—as an artist, I could not pass them by with indifference—but since that unlucky month of March they too are in other hands." Klyuev indicates here that, like the *poema* and the "few lyrics" that he speaks of in the same letter, these books and icons had been confiscated at the time of his March arrest.[53] In other words, the same man who constantly feared starvation or death from hypothermia, and who found himself obliged to change his—generally very modest—lodgings for lack of money, had managed to acquire antiques of undoubted value. Notwithstanding his remarks that nothing of an ancient, ecclesiastical nature was esteemed in Siberia, these purchases cannot have been easy or particularly cheap, and they must have been made with money sent to him—presumably also not without difficulty—by Moscow and Petersburg friends, anxious to protect him from a penurious death. Certainly, the editors of this correspondence are fully entitled to gloss the passage as evidence of the poet using his friends' money not only for physical but also for "spiritual necessities" (*dukhovnye nuzhdy*), but his acquisition of these items in such circumstances is, nonetheless, remarkable testimony of his loyalty to the creation of an integrated poetic and personal life (although, as will be seen below, Klyuev's interest in religious art has received other interpretations).[54] The same editors, preparing the reader, in their preface to this correspondence, for the stylistic features of Klyuev's epistolary manner, suggest that genre models for his letters should be sought among the literary forms of medieval Russia—the petition (*chelobitnaya*), the supplication (*molenie*), fragments of hagiography.[55] While such models may be rather more distant than the editors' remarks suggest, it is undoubtedly true that, like his icon-collecting, the letters themselves show that even when his life was threatened from all sides, Klyuev remained remarkably true to the lives he had created for himself as an artist and as a man. What others made and make of this fact is the subject of the discussion that follows.

From the very beginning of his career, Klyuev provoked radically divergent reactions among those who read or otherwise encountered him.[56] The reasons for some of the more ecstatic reactions have already been suggested, and the caution or hostility of the response of others is equally understandable. Nonetheless, the frequent polarity of attitude toward the poet, even at the very beginning of his career, remains striking. By the Stalinist period, much of the early hostility had been transformed, in the public arena, into the sinister language of ideological persecution, with which the published attacks on Klyuev were armed, while private reactions continued to be divided. After Klyuev's death there was almost total public silence on him in the Soviet Union until the early 1960s, whereupon much of what had been said in his lifetime was reiterated (although a preponderance of treatments relied, without acknowledgment, on details provided by a small number of pieces written in the West after the Second World War). In the 1980s, when it became possible in Russia to publish Klyuev freely and to write about him with equal freedom, a reiteration of the original bitter polemics could be observed. The degree of continuity, and the passion that accompanied much of this reception, were both remarkable, especially in the late twentieth century. After all, it should be remembered that by then Klyuev, despite the attention of prominent Russian philologists and the promotion of some cultural ideologues, was a relatively little-read poet among

Russia's (still large) poetry-reading public. Many nowadays consider him too difficult, too obscure, and sometimes too rebarbative in his themes and preoccupations—the modern reader's idols are more likely to range from Tsvetaeva, Akhmatova, Mandelstam, and Pasternak to Brodsky, or, for a less "sophisticated" readership, from Esenin to Rubtsov. Yet remarkable passion surrounds scholarly and popular treatments of Klyuev—just as was the case nearly one hundred years ago. While the reception and interpretation of his poetry, and his place in the twentieth-century pantheon, are subjects of later chapters, the polemics around the man (themselves, of course, intimately associated with the verdict on his verse) are considered here.

That Klyuev authentically represented and articulated the world of the *narod* was, as has been seen, assumed by many from the start. His second letter to Blok (November 1907) was quoted extensively by the latter in his "Literaturnye itogi 1907 goda" ("Literary Survey of the Year 1907"; published in *Zolotoe runo* [*Golden Fleece*], 1908). For Blok, Klyuev's words were clearly the authentic voice of the Russian people. But others, even at this early stage, treated Blok's reverence for Klyuev with irony, and savagely dismissed Klyuev as a pseudo-peasant. Rozanov, reacting to Blok's article, wrote in a 1908 satirical article that "the 'little peasant' [*muzhichok*] has been plucked from some restaurant, where he had ample occasion to envy 'gentlemen' out on the town."[57] Meanwhile Blok's interest and belief in Klyuev were echoed by many others. The roles of Brikhnichev, Sakulin, and Ivanov-Razumnik in promoting Klyuev and, especially, in promoting a certain image of the poet have already been mentioned. In addition to their articles, the brochure *Obretennyi Kitezh* by B. Bogomolov should also be mentioned (*The City of Kitezh Discovered,* 1917; Kitezh, according to Russian folklore, was the city which drowned itself in Lake Svetloyar to escape the invading Tatars; its story was particularly popular among Old Believers). These treatments of Klyuev, as has been shown, helped to establish and to support a particular image and story, given further credence then and subsequently by Klyuev himself. But just as Blok's early treatment of Klyuev received hostile and ironic commentaries, these later panegyrics, supported by many others, were not the only responses to Klyuev. Indeed, Brikhnichev himself turned from passionate advocate to equally passionate prosecutor within a year, accusing Klyuev of plagiarism and calling him a "new Khlestakov" (the foolish but effectively deceitful hero of *The Government Inspector* by Gogol) in a pamphlet of that title. And even Blok, for all his evident devotion to the idea of Klyuev, remained cautious of the man, while some in symbolist circles were downright hostile.

But the most famous indictment of the Klyuev of the 1910s was not written until the 1920s. It is in Georgii Ivanov's memoirs *Petersburgskie zimy* (*Petersburg Winters;* first published in book form in 1928). Ivanov, a former member of the Petersburg Guild of Poets, was by then an established figure in the Paris emigration. An elegant and witty writer of both poetry and prose, he has frequently been taken to task for his license with the facts. His lines on Klyuev, from the chapter on Gorodetsky, are, however, frequently quoted and have spawned similar treatments.

> But Gorodetsky missed the only real poet of this genre [the "new-peasant poets"]. He read his manuscripts and did not pay any attention to them. It was the "soulless" Bryusov who discovered Klyuev.
>
> Yet, on his arrival in Petersburg, Klyuev fell immediately under Gorodetsky's influence and firmly acquired the manner of a pet travesty of the peasantry [*muzhichok-travesti*].
>
> "Well, Nikolai Vasil'evich [*sic*], how have you settled in Petersburg?"
>
> "Thank the Lord, the Virgin continues to intercede for us sinners. I have found myself a little cell of a room, that is all we need. Come to see me, my son, favor me with your presence. I live on Morskaya, round the corner. . . ."
>
> Once I did go to visit Klyuev. The cell turned out to be a room in the Hôtel de France, fully carpeted with a wide ottoman couch. Klyuev was sitting on the couch, dressed up in a collar and tie, and reading Heine in the original.
>
> "I can manage a bit of their infidel tongue [*marakayu malost' po-basurmanskomu*]"—he said in response to my astonished glance. "A little bit. But there's no soul in it. Our nightingales have better voices, oh, much better. . . ."
>
> "But what am I thinking of," he said anxiously, "what sort of reception is this for an honored guest. Sit down, my son, sit down, my dear. What may I offer you? I do not drink tea, nor smoke tobacco, and have no gingerbread. But," he winked, "if you are not in a hurry, perhaps we should take luncheon together. There is a little tavern here. The owner is a good man, even if he is French. Just round the corner. He is called Albert."
>
> I was not in a hurry.
>
> "Well, that is fine, that is wonderful—I will get dressed."
>
> "Why get changed?"
>
> "Come now, come now—surely I could not go out like this? The dogs would make me a laughingstock. Wait just a minute, I'll be back straightaway."
>
> He emerged from behind a screen in a peasant coat, waxed boots, and a scarlet peasant shirt: "Well now, that's better."
>
> "But you'll not get into a restaurant dressed like that."
>
> "We won't be asking for the main dining room anyway. We peasants know our place is not among the gentlemen. Everyone should know their place [*znai, sverchok, svoi shestok*]. We won't be in the dining room, we're going to a little cell, that is, to a private room. They will allow that."[58]

That there are manifest inaccuracies in this intriguing account is signaled by the mistake with Klyuev's patronymic (which was Alekseevich, of course, and not Vasil'evich). And neither Gorodetsky nor Bryusov "discovered" Klyuev, although the latter did write a preface to *Sosen perezvon.* But Ivanov's general portrait certainly has some factual support: Klyuev may well have known German; he did like Heine; he did wear peasant clothes often in Petersburg; his manner of speaking was marked (and disliked) by many. In his treatment of these details, Ivanov's point of view is clear—Klyuev has fabricated himself; he is a *muzhichok-travesti.* Unspoken but assumed in this portrait is the poet's homosexuality, possibly, it would seem, the root of the "travesty."

Ivanov's description, which continues to be quoted to this day, represents, albeit in somewhat parodic form, a widespread view of Klyuev, and effectively summarizes the attitudes of those in whom Klyuev provoked hostility during his emergence as a major poet. Moreover, it provides one of the most vivid examples of a remarkably consistent portrait of Klyuev—the polar opposite of the image found in his admirers. In fact, it is not far removed from one of the earliest hostile reactions to Klyuev, Rozanov's savage irony of 1908, noted above. Rozanov, of course, was reacting only to Blok's citation of Klyuev's letter, but Klyuev's early epistolary manner anticipates other features of his behavior which will become more pronounced later and will draw the ire or irony of his critics. That Ivanov's account belongs to a consistent, established, and continuing tradition in treatments of Klyuev is further indicated by the fact that it is quoted, and glossed with a rather more sophisticated commentary, by another great poet of the Paris emigration, Vladislav Khodasevich, in his chapter on Esenin within his own book of memoirs, *Nekropol'* (*Necropolis,* 1939).[59] From Rozanov, to Ivanov, and on to Khodasevich, the line is clear and consistent: Klyuev is a fabrication.

Both Ivanov and Khodasevich were, of course, writing in emigration, where the act of memory and the articulation of that act in memoirs were already of great cultural significance by the late 1920s. Subsequently, the destructive forces of Stalinism and of other rapid, often violent social transformations rendered the recovery in memory and in literature of the irretrievably lost reality of the *recent* past one of the most culturally significant—and contentious—processes in Russian writing, whether metropolitan or émigré. For much of the Soviet period, the public (published) and private versions of these processes tended to be at variance. Hence the publication only in recent decades of so many memoirs composed long ago, including significant recollections of Klyuev himself. And hence, perhaps, the popularity of that singularly Russian form, the self-consciously fictionalized memoir.

Klyuev, in fact, is a prominent figure in an early and intriguing example of the fictionalized memoir, *Sumasshedshii korabl'* (*The Crazy Ship*) by Ol'ga Forsh. This evocative and dislocated narrative is based on the story of the House of Arts (Dom iskusstv), a short-lived but vibrant cultural institution in Soviet Petrograd. The book was published in 1931—hardly an auspicious year for the appearance of such a work—and was not published again in the Soviet Union until 1988. Forsh devotes some ten pages to Klyuev, who appears under the transparent moniker of "Mikula." She portrays three episodes from his biography: a reading at the Free Philosophical Academy (Vol'naya filosofskaya akademiya, founded by Ivanov-Razumnik in 1919); his appearance at a memorial evening for Esenin; and his appearance among a group of young writers at the House of Arts. The general portrait of Klyuev is sophisticated and ambivalent—the universally supported image of the brilliant reader, here with a sinister edge; the feminine tenderness, combined with powerful, peasant aggression; the self-consciously inappropriate behavior among the urban literati; the suggestion of theatricality in his appearance and conduct.

Forsh's portrait in her strange and enthralling novel is very much the exception among Soviet-published treatments of Klyuev in the 1920s and 1930s. As will be seen, most such treatments were of a quite different nature. And her version, intriguing and ambiguous, seems to have been shared by fewer memoirists and other writers than the ecstatic or the skeptical.

Within a few years of the establishment of Soviet power a new hostility to the poet emerged, fed first of all by the intense and aggressive debates over the place of literature and literary politics in the new state, and then supported by the establishment of an ideology and doctrine of Soviet literature. In the early 1920s, Klyuev was a particular target of two literary ideologues: Trotsky and Vasilii Knyazev. The former initiated his criticism in articles published in *Pravda* in 1922, repeating them verbatim in his famous *Literatura i revolyutsiya* (*Literature and Revolution,* 1923); and the latter in *Rzhanye apostoly: Klyuev i klyuevshchina* (*Rye Apostles: Klyuev and Klyuevshchina* [the Klyuev phenomenon], 1924). Trotsky's comments are, as might be expected, sophisticated and, in many ways, accurate. He sees Klyuev as a "peasant poet" of a very particular and novel sort, noting that Klyuev decorates his poetry with exotic references as a peasant might decorate his house with urban paraphernalia. Klyuev, he adds, is hostile to the city and welcomes the Bolshevik Revolution very much on his own, peasant, terms, and predicts that Klyuev will henceforth move away from, not toward, the ideology of the new state. Knyazev's book is, in essence, a 140-page review of *Pesnoslov,* in which Knyazev, a "proletarian poet" and member of the group Proletkul't, attacks Klyuev (in particular the recent Klyuev) for his mystical, semireligious treatments of nature and history, for his patriotic poems at the beginning of the First World War, for his proximity to the old intelligentsia, and for other such sins. Knyazev's book, savage but not totally ignorant in its criticism, of course predates the period when published attacks presaged imminent arrest (indeed, Knyazev, like most of the other "proletarian" writers, was himself to fall victim to the purges, evidently perishing in the same year as Klyuev, 1937), but its polemic with Klyuev's "ideology" anticipates the later attacks.

> In private conversations Klyuev says that *skopchestvo* [the cult and state of castrati] is his ideal. Too bad! The presence of such an ideal excludes any possibility of further growth and flowering of the soul. . . .
>
> Klyuev did not know that he was a poet, yet he was a magnificent poet. The forest, the silence, the isolation—spiritual-ascetic seclusion—all that helped the growth of his talent, gave his verse wings—distributed them in hundreds and hundreds of copies all over the endless expanse of sectarian Russia. They were used in prayers on the Volga, they were used in rituals in the Onega region, they were used to praise god [the Soviet usage, without a capital letter] among the snows of Siberia.[60]

What is signally lacking here is any sense of Klyuev the man as a fabrication (and that criticism is muted, at best, in Trotsky's commentary too). Knyazev takes for granted the facts of the biography, repeatedly refers to the "sectarian" elements in Klyuev, and even takes up the Rasputin association cultivated by Klyuev in prose and, especially, in his "Menya Rasputinym nazvali":

> You were called Rasputin for your *spiritual* proximity to him. Not because in your "spellbinding eyes" were the "souls of the stove and the wagon" and the "icy sparkle of Onega was in your self-immolating verses" . . .
>
> You were called Rasputin for your "adventurism," for your dexterity, which is truly unusual, and which allowed you to turn the communist revolution into some kind of flagellant ritual.[61]

In other words, the very things which provoked skepticism and the suspicion of inauthenticity among those who encountered Klyuev in the 1910s now form part of the basis for the assault from Soviet critics, for whom Klyuev's proximity to the peasantry, not distance from them, is evidence to convict. Knyazev repeatedly "buries" Klyuev, announcing his death for the last time on the final page of his book. This savage and violent polemic must have seemed foreboding even in the early 1920s. But there were voices in support of Klyuev, most notably L'vov-Rogachevsky, whose major statement on the "new-peasant poets" (a term he is credited with coining) is his book of 1919, *Poeziya novoi Rossii* (*Poetry of the New Russia*). Klyuev and the other poets whom L'vov-Rogachevsky was to style "new-peasant" had been, even before the Bolshevik takeover, the subject of lively discussion for reasons already explored: the nature and cultural potential of the *narod;* the relationship between people and intelligentsia (famously discussed by Blok); the religious profile of the Russian peasantry (supposedly both "pagan" and Christian); the relationship of the peasantry to nature and to folklore; the contribution of the peasantry to national identity; and so on. With the establishment of Soviet power, these issues took on a more directly ideological coloring, which, in turn, made more acute the debates around the merits and (now) the acceptability of the poets themselves. And added to this already explosive mixture was the remaking of Russian agriculture—in economic, social, and ideological terms—which the Soviet government was to undertake. Consequently, while the "new-peasant" poets were gradually pushed to and beyond the periphery of the acceptable in Soviet literature, they remained very prominent in literary polemics. And Klyuev, despite his enthusiastic (although somewhat eccentric and even millenarian) initial welcome of the revolution, was soon the major target. The combination of evident talent, established reputation (he was somewhat older than most of the other "new-peasant" poets), and "mystical" attachment to "patriarchal" Russian culture rendered him especially vulnerable. Equally, his "eccentric" character and behavior—that is to say, his dress, speech, and almost certainly his homosexuality—made him stand out all the more.

By the end of the 1920s Knyazev's criticism had become a model for the universal savagery with which Klyuev was treated in print. In the fifth volume of the 1931 *Literaturnaya entsiklopediya* (*Literary Encyclopedia*), the two-and-a-half column entry on Klyuev has but two lines of biography (and those inaccurate):

> KLYUEV Nikolai Alekseevich [1887-]—poet. Born in a peasant family; began literary activities in 1912.

The entry continues:

> K. is one of the most prominent representatives of the *kulak style* (q. v.) in Russian literature. . . . The poetic characteristics of this style are the desire to deny the importance of the class struggle in the countryside by representing that countryside as an idyllic patriarchal whole; acute hostility to the city, which destroys this idyll, itself depicted in religio-mystical and fantastic tones, and the desire to replace those class conflicts which are in fact unfolding in the real countryside with conflict between city and countryside—taken out of their social stratification (it is this which leads to the break with reality and to the fantastico-mystical depiction of a nonexistent countryside); finally, an emphatically hostile attitude to the socialist revolution and to the social reconstruction which it has brought.[62]

And so on. The familiar neo-ecclesiastical rolling periods of Stalinist rhetoric condemn Klyuev, clause after accumulated clause. So does the bibliography of secondary material appended to the entry: it lists uniquely hostile treatments, including not only Trotsky and Knyazev but also the more recent and more violent Beskin (*Kulatskaya khudozhestvennaya literatura i opportunisticheskaya kritika* [*Kulak Literature and Opportunistic Criticism*]; Moscow, 1930)—one of several such attacks.

In other words, the attacks on Klyuev's personal and social authenticity (a key concept throughout this discussion) of the pre-Soviet period have been replaced by much more threatening attacks on his ideological probity, sustained, however, by comparable criticism of his aesthetic authenticity—now he has created a "nonexistent countryside," rather than a nonexistent self. Hence, the lives of the poet have ceased to play any role in the public discourse of his critics. It is against this background that Klyuev himself continues to develop and feed what Azadovsky calls his "myth"—in part, it may be suggested, as a vivid (and not uncourageous) alternative to the oppressive mythological structures of Stalinism. Meanwhile, privately in Russia and publicly in emigration, the dispute over the poet's lives continued. And the fascination with the created lives was only increased by the relative public silence in the Soviet Union.

Klyuev's persecutors of the 1920s and 1930s left few records of the poet beyond their own published attacks of the time, in part because so many of them shared the poet's own fate in the Stalinist Terror. But there is one exception: the literary functionary Ivan Gronsky, who edited the newspaper *Izvestiya* from 1928 to 1934 and the journal *Novyi mir* from 1932 to 1937, and who is credited with the invention of the term "socialist realism." He took an active interest in all of the "new-peasant poets," not least because one of the youngest such poets, Pavel Vasil'ev, was related to him by marriage. Gronsky was arrested in 1937, and spent the next sixteen years in the Gulag. When he returned to Moscow after the death of Stalin, he became a senior research fellow at the city's premier institute of literary studies, the Institute of World Literature. In 1959, during the period of "thaws" under Khrushchev, he gave a talk at the Central State Archive of Literature and the Arts (TsGALI, now RGALI) on the "peasant poets" in which, among other things, he discussed his relations with Klyuev. This talk was published by the French scholar Michel Niqueux in 1989, and provides an intriguing insight into the world and views of an unreconstructed Stalinist apparatchik. Taking the dicta of Stalinist cultural policy for granted, Gronsky carefully categorizes the poets under discussion, identifying the later Klyuev as right-wing and bourgeois (although talented); Esenin as weak in character and led astray by others, including Klyuev; Sergei Klychkov as relatively well-intentioned (but drunken); Oreshin as a solid poet who toed the party line;

and Vasil'ev as talented, reformable, but led astray by Klychkov and others whose company encouraged Vasil'ev's "hooliganism" and bohemian conduct. Although it was Vasil'ev's personal conduct that attracted public censure in the 1930s (his drunken brawls and the like), while Klyuev was attacked largely for the presumed ideological content of his work, Gronsky's memoirs paint a more personal portrait of Klyuev than of any other "new-peasant poet." As in so many other hostile or cautious portraits, the "masquerade" in his behavior is emphasized: in 1932, Gronsky, having heard that Klyuev is begging for alms at a church visited by foreigners, summons the poet to his office at *Izvestiya:*

> The door opened. In came a man of average height. Poorly dressed. A scruffy jacket, a shirt tied at the waist with a belt, scruffy trousers, Russian boots. A beard. A cap in his hand. His eyes were narrow, clever, sly, penetrating. He stood, arms folded, by the door. He did not move further into the room.
>
> "So, God has contrived that we meet, Ivan Mikhailovich, the Lord God has contrived it. Well, your accommodation is very pleasant indeed, tra-la-la, very pleasant indeed! Just like paradise, just like paradise!"
>
> I approached him.
>
> "Nikolai Alekseevich, we are acquainted."
>
> "Well, of course, we met both at Blok's and at Gorodetsky's."
>
> So I said, "So, then, we will talk like adults or I won't talk to you at all."
>
> "All right, we will talk like adults."
>
> And then before me sat a highly educated man of our times. If you spoke to him of philosophy, he would talk like a specialist. He quoted from memory the German philosophers Kant and Hegel, and Marx and Engels.
>
> "I know folklore better than anyone else in the Soviet Union," he said, "I know old Russian painting better than anyone else."
>
> And those were not empty words.[63]

Gronsky tells Klyuev that, instead of begging, he need only sell a single item from his icon collection (according to Gronsky, Klyuev owned works by Rublev), and then supplies him with an "Academy ration" card and five thousand rubles. Klyuev then asks Gronsky to issue him tickets for himself and his "nephew" to travel to the country, and Gronsky gives him tickets to Vyatka (where Klyuev, indeed, spent several summers at the turn of the 1930s with Anatolii Yar-Kravchenko). From there, according to Gronsky, Klyuev wrote to him, and sent a *poema,* which the naive recipient found incomprehensible, until Vasil'ev explained to him that it was a love poem addressed to another man. Gronsky, disgusted, then arranges for Klyuev's removal from Moscow with a quick telephone call to Yagoda, head of the secret police, a decision rapidly conveyed to Stalin, who approves it. Klyuev was a "very talented man, who had totally abandoned the revolution," and who "forcibly pulled young poets to the right." Klyuev was indeed an "enemy of Soviet power," Gronsky concludes, and "when there was talk of his [posthumous] rehabilitation . . . I refused to write a letter of recommendation."[64]

Many of Gronsky's reminiscences of Klyuev seem dubious—the value of the icon collection is surely exaggerated; certainly, the circumstances of Klyuev's arrest were different from Gronsky's recollections. And his memoir is at odds with the facts on many points concerning other poets he discusses. Yet there is a remarkable consistency with the Ivanov line: Klyuev's "masquerade" (although here rendered in a far less intriguing portrait); his language; and the implied association of the mask with his homosexuality. Even the preoccupation with things German recurs here (as it does, indirectly, in Ol'ga Forsh's novel). But this version of the hostile line supports other conclusions too: once again, it provides ample evidence of just how preoccupied with Klyuev the Stalinist apparatus was (even given its general literary preoccupations); it suggests how provocatively attached Klyuev was to his own, supposedly invented, version of himself; and it suggests that Klyuev may even have intensified such self-presentation in the face of official hostility.

The power and persistence of Ivanov's version of Klyuev is attested by an account of an incident which must have occurred earlier than the subject of Gronsky's narration, but which was certainly written up later than his, and was published (in the Soviet Union) in 1977: here the ironic account of the peasant-travesty is combined again not only with an overt and hostile signaling of Klyuev's homosexuality but also, astonishingly, with the language of Stalinist persecution. This treatment is the work of Igor' Bakhterev, erstwhile member of the "absurdist" grouping OBERIU, in his "Kogda my byli molodymi" ("When We Were Young"; published in a collection of memoirs of the poet Nikolai Zabolotsky). Bakhterev describes how he, Zabolotsky, and Aleksandr Vvedensky were taken by Daniil Kharms to meet Klyuev:

> We found ourselves not in a room, not in the study of a well-known city-dweller, but in the peasant house of some kind of kulak bloodsucker [*miroed-kulak*], with oak benches, iron chests, icon cases with flickering lamps, extravagant birds of paradise and roosters sewn on curtains, tablecloths, and towels.
>
> We were met by a serious, kindly-looking bearded man in a hempen peasant shirt, his hands folded together as if in prayer. On a bench by the window sat a young man with a "pudding-basin" haircut, wearing a similar hempen shirt.
>
> Klyuev kissed everyone and said, "Now, my dears, we will dispatch the youth [*otrok*] to the pastry shop and put our little samovar [*samovarchik*] on."
>
> The youth departed.
>
> "I've heard lots about you, Mikolushka," he said to Zabolotsky, "such a

> nice-looking boy, pink and well-nourished [*ya pro tebya ponaslyshan, Mikolushka . . . yasen svet kakov, rozoven'kii da v tele*]. So good looking, Mikolka!" And he was ready to embrace Nikolai, but the latter pushed away his sweet-voiced host.
>
> "Forgive me, Nikolai Alekseevich," said Zabolotsky, "you are my namesake, and I'll be straight with you."
>
> "Go ahead, Mikolka, I'll even accept a crown of thorns from you."
>
> "I didn't bring a crown with me, but I will say what I think, only let's agree that you won't get angry. What the devil do you want with this masquerade? It was a poet I came to see, my colleague, but I've ended up God knows where, with some old man from the fairground. You have a university degree, you know languages, why on earth play the fool. . . ."
>
> Vvedensky and Kharms exchanged glances.
>
> "So much for the tea," Kharms whispered to me.
>
> And indeed, something extraordinary took place with our host. The seventy-year-old turned into a middle-aged man (and indeed, he was less than forty), with sharp, cold eyes.
>
> "Whom have you brought to me, Daniil Ivanovich and Aleksandr Ivanovich? Am I at home or not? Am I not free to behave as I see fit?"
>
> Not a trace of the northern accent and mildness was left.
>
> "If I like, I'll sing a psalm, and if I like, a French chanson," at which he demonstrated his knowledge of the cancan.
>
> We did not wait for him to finish, but edged towards the door and out into the corridor, where we saw standing in the darkness the youth with a bundle of rolls.
>
> "What on earth have you done, gentlemen [*grazhdane*]? He is irritable and vengeful. You had better be off."[65]

Klyuev, of course, did not go to university, as Zabolotsky is reported here as saying, and he could not have been under forty at the time of the reported incident (which must have been no earlier than 1928, the year when Klyuev met Yar-Kravchenko, who is clearly the *otrok*). While memoirs in general are notoriously unreliable—as the example from Ivanov's *Petersburgskie zimy* has vividly illustrated—Bakhterev's recollection of Klyuev is striking for more than its evident inaccuracies. That a memoirist publishing his work in the 1970s could condemn Klyuev as a "bloodsucking kulak" and more or less overtly associate his supposed peasant masquerade with his homosexuality surely invites a reaction of distaste from the informed reader (even if editorial pressure on the memoirist is assumed). After all, Klyuev had fallen victim to Stalinism partly because he was labeled a "kulak poet" and partly because he was denounced as a homosexual. As a document, Bakhterev's recollection seems a distorted, even degenerate version of Ivanov's memoir, with a latter-day Stalinist admixture, and it provides a fascinating example of the transmission of images and ideas from territory beyond the culturally permissible into the area behind the Soviet cordon, and then into print there. Nor should it be forgotten that the *average* reader of the volume of memoirs in which this text was published could not have been "informed" in the sense intended above, and would probably not have known the provenance of this version of Klyuev. The prose of Georgii Ivanov and Khodasevich, although available to the members of the literary and scholarly elites, both official and unofficial, who constituted the "informed readers" of the time, was, of course, inaccessible to the vast majority of Soviet readers in the 1970s. Thus most readers would have had no means to measure the plausibility of Bakhterev's account. Indeed, his portrait is cited by the editors of a glasnost-era publication of Ivanov's memoirs as support for Ivanov's version, although the latter is surely one of the sources for Bakhterev—an example of the vertiginous chronological reversals of Russian literature in the Soviet period.[66] However, once again, even in this degenerate version of the Ivanov portrait, it must be said that one finds, beside the evident distortions, much that is plausible: the decor of Klyuev's apartment is well attested; the description of the "youth" matches pictures of Anatolii Yar-Kravchenko; the theatricality and the homosexuality of Klyuev are equally well known.

Three other features of this memoir deserve commentary. First, Bakhterev (like Gronsky before him) assumes a strict stylistic diglossia in Klyuev's speech, which, while surely exaggerated here, is certainly evident in Klyuev's writings and might well have been present to a degree in his speech (although polyglossia seems even more plausible on the evidence of newly available sound recordings).[67] Moreover, in Klyuev's poetry (and to a lesser extent in his prose) the movement between stylistic levels, the sudden incorporation into stylized, dialectal, or other "ornate" constructions of contemporary lexicon, and related devices function repeatedly as part of an active and disorienting aesthetic, not as the intrusion of the "true" into a discourse of falsehood. A more sympathetic memoirist would assume this to be equally the case with the poet's speech, and the result would be a quite different (and more sophisticated) portrait. The second observation invited by Bakhterev's story concerns Klyuev and his created life: *unexpected* guests are reported as finding the poet and his lover dressed in peasant garb *at home* (contrast the Ivanov memoir). Consequently, one might once again observe that Klyuev's sartorial habits indicate something more than a desire for "masquerade," while historical circumstances again encourage an interpretation that is attentive to social and even political context. Third, Bakhterev's memoir suggests that Klyuev knew Kharms and Vvedensky reasonably well. There are grounds for arguing a certain typological similarity between the Olonian poet and the Petersburg "absurdists" both in poetics and in "theatricality," notwithstanding the obvious distinctions, and even for suggesting that they represent parallel developments in late Russian modernism.[68] Tempting though it is to take these aspects of Bakhterev's memoir as informationally significant, there can, however, be no certainty about the reliability of a text that is covert in its literary density, but overt in its ideological affiliation.

Nor is this the end of the line descended from Georgii Ivanov. In its turn, Bakhterev's story appears, without citation, in Nikita Zabolotsky's biography of his father, where it is treated as totally reliable. And in the English translation of that biography, the erroneous remark ascribed to Zabolotsky that Klyuev had completed a university degree is loosely rendered as "you're an educated man," thereby yet further obscuring the fabrication of which Bakhterev, not Klyuev, is guilty.[69]

Bakhterev's Brezhnev-era piece thus seems to merge the "Ivanov line" on Klyuev with traces of the ideologically driven criticism of the 1920s and 1930s. And like a number of other such pieces, it seems shot through with an unspoken hostility to Klyuev's homosexuality, which is implicitly associated with many of the poet's supposedly most "travestied" features.

Konstantin Azadovsky, in the second version of his biography of Klyuev, cites extracts from yet another hostile memoir of Klyuev in St. Petersburg—the page-and-a-half portrait "Eleinyi Klyuev" ("Unctuous Klyuev") by the art historian Erikh Gollerbakh, published in a 1998 collection of Gollerbakh's writing, but written no later than 1942, the year of the author's death.[70] Azadovsky points out some of the obvious errors in Gollerbakh's hostile account, but uses it principally to explore the theme of Klyuev and Old Russian art (Gollerbakh has Klyuev actively trading icons, and cites Mikhail Kuzmin as asserting that Klyuev even helped fabricate "antiques"—yet another version of the paradigm of falsification). However, it is also intriguing to note that this very hostile (and evidently inaccurate—Gollerbakh, like Ivanov, gives Klyuev the wrong patronymic) account ends with the following lines:

> Klyuev died in exile. In his time he wrote:
>
> Lenin has the spirit of Kerzhenets,
> An abbot's roar in his decrees . . .
>
> That got printed, and Klyuev thought: "Ah-ha, they've taken the bait!" But the bait worked only for a time. Soon he was removed. They didn't need to look for an excuse: they were cleaning all the queers out of Leningrad.[71]

Explicitly Gollerbakh links his own hostility (and Klyuev's death—albeit inaccurately presented) to the poet's homosexuality in a gesture that is often present, but rarely explicit in other accounts. However, as is typical of such accounts, Gollerbakh makes no attempt to link the poet's protean identities with his sexual orientation. Indeed, nowhere in treatments of Klyuev, hostile or sympathetic, has this association been explored, however intellectually and culturally inviting it might seem (especially to Western readers).

Gollerbakh, writing no later than 1942, knew that Klyuev had "died in exile," but, of course, it was Ivanov-Razumnik's posthumously published *Pisatel'skie sud'by* (*Writers' Fates,* New York, 1951) which provided the summary of Klyuev's life and death on which many subsequent authors relied, and, as an alternative to the Stalinist Klyuev, it had a powerful, although usually unacknowledged, effect on those in the Soviet Union who wrote about the poet in and after the period of the "thaws." When, in 1965, *Literaturnaya Rossiya* (*Literary Russia*) provided the first publication of poems by Klyuev in the Soviet Union since 1932, they were accompanied by a preface from V. Orlov, which, as Azadovsky points out, takes, without acknowledgment, of course, Klyuev's biography straight from Ivanov-Razumnik.[72] It is intriguing that one of the poems published then was "Menya Rasputinym nazvali," thereby mirroring Knyazev's early Soviet hostility, and sustaining the same collapse of created lives and fact into a seamless and unproblematic whole.[73]

By the 1970s, however, the beginnings of a more cautious approach to the assumed biography and image of the poet can be detected—in the archival publications of Gruntov and the young Azadovsky, and to some degree in the analyses of Vasilii Bazanov. In their different ways, each scholar interrogated aspects of the assumed chronologies and shed light on many aspects of Klyuev's life and work which were hitherto unknown or long forgotten. The expected result of this process would be a gradual integration of the documentary and created lives, as discussed separately above, with intellectual structures emerging to explain whatever points of dissonance remain. Yet such a process of integration, comprehension, and, of necessity, consensus has only taken place to a limited degree. Memoirs, some written long ago but only published in recent decades, often sustain early polarities, while the more popular (or popularizing) treatments of Klyuev continue to depict him very much in terms of the created life. For example, an article of 1988, entitled "Pevets severnogo kraya" ("Singer of a Northern Land"), informs the reader that Klyuev

> was born in 1887 [*sic*] in the small settlement of Koshtugi, in the Vytegra district of the Olonetsk *guberniya* (now territory of the Vologda oblast). There, on the banks of the river Andoma [*sic*], surrounded by deep forests and impenetrable swamps, his childhood was spent.
>
> . . . Praskov'ya Dmitrievna, herself from an Old Believer family, sent her son to the elders of the Solovetsky Monastery as a pupil. In their library he

> first encountered ancient manuscripts and early printed books. But the ascetic way of life did not suit the young man, and he left the monastery.
>
> . . . The poet greeted the October Revolution with delight. He moved from the village to the city of Vytegra and energetically took part in cultural and propaganda work with the population. . . . The poet died in 1937.[74]

This is by no means the only example of its kind, but it provides a good illustration of the general trend. The compression of Klyuev's own autobiographies with the evident half-truths and clichés of late Soviet appropriations and accommodations provides a rather extraordinary text. On the one hand, the reader encounters the romance of the north (deep forests and impenetrable swamps—with the Andoma apparently moved the best part of 100 kilometers southwest to Koshtugi); the Old Belief; the Solovetsky Monastery and asceticism. On the other hand, the poet's "delight" (*vostorg*) at the Bolshevik coup; his energetic participation in propaganda work; his commentary-less "death in 1937." The author even contributes his own creations—Klyuev's encounter with Old Russian culture takes place on the Solovetsky Islands. In a book published in the same year as the article—1988—the author corrects the date of birth to 1884, but repeats most of the other biographical assertions made in his article.[75] As has been noted, the increasing numbers (and openness) of memoirs did not put an end to the polar views of the poet. Klyuev's own accounts of himself found their way into some, while others retained a certain neo-Stalinist hostility, and yet others managed to establish something approaching a rounded portrait of the man.

Typical is the memoir of Igor' Zapadalov, published in 1992. He makes ample use of recently published materials in his generally sympathetic and often informative account, but he quotes without commentary Klyuev's statements that he had been in India, Iran, and China; that he had visited Tolstoy; that he and Esenin had together read their verse before the imperial family and that he had received a gift from Rasputin.[76] Zapadalov, who as a small child knew the poet personally, also reports that his mother was shown artifacts Klyuev had obtained during visits to the Solovetsky Islands. But the same memoirist is at pains to correct the death myths inherited from Ivanov-Razumnik, takes issue with the misogynist image of Klyuev propagated by Leonid Borisov in his memoirs of 1971, and disputes the story that Klyuev was unsympathetic to the distressed Esenin on the day before the latter's death. Zapadalov also quotes and disputes Ivanov's famous lines on Klyuev, lines which Zapadalov himself first heard quoted in a lecture course on Soviet literature at Leningrad State University in the 1950s (yet another example of the many conduits by which such notionally forbidden material entered and remained within literary—but mostly *oral*—discourse in the Soviet period).[77]

Relatively few memoirists seem to take a sympathetic but cautious line—one exception being the poet Ryurik Ivnev in his posthumously published recollections of Klyuev (1984). He provides a generally thoughtful portrait, in which Klyuev's created selves are seen as aesthetic and (if one reads between the lines) ideological evasions.[78]

Of course, divergence among memoirists is a universal. The specific context of Russian literature of the Soviet period provides other complexities, among them the delay in the publication (and often the writing) of many memoirs. But most significant of all is the very importance attached to such memoirs as testimony to events and personalities which the state had attempted to erase. For this reason, above all, it is with such passion that memoirists dispute among themselves versions of events. It should also be remembered that, in the late Soviet and post-Soviet periods of Russian literature, for these and other reasons, the memoir has become one of the most important genres of prose. The cultural process of recalling and restating a lost cultural heritage, initiated by such émigré authors as Ivanov and Khodasevich, produced in the late Soviet period some of the finest and most important Russian writings of the century. Nadezhda Mandelstam's memoirs are the most vivid example of the prominence of the genre, yet they form but a single example of a genre that is extraordinarily rich and varied. It is sometimes suggested that, in the English-speaking world, biography now fulfills the role once played by the long novel, while long novels themselves are now largely the arena for popular and genre fiction. In the Soviet period, the Russian version of the latter-day long novel was often an arena for highly tendentious art (be it socialist realism or its opposite), while biography per se, although popular, did not seem to reach the same prominence as in the Anglophone world. But the memoir—essentially the testimony of survivors about a world felt to be lost (and often shaded in particular exemplars with personal tragedy)—has achieved an importance and centrality in Russian literature that surely rivals that of the biography in Great Britain and North America. Hence, the insistence and persistence of contradictory versions of the poet in later memoirs are testimony both to the recurrence of the same Klyuev questions and to the extraordinary general cultural context in which those questions have been raised.

But Klyuev's life is not only contentious to modern memoirists. The same energy which has, in recent years, revealed a far more detailed documented life than was previously available, has also produced astonishingly savage polemics about the poet among those who have devoted considerable time and industry to Klyuev scholarship. To understand why the disputes around Klyuev go beyond the bounds of normal scholarly polemics, these disputes too must be seen in a general social and cultural context.

The meaning and ownership of pre-Stalinist Russian culture in general remains, of course, one of the most divisive and problematic issues for Russia today—hence the significance and variety of memoirs. A more local issue, however, is especially provocative: the meaning and ownership of the history of the Russian peasantry and its culture. These questions, first raised in the nineteenth century, have continued to be fought over in Russia long after Stalinism and other more benign aspects of the twentieth century put paid to most of the Russian peasantry and its culture as facts of contemporary life. This fight has, indeed, reiterated some of the familiar positions of nineteenth-century debates in which "Westernizers" and "Slavophiles" contended for the correct interpretation of Russia's history and for the right to direct its future. In particular, a neo-Slavophile Great Russian nationalism has long claimed power over the heritage of the Russian village, and has made its most powerful (and often provocative) statements in the works of the so-called *derevenshchiki* (country-prose writers). While it would be otiose to rehearse their positions in detail, it is worth recalling that they represent a position that is (still) anti-Western, anti-urban, ethnically unitary, and culturally introspective. Hence such writers as Astaf'ev and Rasputin continued (although, by the 1990s, rather peripherally) to inveigh against rock music, popular youth culture, moral decline, and, usually by implication, heedlessness of the values and practices of Russian Orthodox Christianity. The ideological matrix of many of these neo-Slavophiles also incorporates two other significant elements—ecological concerns, often blended with a degree of nationalism (the natural history of Russia has been damaged by non-Russians); and a sympathy for at least some of the achievements of the early decades of Soviet power (including, above all, victory in the Second World War, which is presented as a special demonstration of the Russian people's ability to suffer, endure, and overcome, and which is part of the acceptable side of Stalinism).

Neo-nationalist, neo-Slavophile writers appropriate Klyuev as a tragic articulator of many of those positions (his initial exclusion from Soviet culture and then his martyrdom being evidence of the unacceptable side of Stalinism). Indications of such appropriation are abundant. As ever, place of publication can be very telling, although sometimes very misleading, and students of Klyuev will find that a significant number of items have appeared in such leading neo-nationalist journals as *Nash sovremennik* (*Our Contemporary*) and *Moskva* (*Moscow*). At least one item appeared in what was often regarded as an extremist newspaper: *Den'* (*Day;* the article—a publication of fragments of the *poema Kain* [*Cain*]—was subsequently published in *Nash sovremennik*).[79] Of these conservative publishers and promoters of Klyuev, by far the most active have been the father-and-son team Stanislav and Sergei Kunyaev, who, among other things, produced *Stikhotvoreniya i poemy* (*Short and Long Poems*, Archangel, 1986), the first major edition of

Klyuev since 1977, when the edition of Bazanov and Shevtsova, which was also entitled *Stikhotvoreniya i poemy*, was published in the *malaya seriya* (small series) of the famous Biblioteka poeta (Poet's Library). In the introduction to the Kunyaevs' edition, Stanislav Kunyaev quotes with approval the "passionate speech" of the village-prose author Fedor Abramov at the sixth congress of Russian writers:

> The age-old foundations are collapsing, the ancient soil in which ripened all of our national culture, its ethics and aesthetics, its folklore and its literature, its miraculous language, is disappearing, for, to paraphrase Dostoevsky's famous words: we have all come from the village—our sources, our roots. The village is the maternal bosom where our national culture was born and formed.[80]

It is against this cultural and ideological background that the Kunyaevs present Klyuev to the Russian reader (and their selection of poetry reinforces this presentation). In another publication, Stanislav Kunyaev identifies Klyuev among Russia's writers as the most tragic victim of the Stalinist terror, and, in his enumeration of its famous victims, qualifies the martyrdom of the Jewish Meyerhol'd and Babel' by noting their proximity to the Soviet bureaucracy, while also observing that Mandelstam was not persecuted as thoroughly as Klyuev in his lifetime, and was published more or less fully in the Soviet Union in the 1960s and 1970s.[81] In the context of the intricate and sometimes slightly cryptic cultural and political polemics of the period, the Kunyaevs' position is clear: Klyuev is an ethnic Russian martyr, and a representative of a cultural treasury that was first willfully ignored and then violently destroyed by others. His fate was and remains worse than the famous Jewish victims of cultural Stalinism.

Kunyaev published a revised version of his 1987 preface as the introduction to a small paperback edition of Klyuev which came out in 1991, also under the title *Stikhotvoreniya i poemy*. In his revised text another clear stylistic marker of ideological position is evident, as he provides newly available data on the poet's 1934 arrest: "In February 1934 Nikolai Klyuev was arrested in his little room on Granatnyi Lane, on a warrant signed by the deputy chairman of OGPU, Yakov Saulovich Agranov (Sorendzon)."[82] Providing the full name, patronymic, adopted and original surnames of the man who signed the warrant would be redundant, were it not necessary to signal unambiguously his ethnic origin, which is not Russian, but Jewish. This stylistic gesture, implying in general that the Stalinist terror and the destruction of Russia were the work of non-ethnic Russians, and implying specifically that the great Russian national poet Klyuev was the victim of non-Russian persecutors, is also encountered, for example and in abundance, in

Yurii Khardikov's article on Klyuev's exile and arrests in Siberia, published in *Nash sovremennik* in 1989.

For many writers who do not demonstrate such marked and exclusive ethnic nationalism, Klyuev is still a profoundly *Russian* poet. Vitalii Shentalinsky, who gained access to the file on Klyuev created at the time of his Moscow arrest and held by what had become the KGB in its notorious Moscow headquarters on Lubyanka Square, published from that file not only details of Klyuev's interrogation, but also a text of *Pesn' o Velikoi Materi,* the work long thought lost. In his preface to a publication of fragments of that work, he wrote, "Klyuev is a sanctuary of Russian spirituality and beauty" (*zapovednik russkoi dukhovnosti i krasoty*)—a remark which speaks volumes for the place on the cultural spectrum where Shentalinsky would locate the poet.[83]

Hence it is clear that the life and work of Klyuev, intensely and provocatively discussed and manipulated by the poet himself and by many others during his lifetime, reentered the theater of Russian politico-cultural war in the late twentieth century. The work of the Kunyaevs, especially Kunyaev senior (Stanislav), has attracted a number of hostile reviews, in part, no doubt, because of the ideological agenda stated or implied in such works as the prefaces discussed above. However, the principal targets of published criticism have been, quite deservedly, certain problems of a textological nature, and a general carelessness with the problems of the documented and created lives of the poet. Textological issues are among the topics of the following chapter, and the biographical issues have already been discussed, but it is worth pausing over some other aspects of the polemics provoked by the Kunyaevs. Konstantin Azadovsky published a lengthy and highly critical review of the principal Kunyaev edition of Klyuev in 1987.[84] He enumerated many biographical and textual errors, and even identified examples of apparent plagiarism in the apparatus, but more telling, perhaps, are remarks such as these: "It is impossible not to sense that the author of the preface is far from indifferent to the '*izba* cosmos' of the poet"; "Some of S. Kunyaev's general judgments seem unconvincing to me"; "The Klyuev discussed is the one close to Kunyaev above all in . . . his denunciatory 'peasant' program."[85] In short, although Azadovsky's review is full of specific (and well-founded) criticisms, the underlying theme seems to be that Kunyaev has the wrong Klyuev. This notwithstanding the fact that Azadovsky himself wrote in 1978 that Klyuev "to the end of his days remained a Russian poet (in the fullest and deepest sense of that concept) and vividly sensed his own vital association to his native land."[86]

A year after Azadovsky's criticism of the Kunyaev edition, Sergei Subbotin published a lengthy review of the same edition, in which he too took the Kunyaevs to task, especially for textological errors, while also pointing out many of the positive aspects of their new edition of Klyuev.[87] But the second part of his own review is devoted to a polemic with Azadovsky's review. Here, the textological questions which inevitably arise in any assessment of scholarly editions, and arise in especial quantity and complexity in the case of many Soviet-period authors, give way to a more direct and specific debate with Azadovsky himself. Part of this discussion is dominated by familiar issues of archival, or even personal, politics—Subbotin points out that only Azadovsky has been able to gain access to the full manuscript of Klyuev's *O chem shumyat sedye kedry,* the collection prepared in 1933 by Klyuev, but never published. But Subbotin also challenges Azadovsky's classification of Klyuev as *merely* a *samobytnyi krest'yanskii poet* (original peasant poet)—in which classification Subbotin sees a denigration of Klyuev, whom he considers an appropriate member of the first class of the Russian poetic pantheon. Subbotin here precisely identifies the point on which Azadovsky is at variance with most other scholarly readers of Klyuev. It is clear from Azadovsky's biographies of Klyuev, and clearer still from the lengthy essay which accompanied his publication of the poet's "Gagar'ya sud'bina" (discussed in chapter 4), that Azadovsky sees Klyuev as a remarkable and intriguing cultural phenomenon, and as a gifted poet who used his talent to create a fascinating, but potentially misleading, myth about himself. It is also clear that Azadovsky, although he has devoted many years to the careful study and elucidation of Klyuev's life and work, does not consider Klyuev on a par with some of the other poets on whom he has written (for example, Tsvetaeva and Pasternak). Azadovsky's emphasis on Klyuev's mythmaking, his cautious treatment of Klyuev's sociocultural status, and his accompanying caution in any final evaluation of Klyuev's place in Russian literature all distinguish him quite clearly both from those for whom the poet is the most authentic voice and victim of a national tragedy, and from those who see him as a a poet of almost unrivaled mastery and sophistication (this last being clearly the view of Subbotin). Indeed, the intensely polemical atmosphere in which Klyuev is discussed receives another charge from the very title of Azadovsky's article accompanying his publication of "Garar'ya sud'bina": "On the 'National' [*narodnom*] Poet and 'Holy Russia' [*svyataya Rus'*] (Nikolai Klyuev's 'The Loon's Fate')." The quotation marks around the words *narodnyi* and *svyataya Rus'* are a highly provocative gesture in the direction of the ideologues of Klyuev as a national, popular poet.

These polemics display a remarkable degree of continuity with the original contradictory reactions to Klyuev, and reiterate through Klyuev a good many of the abiding issues of Russian cultural politics.[88] They also illustrate not only how intensely the territories of Russian literature and Russian literary studies (even professional "philological" studies) are disputed but how clearly it is assumed that these debates are a central part of broad cultural and political disputes of a general and public nature. Of course, with the end of Soviet power there came a decline in the general public's interest in "high culture" in general and in the intellectual disputes around that high culture in particular, but it is still the case that literature and philology (that is, professional literary and linguistic scholarship) are much closer to the political "mainstream" of Russia than they are in most countries of western Europe and North America. Moreover, Klyuev can also be found well beyond the political mainstream—he is, for example, the subject of a "radio mystery" by the neo-fascist ideologue Pavel Dugin.[89]

Yet even within these contradictory reactions and passionate disputes further paradoxes are to be found. The first is, to put it simply, that Klyuev probably was and certainly is now a relatively little-read poet. Shentalinsky in 1991 wrote of Klyuev's work that "what has been published [in Russia] is not easy to obtain and has had few readers."[90] In fact, Shentalinsky is only partially correct: several Klyuev editions of the 1980s and early 1990s did not sell out—at the time of their publication a considerable rarity for editions of an author long "problematic" for official Soviet cultural policy. Since the mid-1990s, Klyuev has been published quite actively, but with relatively small print runs. In other words, while debates rage around Klyuev, relatively few of Russia's many (and many very well-informed) readers of poetry actually read him. Nor would this seem to be a phenomenon only of recent decades: as Subbotin points out, Klyuev was widely condemned for poems with (typically) polemical or provocative lines, especially opening lines, which, on a full reading, turn out to be more complex in theme or point of view than the polemical lines would suggest—in other words, even Klyuev's contemporary critics often did not read him.[91]

The second paradox, at least as it would appear to most observers from western Europe and North America, is that in all the heated discussions of Klyuev's identity, nature, and achievement which continue to the present day in Russia, little mention is made of his homosexuality. Even in some post-Soviet scholarly publications of Klyuev materials there appear to be cuts where sexual matters might be discussed, and great caution is exercised when discussing the poet's evidently romantic and sexual associations. The publication, for example, of his confessional "Ochishchenie serdtsa" ("Purification of the Heart"), a text written in 1934–35 for—and perhaps, one might suspect, even to please—his correspondent Khristoforova-Sadomova only hints at what "sins" Klyuev himself might wish to have purified (*Sd* 361–67).[92] Azadovsky skirts the issue in the first edition of his biography, although he faces it more directly in the second version, noting, for example, that Kravchenko was "Klyuev's last love, his unconquerable passion," but still treating the circumstances of the poet's Moscow arrest and conviction with great circumspection.[93] Even Natal'ya Solntseva's book *Strannyi eros*

(*Strange Eros*), devoted to the "intimate motifs in the poetry of Nikolai Klyuev," seems constrained by circumstances. Her book ends with the remark: "I am not calling for the acceptance of Nikolai Klyuev's strange eros, but its existence must be recognized, if only because it is a given of Russian poetry." Her book, moreover, has remained very much on the sidelines of Klyuev studies. Klyuev's homosexuality is, of course, treated by authors interested in alternative sexual orientation and Russian culture, although sometimes here, too, circumspection rules. The witty and pseudonymous K. K. Rotikov in his *Drugoi Peterburg* (*The Other Petersburg*) devotes some interesting pages to the poet, but also notes acidly—if not without justification—that Klyuev's oeuvre is "pleasant nourishment for literary scholars, his poetry is complex and is very unlikely ever to become well known."[94]

Many Russians would respond with surprise or even distress to the suggestion that a person's sexuality and sexual preferences might be an integral part of an identity accessible to public discussion, and even more so to the suggestion that such matters might be directly or indirectly related to the creative impulse and its realization in works of art. Certainly, such attitudes help to explain how Klyuev can be appropriated to a nationalist, romantic conservative (and even to some neo-fascist) agenda, which surely must be—at least publicly—very hostile to homosexuality. But similar attitudes underlie the exploration of Klyuev conducted by scholars with no such "right-wing" agenda. While these silences and elisions—as they must seem to most foreign observers—are but one of many paradoxes in the contemporary reception and evaluation of the poet, they do, perhaps, help to explain why there is still such pressure in the work of many authors to create a singular and unified image of the poet, when so much evidence points to an intriguing combination of contradictory elements and influences.

It would be arrogant in the extreme to venture even the suggestion that a brief survey such as this could provide a totally novel view of the poet, but it is surely worth saying that, while many writers have acknowledged the contradictory and paradoxical nature of Klyuev the man and poet, few have drawn the full conclusions necessary from such an acknowledgment.

Nonetheless, a tentative resolution is called for. Klyuev was intimately linked to the world of the Russian peasantry; he was from a distant and remote area where much was archaic and almost everything was unfamiliar to the educated city-dweller. He was also a highly literate and ambitious man, although without much formal education, and he was shaped both by his origins and by the world that he entered as a novice writer. Given both of these formative circumstances, from the early stages of his career he saw himself as authorized to speak for the Russian *narod* and in a version of their voice and culture, and did so—sometimes notwithstanding the evident indifference or even hostility of that same people—to the end of his days (latterly with considerable courage). As he matured, he acquired more and more cultural knowledge which might appear to strengthen that authority, although to some it also appeared, because acquired, as part of a fabrication, and he provocatively displayed what he had acquired, including an identity which was partially assumed, as a strident (and soon very dangerous) politico-cultural statement. Side by side with this learning may be observed his tendency at times (in poetry and in other aspects of his artistic, cultural, and purely personal activities) toward stylization, which should properly be understood as a product both of the absorption of the folkloric and popular into "high culture" and as a feature very characteristic of the age in general—Russian art and literature of the early decades of the century were especially preoccupied with stylization and with the conscious remaking of identity in the light of myth. Hence Klyuev's aesthetics and image are a product both of origin and of the general sensibilities of the 1910s—and he remained eccentrically loyal to both throughout the rest of his life.

His homosexuality must be seen as one of the characteristics which very early distinguished him from the milieu into which he was born, but which was entirely consonant with the literary milieu he entered in St. Petersburg of the 1910s. Yet, just as he cannot have ever been entirely "at home" when he was literally at home, in part perhaps because of his homosexuality, so too his social and cultural sense of his origins, among other things, rendered him uncomfortable with, even hostile to, much of the established literary world. The creation of multiple identities—seen by some as a superficial masquerade—stems, it might be suggested at least in part, from his homosexuality, and is also profoundly linked to the variety of his artistic output, its diversity over the years, and its recurrent inclination toward dissonance, toward the very breaking of any putative whole—in direct contradiction of the *unitary* myths which others have often created around him.

There are several cultural perspectives in which Klyuev, for all of his evident uniqueness, may be placed. In the nineteenth century, the Slavophiles were ridiculed by their opponents for dressing in archaic Russian dress, and Klyuev's creation of a material self may be seen in this tradition (that is, the tradition of the Russians dressing up as themselves—a phenomenon which says much about the country). Of course, what is intriguing (and provocative) in the case of Klyuev is that a man by origin "of the people" seems nonetheless to be "going to the people." And similarly, yet conversely, his dress habits are, *mutatis mutandis*, not so very far removed from the practices of some of the Russian avant-garde, with their predilection for theatricality.

The fluidity of Klyuev's confessional identity was certainly predicated on popular interest at the turn of the century in all areas of popular religion (and later, in the Soviet period, on the state's hostility to religion in general), but it was also entirely characteristic of the world from which he came, where the boundaries between established religion, Old Belief, and even sectarianism could be fluid. Moreover, the Old Belief, in particular, provided a very important model, since it was both learned and popular. It is worth noting that one of the major modern students of the Old Belief, Elena Yukhimenko, has written sympathetically and with sophistication about Klyuev's association with the old faith.[95] Another "outsider" to these polarized debates on the poet's "authenticity," the American Ronald Vroon, has pointed out that there is more of the Old Belief in the garden motifs (a favorite image in Old Believer writing) of Klyuev than in comparable work of his contemporaries: "In their archaism, as well as in the cultural and ideological position they champion, Kljuev's garden poems reflect most closely the mind set of both the Old Believers and certain sectarians."[96] The lives of such diverse figures as the modernist intellectual Aleksandr Dobrolyubov and the sectarian leader Kondratii Selivanov provided models for Klyuev's life-creation and for his autobiographical texts. At the same time, many authors of the early Soviet period created highly mythologized autobiographies, in which cultural and political considerations seemed to blend to create multiple or synthetic identities (the autobiographical texts of Isaak Babel' provide one of many such examples).

Among the major obstructions to a clear view and understanding of Klyuev even now, when so much more material and information are accessible, are the very powerful drive in Russian culture toward single, homogeneous intellectual structures, and the privileging above most other ethic and aesthetic categories of the notion of "authenticity." The latter concept particularly marks and even disfigures the understanding of the dynamic relation between popular culture (especially folklore) and high culture, leading to a positive evaluation of any appropriation of the former by the latter largely in terms either of its accurate reproduction of the popular original or of its successful transformation of the impoverished source into an acceptable work of sophisticated art. The preoccupation with authenticity dogs not only the examination of Klyuev's work but also the examination of the man himself—for some authors, he is indubitably an authentic voice of the people because of where he came from, while for others he is an educated man who cultivated the entirely inauthentic image of a man of the people. There are signs of a more measured approach to these problems in some treatments of Klyuev's life produced in the last decade or so—for example, essays by Aleksandr Mikhailov and some of the essays by Elena Markova collected in her book on the poet—but Klyuev's life seems likely to remain an arena for impassioned debate and polar opinions for some time to come.[97]

To understand Klyuev, his "life-creation," and indeed his verse (as the following chapters will argue), binary oppositions must be left behind, while the context within which Klyuev lived his created lives must be understood. That Klyuev was so committed to certain aspects of his synthetic cultural profile that he continued to sustain that profile at the most dangerous moments or in the most extreme circumstances surely warns the observer that the "inauthentic/authentic" axis is not the most useful guide. As ever, the only possible conclusions seem paradoxical: Klyuev did, indeed, cultivate certain aspects of his image, and many of his autobiographical statements tend toward mythologization, but that does not mean that the image and the autobiographical statements are "inauthentic"; on the contrary, they are not only provocative but also profound assertions of an identity that is simultaneously integral and elusive.

Chapter Two

Text, Time, and Place: What, When, Where, How, and Why in Klyuev's Poetics

THE CONTRADICTORY biographical narratives constructed by and around Klyuev find many analogues in his poetry. The material texts of his work have often been elusive—lost, or brought to light many years after composition—while conceptual fluidity, thematic instability, and stylistic rupture are also typical of his writing. Klyuev's poetry is characterized by shifts which often fracture the putative integrity of the lyric, while individual poems frequently gain entirely new meaning through later modifications or when placed in new contexts (for example, within a newly formed cycle or within a new *sbornik*—a collection of poems, usually marked by relative thematic and chronological unity, and a key feature of Russian modernist poetry). Throughout his career Klyuev's work, like the stories of his life, also makes claims that are signally contradictory. This is perhaps clearest of all in the key matters of time and place. Klyuev's artistic and personal identity is, as the examination of his biography has already indicated, profoundly linked to particular ideas of place—the north, the village. It is equally firmly linked to time—the whole, archaic culture of a frequently evoked past; and, later, the recent past, before the joint cataclysms of revolution and industry. Meanwhile, its actual location in capital-city culture, Russian modernism, and the early Soviet period produces a host of key contradictions. Moreover, while his poetry makes abundant gestures to specific times and places, it also undermines such specificity with frequent and opposite gestures toward quite different cultural referents or toward generalities which militate against the specific. The very label often given to Klyuev—"new-peasant poet"—is redolent of contradictions around ideas of time and place, while contentious claims to particular geographical or historical associations are usually foregrounded in any discussion of the poet and his work. An examination of how text, time, and place interact in and around Klyuev's poetry will highlight key features of his thematics, and provide a context within which to situate the readings of individual texts and forms which follow in the remaining chapters.

Moreover, it is clear that the circumstances in which Russian literature of the modern period has been created and transmitted are different from what has obtained in most of what is now called the "first world," and have had great impact on the content and form of that literature. The literal place of literature—on the page, written or printed—turns out in Russia to be particular, and even peculiar. As is so often the case with Klyuev, his work reveals much that is characteristic of his nation's literature in general, while also revealing features that are unique and defining of him alone.

Textology (more often known in English as "textual criticism"; here the equivalent of the plainer Russian *tekstologiya* is preferred), the most ancient and, perhaps, most "scientific" of the philological disciplines, often seems to address the most intractable problems in literary studies. Even a cursory examination of Old Russian literature (that is, writing in Russia up to the seventeenth century) will confirm the local appositeness of that impression. The student who has struggled with the various versions of the story of Russia's first native saints, Boris and Gleb, or with the most famous of Russian medieval "problem texts," the *Slovo o polku Igoreve* (*Lay of Igor's Campaign*), will have entered an area of intricate and potentially circular argument, where detailed knowledge of the linguistic, historical, and material circumstances of the texts (sometimes as physical objects, sometimes as objects with no clear physical existence) may be marshaled in the cause of speculation—and speculation which often has its own particular and very powerful agenda.

While the printing press and the growth of publishing gradually reduce the prominence of such problems (at least in the literatures predicated upon widespread literacy and industrial distribution of belles lettres), textual issues often remain pertinent to problems of literary evaluation or canonical identification, even in the modern period. Access to an author's drafts, unpublished correspondence, and the like; comparison of different published versions; the posthumous discovery of previously unknown works, and their transcription and editing—these and many other such matters help, of course, to shape and reshape not only an author's reputation but also his or her very oeuvre.

Meanwhile, however, many authors have continued to operate beyond the boundaries of conventional literary systems, even in cultures with high literacy levels and industrial forms of production and distribution. Examples abound: among the most interesting and textologically challenging authors of the nineteenth century in Britain and America one might name Emily Dickinson, whose whole oeuvre might be said to constitute one huge textual problem (indeed, the same might be said about her life and the myths of her lives). The circumstances in which she wrote essentially bypassed the world of printing and publishing, rendering her texts approximate in certain ways to those of authors before the onset of "modernity." Another remarkable poet of the nineteenth century, John Clare (with whom Klyuev invites comparison), composed his poetry in equally "unconventional" circumstances, giving rise to peculiar, although less idiosyncratic, problems of textology—the treatment of nonstandard spelling and punctuation; the rendering of "dialect," and so on; the problem of the "uneducated" author in the modern editorial context. In each case, both the circumstances of composition and the various possible editorial approaches to the texts themselves raise not only specific philological issues but also very broad questions of social history, ideology, and critical methodology: the very way in which the texts are presented makes clear (or sometimes covert) statements not only about the authors but also about the editors, their points of view, and their times.[1]

Russian literature of the nineteenth century provides at least as many classic conundrums—the fragmentary parts of Pushkin's novel in verse *Evgenii Onegin;* the problematic shape of Dostoevsky's *Zapiski iz podpol'ya* (*Notes from the Underground*) and his *Besy* (*Devils*), among many such cases. The examples from Dostoevsky, in particular, also remind one that the circumstances of Russian culture in that century differ from the British or American equivalents. According to Dostoevsky, the censor ruined a vital part of the final pages of part 1 of *Zapiski,* thereby reversing the meaning intended by the author; no manuscript has been found, so there can be no certainty about the nature of the cuts. And in *Besy,* the intended central chapter—Stavrogin's confession to the monk Tikhon, in which the former initially admits to the cynical sexual abuse of a child—was reworked several times by the author at the request of the journal where the novel was being published in serial form, but no version was ever judged acceptable (and therefore, perhaps, no version may ever be judged final); in Dostoevsky's lifetime the various versions of this chapter remained unpublished, leaving an insoluble problem for those who wish, even today, to establish a final and canonical version of the novel. The famous "omitted chapter," first published in 1922, remains a subject of intense academic debate, and is also thought to have provided the source for one of the most powerful (and evidently unfounded) myths of the "demonic" Dostoevsky: that he had himself confessed to the sexual abuse of a child.[2]

And even where circumstances are less problematic than in the cases of Dickinson and Clare, or in politically constrained nineteenth-century Russia, textual issues continue to exercise readers of modern literature. The bitter disputes over the editing of Joyce's *Ulysses,* which began in the mid-1980s and which reverberated even in the pages of national newspapers, provide ample evidence of this, and illustrate how significant and significantly different are the philosophies and cultural assumptions which underpin different approaches to textology (not to mention, in the Joyce case, just how much money can be at stake).[3] Indeed, textual issues are at the root of many intriguing problems about the nature and achievement of twentieth-century authors—for example, editorial decisions about the works which Philip Larkin decided not to publish in his own lifetime and may have preferred destroyed; the multiple and varied redactions of the poems of Auden; and so on.[4] Editorial and publishing decisions in many such examples are, of course, fundamental in generating meaning. According to one reading, Hemingway's *Garden of Eden,* published in 1986 (twenty-five years after the author's death), is, in its published form, more the work of its editor than its announced author; nonetheless, it made Hemingway's estate over one million dollars.[5] Forster's famous, posthumously published novel *Maurice,* addressing in detail issues of homosexual love, emerged in a Britain very different in 1971 from the country of 1914—the year of its primary composition, thereby becoming to its first public readers a very different novel.[6]

Twentieth-century Russia turns out once more to be special, and indeed, far more of an exception than the nineteenth century, with far more—and far more complex—examples of "problem texts" and editorial issues. Many Russian authors of the last one hundred years have worked in an environment where writing and publishing were by no means organically associated, even for "established" (and, in some cases, "establishment") figures. For almost the entire duration of the Soviet period, severe restrictions were applied to the notion of the publishable. At the same time that notion was itself rather fluid. Consequently, authors might find that they had already written and even published works which were now unacceptable. Or they might write in the full expectation that they would be published, only to find out that what they had written was, upon completion, quite unpublishable. Or, again, they might write with the full and clear knowledge that what they were writing was unpublishable at home, but that it might reach readers both at home and abroad by other means. Or they might attempt, in parallel, to write both "acceptable" works (for publication) and "unacceptable" works "for the drawer" (i.e., for posterity), for export, or for unofficial distribution, bypassing the printing press. Or they might revise what they had already written and published to provide a new version, thereby partially eliding the old, to place themselves once more in sympathy with the current orthodoxy. Or, finally, they might write with a clear consciousness of the parameters of the possible, exercising those familiar discursive practices of "self-censorship" or "Aesopian language." And many, during the periods of most severe restriction, chose or found themselves obliged not to write at all—and even this could be very dangerous for a writer's health.

These, then, are many (but not all) of the variations of the consequences of imposed and repressive cultural policy, which must be seen as part and parcel of the history of twentieth-century Russian literature, but they are also the shaping circumstances for many aspects of Russian textual histories and Russian textuality, and they express or generate specific and even strange relationships between time, place, and text. On the one hand, informationally starved and aesthetically hungry Soviet Russia privileged the printed word of high culture far more than did most other countries; on the other hand, no informed reader could treat the contemporary domestically printed word as even a relatively reliable, albeit historically and ideologically bound, statement of canon, in the way most cultures would understand that notion and the processes behind it. In short, the printed word was prima facie untrustworthy, even while it was also one of the highest forms of cultural (or, as many Russians in the later decades of that period would have put it, "spiritual" [*dukhovnyi*]) life.

Moreover, because writers operated in an environment where composition and publication were so radically divorced from one another, other and different processes emerged. Dissemination by oral performance, or in manuscripts and typescripts, led to the proliferation of an author's (and sometimes others') variants, often synchronic, and none accorded the conventional status of canonical by the author's publication (poetry by Mandelstam and Akhmatova provides examples here).[7] The necessity to write "for the drawer" also led to the diachronic proliferation of variants, whereby a text acquired more and more chronological layers of composition as it was written and rewritten without expectation of publication (Bulgakov's *Master i Margarita* [*The Master and Margarita*] being the classic example).[8] The complexities of authorship, meaning, and identity are also brought into sharp relief by the problems in assessing the works of Mikhail Bakhtin and the works attributed to him although published under other names: if he was the author of those pseudonymous texts (as most now assume), what did he intend by them? Russian readers have often answered, "nothing" (that is, he published his "Marxist" works, using the names of friends, in order to make a little money). It is characteristic that many Western readers have come to quite opposite conclusions (he meant what he said), or have dismissed the notion of intention altogether. The debate over authorship, and perhaps even more so, the debate over textual meaning, illustrates the centrality and highly problematic nature of textual questions for twentieth-century Russia and its students.[9] For writers of the later Soviet period, bypassing the world of "official literature" and functioning in one of the many variants of the literary underground could lead to the creation of intensely contextual works, for which the natural readership might well coincide with the members of a literary salon gathered in a Moscow apartment, while the existence of a text in itself might be heavily dependent on a performance aspect predicated upon the presence of the author him or herself (here the practices and poetics of Moscow conceptualism provide a latter-day example, although the OBERIU writers also come to mind).

Thus the ironic formula "pre-Gutenberg conditions," coined to designate a world where writers have no access to the printing press, eloquently expresses the peculiar physical circumstances, but also suggests the peculiar *aesthetic* circumstances in which much of Russian literature existed for some seventy years. For these and for other associated reasons, twentieth-century Russian literature is rich in problematic textual histories, and dizzy with evident textual instabilities. What may be the quarry of careful theoretical dismantling in some cultures is an evident and material fact of literary life here.

Another feature of the cultural environment of modern Russia distinguishes it from most of its Western analogues, adds to the specific problems of Russian textuality, and provides a sense—to the outsider—of historical time having somehow been warped: the survival of many forms of folklore. While elsewhere the conditions of cultural production after the Industrial Revolution were hastening the extinction or near-extinction of those traditional forms of popular culture which were predicated upon collective creativity, oral transmission, and rural society, nineteenth-century Russia retained a very lively and diverse folklore, in part because it remained a predominantly peasant and illiterate society. Given the preoccupation with national popular identity which characterized the Romantic and later periods throughout Europe, Russian folklore thus became an object of great interest to producers and consumers of "high culture" while that folklore was still a very evident and active area of cultural activity, and not only on the geographic periphery. Whereas the British Romantics, for example, tended to look to the past or to the "Celtic fringe" for their folkloric inspiration, a Russian author might look no further than his own servants, or the village adjoining, but culturally remote from, his manor house.

In Russia, as elsewhere, not only the collection but also the *appropriation* of folkloric materials and forms became significant activities for educated society. Thus, belles lettres repeatedly and diversely takes on some of the features of folklore, while of course ignoring others in a process which, among other things, renders folklore perceptible and consumable as *art.* When viewed in retrospect, many such products of the literary appropriation of the popular seem to bear only a superficial resemblance to the "original," but it is a commonplace of the reception of such works that they are in their own time perceived as "authentic"—that is, as reproducing the folkloric original intact—even while their *literary* merits are also recognized. The ideological dimension of national popular identity in which these works were often located plays a crucial role in this contradictory, double identification. Meanwhile, in Russia, and in parallel to such high-cultural appropriations, folkloric forms themselves continued to persist—a situation which enacts the polarities of Russian culture and politics in this period with special drama, and provides further support for the notion that cultural time must be understood differently in Russia from the West.

Even in the twenty-first century, archaic folkloric forms have not been completely extinguished despite the combined efforts of general modernization (mass communications, travel, literacy, social mobility, and so on) and Stalinist attacks on the erstwhile bearers of such culture—the Russian peasantry. Meanwhile, the specific circumstances of Soviet life had already proved especially fertile ground for the growth of modern folkloric and neofolkloric forms. Examples range from the folklore of the Stalinist Gulag to "urban tales," given especial power by the many situations permitting oral narratives and by the many restrictions on the official distribution of information in the Soviet Union.

Hence, in the last two centuries, relations between high culture and various forms of popular culture have been of great importance and complexity in Russia. In some cases they may even be seen as dialogical: high-cultural imitations of the popular come to function as if they were *popular in origin,* or spawn genuinely popular forms themselves.[10]

"Authenticity" is often the most important and misleading category in the perception of folkloric elements in high culture, as has been noted. In the early nineteenth century Zhukovsky, Pushkin, and others wrote *poemy-skazki* ("folk tales in verse"), which took motifs from folk tales, radically modified them, and turned them into works, largely in literary verse forms, that were widely perceived as the authentic voice of Russian popular creativity. In the later twentieth century avant-garde and other authors turned such diverse forms as *barachnye stikhi* (verse of workers' barracks) and urban "incidents" with, *mutatis mutandis,* similar results.[11]

In fact, most such works of high literary appropriation are distinguished by a more or less self-conscious double voice (analogous to that observed in many forms of a similar phenomenon—the *skaz* narrative), and are also marked by many conventional signs of literary stability—individual authorship, unitary form and narrative, stylization, and so on. Nonetheless, as in the case of the special problems of textology in modern Russian letters, the presence in parallel of high-literary and folkoric forms, and the interrelationship between the two, serve to foreground problems of authenticity, identity, and stability as especially marked categories in the problematics of literature. These issues, in turn, are shot through with ideological problems, and invite markedly ideologized treatments from their discussants.

It is also self-evident that certain aspects of the poetics of Russian literature which appear historically (or aesthetically) after the great age of the novel display a preoccupation with various forms of artistic instability as an immanent feature of textuality. The generic and narrative uncertainties of authors originating in the middle of the nineteenth century, but anticipating in their prose the literary sensibility of the next age (Leskov, for example), mark the beginning of this process, while the various stages of Russian modernism, from symbolism to acmeism, mark its apogee, and Russian postmodernism its ironic reiteration. In the Soviet period, these conceptual instabilities (around issues of authorship, fixed or fluid textuality, and so on) meet material circumstances which are equally productive of such instabilities, but for different reasons—the impossibility of publishing, the lack of control over one's own writing, and so on.

Klyuev's texts illustrate abundantly all of these issues and their interrelationship. He was, qualifications notwithstanding, a Russian modernist. Yet he emerged, as has been seen, from a world still marked to some degree by the cultural practices of a preliterate society (most peasants were illiterate or semiliterate; folklore in the north—where, it should be added, literacy was more widespread—continued to thrive into the twentieth century). And he made considerable use of these circumstances, and perhaps even more use of the *perception* of those circumstances among literate Russians. Moreover, he spent the final twenty years of his life getting closer and closer to the pristine state of pre-Gutenberg literature, as one of the many authors whose writing was increasingly divorced from the world of publishing, and predicated instead on quite other circumstances.

As a result of the last of these factors, the only attempt at a collected works produced by the author himself—*Pesnoslov*—came in the middle of his career (but already in the Soviet period, and possibly marked by self-censorship), while a very significant part of his oeuvre grew increasingly unpublishable and remained unpublished well beyond his own life, to emerge from archives only after the Second World War in the West, and mostly after 1985 in Russia itself. Meanwhile much of what he had published up to 1919, when *Pesnoslov* came out, was republished in Russia only at the very end of the twentieth century. His works themselves show many signs of a preoccupation with popular culture and folklore, and, at some stages, of a self-conscious imitation or appropriation of folkloric devices and thematics. The modernist instability of voice, identity, form, and language is abundantly evident throughout his mature work, albeit often in unusual combination with elements less characteristic of the modernist poetic.

It is no surprise, then, to discover that Klyuev presents many examples of the textological problems most characteristic and widespread in twentieth-century Russian letters. Nor is it a surprise to discover that many of these problems continue to shape, and, indeed, distort the general picture of Klyuev's poetry (such as that picture is). At the same time, and as in the works of so many other Russian writers of the first half of the century, Klyuev's oeuvre is shaped into unstable and problematic forms by a striking coincidence of the enforced, external circumstances of the Soviet period, and by intrinsic tendencies to instability emerging from his own (and the period's) aesthetics and poetics long before any return to "pre-Gutenberg conditions."

Meanwhile, as a writer widely perceived to be of authentically "popular" origins, he was not only authorized but also actively encouraged to speak in ways which could be taken as (paradoxically) nonliterary and collective, only for those very "folkloric" texts to become objects of intense and highly critical scrutiny for their *literary* emergence and high-cultural orientation.

Twentieth-century Russia developed its special and unusual sense of time, which both shaped its literature and was also expressed in that literature, as a result of the interaction of earlier native traditions with the dramatic events of that century. Eschatological, apocalyptic, and millenarian preoccupations, which have formed an important strain in Russian culture since at least the fifteenth century, became particularly widespread early in the twentieth century and were very evident among the symbolists, their contemporaries, and their immediate successors. In the Soviet period, these preoccupations gained a sense of literal reality from the massive national disruptions of war, revolution, rapid social transformation, and mass repression. They continue to be much in evidence to the present day, and contribute to Russia's particular concepts of time, not least because they also formed a significant element in the utopian claims of the Bolshevik regime. Meanwhile, the articulation of cultural loss gained special force because that which was irretrievably (and very evidently) lost was often close in time to the present. After the dramatic breaks of the first half of the century, Soviet society developed another and contrasting sense of time for its postwar experience—time that was standing still, most tangible in the Brezhnev years, which a subsequent period would dub the "period of stagnation." As a consequence of these experiences and perceptions of time, after the early Soviet period linear chronology ceased to provide access to a reliable narrative for the course of cultural history. Thus spirals and parallel and broken lines often seem more appropriate metaphors for any description of that history in the twentieth century. Moreover, the biographies of individuals often reiterate broad sociocultural experience: "unnatural" breaks, cataclysmic interruptions, tragic diversions, and later an ironic certainty that "nothing happens" are important features of individual Russian lives in this period. And for that reason the dramatic and often tragic biographies of public figures—especially from "high culture"—take on, as was suggested in chapter 1, special meaning both as representatives of general historical patterns and as grand versions of all-too-familiar personal, family stories.

Twentieth-century Russia also developed (and, it might seem to an outsider, distorted) its own peculiar notions of place on both a large and small scale.[12] The Soviet state isolated itself from its geopolitical and cultural surroundings so that it became, at least conceptually, as isolated in space as it was in time, giving the general and the particular places of the country an abiding sense of the special, and everywhere beyond the borders of the country a mythical, inaccessible quality. Meanwhile, certain earlier relations predicated upon space or places gained new power. For example, St. Petersburg/Leningrad remained a much-mythologized city, and although it lost its central place in Russian politics, its role as an opposite in the cultural polarity with Moscow was frequently evident, albeit qualified now by the new superiority in secular (and often artistic) authority of the latter. Other familiar places of nineteenth-century Russia were more radically transformed, and some eliminated. The noble estate—its decline already lamented in the later nineteenth century—features in twentieth-century writing largely as a memory (and after 1917, most often as a memory of a pre-Soviet, sometimes idyllic childhood, recalled in the dual displacement of mature foreign exile for writers from landowning families). The attenuation of the cultural image of the noble estate provides no surprises, given the liquidation of its owners as a class, but the fate of another favorite literary site, the provincial town, is rather more complex. It was prominent in the fiction of the later nineteenth century, where it was often treated with a mixture of irony and affection. If Moscow and St. Petersburg are generally presented with reference to their specific qualities and even specific topography, the provincial town has a much more generic and abstract profile in Russian writing of the period, sometimes functioning as a negatively colored or humorous microcosm of Russian society in general. Yet no reader of Russian fiction of this period can doubt the importance of the provincial town in the cultural and economic map of the country. Elements of this profile recur throughout the twentieth century, but the centralization of Russian culture (and economics) drained much of that erstwhile energy from all but the largest urban centers. Separate from the provincial town, the countryside and the Russian village, ideologically and culturally problematic for nineteenth-century writers, became, with collectivization and subsequent demographic changes, even more marked arenas of cultural polemics, while also providing powerful physical evidence of the cost of projects of utopian transformation. The status and authenticity of rural culture—ever especially loaded issues in Russia, because of their proximity to questions of nationality and national identity—became even more problematic issues with rapid urbanization. After all, Soviet Russia, while retaining its peasant memories, was not only ideologically and culturally expressly urban, but also demographically so (especially after the Second World War). Moreover, that urban population was not so much Russian as Russophone—it was, by national origin, very cosmopolitan, while the remnants of the *Russian* village remained almost exclusively

Slavic. Thus, in the later twentieth century, partly as a result of urbanization and other developments characteristic of modern societies, the disputes over national identity and the role of the rural, ethnically Russian peasantry in defining it became particularly charged.

In general, the demographic and cultural movement of twentieth-century Russia was first and foremost toward the center (which means, above all, Moscow), so that everywhere else defined itself, at least in part, with reference to that center. This had been true of the nineteenth century, too, but it was even more marked in the Soviet period. For example, the typical twentieth-century writer's biography may well include provincial birth and upbringing, but it usually continues with a journey away from the birthplace to the center. Subsequent journeys out from the center, even journeys home, have the quality of excursions, even if they are journeys to discover an "authentic" Russia (and this would be true even for some of the writers of expressly provincial, especially rural, prose in the later Soviet period). Lateral movement across the provinces is less characteristic of the period. And, of course, what is true for Russian writers and writing in the later twentieth century is also true, to a large extent, of the Russian intelligentsia in general (for whom lateral movement across the provinces or from the center into the provinces was often *enforced*). It is also important to recall that Russia, in terms of extent of territory by far the largest country in the world, was largely inaccessible to its own population throughout the twentieth century and remains so today. While mass travel, including individual leisure travel, characterized most of the first world in the twentieth century, with first public and then private transport rendering every part of western Europe and North America more or less easily accessible to its citizens, travel in Russia sometimes looks as difficult now as it was early in the nineteenth century, when the country's roads were notorious among travelers for their poor quality. And individual travel in Russia, especially to destinations other than major cities and popular vacation spots, still retains much of the quality of the adventurous journeys undertaken in earlier centuries by western Europeans seeking to discover the remote corners of their own and other countries, while ethnographic expeditions continue to take Russian folklorists, ethnographers, and anthropologists from big-city universities into the exotic world of their country's past *in their own "backyard."* Moreover, economic and legal restrictions added to problems of mobility and guaranteed that exposure to new parts of Russia was, for many of its citizens, far from pleasant (Gulag and exile), while the economic opportunities which drove the socially and financially ambitious to outlying or inhospitable regions in the later twentieth century did little, in most cases, to distract those pioneers from their capital-city orientation.

The special circumstances of modern Russia also shape the physical evidence of the relationship between time and place, for whereas the western European traveler has been encouraged to see continuity with the past in his or her places of cultural pilgrimage and leisure travel (the demands of tourism, the practices of town planning, habits of restoration, and consequences of economic prosperity have often tended to elide or disguise signs of dramatic change, while preserving, or claiming to preserve, physical evidence of the past), the Russian visitor to another town, to a village, or to the countryside is almost certain to see abundant evidence of dramatic, time-breaking change—abandoned houses, largely empty villages, destroyed or politically appropriated churches, relics of war, whole urban areas razed for Stalinist reconstruction, and so on. For example, as political and demographic changes continue radically and rapidly to reshape the Russian countryside, whole villages disappear. It is not at all uncommon to hear Russians born in rural areas announce that their native villages no longer exist, or now consist solely of houses used by vacationing city-dwellers. In western Europe, remarks on the wholesale disappearance of one's native domestic environment are far more likely to be heard from people who grew up in *urban* areas subsequently cleared for "redevelopment" or for road building.

Of course, given the nature of this large-scale cultural geography and demographics, it is no surprise that the smaller-scale places which distinguish Russian writing of the Soviet period are mostly urban: the apartment, places of collective endeavor and encounter (mostly workplaces), the street. Meanwhile, in expressly ruralist prose, the construction of place is often in terms of some postcatastrophe landscape, or else much more abstractly, in terms of character and language stylized to represent rather than describe place.

It is against these general phenomena that the specifics of Klyuev's relations to time and space, and the subsequent relocating of the poet and his oeuvre, must be read. Klyuev's biography demonstrates many of the paradigms elaborated above: at the very beginning of the Soviet period, a few years in a provincial town (Vytegra), described with some acidity in a number of works of the period, and barely present in his work after his departure from it; in the early 1920s, a move to one of the cultural centers (Leningrad), and then, at the end of that decade, resettlement in the capital; exposure to the countryside in the Soviet period during *vacations* (and not in his native area); in the 1930s, enforced displacement from the center to remote exile; big-city life in small apartments; limited opportunities for individual travel. His works, too, share many of the characteristics of their period. His early poems are often marked by preoccupations with time and space which are typical of the symbolist period in general, while his works of the 1920s and 1930s both testify to and are victims of the early Soviet remaking of both categories. And the posthumous fate of poet and poetry is both shaped by and illustrative of the consequences of that remaking. Meanwhile, individual, even idiosyncratic notions of time and space are abundantly evident throughout his life and work.

Moreover, the rudimentary chronological divisions invited by history itself (Klyuev before 1917; Klyuev in the Soviet period; posthumous Klyuev) must themselves be treated as highly provisional, since the story of the reception of poet and poetry has, as has been seen already, its own peculiar chronology. Since Klyuev's later works enter Russian letters in the late Soviet period, any account of changing attitudes to the poet—or the absence of such—in the last decades of the twentieth century and beyond must observe, as has been argued, not only the usual issues of changing tastes and evaluations but also the elementary fact that the poet's own available work expanded very significantly in this period, with the discovery and publication of many new poems.

In Klyuev's poetry, time is a prominent yet elusive category—from the cyclical, calendar time of nature and of man-in-nature to the apparently timeless world of the idyllic northern village or to the apocalyptic time of that idyll's destruction; from the "natural" chronology of the ages of man to the "unnatural" interventions in human life of the mass violence of the twentieth century; from the evasion of time through the anticipated utopias of popular spirituality to the millenarian claims of political movements. It is not surprising that apocalyptic chronologies are frequent in the poet's later works, but it is also true that some of the most historically scarred works are marked by a striking achronicity. However, it is not only historical but also personal time that is foregrounded and disrupted in the later poetry (especially the later love poetry).

The places of Klyuev's poetry are equally revealing, and a preoccupation with places, specific and general, is even marked in the very titles of many of Klyuev's publications. The collections *Sosen perezvon, Lesnye byli, Izbyanye pesni, Izba i pole*; the sections of *Pesnoslov* entitled "Sosen perezvon," "Lesnye byli," and "Pesni iz Zaonezh'ya" ("Songs from the Trans-Onega Region"); the *poemy Chetvertyi Rim, Zaozer'e, Derevnya, Solovki, Pogorel'shchina*; and a number of his individual lyrics and cycles all indicate very clearly an orientation to place or places. Above all, however, Klyuev and his poetry may be associated with two sites. The first is the village or countryside (*derevnya* means both in Russian). Understood both as the residence of the peasant and as the site of unique—but also universal—values, it is often depicted as the arena of idyllic interaction between nature and culture. The second is the north, a concept as evocative and elastic as *derevnya*, and, as has been seen, of great cultural significance in the early twentieth century, but most often in Klyuev's work reserved for two related regions: the area around Lake Onega, and the White Sea coast. In the poet's cultural geography, both are peopled almost exclusively by *Russians* (notwithstanding the historically diverse demography of these regions, and despite the "Lapp" motifs in *Pogorel'shchina* and *Pesn' o Velikoi Materi*), but many of these Russians are Old Believers or religious schismatics, rather than members of the established church. Gestures made to the Finno-Ugric elements of northern culture remain, however, extremely noteworthy, and, in the opinion of some, shape much of his poetics.[13] These favored regions are also characterized in his work by an extraordinary expansiveness and not infrequently by an explicit Orientalism (that is, they are linked to the culture and religion of the Orient), while being expressly presented as treasure houses of unique artifacts and values. As might be expected, the poet's core places are where the village and the north coincide, often as realized in specific objects, for example, the northern peasant hut, even the peasant stove. On the other hand, many such particular locales are rendered vague and ambiguous, endowed with qualities which contrast with their notional spatial specifics—for example, natural sites frequently and explicitly become "texts" to be read or places of worship.

In Klyuev's biography, his own places of residence, and especially his own *rooms* are, as has been noted, intriguing and self-consciously framed and decorated spaces, while the geography and topography of his autobiographical texts are intriguing and paradoxical in their relationship to him and his work.

Finally, it must be noted that, in any broad history of Russian letters, Klyuev's "place" is highly problematic, since his poetics and his biography, as has already been seen, associate him with movements in Russian letters which are apparent opposites in terms of time and space (as well as culture)—that is to say, crudely speaking, modernism (first and foremost present- and future-oriented, and urban) and ruralism (oriented to the countryside and to the past).

The multiple and contradictory interactions of the various concepts of time, place, and text suggested above are central to the identity of the poet and his poetry, and equally central to the often highly polemical disputes upon which discussion of that identity remains predicated. Klyuev's life and his life-text have already been seen to contribute to and reiterate many of these problems, while features of his poetics also enunciate analogous issues in terms of direction and formal modifications (in allusions, thematics, metrics, and so on). Among the consequences are the acutely disputed questions of the poet's time and place in literary history and in poetic canons, raised throughout his life and revived in new forms later.

Time and place may also be seen as physically expressed in the most significant markers of his work as a poet—his books, where the two visibly intersect. Lyric collections, as has been noted, were, for the publishing environment of the symbolist period, the principal landmarks of the individual and general poetic landscape, and they were almost always not only the primary (if not the first) *place* of publication for lyric poems but also the most eloquent markers—and sometimes eliders—of *time* for individual poets. Thus the interrelationship of time and place as themes and as instrumental forces can most fruitfully be explored by a narrative outline of Klyuev's treatments of these themes, keyed to the chronological sequence of publication of the author's own books, which themselves, in their overall shape and history, articulate major issues of time and space. At least until the mid-1920s, it is possible to provide a quite thorough reading of Klyuev through the sequence of his collections (although the chronology of this sequence is not always transparent). Moreover, as physical places of assembly for lyric poems, collections not only provide a series of distinct bodies but also tend toward individual thematic unity (often, as has been suggested above, implicit in titles which themselves designate *places*). However, just as their chronology is far from transparent, so too the location of a poem within one bounded area is often provisional (poems turn out to be somewhat mobile, notwithstanding the physical solidity of the collection as a form). Many of these problems will be encountered in the exploration of Klyuev's second major lyric collection, *Bratskie pesni,* attempted in chapter 3. The following pages will illustrate how broadly they are encountered in an overall narrative of Klyuev's poetic production.

In other words, by reading Klyuev's verse for its treatment and enactment of time and place, while paying attention to the times and places where the poet (and sometimes others) physically located his poetry, it will be possible to reveal not only the major lines of poetic development throughout his oeuvre but also the impact of material context on the overall profile of that oeuvre. It is hoped that such a reading, intended to be spatially and chronologically self-conscious, will provide the framework for the approaches to individual works attempted in more detail in chapters 3 to 6.

In Klyuev's early verse most aspects of time and place are abstract and often conventional. The original version of *Sosen perezvon* (*Peal of the Pines*), as its title suggests, is preoccupied with the poetic and religious potential of nature, and of its relationship to the social struggles of its human denizens. Familiar attributes of village and peasant life recur, often in a context of implied social protest and generalized utopian yearning:

На песню, на сказку рассудок молчит,
Но сердце так странно правдиво, —
И плачет оно, непонятно грустит,
О чем? — Знают ветер да ивы.

О том ли, что юность бесследно прошла,
Что поле заплаканно-нище?

Вон серые избы родного села,
Луга, перелески, кладбище. (149)

Reason says nothing to song or to tale,
But the heart is so strangely truthful—
And it weeps, incomprehensibly mourns,
For what? Only the wind and the willows know.

For a youth that has passed without trace,
For a meadow so lamentably poor?
There lie the gray houses of the home village,
The fields, copses, cemetery.

Here the very general quality of the *rodnoe selo* (home village) is emblematic of the abstract representation of place which is predominant in the early verse, and which remains an abiding characteristic of Klyuev's poetry—although later in combination with quite different, even opposite features. This *rodnoe selo* could be anyone's home village, a point reinforced by the absence of personal pronouns in the poem, except for the reflexive *sebe* in the penultimate line "I gor'ko v sebe posmeetsya dusha" ("And bitterly the soul will laugh to itself"). Similar is the general, even universal, lyric statement of the passing of personal time ("yunost' bessledno proshla . . ."), especially commonplace, of course, in the writing of the young. Sometimes such personal time is linked to an equally conventional seasonal calendar, as in another poem from *Sosen perezvon,* "Lyubvi nachalo bylo letom,/Konets — osennim sentyabrem" ("Love's beginning came in summer,/The end—in autumnal September," 96–97).

Another abiding characteristic in Klyuev's writing is the reuse of titles and the relocation of poems. The first section of *Pesnoslov*—a cumulative statement of his poetry to date (1919)—is also entitled "Sosen perezvon," but in it the poet returned to his own literary beginnings and remade them, in part by raiding later work. For example, "Ya molilsya by liku zakata,/Temnoi roshche, tumanu, ruch'yam," ("I would pray to the sacred face of the sunset,/To the dark wood, to the mist, the streams," 172–73), which provides a paradigmatic statement of nature as place of worship, was originally part of the large version of *Lesnye byli,* but appears in the "Sosen perezvon" section of *Pesnoslov*—and provides yet another illustration of after-the-fact modification of the poet's professional chronology, not least since it was written after the publication of the first version of *Sosen perezvon.* Although the reader was likely to infer that each new collection marked a new stage in the poet's career (poems are presented undated), thematic association is, in fact, as important as chronology of composition in the shaping of the early collections, for poems from the same year may find themselves in any one of the first three collections, and may also move between the collections in their various versions. Again, some of the strategies the poet seems to have employed in the construction of "life-texts" are also applied to the construction and reconstruction of literary texts, and especially of the contexts within which they are organized (in this case, the sequence of sections within a cumulative volume, linked by name to the chronology of his poetic *sborniki*).

Time and especially timelessness are also prominent themes in the poet's early work. Eternity and apocalyptic time, usually experienced within some more everyday and "natural" chronology and in an abstractly presented natural place of mystical and sensual religious experience, are characteristic elements of many of the poems in the various versions of *Bratskie pesni,* which will be explored in chapter 3. As will be seen, not only did the poet produce two different books under the title *Bratskie pesni*, but he also entitled the second section of the first volume of *Pesnoslov* "Bratskie pesni." In fact, the first volume of *Pesnoslov* reiterates, in its first four section titles, the titles of Klyuev's first four separate poetic *sborniki:* "Sosen perezvon," "Bratskie pesni," "Lesnye byli," and "Mirskie dumy"; they are followed by "Pesni iz Zaonezh'ya," the title of the second section of "Mirskie dumy." However, the *contents* of these sections of *Pesnoslov* do not correspond to the earlier versions they might be assumed to reiterate.

The first poem of the *Pesnoslov* version of "Bratskie pesni," quoting the Book of Revelation, announces in its opening lines:

Я был в духе в день воскресный,
Осененный высотой,
Просветленно бестелесный
И младенчески простой.

Видел ратей колесницы,
Судный жертвенник и крест,
Указующей десницы
Путеводно-млечный перст. (110–11)

I was in the spirit on the Lord's day.
Blessed by elevation,
Lucidly incorporeal
And childlike in simplicity.

I saw the chariots of the hosts,
The judgment altar and cross,
The galactic-directing finger
Of the index hand.

However, the second poem in the *Pesnoslov* version of "Bratskie pesni" (both of these first two poems belonged originally to *Sosen perezvon*) announces:

Я бежал в простор лугов
Из-под мертвенного свода,
Где зловещий ход часов —
Круг замкнутый без исхода . . . (142)

I fled to the meadows' expanse
From deadly vaults,
Where the sinister march of hours
Is a vicious circle with no way out . . .

Thus, while timeless revelation (with no specifics of place) opens this version of "Bratskie pesni," the second poem addresses a quite different, although equally favored, theme—the contrast between the somewhat abstract polarities of nature, to which the speaker flees, and civilization, the "deadly vaults" and mechanically measured time of which he has fled, thereby expressly rejecting organized religion, and finding salvation in the "stones and plants" which whisper "holy, holy, holy" to him. This thematic pair—one devoted to elevated revelation, the other to the transfer of ecclesiastical practice to the natural world—provides a model for much of Klyuev's treatment of spirituality. It also demonstrates how the spatial situation of poems within sections or collections and with reference to the works around them generates meaning—in this case, by providing a pair of opposites, expressing alternative, but equally promoted, versions of spiritual experience.

The title of Klyuev's third collection, *Lesnye byli* (*Forest Tales*), again directs attention to the association between poetry and nature, although in the various versions of this book it is the harmony of the peasant village and the peasant house which is most emphatically stated. A major vehicle for this statement is the lexicon of the collection—here, for the first time, the association between place and language is strong and marked, although by no means ubiquitous. Elements of the calendar year are also prominent, colored by the continuum of nature, folklore, and high culture (from now on a recurring feature of Klyuev's treatment of the countryside):

Месяц — рог олений,
Тучка — лисий хвост.
Полон привидений
Таежный погост.

The moon is a deer antler,
The cloud—a fox's tail.
Full of specters
Is the taiga cemetery.

В заревом окладе	In the dawn's icon cover
Спит Архангел Дня.	The Archangel of Day sleeps.
В Божьем вертограде	In the Lord's vineyard
Не забудь меня. (279)	Do not forget me.

The poems comprising the different versions of *Lesnye byli* share with the preceding collections a topographical vagueness—the village is an abstract place, where the *izba* and the field are general, mythologized sites. In the early Klyuev, the places that he himself came from are barely perceptible: his villages and peasantry are generic, in marked contrast to the specifics of rural representation in other literary traditions, and in equally marked contrast to the specific realization of urban space (especially of the two capitals) in the Russian literary tradition. However, proper names, at least, are more common in *Lesnye byli* than in *Sosen perezvon* and *Bratskie pesni,* and some specific times and places are designated, for example, "Povolzhskii skaz" ("Volga Tale," 192–94) and "Veshnii Nikola" ("Spring Nikola").[14] The latter appears to be the first of Klyuev's poems explicitly to play with mythologies of the poet's own identity through his name, later a significant motif (as, most obviously, in *Pesn' o Velikoi Materi*). It is characteristic that this first statement—"ya Veshnii Nikola" ("I am the Spring Nikola")—is explicitly tied both to time and to place: the "spring Nikola" is the popular, that is, peasant or village, name for the spring feast of St. Nicholas (879). In other words, the poet's claimed identity is more specific than, but quite separate from, any particular place with which he could be linked.

In the *Pesnoslov* version of "Lesnye byli," a greater toponymic specificity may be noted, as may the use of named denizens of Klyuev's countryside (some fictional, some literary, some historical):

Сготовить деду круп, помочь развесить сети,
Лучину засветить, и слушая пургу,
Как в сказке, задремать на тридевять столетий,
В Садко оборотясь, иль в вещего Вольгу.

«Гей, други! Не в бою, а в гуслях нам удача, —
Соловке-игруну претит вороний грай . . .»
С палатей смотрит Жуть, гудит, как било, Лаче,
И деду под кошмой приснился красный рай . . . (251)

Preparing the old man's groats, helping hang the nets,
Lighting the torch, and, listening to the blizzard,
Falling asleep, as in the tale, for three thousand years,
Turning into Sadko, or into the prophetic Vol'ga

"Hey, friends! Our success is not in battle but in song,
The crow's cries disgust the playful nightingale . . ."
From the warming benches Horror looks down, Lache sounds like a
gong,
And the old man under the felt blanket dreams of a fine paradise . . .

Characteristic here is the combination of *bylina* heroes (Sadko and Vol'ga) with the personified Zhut' (Horror), and the specific northern location Lake Lache, famous for its role in the work of Daniil Zatochnik and present elsewhere in Klyuev's poetry. It is also significant, given the general movement between opposite categories here (as so often in Klyuev's poetry), that in the phrase *tridevyat' stoletii* a term usually applied to place has been transferred to time: the usual phrase is *za tridevyat' zemel'* (literally, "across three-time-nine lands," that is, "far away"). Equally telling is that, even with greater toponymic specificity, Klyuev's poetry of place remains largely abstract and mythological, rather than attentive to the description of actual locale. If Klyuev is to be read as a poet of place, then it is of a *conceptual, not physical,* place.

"Galka-staroverka khodit v chernoi ryaske" ("The Old Believer jackdaw walks in its black cassock," 282–83) illustrates these points well. In general, Klyuev's mature poetry abounds in animals and birds, many of them specific to or often associated with northern Europe, like the loon, discussed in chapter 4 (ninety-eight birds are said to occur in Klyuev's verse).[15] But the birds of this poem, as often elsewhere, tend to be presented not so much in association with a particular natural habitat, but rather in terms of their role in Klyuev's highly mediated and mythologized version of the "natural" environment—in other words, the poem does not claim to present the special, local insight of the observant countryman (contrast, for example, John Clare), but rather the spiritually informed view of a sometimes distant lyric observer. Equally, the human environment may be presented in avian terms, as in the conclusion of "Razokhalas' starukha" ("The old woman sighed deeply"):

Изба — гнездо тетерье,
Где жизнь, как холст доткать . . .
А тучи ронят перья
В лесную темь и гать. (215)

The peasant house is a black grouse nest,
Where life must be woven like canvas . . .
And the clouds drop feathers
Into the woodland dark and path.

Here again it is the generality of imagery (and the generalized picture of tired old age in the poem as a whole) which is reinforced by the natural references, and in fact the specificity of the avian allusion is immediately undermined not only by semantics—why, after all, should the peasant hut, site of such toil, be associated specifically with the nest of a galliforme—but also by the very abstract image of the clouds dropping feathers into the forest. It might be noted, moreover, that the old woman of the poem's opening line is not, it would seem, a denizen of any Olonian locale, since her beloved seems to have perished beneath a "*taiga* bear" ("Pod *taezhnym* medvedem/Pogib likhoi lesnik" ["Under a taiga bear/Perished the bold forester"]).

The opening and closing poems of Klyuev's collections and of the sections of his larger books are often not only especially striking but also, as "bookends," important thematic markers and thus indicators of the significance of the physical situation of poems, their place in books. The final poem of the *Pesnoslov* "Lesnye byli" illustrates a very characteristic presentation of place: nature as a site of religious worship. The poem quite specifically appropriates elements of the liturgy to nature, while presenting the speaker in a characteristically ambiguous role as the object of a prophecy in which he is the apparent Abraham-like progenitor of an all-encompassing song:

Ель мне подала лапу, береза серьгу,
Тучка канула перл, просияв на бегу,
Дрозд запел «Блажен муж» и «Кресту Твоему» . . .
Утомилась осина вязать бахрому.
В луже крестит себя обливанец-бекас,
Ждет попутного ветра небесный баркас: . . . (253)

The fir tree offered its bough, the birch a catkin,
The cloud dropped a pearl, shining as it ran,
The thrush sang two hymns "Blessed the man" and "To Your cross" . . .
The aspen grew tired of weaving velvet.
The snipe, baptized without immersion, christens itself in the puddle,
The celestial longboat waits for a following wind: . . .

The solipsistic vision of the lyrical speaker communing with nature and apparently receiving a vision of his special powers is reinforced and also dislocated by explicit and implied referents. Three trees are mentioned in the opening lines—the fir, the birch, and the aspen, all typical of the Russian forest, and widely celebrated in literature. But between these references a cloud drops a pearl, and a thrush sings liturgical lines. The figurative progression of the opening lines is also characteristic of the poet's movement between nature and culture, landscape and man: *lapa* is literally an animal's paw, but the word is widely used to designate the bough of a coniferous tree; *ser'ga* is literally an earring, while its diminutive *serezhka* frequently designates a catkin; however, the "pearl" of the second line has no widespread botanical usage, and is strictly metaphorical (for a raindrop). And no sooner has the snipe (an *oblivanets*—that is, baptized by the scattering of water upon it, not by immersion, as is usual in Russian Orthodoxy) christened itself, than the major image changes from this natural liturgy to the departure of a boat which will apparently cross "the Lord's seas" (*Gospodni morya*) and which, as subsequent lines suggest, will carry the lyrical speaker. That image too is soon abandoned, as the speaker asserts that his *kobylitsa-dusha* (mare of a soul) longs for flowery meadows. Those meadows, supremely abstract, are the site of the final images of the poem:

> Там, под Дубом Покоя, накрыты столы,
> Пиво Жизни в сулеях, и гости светлы —
> Три пришельца, три солнца, и я — Авраам,
> Словно ива ручью, внемлю росным словам:
> «Родишь сына-звезду, алый песенный сад,
> Где не властны забвенье и дней листопад,
> Где береза серьгою и лапою ель
> Тиховейно колышут мечты колыбель».
>
> There, beneath the Oak of Peace, tables are set,
> The Ale of Life is in flagons, and the guests are bright—
> Three visitors, three suns, and me—Abraham,
> As a willow attends to a stream, so I to the dew words:
> "You will bear a star-son, a scarlet song garden,
> Where neither oblivion nor the autumn of days shall have power,
> Where the birch with its catkin, and the fir with its bough,
> Will quietly rock the cradle of dream."

This vision of timelessness (*gde ne vlastny zabven'e i dnei listopad*) is set in a natural world very evidently tied to the seasons, but where the opening images of the poem are finally recast in the eternity of the "cradle of dream," and where the "autumn of days" is powerless. Cutting across the reiteration of images from the opening is the emergence of a quite different referent—the visit of the angels to Abraham in Genesis 18 (873). The ambitious solipsism of the speaker is strongly reinforced by this allusion to a highly significant moment in Genesis, which, of course, Christian tradition sees as anticipating the New Testament: three unknown visitors come to Abraham, who welcomes them with customary hospitality, whereupon one predicts that Sarah, in old age, will bear a son. In Klyuev's poem the speaker, identifying *himself* as Abraham, hears a prophecy that *he* will bear a son—the *alyi pesennyi sad,* which will conquer time (in other words, the speaker's verse is assigned a semi-messianic future, according to the speaker's own account). The ambitiousness of this appropriation of sacred text to individual poetic manifesto is further reinforced when it is recalled that the visit of the men to Abraham is often seen as the principal subject of the most famous object of Russian sacred art—Andrei Rublev's *Trinity*. Iconography is a very common referent in Klyuev's work, and the poet himself collected icons, of course; the name Andrei Rublev has been said to occur twenty-two times in Klyuev's poetry.[16] The movement of this poem through time, space, and referential arenas is characteristic of Klyuev's poetry of this period and later, and illustrates well how the relatively specific implied environment of the Russian landscape may quickly be replaced with or transformed into something quite different (for example, the *Dub Pokoya* calls to mind the oaks of Mamre [Genesis 18:1], rather than any northern European site). Moreover, birch, spruce, aspen, willow, thrush, and snipe, while entirely characteristic of Russia, are not, it should be noted, peculiar to any particular northern landscape, and are notable more in their enumeration and their denomination than for their ecology. Here too is a fundamental characteristic of much of Klyuev's treatment of time and particularly space, where cataloguing, enumeration, and specific designation, rather than complex individual referential association, often seem predominant. Lastly, it could be argued that Klyuev's poetry not only abounds in allusions to icons (above all—as is characteristic of the poet—to the *names* or types of icons) but also itself is often characterized by attitudes to time and place which are reminiscent of the iconic: achronicity, or at least the simultaneous presence of different historical or narrative moments; movement between concrete and abstract in the representation of place; the incorporation of local detail into biblical stories; and so on.[17]

The countryside and village are not only distinguished by what they are (place of worship, site of a happy peasant's calendar, with the *izba* as its heart) but also by what they are not—that is to say, by their freedom from urban elements. The latter, however, are threatening, and "Lesnye byli" in *Pesnoslov* contains three successive poems which identify the coming threat of the railway: "Pushistye, teplye tuchi" ("Fluffy, warm clouds," 203–4), "Vrazh'ya sila" ("Enemy Forces"), and "Obozval tishinu glukhoman'yu" ("He called quiet the backwoods," 248–50). The first of these poems explicitly identifies the threatened area ("Osennyaya yav' Obonezh'ya/Kak skazka, bayukaet dukh"; "The autumn clarity of the Onega lands/Sings a lullaby to the spirit, like a folk tale"), while the diabolical threat is definitively identified in the final lines of the third poem:

Светлый отрок — лесное молчанье,
Помолясь на заплаканный крест,
Закатилось в глухое скитанье
До святых, незапятнанных мест.

Заломила черемуха руки,
К норке путает след горностай . . .
Сын железа и каменной скуки
Попирает берестяный рай.

A bright youth—forest silence,
Praying to the tear-stained cross,
Has gone off on distant wandering
To sacred, untouched places.

The bird cherry has wrung out its hands,
The ermine disguises the track to its hole . . .
The son of iron and of stone tedium
Is crushing the birch-bark paradise.

These poems anticipate the later treatments of apocalyptic Soviet urbanization and industrialization (for example, *Pogorel'shchina* and "Razrukha"), but lack their specific referents. A recent editor observes that Klyuev's anti-railway poetry was inspired by the construction of the main line to Murmansk (860). However, it is also worth recalling that Klyuev's own home region—south and east of Lake Onega—remains to this day probably the largest area in European Russia without a passenger railway. In other words, the line to Murmansk (from Petersburg) did not actually pass close to Klyuev's own region and could not be seen as threatening his native, local "birch-bark paradise," while the line to Archangel, in fact somewhat closer to that region, had been built some time before.[18] However, the Murmansk railway did pass by Lake Vyg, and relatively close to the area where the Old Believer community of that name had been located. In other words, the railway could be conceived as threatening not Klyuev's own *petit pays,* but one of his favorite sites of northern spirituality—that is, it was a threat to an aspect of his mythologized, spiritual homeland, not to his literal native area.

The peasant calendar is abundantly reflected in the poems in the various versions of *Lesnye byli* (examples include "Mesyats — rog olenii," "Oktyabr' — petukh medyanozobyi," "Radost' videt' pervyi stog," "Cherny protaliny, navozom," and "Ya doma. Khmaroi tishinoi" ["The moon is a deer antler," "October is a copper-throated rooster," "The joy of seeing the first hay rick," "Dark are the thawed patches. The smell of manure," and "I'm home. Dark silence"]; 279–80, 248, 197–98, 200–201, 198–99). Many calendar poems, although observing the seasons of the countryside and the peasant year, are marked by the same mythologizing and even solipsistic elements observed elsewhere, so that, once more, it is not the specific and local which takes pride of place.[19]

The same could be said of the poems which celebrate that central locus of the Klyuev village, the *izba* or peasant hut. Most notable is the poem entitled "Rozhestvo izby" ("Birth of the Peasant Hut") in posthumous publications, yet another poem composed after the publication of the two books called *Lesnye byli,* but included in the *Pesnoslov* section of the same name. Even the title, with its Church Slavonic form *rozhestvo,* giving the birth of the peasant house an especially, but, for Klyuev, characteristically sacred coloring, is not without problems of time and space: that title does not appear in *Pesnoslov,* nor did he use it the only other time he published the poem himself, but is taken from a manuscript copy of the poem (878). The opening stanza is in marked contrast to that sacred tone set by the title, providing rather concrete details of the construction of a peasant log house:

От кудрявых стружек тянет смолью,
Духовит, как улей, белый сруб.
Крепкогрудый плотник тешет колья,
На слова медлителен и скуп. (280)

The curly shavings smell of resin,
The white wood frame is aromatic as a beehive.
The broad-chested carpenter hews the stakes,
Slow and scarce with words.

But this concrete site is rapidly transformed into something quite different, and the poem concludes with an almost messianic message:

Крепкогруд строитель-тайновидец,
Перед ним щепа, как письмена:
Запоет резная пава с крылец,
Брызнет ярь с наличника окна.

И когда оческами кудели
Над избой взлохматится дымок—
Сказ пойдет о Красном Древоделе
По лесам, на запад и восток.

Broad-chested is the builder-visionary,
Before him splinters are as letters:
The carved peahen will sing from roofs,
Green will splash from the window lintel.

And when, like shavings of tow,
Above the house smoke curls,
The tale of the Fine Woodworker
Will go to east and west across the woods.

Here, in the line "Pered nim shchepa, kak pis'mena," is another clue to Klyuev's presentation of place: it is very frequently oriented toward textualization. Fields and peasant houses become things to be *read.* And here the builder, a *tainovidets,* is clearly also a *writer.* The capitals given (in *Pesnoslov;* they are absent in posthumous publications) to *Krasnyi Drevodel* are also striking, adding to the messianic tone of the conclusion. It is also entirely characteristic of Klyuev's presentation of the peasant world that readers may be tempted to list among the sources for his concept of the peasant house not only his own long residence in an *izba* but also the mythological approach to the peasant world established in such works as the famous article by the nineteenth-century folklorist Aleksandr Afanas'ev on the "Pagan-Religious Significance of the Slav's *Izba,*" first published in 1851.

The clearest assertion that the peasant world is a text to be read comes, perhaps, in the opening line of "Ryzhee zhniv'e — kak kniga," a poem of 1915, subsequently included in the collection *Mednyi kit,* then in the "Dolina edinoroga" section of *Pesnoslov,* and finally presented as the opening poem of the "Pole" section of his last published collection, *Izba i pole* ("The ginger stubble field is like a book," 260). The mobility of this lyric, recontextualized at the heart of successive collections of verse, indicates, among other things, the significance within Klyuev's oeuvre of the statement it makes, and suggests that the poet himself saw it as a programmatic work.

Klyuev's fourth collection, *Mirskie dumy* of 1916, was divided into two sequences, "Mirskie dumy" and "Pesni iz Zaonezh'ya."[20] As noted, those titles recur in *Pesnoslov* as the names of the fourth and fifth sections of that collection, but again, with contents somewhat different from the original versions. The two versions of the "Mirskie dumy" sequence are notable for their references, in a series of folk-epic stylizations, to the First World War (these poems are from the period when Klyuev and Esenin read patriotic poetry in Petrograd, and possibly in Tsarskoe Selo, during Klyuev's association with Feodorovsky Gorodok, discussed in chapter 6). The prominence of this obvious referent clearly distinguishes *Mirskie dumy* from the preceding collections, where allusions to contemporary events (for example, railway construction) were vague at best. The war poems, predictably, attracted especial criticism in Soviet scholarship of the 1970s and early 1980s, although they are far from unequivocally chauvinistic, notwithstanding the lines about imperial Germany from the last poem of the sequence:

Народилось железное царство
Со Вильгельмищем, царищем поганым. —
У него ли, нечестивца, войска — сила,
Порядового народа — несустетно;
Они веруют Лютеру-богу, . . . (273)

There was born the iron kingdom,
With Wilhelm-giant, godless emperor. —
He, the impious creature, has mighty armies,
Countless men for call-up;
They believe in the god Luther, . . .

More significant in these poems is the combination of contemporary realia of time and space (even if sometimes folklorized, as in the lines above) with allusions to a peasant calendar of ever-recurring saints' days and to the geographically generalized peasant locations of the earlier poetry. At the same time, two other features which will be very prominent in much of the later poetry become evident here: the use of a very wide range of highly specific Russian toponyms, often in lists and catalogues; and the incorporation of fictional characters and even places into environments shaped by familiar "real-world" proper names for places and people.

The poem "Mirskaya duma" ("Secular Meditation," 264–65) narrates in stylized folk-epic manner a gathering of northern peasants, combining a catalogue of specific places with mythological and popular-religious referents:

Не гуси в отлет собирались,
Не лебеди на озере скликались, —
Подымались мужики — пудожане,
С заонежской кряжистой карелой,
С каргопольской дикой лешнею,
Со всей полесной хвойной силой,
Постоять за крещеную Землю,
За зеленую матерь-пустыню,
За березыньку с вещей кукушкой . . .

Из-под ели двадесять вершинной,
От сиговья Муромского плеса,
Подымался Лазарь преподобный
Ратоборцам дать благословенье,
Провещать поганых одоленье . . . (264)

It was not geese gathering for departure,
Not swans calling one another at the lake—
Countrymen have arisen—men of Pudozh,
With the thick-set Karel nation,
With Kargopol''s wild Wood Spirits,
With all the forest pine force,
To stand and defend the baptized Land,

The green wilderness-mother,
The birch tree with the prophetic cuckoo . . .

From under the giant fir,
From the whitefish Murom reach,
The Venerable Lazarus rose
To give the warriors his blessing,
And to prophesy the vanquishing of the impious.

Here the toponymic catalogue is very typical of Klyuev, blending the concrete and specific (men of Pudozh) with the mythologized (Wood Spirits of Kargopol'). It is also noteworthy that while the specific places listed above—Pudozh, Kargopol', and the Murom Promontory—are all relatively close to Klyuev's home villages, his actual native sites (for example, the villages of Koshtugi and Zhelvachevo, or, more likely, the rivers they lie on; or the city of Vytegra) do not appear.

In "Gei, otzovites', kurgany—" ("Hey, answer, burial mounds," 256–57) three of Klyuev's favorite sacred places are listed, again in a general context created by the combination of the legendary and the very general: descendants of *bylina* (folk epic) heroes meet mythologized nature. This collage of times and places, but with reference to contemporary events, anticipates Klyuev's address to the Soviet catastrophes so amply treated in his verse of the later 1920s and the 1930s:

Муромцы, Дюки, Потоки Русь и поныне блюдут . . . Чур нас! Вещуньи-сороки Щокот недобрый ведут,	Heirs of Ilya, Dyuk, and Potok Even now watch over Rus' . . . Beware of us! Magpie-prophets Sound a sinister chatter,
В сутемень плачут гагары, Заяц валежник грызет, — Будут с накладом товары, Лют на поганых поход.	Loons cry in the twilight, The hare gnaws fallen branches— Goods will be taxed, Wild the campaign against the infidel.
Гром от булатных ударов Слаще погудной струны . . . Радонеж, Выгово, Саров, — Наших имен баюны. (256)	Thunder from the strike of steel Is sweeter than the melodious string . . . Radonezh, Vygovo, Sarov— The singers of our names.

The enumeration, in a single line, of Radonezh, Vygovo, and Sarov is very revealing of Klyuev's toponymic references in general. The places form an elegant dactylic triptych, in parallel with the descendants of Il'ya Muromets,

Dyuk Stepanovich, and Potok (Mikhail Ivanovich) of the opening line quoted above: "Muromtsy, Dyuki, Potoki" (872). Yet the places are confessionally very diverse in their associations: St. Sergii of Radonezh was a major figure of the fourteenth century, contributing to the transformation of Russian monasticism in the Muscovite period (and particularly relevant in this context because of his association with Dmitrii Donskoi's victory over the Tatars at Kulikovo Field); Vyg was one of the great centers of the Old Belief, north of Lake Onega, flourishing in the eighteenth century; St. Serafim of Sarov (ca. 1754–1833) is one of the most popular figures in modern Russian Orthodoxy. The triumvirate of places, in fact, privileges rhetoric and general national symbolism over any specifics of place; for example, it is hard to conceive of any actual or potential theological point of view—popular or conventional—from which those three places would be regarded with equal admiration. On the contrary, it is extent—in geography (the Moscow region; the Russian north; the Volga region), history, and theology—which is evoked here. Such rhetoric and symbolism will be characteristic of much of Klyuev's later toponymic poetry, and provides another key to an understanding both of the thematics and the poetics of his verse. And once again, despite Klyuev's presentation of himself as a poet of specific beliefs and places, his poetry suggests opposite tendencies: toward collage; poetic, rather than programmatic, coherence; and mythologization outside of conventional geography and history.

Thus named fictional characters keep company with saints in several poems of the "Mirskie dumy" sequences. A striking blend of proper names occurs in the long "Besednyi naigrysh." One passage provides a colorful aetiology for geographical features:

От словес апостольских Планида
Как косач в мошище, встрепенулась,
Круто буйну голову здынула,
Откатила скуфью за Онего.
Кур-горой скуфья оборотилась,
Опушь стала ельником кромешным,
А завязка речкою Сорогой . . . (276)

At the words of the apostle, Planida
Started, like a reaper in a soaking pool,
Sharply raised her wild head,
Cast her skullcap beyond Onega.
The skullcap turned into a smoke-mountain,
The edge a dark fir grove,
And the knot the little river Soroga . . .

Thus the mythological Planida (fate) encounters the popular and local form of the name of Olonia's principal lake (Onego), and the river name, Soroga, in a passage which, as it describes magical transformation, could stand for Klyuev's own poetic wizardry. On the one hand, parts of this passage have much in common with folk aetiologies, but on the other hand, the movement between northern, prominent, and very large Lake Onega and the little Soroga hundreds of kilometers to the south in the Valdai region is expressly eclectic, characteristic of Klyuev, not folklore, and expressive of a mythologized totality of the (modern) Russian land.[21]

The *Pesnoslov* "Mirskie dumy" also includes the lengthy folkloric stylization "Obidin plach" ("Obida's Lament"), in which a female speaker narrates her ill-omened vision of destruction (unable to sleep, she walked to the lake at night and saw many mutilated bodies on its floor; for that reason she will not join the peasant festivities about to take place):

Я поведаю на гульбище
Праздничанам-залихватчикам,
Что мне виделось на озерышке,
Во глуби на самом донышке:
Из конца в конец я видела
Поле грозное, убойное,
Костяками унавожено.
Как на полюшке кровавоём
Головами мосты мощены,
Из телес реки пропущены,
Близ сердечушка с ружья паля,
О бока пуля пролятыва,
Над глазами искры сыплются . . . (100)

At the gathering I shall tell
To the revelers celebrating,
Of my vision in our lake,
In its depths, on its very bottom:
From end to end I saw
A fearful, murderous field,
Enriched with skeletons.
And on the bloody field
Bridges were laid with heads,
From bodies rivers flowed,
Near the heart, firing from a rifle,
Bullet flying against flanks,
Under eyes sparks scatter . . .

This poem was first published in 1909 as "Sovremennaya bylina" ("Contemporary Epic Tale"); it appeared in *Sosen perezvon* as "Lesnaya byl'" ("Forest Tale"); then as "Sovremennaya bylina" in the first, small *Lesnye byli;* and as "Lesnaya byl'" in the second, larger version of that collection. Then it migrated to the "Mirskie dumy" section of *Pesnoslov* as "Obidin plach," under which title it appeared in the booklet *Pesn' Solntsenostsa: Zemlya i zhelezo* (*Hymn of the Sunbearer: Land and Iron*) of 1920. It also appeared in Klyuev's last published collection, *Izba i pole* of 1928, as one of the final poems of that collection's third and concluding section, "Urozhai" ("Harvest"). Thus, the poem of the fourth section of *Pesnoslov* is a later variant of one of Klyuev's very early lyrics (it is the twenty-ninth poem in *Serdtse edinoroga,* with the initial date of composition noted as 1908). In addition to the highly significant changes of title among these various versions, there are also very telling textual variants. Moreover, a manuscript of the poem was among five lyrics sent to Blok in 1908: in that version the poem appears as "Pesnya devushki" ("Song of a Maiden"), with extensive variants.[22] In its original published role as a "*contemporary bylina,*" the poem clearly presented a vision of sociopolitical martyrdom, in line with much of Klyuev's thought during those years, and with his presentation of himself in the letters to Blok. The early versions of the poem contain lines referring to the gallows which are absent in the later versions, while lines which emphasize the brutality of the martyrdom were censored (832). As "Lesnaya byl'," it is the poem's association with place, rather than time, which is emphasized in the title, although the text remains substantially the same. Its first appearance as "Obidin plach," with its title exemplifying the now ubiquitous allusions to *Slovo o polku Igoreve* (*Lay of Igor's Campaign*) in Klyuev's poetry, is in a 1919 revision of the 1916 First World War sequence (that is, the *Pesnoslov* version of "Mirskie dumy"), and here the allusions to the gallows are absent. Thus the poem, originally associated with martyrdom in political struggle, presumably against the political order of the day, becomes part of a sequence dominated by images of national courage and military martyrdom on behalf of the motherland during the First World War, but in doing so modifies, after the event, the original version of that sequence by adding further emphasis to the images of death and destruction. Given the time and place of publication (1919, early Soviet Russia), historical and political interpretations of this revision are possible: the cycle has been modified in the light of subsequent events—Russia's losses, the horror of the war—or the cycle has been modified in the Soviet period to emphasize the political senselessness of that "imperialist" war. When the poem reappears yet again in Klyuev's last collection (thereby indicating, among other things, the poet's continuing preoccupation with this early work), a further transformation of its role in time and place might be said to have taken place, as the poem by then fits with many of Klyuev's later apocalyptic visions of contemporary Soviet Russia (and is compatible with the programmatic, even provocative content of much of *Izba i pole*).

The story of "Obidin plach" thus illustrates not only the elusive mutability of Klyuev's work (consistent with the protean character of his thought, image, and even, perhaps, character) but also how the instability of poetic time and place is to a certain degree enabled by the mutability of historical time and place, which that poetry itself expresses, not least in its relationship to its physical place on particular pages at particular times. A single poem, as it is modified and relocated in time and space by the poet, seems to change (and be changed by context) in quite radical ways, just as some of the key motifs of the poet's "life-creation" mutate over time and space, partly in response to changing external circumstances. In short, verse has a complex biography, while the poet's life is evidently *textual.*

The second half of the book *Mirskie dumy* consists of a sequence of poems entitled "Pesni iz Zaonezh'ya" (the "Trans-Onega region" denotes, among other things, the area east of Lake Onega—that is, on the far side of the lake from St. Petersburg). This is also the title of a larger sequence of poems, forming the fifth part of *Pesnoslov,* and consisting of twelve poems from the original version of the sequence, one poem from *Bratskie pesni,* and fifteen poems from *Lesnye byli.* The same title also heads a selection of five poems published in the periodical *Ezhemesyachnyi zhurnal* in 1914.[23] The title illustrates again the combination of abstract and concrete in Klyuev's toponymics—on the one hand, these poems may indeed claim to be songs from the "Trans-Onega region," being the work of a lyric poet from near that part of Russia; on the other hand, they are *metaphorical* songs (but actually poems, although some are stylized as folk songs), from a world beyond the physical realities of actual time and place, from somewhere *beyond* the Lake Onega of geography.[24]

The various versions of these "songs from beyond Onega" are marked not only by the prominence of highly stylized folklore, but also by the prominence of female speakers—unusual in other parts of Klyuev's oeuvre. A few poems, such as "Stikh o pravednoi dushe" and "Proslavlenie milostyni" ("Poem About the Righteous Soul," "Praise of Alms," 229–30, 222–23), the final two works in both book versions of "Pesni iz Zaonezh'ya," show clear signs of proximity to folklore (in this case religious), but most of the "songs" lack the devices of actual folk song and are infrequently colored by dialectisms, notwithstanding the geographical allusion of the title. In sharp contrast to other poems of this period, with their preoccupations with contemporary events, but in accordance with the poetics of the folk song, the poems in "Pesni iz Zaonezh'ya" are almost completely free of concrete geographical or chronological references. The settings are, for the most part, generalized villages, with quite unspecific characters (despite the occurrence of occasional fictional first names). The "peasant's calendar," so noticeable in other areas of Klyuev's poetry from this period, is also a muted presence at best, but another aspect of the experience of time is newly prominent—many of the poems address specific, albeit generalized, moments in the life of man, and particularly of woman. Several poems treat such favorite folk song and folk song-stylization themes as attitudes to courtship, marriage, and family relations, most often from the point of view of a young woman—"Svadebnaya," "Ivushka zelenen'ka . . . ," and "Na sele chetyre zhitelya," among others ("Wedding Song," "Green Willow," "The village has four residents," 167, 228–29, 216–19).

Mednyi kit (*The Copper Whale*) was Klyuev's fifth new collection. Dated "1919," it came out, in fact, at the end of 1918.[25] It was his first book to be published after the Bolshevik Revolution (although by no means his first publication—the years 1917 and 1918 saw the appearance of numerous poems in periodicals and almanacs, including, most notably, the almanac *Skify*). Many of the forty-one poems in *Mednyi kit* reflect directly or indirectly events of the revolutionary period. However, it is a different sort of collection from the first four, since it does not in fact represent, first and foremost, the poet's work of the present and recent past, as earlier collections had done, but instead combines recent work with earlier, sometimes much earlier poetry. As usual, the poems in the collection are not dated, so only a reader already attuned to Klyuev's style and thematics might guess that the collection contains poems written as early as 1905, as well as poems from the revolutionary years. The order in which the poems appear is—as ever—not determined by chronology of composition, nor yet quite by theme, although a certain "narrative" movement (away from initial revolutionary enthusiasm) may be detected. The collection opens and closes with long, programmatic works. "Pesn' Solntsenostsa" (363–66), the first work in the collection, celebrates the union of East and West in Russia, and of Russia with the speaker in a series of characteristic oratorical gestures. (Boris Filippov uncharitably termed this work an *alyapovataya oda* [clumsy ode, 1:562].) It is closely associated with Klyuev's Scythian episode, in which the poet's preoccupation with the inherent universalism of his rural Russia becomes more pronounced.[26] *Mednyi kit* ends with two more long works—"Poddonnyi psalom" ("Psalm from the Depths," 288–92) and "Mednyi kit" (392–95).[27] The former combines language and toponyms drawn from the Bible and the church with contemporary sociopolitical aspirations and with elements from the poet's own favored geography. The latter is especially eclectic in its combinations of times and places, and sounds a distinctly prophetic note (past and present combining to anticipate the future—a very typical gesture for Klyuev's mature verse), as the opening and concluding stanzas clearly indicate:

Объявится Арахлин-град,
Украшенный яспием и сардисом,
Станет подорожник кипарисом,
И кукуший лен обернется в сад.

Братья, это наша крестьянская красная культура,
Где звукоангелы сопостники людских пабедок и просонок!
Корноухий кот мудрей, чем Лемура,
И мозг Эдиссона унавозил в веках поросенок.
. . .
Матросы, матросы, матросы, матросы —
Соленое слово, в нем глубь и корал,
Мы родим моря, золотые утесы,
Где гаги — слова для ловцов-Калевал.

Прости, Кострома, в душегрейке шептухи!
За бурей «прости», словно саван, шуршит.
Нас вывезет к солнцу во Славе и Духе
Наядообразный, пылающий кит.
(392, 395)

Arakhlin-town shall appear,
Decorated in jasper and cornelian,
Plantain shall become cypress,
And cuckoo moss will turn into a garden.

Brothers, this is our red peasant culture,
Where sound-angels are the spiritual brothers of human failings and
sleep!
The crop-eared cat is wiser than Roman spirits,
And a piglet has fertilized the mind of Edison for the ages.
. . .
Sailors, sailors, sailors, sailors—
The saline word, in it the depths and coral;
We shall bear seas, golden cliffs,
Where eider ducks are words for the hunters of Kalevalas.

Forgive us, Kostroma, in the blouse of a horse-whisperer!
Through the storm "forgive" rustles like a shroud.
We'll be carried to the sun in Glory and Spirit
By a flaming whale in the form of a naiad.

In between these striking, if sometimes rebarbative, bookends to the collection, the tone varies from enthusiastically revolutionary to ambiguously archaic. At times the present seems millenarian, at others more brutally apocalyptic. For example, "Zhil'tsy grobov, prosnites'! Blizok strashnyi sud," "Millionam yarykh rtov," "Prostyatsya vam stoletii igo," "Pust' cheren dym krovavykh myatezhei," and "Na bozhnitse tabaku os'mina" demonstrate the variety of apocalyptic interpretations offered for the present ("Dwellers in coffins, awake! The last judgment is nigh," "For millions of wild mouths," "You'll be forgiven the centuries-old yoke," "May the smoke of bloody revolts be black," "On the icon shelf is an ounce of tobacco"; 379–80, 383–84, 184, 378–79, 369–70). As the last work indicates, anti-urban notes are also struck in the collection (other examples include "Vecher rzhavoi pozolotoi," "Iz podvalov, iz temnykh uglov," "Gospodi, opyat' zvonyat" ["Evening with its rusty gilt," "From cellars, from dark corners," "Lord, they're ringing again"]; 371–72, 362–63, 349). The East-West conjunction, often made through the everyday culture of the northern peasantry, is also abundantly evident here, in "Nizkaya derevenskaya zarya" ("A low village dawn," 389–90; entitled "Revolyutsiya" ["Revolution"] in *Pesnoslov*), "Svit' sennyi voz mudree, chem sozdat'" ("To tie together a cart of hay is finer, than to create," 386–87; entitled "Trud" ["Labor"] in *Pesnoslov*), and "Fevral'" ("February"), 360–62. Perhaps the most striking poem of the collection is its second one, "Lenin," which was also to open the cycle of the same name, addressed to the Bolshevik leader. That cycle would be the penultimate work in the final section of *Pesnoslov,* and, later, the first of two cycles in Klyuev's thrice-published collection *Lenin,* as discussed below. In the individual lyric "Lenin" the familiar spectrum of diverse historical, cultural, and geographical references is deployed to produce a highly idiosyncratic portrait of the revolutionary, opening with the Old Believer associations of the first stanza:

Есть в Ленине керженский дух,
Игуменский окрик в декретах,
Как будто истоки разрух
Он ищет в «Поморских ответах». (377)

Lenin has the spirit of Old Believer Kerzhenets,
An abbot's roar in his decrees,
As if he seeks the sources of destruction
In the *Answers from the White Sea Shore.*

Klyuev's portrait of Lenin makes it easy to anticipate the poet's rapid disillusion with Bolshevism (and its with him), but is also telling in the nature of its deployment of various times and places. Here they are essentially attributes, thematic designations marked by denominational precision (Kerzhenets, an Old Believer center, rather than "the Old Belief as a whole"), but with relatively little independent, specific resonance—Klyuev's times and places are still, first and foremost, abstract, even when defined—a feature which links him to a premodern poetics. Equally telling is the allusion to Denisov's *Answers from the White Sea Shore,* one of the classics of Vyg literature, and a favorite referent of Klyuev's—in other words, at least one of the functions of this reference (and other such allusions) is expressly to appropriate the subject of the poem to an aesthetic and social agenda peculiar to Klyuev. This function is often evident in the more arcane of the poet's historical and geographical allusions, which the dutiful reader may elucidate only with the help of quite detailed reference books or commentaries, and is particularly characteristic of his employment of toponyms and personal names related either to the Russian north or to the confessional models with which he sympathizes (the Old Belief; popular Orthodoxy, and so on).

Klyuev's sixth collection is his most important, the two-volume *Pesnoslov* (*Hymn Book*) of 1919. It provides both a summary of his work to date and, as has been seen, a retrospective remaking of his early self. As so often in this period, that remaking may be viewed as expressing the foregrounded interaction of the aesthetic and the political. The collection clearly demonstrates the general tendency of modernism to return to texts already completed, to revise, and to elide earlier versions and records. For example, it will be recalled that the first volume of *Pesnoslov* reiterates the sequence of Klyuev's first four collections in its five divisions ("Sosen perezvon," "Bratskie pesni," "Lesnye byli," "Mirskie dumy," and "Pesni iz Zaonezh'ya"), but presents different contents for these later versions of earlier collections.[28] Meanwhile, it has also been suggested that both the overall contents of the collection and some of the transformations of earlier works are in response to, and even under pressure from, the new social order introduced by the Bolshevik coup.[29] In any event, a clear, if unfortunate, marker of time and place is the presence of a considerable number of typographical and similar errors—the collection is littered with misprints, poems are omitted from the contents pages, and some pages even bear the reversed imprint of others.

The composition of *Pesnoslov* has been studied at some length by Eduard Meksh, who charts the emergence of the collection from an initial plan of 1916 to combine (new) versions of previously published volumes into a single book.[30] In early October 1917 Klyuev sent the intended publisher the manuscript of that book, which differs significantly from the first volume of *Pesnoslov,* published some two years later, when it had been reshaped, like the second volume, by the new circumstances in which the poet and his country found themselves. Meksh notes, among other things, that the original version was in one volume, and opened with a *kovchevets* (little arc) consisting of "Mirskie dumy" alone, followed by a second *kovchevets* consisting of "Sosen perezvon," "Bratskie pesni," and "Lesnye byli." Moreover, not only the order of these sections, but also their contents are very different in the 1917 version from the final version presented in the first volume of *Pesnoslov,* to which has been added a fifth section, "Pesni iz Zaonezh'ya." Meksh notes the fluidity of Klyuev's compositional practice, and his research again warns against treating any published version as abstract and final, rather than as a product of processes partially dependent on circumstances (for example, Klyuev's 1917 book might well have been published, but its nonpublication led to the production of *Pesnoslov*). Klyuev's own ordering and reordering of his poetry also illustrates how the poetic collection variously embodies and materially represents time as sequence—analogous at a more abstract level to the reiterations (of meter, rhythm, rhyme, image, and so on) which materially constitute an individual poem. Or, to put it less abstractly, placing "Mirskie dumy," the newest poems, first in the book would have had quite a different effect from preserving the order of the publication of collections to date, as is done in the first volume of *Pesnoslov* (although, of course, both the contents of those sections representing previously published collections and the contents of individual poems often differ considerably from the originals). Moreover, the addition of a second volume, containing newer and mostly previously uncollected poetry, again radically changes the nature of the book as a whole.[31]

The use of earlier titles to designate sections of the book suggests both thematic and chronological progression. As ever, however, the poems are presented undated, and an alert contemporary reader would have quickly noted that thematic association sometimes predominates over chronological sequence, and that the thematic/chronological associations of the past are often remade quite dramatically. This is clear not only in the first volume but also in the second, which is divided into only three sections: "Serdtse edinoroga," which consists of a version of Klyuev's memorial cycle to his mother, "Izbyanye pesni," and the longer "Belaya povest'" ("White Tale"); "Dolina edinoroga," containing fifty-eight poems, some from *Mednyi kit,* but most newly collected; and "Krasnyi ryk" ("Red Roar"), consisting of forty poems, sixteen of them from *Mednyi kit,* the thematics of which "Krasnyi ryk" restates and remakes.

The second volume of *Pesnoslov* presents most of Klyuev's poetry from the years 1916, 1917, and 1918, although the poems are not dated in the collection itself (with very rare exceptions), and there are also poems from earlier years, including most of the "Izbyanye pesni" poems. This volume represents, among other things, the fullest version of the poet's immediate but complex response to the events of those years. Indeed, it is strongly marked by evidently competing ideas and images, many of which coalesce around the ever-problematic issues of time and place. The very structure of the volume and the order of poems within each section illustrate the singular importance and complexity of this combination. The fourteen-poem cycle "Izbyanye pesni" and "Belaya povest'," comprising "Serdtse edinoroga," are justly admired by Klyuev's readers, and are intriguing as portraits of a sort of mythologized calendar and description of village life.[32] While the heroine's death is an obvious and very significant marker of individual time, the poems occasioned by that death present, in fact, a very stable and *timeless* world in which rural rituals related to calendar, event, or routine are denoted by orderly repetition and by a striking combination of Christian and popular, "pagan" belief and practice. It is also highly characteristic of Klyuev's presentation of place in general, and place with apparent personal association in particular, that the village life depicted is almost entirely without geographic specifics. While the proper names of saints and biblical places abound, and are accompanied by many allusions to the domestic animals of the Russian village, to the liturgy and to popular apocrypha, and by enumerations of the contents of the *izba* and the rituals of "mother's" burial, characters are identified either by generic denomination of relationship ("mother," "grandfather") or by striking but fictional and short-lived specificity. For example, the lines "I khochetsya malen'koi Mashe/Sytovogo khlebtsa poest'" ("And little Masha wants to eat/Honey-mix bread") from "Kovriga svezha i dukhmyana" ("The rye bread is fresh and fragrant," 243–44) provide the only appearance of "little Masha," whose name functions no more individually than the generic labels encountered elsewhere.[33] And the only plausible Russian place name in the cycle is Krasnyi Volok, which, notwithstanding this apparent indication of concrete and specific reality, is, in fact, an idealized village where a rural epiphany may be expected:

В селе Красный Волок пригожий народ:
Лебедушки девки, а парни, как мед,
В моленных рубахах, в беленых портах,
С малиновой речью на крепких губах
. . .
Рундук запорожный — пречудный Фавор,
Где плоть убелится, как пена озер.
Бревенчатый короб — утроба кита,
Где спасся Иона двуперстьем креста.
. . .
Озерная схима и куколь лесов
Хоронят село от людских голосов.

По Пятничным зорям на хартии вод
Всевышние притчи читает народ . . . (242)

In the village of Krasnyi Volok the people are fine:
Swans—the girls, and the boys like honey,
In long feast-day shirts, in bleached trousers,
With melodic speech on firm lips
. . .
The Ukrainian linen chest—is a wondrous Mount Tabor,
Where flesh will whiten, like lake foam.
The wooden case is the belly of the whale,
Where Jonah was saved by the Old Belief cross.
. . .
The lakeland order and the cowl of the woods
Protect the village from human voices.
By Paraskeva's dawns, on the waters' charter,
The people read celestial parables . . .

The ideal nature of the village is abundantly clear, while its abstract, programmatic nature is indicated by the combination of diverse religious and cultural references, and by the radical ahistoricity of the combinations (*molennye rubakhi*—festive wear of Old Believers; *runduk zaporozhnyi*—presumably a chest of Ukrainian linen, which itself is a Mt. Tabor; the *korob* which is a whale, where Jonah from the Old Testament saved himself by making the sign of the cross with two fingers, like a Russian Old Believer). However, there is perhaps one disguised marker of the very personal and specific. The dawns belong to St. Paraskeva Pyatnitsa, a favorite saint in Orthodoxy. She, of course, is the patron saint of Klyuev's mother, Praskov'ya, whose death is the occasion of the entire cycle (and the main Makachevo church—that is, the principal church of the poet's childhood—was consecrated to St. Paraskeva).[34]

As these examples illustrate, "fictionality" in the presentation of time and place, as of character and event, is constructed and subverted in most unusual ways in Klyuev's verse. Equally characteristic of his construction of time and place is the concluding poem of the section "Serdtse edinoroga," the long "Belaya povest'" (303–7), in which it is not the heroine's death, but her giving birth to the poet, which is the subject of an elaborately constructed myth associating the poet's verse with her bread baking.

The contrast between "Serdtse edinoroga" and its larger counterparts within the volume is striking. "Dolina edinoroga," in particular, presents a series of unpredictably competing thematic and poetic moments in which different and contrasting features of time and space are especially evident, while "Krasnyi ryk" both reiterates these combinations and restates—partly by means of the sequence in which its composite poems are ordered—the exploration of revolutionary thematics encountered already in *Mednyi kit.*

Meanwhile, the titles "Serdtse edinoroga" ("Heart of the Unicorn") and "Dolina edinoroga" ("Valley of the Unicorn") indicate association between the first and second sections of the volume, although of what kind is far from clear. The unicorn is not only a mythical beast, symbolic of purity, but also a very un-Russian creature. Locating its *heart* in the Russian *izba* in the first section is, however, entirely consonant with the universalist imagery encountered abundantly in the second volume of *Pesnoslov.* As for its *valley*—yet another elusive place name in a Klyuev title—it is perhaps to be associated with the rhinoceroses of the opening line of the sixth poem in the "Lenin" cycle (in "Krasnyi ryk"), where a characteristically striking image begins an emblematic enumeration of Klyuev's syncretism (an archaic meaning of *edinorog* is "rhinoceros"):

Стада носорогов в глухом Заонежье,
Бизоний телок в ярославском хлеву . . .
Я вижу деревни, седые, медвежьи,
Где Скрябин расставил силки на молву.

Herds of rhinoceroses in distant land beyond Onega,
A bison calf in a Yaroslavl' barn . . .
I see villages, gray, haunts of the bear,
Where Scriabin set traps for talk.

Millenarian and apocalyptic time, already favorite categories, are among the principal referents for the revolutionary poems, as in *Mednyi kit,* but in *Pesnoslov* the apocalyptic predominates and is increasingly evident in "Krasnyi ryk" as a major metaphor for the revolutionary period, notwithstanding the fact that the section, and with it *Pesnoslov,* ends on the utopian tones of the Lenin cycle and the long poem "Mednyi kit."

At times, it is true, an anticipated golden age coming after the present seems to be predicted. Indeed, the poem immediately preceding "Lenin" announces:

На ущербе красные дни,
Наступают геенские серные, —
Блюдите на башнях огни,
Стражи-товарищи верные!

Слышите лающий гуд,
То стучится в ад Григорий Новых . . .

У Лючифера в венце изумруд,
Как празелень рощ сосновых.

Не мой ли «Сосен перезвон»
И радельных песен свирели
Затаили Распутинских икон
Сладкий морок, резьбу и синели?

В наговорной поддевке моей
Хлябь пурги и просинь Байкала.
За пляской геенских дней
Мерещится бор опалый.

В воздухе просфора да кагор,
(Приобщался Серафим Саровский),
И за лаптем дед-Святогор
Мурлычет псалом хлыстовский.

Ковыляет к деду медведь,
Матер от сытной брусники . . .
Где ж индустриальная клеть,
Городов железные лики?

На ущербе красные дни,
К первопутку лапти-обнова,
Не тревожит гуд шестерни
Рай медвежий и сумрак еловый.

Только где-то пчелой звенят
Новобрачных миров свирели,
И душа — запричастный плат —
Вся в резьбе, жемчугах и синели. (414–15)

The red days are on the wane,
Sulphurous days of Gehenna are coming—
Watch the fires on the towers,
Faithful comrade-guards!

Hear the barking groan,
That's Grigorii Novykh knocking on hell's doors . . .
Lucifer has an emerald in his crown,
Like the first green of the pine grove.

Was it perhaps my *Peal of the Pines*
And the pipes of my songs of ecstasy
That hid the sweet darkness, carving and blue
Of Rasputin's icons?

In my magical peasant coat
Is the blizzard's sleet and Baikal's azure.
Behind the dance of Gehenna's days
The shameful grove can be glimpsed.

There is communion bread and wine in the air
(Serafim of Sarov has taken the host),
And old Svyatogor making bast shoes
Purrs a flagellant psalm.

A bear hobbles toward the old man,
Strong from rich whortleberry . . .
Where now is the cage of industry,
The iron visages of towns?

The red days are on the wane,
New bast shoes lead to fresh snow tracks,
The hum of gears cannot disturb
Bear heaven and fir twilight.

But somewhere, like a bee, hum
The flutes of newly wed worlds,
And the soul—communion scarf—
Is all carving, pearls, and blue.

Characteristic here are the eclecticism in references (Rasputin [Grigorii Novykh], a figure frequently encountered elsewhere in his work, including, as will be seen, "Gagar'ya sud'bina"; Serafim of Sarov, Svyatogor); the reiterated suggestion of the importance of heresy and apostasy—implied in the figure of Rasputin, and announced in the flagellant song sung by the folkloric hero Svyatogor; hostility to urban civilization and alarm at the hellish present; the somewhat uncertain prophecy of a brighter future, explicitly associated with nature and rural life; and the identification of the poet Klyuev within this matrix, as the third stanza speculates on the role of his first two collections in predicting recent events, while the final stanzas anticipate an unequivocally Klyuevan idyll for the future by poetic fiat.

The movement between self-definition and a broad ideological and aesthetic agenda is often vertiginous in the poems of this period, and is frequently facilitated or, at least, marked by allusions to time and place. In "Dolina edinoroga" the speaker declares (in a relatively rare direct allusion to the non-Russian heritage of the poet's home region):

Я потомок лапландского князя,
Калевалов волхвующий внук,
Утолю без настоек и мази
Зуд томлений и пролежни скук. (367)

I am the heir of a prince of Lapland,
The spell-casting grandson of the Kalevala,
I will soothe without tinctures and ointment
The ache of yearnings and the sores of boredom.

Characteristic both in these opening lines and throughout the poem is the movement between high culture, with its aristocratic and exotic version of the poet's lineage (descended from a Lapp prince), and the contradictory image of the poet as a rural seer and curer. This contradictory assertion of identity also serves as a reminder that statements of relationship in Klyuev's work may often be metaphorical (compare the claims to be descended from Avvakum, the family histories of the autobiographical texts, and the mythologized treatment of the poet's family and youth in *Pesn' o Velikoi Materi*). Moreover, the northern and rural features are contrasted with the inadequate civilization of the western city (in this case represented by Washington and Riga: "Vashington, cherepichnaya Riga/Ne vmestyat kashalotnoi volny" ["Washington, tile-roofed Riga/Will not accommodate the sperm-whale wave"]), while the poem concludes with an invitation to join the speaker in eclectic cultural union:

Уплывем же, собратья, к Поволжью,
В папирусно-тигриный Памир!
Калевала сродни желтокожью,
В чьем венце ледовитый сапфир.

В русском коробе, в эллинской вазе,
Брезжат сполохи, полюсный щит,
И сапфир самоедского князя
На халдейском тюрбане горит.

Let's sail away, brethren, to the Volga's banks,
To the papyrus-tiger land of the Pamir!
The *Kalevala* is akin to yellow-skinned folk,
In whose crown is an arctic sapphire.

In the Russian basket and the Hellene vase,
Flash the northern lights, the polar shield,
And the sapphire of a Samoyed prince
Burns on a Chaldean turban.

Here, and in a number of other poems from this volume of *Pesnoslov,* the poet's relocation of his identity *further north* is to be noted (the opening poem of the Esenin cycle in "Dolina edinoroga" refers to *rodnoi, belomorskii prostor* [native White Sea expanse], 297), in combination with the geographic universalism of his aesthetic manifesto. This relocation, already suggested in the Esenin poem of 1916, will become more and more marked in his work of the Soviet period, achieving its strongest statement in *Pesn' o Velikoi Materi.*

Other poems in the second book of *Pesnoslov* present a rural account of the seasons (for example, "Na ovinnoi paperti Paskha," "Kak grob episkopa, gde ladan i parcha" ["Easter is at the barn's church porch," "Like a bishop's coffin, where incense and brocade"; 320, 327–28] in which the peasant, even pagan, calendar is blended with that of the church. On the other hand, both "Dolina edinoroga" and "Krasnyi ryk" contain allusions to and suggestions of sectarianism, not least the *skoptsy.*

A targeted polemic is conducted in the two-poem cycle in "Vladimiru Kirillovu" ("To Vladimir Kirillov," 396–99). Here characteristic aspects of Klyuev's deployment of time and space are especially noteworthy:

Твое прозвище — русский город,
Азбучно-славянский святой,
Почему же мозольный молот
Откликается в песне простой?
. . .
Убегай же, Кириллов, в Кириллов,
К Кириллу — азбучному святому,
Подслушать малиновок переливы,
Припасть к неоплаканному, родному.

Your sobriquet is a Russian town,
An alphabetically Slavic saint,
Why then should the callous hammer
Echo in a simple song?
. . .
Run off, then, Kirillov to Kirillov,
To Kirill—the alphabet saint,
To listen to the trills of robins,
To fall before the unlamented, the native.

The rebukes and advice to the proletarian poet are typical of Klyuev, not least for the open play with redundancy and repetition and for the investing of the Cyrillic alphabet (a common referent in his work of this period) with especial significance, akin to the natural, rural world where the addressee should worship—again, nature and text intersect. However, it is also significant that the polemic plays not so much with the place to which it refers (the Monastery of St. Cyril of Belozersk, at the town of Kirillov near Beloe Ozero, and only a couple of hundred kilometers from Klyuev's native villages) as with the *name* of that place. That it is designation and lexical association which are predominant is emphasized by two other facts relevant to this poem, both of which undercut the apparently unproblematic assertions it makes: the opening line announces that the addressee's sobriquet is a "Russian town," while Vladimir Kirillov actually bears the names of *two* ancient Russian towns—not only little Kirillov, but also Vladimir the Great—and St. Cyril of Belozersk (1337–1427) is *not,* of course, the saint who gave his name to the alphabet used by the Russians—that, as every Russian knows, is the ninth-century St. Cyril, who, with his brother St. Methodius, brought Christianity to Moravia. In other words, Kirillov's recommended flight to the town of Kirillov would take him, literally and geographically, to one Cyril, but figuratively—with no regard for historical detail or geography—to another (although, to add to the complexities of name play here, it should be remembered that St. Cyril of Belozersk derived his monastic name from his ninth-century predecessor).

Equally characteristic is the employment of very specific historical references in the context of an all-embracing, if unstable, mythology of nature. Thus one poem in "Krasnyi ryk" opens by noting the rather arcane information that Neil of Sora (Nil Sorsky), a monastic follower of St. Cyril of Belozersk, forbade the cutting of trees on the territory of his spartan monastic community, founded at the end of the fifteenth century:

Нила Сорского глас: «Земнородные братья,
Не рубите кринов златоствольных,
Что цветут, как слезы в древних платьях,
В нищей песне, в свечечках юдольных.

Низвергайте царства и престолы,
Вес неправый, меру и чеканку,
Не голите лишь у Иверской подолы,
Просфору не чтите за баранку.

Притча есть: просфору-потеряшку
Пес глотал и пламенем сжигался.
Зреть красно березку и монашку —
Бель и чернь, в них Руси дух сказался.

Не к лицу железо Ярославлю, —
В нем кровинка Спасова — церквушка:
Заслужила ль песью злую травлю
На сучке круживчатом пичужка?

С Соловков до жгучего Каира
Протянулась тропка — Божьи четки,
Проторил ее Спаситель Мира,
Старцев, дев и отроков подметки.

Русь течет к Великой Пирамиде,
В Вавилон, в сады Семирамиды;
Есть в избе, в сверчковой панихиде
Стены Плача, Жертвенник Обиды.

О, познайте, братия и други,
Божьих ризниц куколи и митры —
Окунутся солнце, радуг дуги
В ваши книги, в струны и палитры.

Покумится Каргополь с Бомбеем,
Пустозерск зардеет виноградно,
И над злым похитчиком-Кащеем
Ворон-смерть прокаркает злорадно». (408–9)

The voice of Neil of Sora: "Earthborn brothers,
Do not cut the crowns of the gold-trunked trees,
That flower, like tears in ancient dresses,
In an impoverished song, in mournful candles.

Overturn kingdoms and thrones,
Unfair weights, measure, and coinage,
Just don't bare the skirt tails of the Iberian Virgin,
Don't treat communion bread as tea rolls.

There is a tale: a dog swallowed
A lost piece of communion bread and caught light.
It is fine to see a birch tree and a nun—
White and black, in them the spirit of Old Russia was stated.

Iron does not suit the face of Yaroslavl',
It has the Savior's blood—a church:

Has the bird upon the lace branch
Deserved evil, dog-like persecution?

From Solovki to burning Cairo
The path is laid—the Lord's prayer beads,
Beaten by the Redeemer of the World,
By the soles of elders, maids, and youths.

Old Russia flows toward the Great Pyramid,
To Babylon, to the Gardens of Semiramis;
Within the peasant house, in its cricket requiem,
Are the Wailing Wall, the Altar of Offense.

O recognize, brethren and friends,
The cowls and miters of the Lord's sacristies—
The sun, the arcs of rainbows will bathe
In your books, strings, and palettes.

Kargopol' shall befriend Bombay,
Pustozersk shall blush like grapes,
And over the evil thief Kashchei
Raven death shall caw maliciously."

As is so often the case, the poem raises intriguing questions about Klyuev's interests and knowledge. Neil's ascetic community on the Sora River, not far from Kirillov, may reasonably be considered within the regional orbit of Klyuev's home region. In decay for a long time, the *skit* (community of hermits) had undergone something of a revival in the nineteenth century, when a monastery of some size thrived on the site. Neil did, indeed, forbid the cutting of trees there—a fact which Klyuev could have learned from local sources or oral tradition (although there is no evidence that he visited the site itself), or yet, perhaps, from manuscript sources, since it appears that this particular detail of life at the *skit* was not available in print at the time.[35] The problem is emblematic of the questions of Klyuev's identity—did he know this fact about Neil because he was a member of a community for whom it was traditional knowledge, or did he read it as a learned investigator of old texts when he developed his cultural interests as a mature author?

In fact, the poem, although nominally the discourse of the historical Neil of Sora, moves far in place and time from him: soon the great specificity of the opening lines, alluding to instructions for the maintenance of a single religious community, established by a named historical figure, has been abandoned for eclectic combinations, many of them commonplaces of European culture, and for programmatic statements characteristic of the poet, rather than the ascetic. Other elements in the poem quite clearly allude to the political and religious situation of Russia at the time of the poem's composition (1918–19)—in particular, the threat to national religion from Bolshevism. This sort of referential movement between times and places is, moreover, achieved in the compressed poetic time and space of an eight-stanza lyric—another abiding characteristic of the mature poet's work. Here the compressed time of the lyric both facilitates the vatic, obscure pronouncements of the notional speaker and contrasts with the temporal expansiveness of the referents, which itself is analogous to their geographical expansiveness. Emblematic of this paradoxical movement between opposites is the assertion made in the penultimate stanza: Russia flows to the pyramids, to Babylon, and to the Gardens of Semiramis, while the peasant hut *contains* the Wailing Wall and an altar to Obida (the embodied offense in *Slovo o polku Igoreve*).[36]

Pesnoslov was followed by three small collections published in 1920. The thirty-page *Izbyanye pesni,* the nineteen-page *Pesn' Solntsenostsa: Zemlya i zhelezo,* both published in Berlin, and *Neuvyadaemyi tsvet,* published in Vytegra, do not function as landmarks in his oeuvre in the same way as the volumes examined in the preceding pages. The original *Neuvyadaemyi tsvet,* subtitled *Pesennik* (*Song Book*), is an extreme bibliographic rarity—according to Azadovsky, only three copies are known. It was republished (but not as a photo-reprint) in 1995.[37] *Neuvyadaemyi tsvet* (*Unfading Flower*)—the title is the name of an icon—contains seventeen poems, all previously published in other collections. As Azadovsky again observes, this collection is distinguished from all Klyuev's others by its inner unity, since it consists entirely of the poet's folkloric stylizations, many of them narrative in character (for example, "Ivushka zelenen'ka . . ." and "Obidin plach"). Such poems were not, in fact, characteristic of his writing by the time of the publication of *Neuvyadaemyi tsvet* (but were, perhaps, the most likely exemplars of his oeuvre to appeal to readers in his hometown).[38] As highly self-conscious, literary stylizations (of which there is a long tradition in Russian belles lettres), they also provide the clearest indication of the relatively great distance Klyuev's poetics may take him from the major forms of Russian verbal folklore, notwithstanding the presence of abundant motifs and other features drawn from it. Indeed, the strong ethnographic element frequently evident in his work, while indicating considerable interest in folklore, also proclaims relative poetic distance from it.[39] Around this issue, as around the even more complex matter of Klyuev's poetic language, are seen many of the problems and conflicts which have always been characteristic of the reception and interpretation of the poet and his work. The tendency to reductive arguments about the "authenticity" of Klyuev's voice, however, has often obscured, rather than illuminated, his poetics and, for that matter, his achievement as a poet.

L'vinyi khleb (*Lion's Bread*), published in 1922, contains the majority of Klyuev's lyrics known to have been written between the completion of *Pesnoslov* and that year. It thus represents the poet's largest statement of his years in Vytegra—years which were perhaps the most productive in his career. It was there that Klyuev wrote not only the poems in *L'vinyi khleb,* some of the later lyrics in *Pesnoslov,* much of *Mednyi kit,* and a considerable number of lyrics not placed in any collection but also a significant amount of (partly occasional) prose and his first *poemy, Chetvertyi Rim* (1921) and *Mat'-Subbota* (1922). Among these achievements, *L'vinyi khleb* stands out, not least because it concludes the series of published, major collections which link a rough chronology of the poet's career with particular themes. Moreover, Klyuev seems to have written no lyric poetry at all between the end of 1922 and mid-1925, while the lyric poetry written after 1925 not only has a different story to tell but also itself forms part of a quite different narrative (the poet outside of the "official" world of literature; manuscripts without publishing; poetry of resistance and of last things; and so on). Thus, *L'vinyi khleb* is an especially important volume, and is effectively, if not intentionally, the culmination of the series which begins with *Sosen perezvon.* Its poetic and thematic integrity is striking, as is its ordering of contents (not based upon chronology of composition, although limited to the period 1919–21).

Moreover, the history of *L'vinyi khleb* is complex indeed: in the manuscript version of the collection of 1922, held in RGALI, the order of poems is quite different from the published version, and there are three more poems ("Uragany vpryaglis' v sokhu —," "Oni smeyutsya nad moei poddevkoi," and "Proklyata verba, slezinka" ["Hurricanes have been harnessed to the plow," "They laugh at my peasant coat," "Accursed is the willow, the teardrop"]; 451–53, 456–57).[40] It is not entirely clear who is responsible for the final shape of the published version. However, the facts that the three poems present in the manuscript but omitted from the published book do not seem likely candidates for simple censorship or self-censorship, and that the published order of the poems is certainly characteristic of Klyuev, suggest that it is legitimate to regard the shape of the published *L'vinyi khleb* as primarily the work of the author's own hands. Klyuev worked again on *L'vinyi khleb* after its publication, preparing a second edition at least twice: once shortly after the original publication, in 1922, and again in 1924.[41] Each of these new, unpublished versions is based on the published collection, but with revisions, and, again, the order of poems is significantly different, while four more poems have been added: "Dremlyu s medvedem v obnimku . . . ," "Potemki — podzharaya koshka . . . ," "Gitarnaya," without its title, and "Starikom v lokhmot'ya odetym" ("I doze in the bear's embrace," "Darkness—a wiry cat," "Guitar song," "As an old man, dressed in rags"; 506–8, 509–11, 937, 938). The manuscript with these revisions is in a private archive, and currently unavailable.[42] Moreover, in the newspaper *Nakanune* (*On the Eve;* published in

Germany) for March 26, 1922, the Berlin publishing house Skify announced among its books in preparation "Nikolai Klyuev, *L'vinyi khleb* sbornik stikhotvorenii." Although no physical evidence of the publication of this book has been found, it is entered in Tarasenkov's bibliographic guide.[43] Moreover, Tarasenkov provides the pagination of this book (thirty-eight pages)—a detail which suggests that he had seen more than the announcement in *Nakanune,* where no pagination is given, and that this version, if it did indeed exist, probably contained significantly fewer poems than the published version of 1922, which is 103 pages long. Tarasenkov's entry on Klyuev is particularly tantalizing, because he does not include in his guide any other collections of poetry announced in the same *Nakanune* advertisement as forthcoming, but apparently never published—hence it seems quite possible that this version of *L'vinyi khleb* did have some kind of material existence. As these various details indicate, the collection which provides the most important statement of the most productive period of Klyuev's career, and which effectively marks the end of his relatively unproblematic relationship with the printed word, is itself highly problematic: the manuscript version differs from the published; two further attempts at publication suggest significant authorial revisions; and a foreign phantom haunts the known published and manuscript versions.

On the one hand, *L'vinyi khleb* turns out to be a somewhat unstable entity, with the published version haunted by planned, alternative versions that have remained phantoms because of extraneous circumstances. On the other hand, the published version has a clear thematic structure, marked by the organization of poems. As in many of the later collections, the "bookend" poems with which the published collection opens and closes are especially significant in announcing and summarizing themes, and they may be clearly associated with one another. The first poem of the collection, "Psaltyr' tsarya Aleksiya" ("A psalter of Tsar' Aleksii," 475–76, 930), strikes notes which will be heard throughout *L'vinyi khleb,* and which are clearly reiterated, in modified form, in the last poem, "Pole useyannoe kostyami" ("A field sown with bones," 472, 930). In these exemplary poems, the present and the past are combined, both to provide an allegory for the future and to abolish temporal specificity; the validity of the rural idyll is asserted, as is its evident endangerment; the (contextually surprising) prospect of rebirth and renewal is announced; and ethnographic detail (often northern Russian) is combined with geographic expansiveness or universalism. "Psaltyr' tsarya Aleksiya" provides a striking opening to the collection:

Псалтырь царя Алексия,
В страницах убрусы, кутья,
Неприкаянная Россия
По уставам бродит кряхтя.

Text, Time, and Place

Изодрана душегрейка,
Опальный треплется плат . . .
Теперь бы в сенцах скамейка,
Рассказы про Царьград,

На столе медовые пышки,
За тыном успенский звон . . .
Зачураться бы от наслышки
Про железный неугомон,

Как в былом, всхрапнуть на лежанке . . .
Только в ветре порох и гарь . . .
Не заморскую ль нечисть в баньке
Отмывает тишайший царь?

Не сжигают ли Аввакума
Под вороний несметный грай? . . .
От Бухар до лопского чума
Полыхает кумачный май.

Заметает яблонным цветом
Душегрейку, постный Псалтырь . . .
За плакатным советским летом
Расцветают розы, имбирь.

В лучезарье звездного сева,
Как чреватый колос браздам,
Наготою сияет Ева,
Улыбаясь другим мирам.

A psalter of Tsar' Aleksii,
Its pages—scarves, funeral groats,
Restless Russia
Wanders, wheezing, through decrees.

The peasant jacket is torn,
The disgraced headscarf flaps . . .
Now a bench by the door would be good,
And tales about Constantinople,

Honey buns on the table,
The bells of Dormition across the fence . . .

Oh, to hide from the rumors
Of the indefatigability of iron.

To take a nap, as before, on the stove bench . . .
Except that gunpowder and smoke are in the wind . . .
Is it foreign devils that the quietest Tsar
Is washing off in the bathhouse?

Aren't they burning Avvakum
To the cawing of countless crows? . . .
From Bukhara to the Lapp tents
Calico May is flaming.

Under apple blossom, the jacket and
The lenten Psalter are swept away . . .
Behind the Soviet summer of posters
Flower roses and ginger.

In the luminescence of astral sowing,
Like an ear of grain to its furrows,
Eve gleams in her nakedness
Smiling at other worlds.

The anti-urban notes sounded here (the fear of "the indefatigability of iron") and the various signs of apocalyptic destruction are encountered almost ubiquitously in the collection, but the specific contemporary, political reference to the *Soviet* summer in the penultimate stanza is relatively uncharacteristic of *L'vinyi khleb* (making its occurrence in the opening poem especially noteworthy). Indeed, if the fifty poems of the collection are compared with lyrics contemporaneous to it but not included within it (of which there are some thirty-five, many of them originally published in Vytegra periodicals), it is clear that those with the most evident and specific contemporary references, including all occasional pieces, have been excluded. When specific allusions to the present are made in *L'vinyi khleb,* they stand out as exceptions, and are never consistently reiterated even within a single poem. For example, the poem which opens with the line "Po mne Proletkul't ne zaplachet" contains only two other references unique to contemporary Russia after that first line, with its allusion to a Soviet cultural group; rather, the poem states a self-definition of the poet in terms of association, by turns, with Africa, with Mecca as dreamed by a gray Olonian *izba,* with Arabian decoration as the picture of a future Russia, and with gorillas and parrots in the taiga ("Proletkul't won't cry for me," 421–22). Such referential movement is typical—the overall thematics of *L'vinyi khleb* are dominated by a syncretic approach to time and place, by a synesthetic presentation of experience, and by a marked solipsism, in which the cultural identity of the poet-speaker is expressly tied to both the syncretic and the synesthetic.

The last poem of the collection, "Pole useyannoe kostyami," presents its concluding apocalyptic interpretation of the present, drawing on, among other things, the visions of the prophet Ezekiel, Old Russian literature, and in the version published in *L'vinyi khleb,* Esenin and the chemist Mendeleev.[44] But especially characteristic of the collection is the explicit association here of eclectic and contrasting images of time and place with the expressed contradictions in the poet-speaker's own situation:

> Я — ворон кружусь над великой гробницей,
> Где челюсть осла с Менделеевым рядом.
>
> Мой грай почитают за песни народа . . .
>
> I'm a raven, circling above the great sepulcher,
> Where the jaw of an ass lies next to Mendeleev.
>
> My cawings are thought the songs of the people . . .

Equally typical of the collection is that this final poem, which presents such an alarming vision in its first twenty-two lines, concludes with six lines which seem to anticipate a future of renewal, uniting past and present, pagan and Christian:

> Глядь, в черепе утлом — осиные соты,
> И кости ветвятся, как верба в цвету!
>
> Светила слезятся запястьем перловым,
> Ручей норовится облобзаться с лозой,
> И Бог зеленеет побегом ветловым
> Под новою твердью, над красной землей!
>
> Look, in the decaying skull lie wasp nests,
> And bones are now sprouting like willows in bloom.
>
> The stars weep tears of pearl bracelets,
> The stream is attempting to kiss the vine,
> And God becomes verdant in rushing of willows
> Beneath a new firmament, above a red land!

Here, as so often, the thematic movement between past (often as a model for the present), present, and predicted future generates a particular kind of timelessness—achronicity, rather than eternity—which is enacted in the fabric of the poem by the sudden shifts of perspective, rendering any kind of notional integrity of time and space in the poem as performed text impossible.

It is also characteristic of the collection that these very telling opening and concluding poems are not placed in chronological order of composition among the fifty poems of *L'vinyi khleb.* The first poem, "Psaltyr' tsarya Aleksiya," was in fact written one year *after* the last poem, "Pole useyannoe kostyami." Nonetheless, in the collection, the last poem echoes the first, thereby inverting their literal chronological relationship. In other words, in a very concrete manner the collection as a physical object may be seen, in its composition, to enact the complex manipulation of time and place which is typical of its thematics and poetics.[45]

Most of the dominant themes of the collection are directly (and sometimes paradoxically) associated with ideas of time and space. Orientalism in general and, in particular, an association of the Russian north with the Islamic East represented by familiar ciphers such as Mecca (as in "Po mne Proletkul't ne zaplachet") are ubiquitous, and generally consistent with previous collections, but here these combinations are often expressly tied to one of the collection's other master-themes—self-conscious poetic and cultural self-definition (as in "Prostit'sya s laptem-milyagoi," "Zurna na zyryanskoi svad'be," "Teper' by Kazbek-kovriga" and many other lyrics ["Farewell to them dear bast shoe," "A *zurna* at a Komi wedding," "Now for a Kazbek-sized rye loaf"]; 477–78, 479–80, 482–83). In this and other contexts where poetry and the poet are explicitly discussed, the former is often presented as a means, sometimes ambiguous, for healing and renewal. This is the case too in some of the poems where rural idylls and their destruction are the dominant themes, for example "Osypalas' izbyanaya skazka —," "Zhelezo," "Poselit'sya v lesnoi izbushke," and "Na zavodskikh zadvorkakh, gde ugol'nyi ad" ("The tale of the peasant house is scattered," "Iron," "Settling in a forest hut," "In the backyards of factories, with their coal hell"; 481–82, 448–49, 431–32, 485–86). The last-named poem's opening and concluding stanzas are illustrative:

> На заводских задворках, где угольный ад,
> Одуванчик взрастает звездистою слезкой;
> Неподвластен турбине незримый Царьград,
> Что звенит жаворонком и зябликом-тезкой.
> . . .
> Стих — черпак на родной соловецкой барже,
> Где премудрость глубин, торжество парусов . . .

Я в историю въеду на звонном морже
С пододонною свитой словесных китов!

In the backyards of factories, with their coal hell,
A dandelion grows like a celestial tear,
Turbines have no power over unseen Constantinople,
That rings out like a lark and its chaffinch namesake.
. . .
Verse is a scoop on a native barge from Solovki,
With the wisdom of depths and the triumph of sails . . .
I shall enter history on a walrus of sound
With a suite below of verbal whales!

In *L'vinyi khleb,* what was to be one of the primary geographic associations of Klyuev's post-Vytegra career, encountered already in the later poems of *Pesnoslov,* is much in evidence—the now familiar claim to an affiliation with the far north, specifically, with the White Sea coast. That affiliation itself is complex and multiple (as well as fictitious), for it ties the poet not only to something more remote and perhaps more exotic than his native Onega region (and something culturally and geographically very different from it), but it also makes another appeal to the Old Believer heritage, in this case to the White Sea groupings, and furthermore, by strong implication, to the model provided by the most famous cultural figure to emerge from that region—Mikhail Lomonosov. As has been noted, the latter's birth as the son of a prosperous fisherman, and his supposed early association with Old Believers provide some of the background for the mythologized autobiographies encountered in *Pesn' o Velikoi Materi* and elsewhere. Of course, the association with the Solovetsky Islands had occurred very early in Klyuev's claimed autobiographies, as has also been seen, and it too will become more prominent in his later work (as will the association with Avvakum and his martyrdom, which itself took place in the far north).

In "Zadvorki Rusi — matyugi na zabore" ("The backyards of old Russia—profanities on fences," 492–93), the far north is seen as the location of spiritual purity, apparently betrayed in the interests of poetry:

Задворки Руси — матюги на заборе,
С пропащей сумой красноносый кабак,
А ветер поет о родимом Поморье,
Где плещется солнце — тюлений вожак,

Где заячья свадьба, гагарьи крестины
И ос новоселье в зобатом дупле . . .

О, если б в страницах златились долины,
И строфы плясали на звонкой земле!

The backyards of old Russia—profanities on fences,
The red-nosed inn with beggar's bag,
But the wind sings of the native White Sea coast,
Where the sun splashes, leading the seals.

Where hares marry and loons are baptized
And wasps hold housewarmings in a large-cropped tree hole . . .
O, if only these pages had golden valleys,
And stanzas danced on the echoing earth!

In the programmatic "Drevnii novgorodskii veter" ("Ancient wind of Novgorod," 494–95), the broad associations of nature, text, north, and Orient abound, while the link to Lomonosov is explicit:

В стране холмогорской, в нерпячьем снегу,
Под старым тресковым карбасом
Нашел я поющий берестяный след
От лаптя, что сплел Ломоносов . . .

In the land of Kholmogory, in the ringed-seal snow,
Beneath the old cod boat
I found a singing birch bark trace
Of the bast shoe woven by Lomonosov . . .

L'vinyi khleb is full of references to places near and distant from the poet's own, as is his mature poetry in general. But just as the occasional poems of this period, linked to his activities in Vytegra, are absent from the collection, so too are, for the most part, any locations particularly and specifically linked to his autobiography. Neither Koshtugi, the poet's birthplace, nor Zhelvachevo, where his parents moved after the poet's birth, are mentioned by name in his poetry (although the Megra River, which flows by Koshtugi and renders it especially picturesque, and the Andoma, which arcs around Zhelvachevo to similar effect, are among his very numerous hydronyms). Vytegra, the center of his home region, where the poet lived and worked productively in the years covered by *L'vinyi khleb,* is itself a very rare presence in his lyrics. "Krasnyi orel" ("Red Eagle," 415) of 1919, one of the many occasional poems of that period absent from *L'vinyi khleb,* begins with the line "Glukhaya Vytegra ne slyshit uragana" ("Remote Vytegra does not hear the hurricane"), and explains that such a place is too remote and provincial for its revolutionary addressee, whereas the remoteness of many northern locations is given a positive value in Klyuev's mythological re-creations—if not in his professional practice. The town is also characterized, if not named, in the lyric, untitled in *L'vinyi khleb,* which begins:

> Глухомань северного бревенчатого городишка,
> Где революция как именины у протопопа.
> Ряд обжорный и каланчи вышка
> Ждут антихриста, сивушного потопа. (422).
>
> The backwoods of a northern, wooden town,
> Where the Revolution is like the archpriest's birthday.
> The greedy market and the fire watchtower
> Wait for the Antichrist and a flood of moonshine.

This poem was published, with variants, in the local newspaper under the title "Vytegra," and appears with the same title in some manuscript sources (912), but in *L'vinyi khleb* the link to autobiographical and geographical specificity has been erased. It is also curious that the now-unnamed town's principal church is characterized thus:

> Собор же помнит Грозного, Бориса,
> На створах врат Илья громогласный . . .
>
> But the cathedral remembers Ivan the Terrible and Boris,
> On its gates is Elijah, the thunderous prophet . . .

Vytegra is not in fact an ancient town. The first written reference to a river quay on the site of the modern town is from 1710, while the town itself was named and founded by imperial decree in 1773. Its principal church in Klyuev's time, as now, was the Church of the Feast of Candlemass (Purification—Sretensky sobor), which dominates the city's left bank, standing on Krasnaya Gorka. That church was erected in 1873 to commemorate the centenary of Vytegra's founding. One commentator glosses the lines quoted above not as referring to a church in Vytegra, but to the Church of the Feast of the Protection of the Virgin (Pokrov) at Vytegorsky Pogost in the village of Ankhimovo, seven kilometers from Vytegra (912–13). This church was justly famous, and Klyuev wrote to Shiryaevets in 1914 that "this twenty-four-domed church from the time of Ivan the Terrible breathes inexpressible charm" (*Sd* 223). Here, too, several observations about the interrelationship of time and place are apposite: this splendid wooden church was at Ankhimovo, not Vytegra; it most certainly could not "remember Ivan the Terrible and Boris Godunov," since it was built in 1708; the Petrozavodsk author Vasilii Firsov points out that Klyuev consistently gave the church an earlier date than is historically accurate (as Klyuev's remarks to Shiryaevets illustrate), and equally consistently described it as possessing twenty-four cupolas, as it originally had, whereas by the beginning of the twentieth century it had only twenty-one; and finally, it is emblematic of the transformations which render all such discussions especially complex now, more than eighty years after the composition of this poem, that it must also be noted that this church, the finest piece of sacred architecture in the entire region, burned to the ground in 1963, a fact which continues to draw sad commentary from locals, and which seems especially in keeping with Klyuev's views of the fate of his country.[46]

Perhaps that last fact, more than anything else, illustrates the complexities of any consideration of time and place in Klyuev's work, particularly in relation to the Russian north. As was noted in chapter 1, the world from which Klyuev came, to which he refers, and which he undoubtedly transforms in his work, was relatively remote from urban intellectuals in the early years of the twentieth century. In the early years of the twenty-first century that world is far *more* remote—depopulation, urbanization, the failure of Russia to develop a modern "infrastructure," the ideology-inspired ravages of the Soviet period (antireligious campaigns, forced collectivization, purges, exile, imprisonment, and so on) have all placed an enormous distance between it and the present. Thus discussions of Klyuev's place in his own world (or worlds) are especially difficult, and inevitably loaded with issues which are characteristic of the time of discussion. Meanwhile, elements in Klyuev's work and in his conduct may be seen, after the event, as strikingly prophetic: the accidental burning of the Ankhimovo church seems to literalize the figurative, fictional "burnt ruins" of *Pogorel'shchina.*

It remains true, however, that the total absence from Klyuev's work of specific references to the villages of his childhood is as significant as the limited and less-than-specific references to Vytegra. While the general landscape of the area may well be seen in some of his nature poetry, an author anchored in the concrete realities of individual rural experience might have made more of Koshtugi and Zhelvachevo. So might an author more interested in the description of specific and concrete landscape, for both villages are marked by many particular features, and to the outside eye have elements of the picturesque, by any definition, about them, not least in the presence of their rivers. Zhelvachevo was certainly small and relatively remote even in Klyuev's day, but it stands on a bend in the Andoma River and contains even now a number of fine old wooden houses (it had no church—

the nearest being in Makachevo, the *selo* of which the *derevnya* Zhelvachevo forms a part). The house where Klyuev's family lived and worked stood beside a relatively large merchant house. Koshtugi, a larger *selo,* consisting in Klyuev's day of almost twenty separate villages (*derevni*), has two rivers snaking through it (the Megra and the Kimreka), and must have been relatively prosperous in the 1880s and 1890s. Although heavily Russified, the area in general retained at least memories of ethnic diversity, as of confessional diversity.[47] Notwithstanding Klyuev's silence on the specifics of the villages of his birth and childhood, any search for the local roots of his poetic world must attend to the general characteristics of these places—the significance of rivers; the confessional and ethnic diversity of the area; the linguistic blend (Slavic and Finno-Ugric) of the area's toponyms; the peasant economy; and so on. But it is also clear that his work is not predicated upon the evocation in precise detail of his own *petit pays,* narrowly defined, as the many examples cited of universalism, abstract play with toponyms, mythologized autobiographies, and so on have already illustrated. Lake Onega, its shores, and islands appear many times in his work (but not the lake's principal city, Petrozavodsk, where Klyuev spent some time in the first decade of the twentieth century)—as do the island of Kizhi with its spectacular wooden churches, and the island of Palei, where Old Believers set light to themselves to avoid persecution. Yet Vytegra, as has been seen, barely figures by name in Klyuev's poetry, whereas other nearby towns on the eastern side of Onega are prominent. Kargopol', 152 kilometers from Vytegra (234 by road), appears nine times, for example.[48] Pudozh (90 kilometers from Vytegra, but, until road improvements in the late 1990s, 397 by road) appears eight times. The appearance of Kargopol' in "Mirskaya duma" and in "Nila Sorskogo glas: 'Zemnorodnye brat'ya . . .' " has been noted above. The town also occurs twice in *L'vinyi khleb:* in "Solntse izbu vznuzdalo" and in "U vecherni dva cheloveka" ("The sun has bridled the peasant house," "There are two men at vespers"; 483–84, 489–90). In both instances it serves as the northern Russian polarity of a utopian universalist pronouncement:

> И когда огневой возница
> Взнуздывает избу,
> Каргопольским говором Ницца
> Провещает Руси судьбу: . . .
> . . .
> Выстроит Садко Избу соборную,
> Подружит Верхарна с Кривополеновой
> И обрядит Ливерпуль, Каабу узорную
> В каргопольскую рубаху с пряжкой эбеновой!

And when the fiery coachman
Bridles the peasant house,
Nice will prophesy old Russia's fate
In the accent of Kargopol': . . .
. . .
Sadko will build a Meeting House,
Will introduce Verhaeren to Krivopolenova
And will dress Liverpool, decorated Kaaba,
In a peasant shirt from Kargopol', with an ebony clasp!

On the one hand, the word "Kargopol'" could be replaced by any other (northern) Russian toponym to very similar general effect in order to denote, respectively, the northern Russian accent and northern Russian popular dress, a fact which illustrates the relatively abstract employment of denominations of place in Klyuev's work. On the other hand, specific features of the town must also be noted: Kargopol' is relatively close to the poet's own native region and has the distinction of being old, beautiful, historically significant, adorned with very fine churches, yet small and relatively inaccessible (almost 100 kilometers from the nearest railway station), facts which render the city appropriately emblematic of a particular image of the Russian north frequently propagated in Klyuev's work and which illustrate the paradoxical richness of his synthetic, yet authentic geography.[49] Kargopol' is also very close to Lake Lache, which itself occurs four times in Klyuev's verse (most tellingly in the opening line of a poem from the cycle "Razrukha," discussed in chapter 5). Lastly, it should be noted that Kargopol' was the place to which Bryusov's sister Nadezhda retreated in 1911, partially, it would seem, under the influence of Aleksandr Dobrolyubov. The biographical matrix for the town is thus characteristically synthetic: it is indeed near to Klyuev's own native region, and it seems that the poet knew the town personally (he wrote to fellow revolutionaries sent into exile there in 1906, and his letter indicates some local knowledge); yet it may also be associated with Klyuev's observation of the intelligentsia's "re-Russification" of itself in the "retreats" of Dobrolyubov and others.[50] Hence the poet's personal ties to Kargopol' are both direct and, as it were, through the capital-city culture with which he polemicized, but to which, *mutatis mutandis,* he belonged and which helped to shape his mature poetics. Pudozh, while perhaps less appealing to the aesthetically attuned and adventurous tourist, is also older and less accessible than nearby Vytegra, and more unambiguously tied to Karelia (forming part of the modern Republic of Karelia). Like Kargopol', and unlike Vytegra, it was quite close to a well-known monastery.[51] These examples also remind the reader that the idea of northern identity, so prominent in Klyuev's work, is primarily significant not in and of itself, but in a series of other (and sometimes contradictory) contexts—universalism, Orientalism, ruralism and anti-urbanism, Orthodoxy, the Old Belief, the geographical and political periphery, spiritual and natural purity, and so on.

Without doubt, a map truly representative of Klyuev's north would require several extra dimensions, and would be conceptually complex. It would also deviate frequently from the actual topography and demography of northern Russia. On the other hand, certain features of the poet's home region, while not described in his poetry, would certainly help to explain the particular features of such a map. In addition to those details noted above, a crucial constituent element of the poet's native geography is the Vytegra region's status as a *border area.* This status is reflected in the mutability of its politico-administrative affiliation: originally part of the Novgorod *guberniya,* Vytegra entered the reformed Olonian *guberniya* in 1784, returned to Novgorod in 1794, and then went back to Olonia in 1801. In the 1920s the Vytegra region became part of the Leningrad oblast, and finally, in 1937, part of the Vologda oblast, where it remains, a little uncomfortably, to this day.[52] In other words, the area has moved, administratively, between ancient Novgorod, north-central Vologda, modern St. Petersburg, and Finno-Ugric Karelia. These multiple affiliations and the town's uncertain identity among them have clear analogues in Klyuev's own literary identity. Similar observations might be made about the region's confessional identity, even today. Orthodox Vytegrans (*vytegory*—the Russian term itself is slightly unexpected) to this day possess the folding icons more characteristic of Old Believers, and are often buried with Old Believer crosses.[53] Again, the simple binaries of "fact and fiction," reality and invention, authenticity and inauthenticity seem reductive in the face of such actual complexities of time and place.

There are many other features of the cultural geography of Klyuev's native region which may also shed some light on the poet's programmatic claims. For example, healing and holy springs in the area are termed *iordany* (Jordans)—as if the landscape of the Holy Land and the story of the Gospels had been literally mapped on to the area. In other words, the everyday practice of Klyuev's home region provides an example of precisely the sort of gesture made frequently in his own work. In the past, these *iordany* (the term is still used) were sometimes surrounded by structures which facilitated the collection of water for immersion, so visitors could bathe in the waters of "Jordan" (in 2003 a model of such a structure could be seen in the Koshtugi school museum). It is also worth comparing Klyuev's frequent claims to have some kind of secret knowledge of a "hidden Russia" (discussed in the context of sectarianism in chapter 3) with a feature of the toponyms of his *petit pays.* Place names are the cause of some confusion in the documenting of his biography, and not without reason: for example, Koshtugi is, as noted above, a *selo,* consisting of a large number of adjacent *derevni;* each *derevnya* has two names—an "official" name, used in legal documents, on maps, and so on; and a colloquial name, used by the locals, who never employ the "official" term.[54] Thus, the inhabitants of Koshtugi may be seen as inhabiting a "secret" toponymic landscape, hidden from the uninitiated outsider. The example is not unique in the region. Similar complexities of denomination may even have led one scholar, writing in 2003, to describe Zhelvachevo as a village *nyne ne sushchestvuyushchaya* (no longer existing), even though, as of summer 2000, it counted three permanent inhabitants, and a significantly larger number of "summer folk."[55] Other features of Klyuev's home region are also worth noting in this context. Beyond the larger villages, more or less accessible today by motorized transport (although not always by passenger car), in the thickly forested interior of the Vytegra region, lie smaller, rapidly emptying settlements that, although certainly much more densely inhabited in Klyuev's day, can hardly have been much more accessible to the outsider than they are today. Some of them are remarkable for the survival of pockets of Finno-Ugric population, or for striking wooden churches, seen by very few people (for example, the village of Syargozero, some twenty kilometers further inland from Koshtugi). And Zhelvachevo, the village where Klyuev grew up, is still considered to be a place for sorcerers and spells.[56] At the annual Klyuev meetings in Vytegra, local schoolchildren working under the direction of Nina Mitroshkina, a teacher at Vytegra High School no. 1 and director of the folk and ethnographic group Olonia, regularly present papers which explore local specifics of language and ethnography in Klyuev's work.[57] During the Klyuev meeting in October 2002, children at the Koshtugi village school (now closed—another sign of the village's terminal decline in the twenty-first century) gave a presentation on local dialect which indicated, among other things, that many elements of the Veps language could still be found in the speech of locals. The result was a Russian at times almost incomprehensible to the native speakers present—a striking analogue to some of the more arcane linguistic features of Klyuev's poetry. In other words, while a great deal of Klyuev's construction of place and space is highly abstract and very evidently mythologized, much of his approach to cultural geography may also—and paradoxically—be associated with the specifics of his own home region.

Like place, time also finds different and often paradoxical expressions in *L'vinyi khleb*. The collection has relatively few unambiguous and specific references to the present, yet its overall preoccupation with imminent apocalypse and potential renewal obviously echoes the time of its composition. The pastoral idylls recalled or desired in a number of lyrics are equally timeless, yet colored by the same context of imminent demise which generates the poems lamenting the advance of urbanism. Remarks on the ages of man also occur in a number of poems (for example, " 'Tridtsat' tri goda, tridtsat' tri," "V shestnadtsat' — kudri da posidelki" ["Thirty-three years, thirty-three," "At sixteen—curls and gatherings"]; 496–98, 480–81) and are, as is characteristic of the collection, often linked both to the identity of the poet-speaker and to his role and mission. In "Menya khoronyat, khoronyat" ("They're burying me, burying," 502–3) the speaker defends his aesthetics and resists his cultural enemies, mxing the abstract and the concrete in typical fashion—the concrete includes two hostile references to the poet Bryusov, as well as an allusion to the poet's own *Pesnoslov,* while, among many abstract descriptions, the speaker characterizes himself as "iz sta millionov pervyi/Gurtovshchik zlatorogikh slov" ("among one hundred million/The best herdsman of gold-horned words"). At one point in this polemical self-defense, the speaker declares "Pogrebayut menya tak rano/Tridtsatiletnim borodachom" ("They're interring me early/A bearded thirty-year-old"), apparently another specific and concrete allusion to himself. But even this most personal of times is slippery in the case of Klyuev. At the time of the composition of this lyric the poet was certainly bearded, but he was also thirty-seven years of age (it will be recalled that many of his autobiographical statements are elusive on the matter of his age, as on many others).

As has been noted, *L'vinyi khleb* does not include all the lyrics which Klyuev composed between 1919 and 1922. In addition to the occasional pieces, some of an almost agitprop character, a number of poems reiterating themes found in the collection itself were also omitted. Of particular note is the elaborate "Ot berezovoi zhily povytekla Volga" ("From a birch vein out flowed the Volga," 515–17), written in 1921 or 1922, but published in its full (but incomplete) form only in 1990. This work, of some ninety lines, exemplifies, among other things, the ekphrastic tendency in Klyuev's poetry, most often seen in the descriptions of objets d'art, craft items, and so on. Here it is iconography, especially the work of Andrei Rublev, which is described, but in characteristic association with images of nature, geographic catalogues, Orientalism, and technical language:

От березовой жилы повытекла Волга,
Из медвежьего зуба Звенигород слажен . . .
Аксамиты напевов коротко иль долго
Будет мерить оравами бумаж[ная] сажень . . .

Я хочу песнословить рублевские вапы,
Заозерье перстов под гагарьим туманом . . .

From a birch vein out flowed the Volga,
Zvenigorod is formed from the tooth of a bear . . .
The velvet of refrains—long or short—
Will be measured in hordes by the paper furlong . . .

I want to sing praises to the paints of Rublev,
His fingers' land beyond lakes in the loon mists . . .

In addition to the toponyms of the lines above, the poem also mentions Russia (as *Rasseya* and as *Rus'*); Rome, Prague, the Baraba steppe in Siberia, the Turanian plateau in Central Asia, the Pechora and Nile rivers, Matochkin Shar and Vaigach Island above the Arctic Circle, Vyg and Leksa—sites of Klyuev's favorite Old Believer communities in Karelia—and Lake Baikal (939–40). Other proper names encountered include those for icons (such as "Ne rydai mene Mati" ["Weep not for me mother"]), an apparently nonexistent "Tale of Seth," and a series of historical figures, from Cyril Chelmogorsky, founder of the monastery near Kargopol', to Stenka Razin. The extraordinary variety of proper names is indicative of the rapid movement between times and places, matched by an equal diversity of vocabulary, evident especially in the names of flora and fauna, and of the colors and techniques associated with iconography. Indeed, iconography, with its very particular depiction of time and space, and its unique relationship to both the concrete and the abstract, provides an enlightening model for much of Klyuev's poetics. In this poem, as ever, not all references are equal: the allusions to the Old Belief and to places in the Onega region, for example, are reiterations of a rich, if contradictory, individual poetic mythology, while the more exotic allusions, although also part of a reiterated pattern, are, in themselves, far less rich in associations (they may freely be exchanged for other terms designating "Orient," "remote," "exotic," and so on). As in so many poems of this period, to the association of nature, culture, history, and Russia must be added the identity of the speaker-poet, solipsistically uniting the diverse referents of the poem in a very striking series of images:

Окунаюсь в стихи, чтобы стать топором,
Чтобы Разина кровь расплескать языком,
О ретивую печень точить лезвие —
Лебединую нежность и сердце мое.

I dive into poetry to become an axe,
To splash the blood of Razin with my tongue,
To sharpen a blade against a resistant liver—
Swan tenderness and my heart.

With the end of Klyuev's Vytegra period comes, as has been noted, a break in his composition of lyrics: he stopped before he left Vytegra in 1923, and only resumed in Leningrad in 1925. Klyuev's most productive and perhaps his greatest period as a lyric poet was over. By the end of 1922 he had also completed the first two works that can be unproblematically qualified as *poemy*—*Chetvertyi Rim* and *Mat'-Subbota.* They were to be followed by the third, *Zaozer'e* (*Beyond the Lake*) only in 1926. *Chetvertyi Rim* (*Fourth Rome*), while polemicizing with Esenin, also shares with much of Klyuev's lyric output of this period a syncretic universalism, a defense of a mythologized peasant Russia, and a certain preoccupation with the northern landscape, rendering the millenarian implications of its title in a manner characteristic of and peculiar to Klyuev. *Mat'-Subbota,* similarly, may be tied to some of the poetry of *L'vinyi khleb* in its movement between, on the one hand, the relative generalities of the peasant calendar, peasant *izba,* and peasant stove (all understood in terms of a merging of pagan and Christian) and, on the other, the specifics of the mythology of the birth of the poet and his poetry. Hence, time and place, as treated in these *poemy,* are much in accord with the lyrics contemporary to them.

Klyuev's journalistic prose, largely restricted to his Vytegra period, is perhaps less rich in echoes of time and place, although his employment of apocalyptic motifs will be remarked, and his defense of the artifacts of vernacular, rural culture in one piece might also be noted ("Slovo o tsennostyakh narodnogo iskusstva" ["Speech About the Values of Folk Art"], *Sd* 158).[58] This period also saw the beginning of the articulation of the elaborate autobiographical narratives, explored in chapters 1 and 4. Their generic fluidity and their relationship as complete texts to the time and place of their composition, and in some cases, to the time and place of their publication, are instrumental in shaping their meaning and reception. In particular, Klyuev's increasing elaboration of a northern, often White Sea, identity may be associated not only with the increasing geographical and historical remoteness of that identity in the Soviet period, but also with the Soviet state's increasing hostility to everything represented by that created identity.

The apparent break in Klyuev's composition of poetry in 1923 and 1924 is the only such example in his career (even in Siberian exile he wrote poetry), and it forms a clear divide between the early 1920s and the beginning of what may quite appropriately be called the "late" period, determined by different circumstances, and characterized by somewhat different themes and forms from the preceding years. It should be noted, however, that Klyuev did not cease to publish in those years. At least seven publications in periodicals and almanacs are recorded for the years 1923 and 1924, some of them in major metropolitan volumes.[59] By far the most important publication of these years was of the collection *Lenin,* in three editions published in 1923 and 1924. It consists of the cycle entitled "Lenin" from "Krasnyi ryk," which is here retitled "Bagryanyi lev" ("Scarlet Lion"), and several of Klyuev's most enthusiastic revolutionary pieces. Notwithstanding its title and Klyuev's dispatch of a copy to Lenin himself, the collection is, it should be remembered, far from standard-issue propaganda—many of the same features evident elsewhere in the period characterize the poetry here: an ambivalent universalism, with its core in the Russian north; an intermittent emphasis on the poet-speaker; and a radical transformation of the Bolshevik agenda to accommodate the rural utopianism of Klyuev's own aspirations.

When Klyuev resumed writing after the break of 1923–24, his professional circumstances were very different: he had little access to the printing press, and wrote in relative isolation from the newly established literary world. Consequently, the physical places of preservation (and destruction) of his later poetry, and the chronology of its publication and nonpublication, could not but have enormous impact on the very fragmentary and largely untimely reception of what he wrote in Leningrad, Moscow, and Siberia. As will be seen in chapter 5, it has been a particular irony that some of the poems articulating a view of the present and future which is "prophetic" in its discursive patterning were not published until long after their composition, by which time it was impossible not to read them, at least in part, as already fulfilled prophecy. Thus, a pattern of apparent concretization of the abstract even informs the after-the-fact reception of much of this later work.

In addition to the limited publications of new poetry in periodicals of the 1920s, Klyuev did publish one more collection, *Izba i pole* of 1928. It contains no previously unpublished works, and only two which had not appeared in earlier collections. As is evident from that fact alone, it is not a collection of recently composed poetry. Indeed, Klyuev provides a brief prefatory remark which draws attention to the fact that the contents are not new. The collection, dedicated to the memory of the poet's mother, is divided into three sections. The first, "Izba," consists of nineteen poems, ten of them from "Izbyanye pesni." As in the various versions of that cycle, most of the poems of "Izba" articulate an historically timeless calendar of peasant life and death, but the cycle ends with the markedly discordant "Vrazh'ya sila," describing the intrusion of industry into the countryside. The second section, "Pole," consists of twenty-five lyrics. It opens with the programmatic "Ryzhee zhniv'e — kak kniga," discussed in the preceding pages of this chapter, and concludes with the anti-industrial "Obozval tishinu glukhoman'yu," followed by the (seasonal?) death poem, "Smertnyi son" ("Mortal Dream," 267–68). In between, an approximate calendar of seasons is charted in a selection of Klyuev's landscape poetry, some of it describing only nature, some the place of the peasant in nature, and some the relationship of the poet to those themes. Overall, the tone is somewhat bleaker than in the first section. "Urozhai" ("Harvest"), the last section of *Izba i pole,* consists of seventeen poems, opening with "V zabornoi shcheli solnyshka kusok" and concluding with "Chto ty, nivushka, cherneshen'ka" ("In the crack in the fence, a piece of the sun," "What, dark meadow"; 447–48, 270–73). As these "bookends" suggest, this last section is more thematically and poetically varied than the first two, containing not only several works of poetic and other self-definition but also works where the predominant theme is, for example, rural utopianism, or anti-urbanism, or love. Also among the poems of this section are several of Klyuev's folklorized narratives, including "Povolzhskii skaz," the sinister "Obidin plach," and "Chto ty, nivushka, cherneshen'ka." The last-named poem was composed and first published in 1915, at which time it would have read unambiguously as a war poem: it consists of four dialogues between a human speaker and, respectively, a meadow, a peasant house, a road, and a fir tree. Each representative of the countryside explains its mournful situation by reference to the absence or loss of menfolk, by implication through warfare. That content remains unchanged in the 1928 publication, but the new context of the poem colors the lamentation quite differently. In the final lines of the poem (and of the collection) a fir tree, earlier praised for constantly weaving its lace foliage, explains its lamentation in a tone consistent with much of the collection:

Я считаю ку-ку покаянные
И в коклюшках, как в Требнике, путаюсь.

I count repentant cuckoos
And get lost in bobbins, as in the breviary.

In other words, the 1915 poem is here deployed to quite different effect, reiterating grief not for the losses of the time of its composition, but for the onset of the destruction of "peasant house and field" of the time of the publication of the collection (not to mention the destruction of the denizens of those places, and of their culture).

Izba i pole has received relatively little attention from scholarly readers, and for understandable reasons: it contains no new materials; where there are revisions, they may be regarded as "enforced" (for example, the reduction of the homoerotic elements in "Puteshestvie" ["Journey"], 338–39, 889). Klyuev himself lamented that the collection had been held up by the publisher for two years prior to publication, and that some ninety pages had been cut from it (*Sd* 262).[60] However, like so much of Klyuev's work in the Soviet period, the collection represents a very interesting engagement with time and place, from its initial, perhaps provocative, defense of the republication of older poems in the preface to the final lines of the last poem. The very fact that a poem of somewhat homoerotic content is included, albeit emasculated, suggests a polemical stance, while the predominance of poems keyed to rural idylls, and of a general tone of regret or lament, is equally significant, given—again—the time and place of the collection's publication. The almost total silence with which the collection was received and the hostility with which it was treated in later commentaries provide ample confirmation of its status as an "untimely" publication. The publication of a reprint of the collection in 2003, accompanied by a learned afterword by Sergei Subbotin, is most welcome.[61]

Like *Izba i pole,* the poetry which Klyuev composed after his departure from Vytegra is equally characterized by an evident "untimeliness." Although he gave public readings of some of the later works, most remained unpublished until the late 1960s. Then the British Slavist Gordon McVay was able to copy a significant number of drafts from Klyuev's notebooks in a Moscow state archive. These drafts appeared in the two-volume *Sochineniya,* published in West Germany in 1969. From there they gradually made their way back to a limited number of readers in Russia. With the political transformations of the Soviet Union in the 1980s came a wave of domestic publications, which led eventually to the publication of the "finished" versions of what McVay had found in draft, and to the discovery and publication of a significant number of new works, including such major poems as the "Razrukha" cycle and *Pesn' o Velikoi materi,* and finally *Kreml'.* This process, like the conditions in which these poems were composed (but often left unfinished, or in multiple versions, or extant only in draft), generated its own dynamics of reception—Klyuev *read* in his homeland long before he was *published* (abroad), and read in variant forms; Klyuev's works published in a chronological sequence that had its own logic, determined by circumstances and by chance and long after the poet's own death. Once more, time and place are significant constructive elements in the images of the poet created over these years.

Many features of the poetry written after Klyuev's departure from Vytegra are shared with the verse of the late 1910s and early 1920s. For example, toponymic catalogues and the vertiginous movement from specific, concrete, and often rich geographic or historical references to broad, universalist, or timeless allusions are as common in the later poetry as before. Also typical of that poetry is the association of the personal identity of the speaker with very broad historical themes, sometimes mediated through the theme of age, variously presented. Hence, the love motifs, which are predominant in the lyrics of the late 1920s and early 1930s, are accompanied by elements drawn from public discourse, often producing a paradoxical statement of "age" (of an individual, as an historical period, and so on).

Many of these features are amply evident in the lyrics examined in chapter 5—for example, the late "Razrukha" abounds in toponymic and historical catalogues, while "Povest' skorbi" ("Tale of Woe") very explicitly links personal and national fate, in a context established by broad historical and geographic references. "Nasha russkaya pravda zagibla" is also typical in its insistent reiteration of diverse markers of disaster, followed by a rather provisional, but emphatically rural, salvation:

Наша русская правда загибла,
Как Аленушка в чарой сказке . . .
Забодало железное быдло
Коляду, душегрейку, салазки.

Уж не выйдет на перены крыльца
В куньей шубоньке Мелентьевна Василиса,
Утопил лиходей-убийца
Сердце князево в чаре кумыса.

Заливай ордынским напитком,
Тверь-вдовица, кос пепелище,
Твой Михайло в шуйце со свитком
Стал вороньей гнусавой пищей.

И боярыни Морозовой терем
В тощей пазухе греет вьюгу,
На иконе в борьбе со зверем
Стратилат оборвал подпругу.

Так загибла русская доля —
Над речкою белые вербы,
Вновь меж трупов на Косовом поле
Узнают царя Лазаря сербы. . . . (543–44)

Our Russian truth has perished,
Like Alenushka in the enchanted tale . . .
Iron cattle have butted
Christmas carols, peasant jackets, hand sleds.

Vasilisa Melent'evna will not come again
To the feathered porches in a marten fur coat,
An evil murderer has drowned
The prince's heart in a goblet of mare's milk.

Drown your sorrows in the drink of the Horde,
Widow-Tver', tresses in ashes,
Your Mikhailo with a scroll in his left hand
Has become the crows' foul food.

And the palace of Boyarynya Morozova
Warms in its emaciated breast a blizzard,

On the icon, in his battle with the beast,
Theodore Stratelates has torn his saddle-girth.

This is how Russia's fate ended—
White willows over the river—
Again among the corpses of Kosovo
The Serbs see King Lazarus. . . .

The range of referents in these opening lines is typical of much of the later poetry: folklore (Alenushka); modern industry (iron); the fourth-century warrior- and martyr-saint Theodore Stratelates; the times of Ivan the Terrible (Vasilisa, his sixth wife and widow, also the heroine of a play by Ostrovsky); twelfth-century conflicts with the Tatar horde (Prince Michael of Tver' and, apparently, Daniil of Galicia—the two seem to be confused here, 946); the famous Old Believer martyr Morozova (well known through Surikov's nineteenth-century painting); and the Battle of Kosovo. Equally intriguing is the apparent confusion: in the folk tale Alenushka is eventually rescued from drowning (water, other liquids, and drowning motifs abound in the poem); Vasilisa is more properly Vasilisa *Melent'eva* (surname, not patronymic); St. George, not St. Theodore, is renowned for combat on horseback, and is usually depicted riding to battle with the dragon (while St. Theodore is usually depicted standing, holding a weapon); two medieval princes seem to have been run together. Only the Battle of Kosovo is presented according to history. Following these multiple and largely apocryphal references to the past, denoting the disasters of the present, a central stanza announces that Swan Russia has flown away, to be followed, however, by three-and-a-half stanzas in which a natural and timeless redemption is presented:

На костях горит мусикия,
Вместо сердца кротовы ходы . . .
Отлетела лебедь-Россия
В безбольные тихие воды.

Но сквозь слезы, звериные муки
Прозревают родину очи:
Забрели по колено буки
В синезер, до питья охочи.

Ловит солнце лещом матерым
Стрекозиных телег вереницы,
По-ребячьи лохматят горы
С голубых просонок косицы.

Исцеленный мир смугло-розов,
На кувшинках гнезда гагар,
И от вьюг, косматых морозов
Только сосен смолистый жар.

Далеко по синим поречьям
Благодатный печерский звон . . .
. . . .
. . . .

Music burns on bones,
Mole tunnels replace the heart . . .
Swan Russia has flown away
To painless, quiet waters.

But through tears and bestial torment
My eyes detect the homeland:
Ash trees have wandered into lake blue
Up to their knees, desirous of drinking.

The sun, like a great bream,
Catches rows of dragonfly carts,
Childlike, the mountains rumple
Tresses from bright blue sleep.

The world, cured, is dark pink,
Loons nest on the lily pads,
And from blizzards and hairy frosts
All that comes is the pines' rich heat.

Far away over blue river stretches
Is the beneficent catacomb chime . . .
. . . .
. . . .

Like so much of Klyuev's mature poetry, in particular that written in and after the early 1920s, the almost hallucinatory quality of this lyric is produced not only by the series of allusions to the past, validating the implied view of the present, and by the apparent vision of the concluding stanzas, but also by the extreme discontinuity between its parts, highly characteristic of much popular prophetic discourse. Yet the discontinuity (the second part has no historical or literary referents, for example, and is not tied by any clear logic of argument or narrative to the first) is itself undercut by the reiteration and modification of motifs from the first part: most obviously, water, drinking, damaged heart, trees, tresses. The poem was not published until 1991, when it came out in the last selected works to be published in the Soviet Union—yet again, a highly suggestive conjunction of time and place. Moreover, the final two lines of the manuscript text have been erased, so that the conclusion of the poem, as it stands, is a literal elision, adding to its provisional, timeless, yet highly time-bound status (947).

Another conjunction of time and place is of particular importance in Klyuev's later work. The places where he spent his summers at the end of the 1920s and the beginning of the 1930s played a special role in his career. Those summers, to judge from his own dating of his texts, seem to have been especially productive, and his correspondence supports the impression that they were times both of creativity and of greater relaxation, away from the ample pressures of metropolitan life and attention. Moreover, they provided the poet with his only significant contact with the countryside after his removal to Leningrad in 1923.[62]

Of these places, the Vyatka area, which he first visited in 1929, is by far the most significant. "Ya leto zoril na Vyatke" ("I waited out summer on the Vyatka," 593–94) evokes the area's characteristics at some length and contrasts the Vyatka area with the Moscow to which the speaker returns. Other works also refer to Vyatka: in all, there are at least seventeen occurrences of the word "Vyatka" and its derivatives *Vyatich* (a resident of the area) and *vyatskii* (of Vyatka) in Klyuev's poetry.[63] The author Vladimir Semibratov, among others, has dealt at length and on several occasions with Klyuev's treatment of the Vyatka theme, and correctly points to the poet's elaboration of a number of characteristics of the region: its "provincial," quintessentially Russian nature; its long rivers (several of which are also encountered in his verse—the Kama seventeen times) and extensive forests; its local crafts; and its non-Russian population (Klyuev refers frequently to the Mari people, sometimes explicitly in the context of the Vyatka region).[64] As Semibratov notes, elements of Vyatka (the river or the region, but not the city [present-day Kirov]) feature prominently in the poetry associated with Yar-Kravchenko, some of which was composed in the village of Potrepukhino near Sovetsk (formerly Kukarka), in the south of the Vyatka region. In "Pis'mo khudozhniku Anatoliyu Yaru" (579–83), the speaker inquires:

Ты помнишь ли на Вятке ели,
Избу над пихтовым обрывом?
Тебе под двадцать, я же сивым
Был поцелован голубком,
Слегка запорошен снежком,

Как первопуток на . . . погост . . .
В закатном лаке Алконост
Нам вести приносил из рая,
В уху ершовую ныряя,
В палитру, кипяток, лазори,
Чтоб молодость на косогоре
Не повстречала сорок пугал —
Мои года, что гонит вьюга
На полюс ледяным кнутом . . . (580–81)

Do you remember the firs on the Vyatka,
The house above the silver-fir ravine?
You were near twenty, but I'd been
Kissed by a gray-blue dove,
And had a covering of snow,
Like the first track . . . to the cemetery . . .
Alkonost in sunset varnish
Brought us news from paradise,
Diving into fish soup made from ruff,
Into palette, boiled water, blues,
So that youth on the hillside
Should not meet forty scarecrows—
My age, driven by the blizzard
To the pole with an icy whip . . .

Here and elsewhere in the poem, geographically and autobiographically specific references blend (and contrast) with more abstract and mythological elements—for example, the allusion to painting mythologizes and renders abstract what Yar-Kravchenko actually did during the Vyatka summers. Yet, as has also been suggested by Semibratov and others, Vyatka is more than an autobiographical reference—its characteristics are especially appropriate for Klyuev. Indeed, it might be added that the region—remote, extensive, "backward" (as the poet observes, "Vyatichi ne lyubyat sapog,/Podavai im batyushku-lapot'" ["Vyatka people don't like boots,/Give them old-man bast shoe"], 537), dominated by rivers and forests, and perhaps crucially, both a border area and a region of considerable, if by Klyuev's time somewhat elided, ethnic complexity—provides a very appropriate analogue to the poet's own native region. One scholar even includes it in her map of Klyuev's "Russian north."[65] The poet's employment of "Vyatka" is revealing in yet other ways. First, the combination of the autobiographically specific, the mythological, and the ethnographic is very typical of the poet's realization of native geography. Second, it is again worth noting that "Vyatka" is much more prominent in his poetry by name than his own Vytegra, not to mention his home villages. And third, it is especially important to note that Klyuev's elaboration of the Vyatka theme begins *long before he visited the area.*[66] Of the seventeen occurrences of the word "Vyatka" and its derivatives, seven are in works written before his first Vyatka summer. They are as follows: the *vyatich v tyurbane* (Vyatka man in a turban) of "Pridet karavan s shafranom" ("A caravan bearing saffron shall arrive"; 505–6); the preference of *vyatichi* for traditional bast shoes, cited above from "Druzhba" ("Friendship"); the beauty of girls, "like birches," along the Vyatka in "Kto za chto, a ya za dvoperst'e" ("Men may support what they wish, but I am for making the sign of the cross with two fingers," 541); two relatively detailed allusions to the crafts of the region in *Pogorel'shchina* (672–73); the wonder of *vyatskii stikh* in "Ya znayu, rodyatsya pesni" ("I know songs will be born," 468), suggested by Semibratov to be associated with Esenin; and the image of wigwams on Vyatka meadows ("Na zavodskikh zadvorkakh, gde ugol'nyi ad," 486).[67] The deployment of Vyatka in these lines is very typical of Klyuev's addresses to Russian cultural geography: universalism through national specifics, expressed locally (the turban-wearing, wigwam-dwelling *vyatichi*); nature and beauty (birches and Vyatka girls); ethnographic cataloguing (crafts of the region); the Vyatka region as a cradle of authentic Russianness (all these examples, and the preference for bast shoes); and, as ever, the programmatic association with the poet himself, implicit in several of these allusions, and explicit, it would seem, in the phrase *vyatskii stikh,* which appears to refer, among other things, to the highly decorative popular arts of the region. In other words, in these examples Vyatka serves as Kargopol' has been seen to have done—on the one hand, as an easily replaceable cipher for "provincial, ancient Russianness," and, on the other, as a place-specific articulation of those values (the particularities of the region have already been discussed, are visibly demonstrated in several of the examples above, and are implicit in others). The relationship of this "Vyatka mythology" to the poet's biography is also instructive: existing before he visited the place, and elaborated in part in the terms discussed above, it is enriched by his own experiences there, and forms a significant element in his treatment of geography, among other themes, in the early 1930s. Once again, this complex of motifs illustrates the poet's synthetic, diverse realization of leitmotifs, and seems to warn strongly against a reading based upon the binary opposition of "authentic/inauthentic" which continues to haunt attacks upon and defenses of the poet and his work.

The *poemy* written after the Vytegra period have much in common with the lyrics, as does the story of their reception. They are discussed at greater length in chapter 6. The "peasant's calendar" of *Zaozer'e* (1926) presents an idyllic and timeless portrait of northern village life, blending pagan and Christian practice—but at precisely the historical moment when forces were gathering to destroy the cultural elements upon which the poem draws. In *Plach o Sergee Esenine,* the identification of the poet-speaker with the *far* North is once again made ("Moi krai, moe Pomor'e," 660). In *Derevnya* (written in 1926, published and savagely attacked in 1927) one of the major tropes of Klyuev's later work is encountered—the association of what would now be called ecological disaster with its politico-cultural equivalent:

> Мы расстались с саровским звоном —
> Утолением плача и ран.
> Мы новгородскому Никите
> Оголили трухлявый срам, —
> Отчего же на белой раките
> Не поют щеглы по утрам? (664–65)
>
> We parted with the Sarov peal—
> The soothing of lamentation and wounds.
> We exposed the crumbling shame
> Of St. Nikita of Novgorod—
> So why do no goldfinches sing
> On the white willows in the morning?

In other words, the loss of the church bells of Sarov, the desecration of relics (a frequent motif in Klyuev's work), and the ominous silence of the birds are all part of a single complex of signs indicating the coming apocalypse, and marked, of course, by the destruction of the title village. The fragmentary *Solovki* (1926–28) catalogues the charms of the islands, associating them both with nature and with culture, then laments their abandonment by Christianity (another common motif in the later verse), thus combining historical celebration with current despair. Of course, as has been noted in chapter 1, the Solovetsky Islands had become by this time a Soviet prison camp, so that the poet's articulation of time and place is once again highly significant, that significance partly indicated by what is *not said* in the poem itself. *Solovki* also stands out as a *poema* about a real, not a fictional place—the major sites in almost all the other *poemy* are not only mythologized, but also invented. *Pogorel'shchina* reiterates at much greater length and in much greater complexity the allegory of destruction seen in *Derevnya,* and once again describes the present as catastrophically breaking the nature-culture unity which characterized the rural idyll of the past in the imaginary village Sigovoi Lob. *Kain* (1929), extant only in fragments, contains several catalogues of fallen sites of Russian spirituality and identity, while also deploying contradictory images of the poet-speaker's own identity (and complicity in the fall). In *Pesn' o Velikoi Materi,* as will be seen in chapter 6, the movement between timeless idyll and apocalyptic present, northern pastoral and urban destruction, unity of nature with culture and destruction of both, mythologized autobiography (semi-Lomonosovian childhood on the White Sea coast) and commentary on the speaker's current situation, provides a culminating point for many of the thematic strands which may be identified in the earlier *poemy.* Meanwhile, the story of the work's partial preservation (as an appendix to a KGB file), and its publication at the end of the Soviet era, is equally emblematic of the problems of physical place and concrete chronology which have shaped and reshaped the reception of Klyuev's work. His last *poema, Kreml',* gives perhaps the most striking, although exceptional, statement of time and place: written in the first months of his exile in distant Kolpashevo, it celebrates the Moscow Kremlin as the center of contemporary Soviet power, rejects the poet's own previously treasured ideal places, and appeals for mercy from those whom the poet had earlier labeled in "Nerushimaya stena" *rogatye khozyaeva zhizni* ("Indestructible Wall"; horned masters of life, 542). And the publication of *Kreml'* in 2006, long after the era of glasnost-inspired "returns" and clarifications, must itself be numbered among the most untimely of Klyuev's reappearances.

Time and space in Klyuev's poetry, and the times and spaces within which that poetry was created, published, and read, form a complex matrix, offering simultaneously a number of different locations for the poet. The association of Klyuev with the north of Russia, clearly important for his first serious readers and amplified (and complicated) by the poet himself throughout his career in biographical statements of various kinds, remains one of the principal vectors of interpretation and dispute. Indeed, in the rapidly expanding scholarly literature on the poet, studies of place occupy a prominent place. Perhaps the most active center for the study of Klyuev in recent years has been the city of Vologda, capital of the oblast in which the poet's home region now finds itself. There, at the Department of Russian of the Vologda State Pedagogical University, Professor Lyudmila Yatskevich heads a group of scholars working on a *Poetic Dictionary of N. A. Klyuev.* That group of scholars (above all Yatskevich herself) has published very extensively since the mid-1990s.[68] One of the most frequent objects of their attention has been Klyuev's terminology for space and place. The works of the group address, among other things, Klyuev's "cultural geography" in general; his use of hydronyms; his designation of *svoe prostranstvo* (person-specific space); the mythical city of Kitezh; and the "thematic paradigms" of space, and of the *izba.* The foundations for this scholarship are provided by the group's work on a frequency dictionary of Klyuev's poetry, and by the general principles of Russian linguistic studies, deriving, crudely speaking, from structuralist concepts of language. Even the most basic of frequency data are very revealing: by far the most widely used pronoun in Klyuev's poetry is the first-person singular, while the four most frequent nouns are *dusha* (soul, 203 occurrences), *serdtse* (heart, 178), *pesnya* (song, 145), and *izba* (peasant house, 130).[69] Among the most significant conclusions reached by these scholars are observations on the centrality of the Russian north, especially when conceived as a sacred space, and associated with the broader concept of *svyataya Rus'* (holy Russia), in Klyuev's poetic geography. Among many other significant observations, they also note the poet's tendency to use expressions of extent ("from . . . to . . ."), to create "verbal maps," and to combine the real with the mythological in the creation of a concept of "sacred space." A series of oppositions (heaven/hell; East/West; Slavdom/the rest of the world; holy Russia/the non-Christian world; the Old Believer north/the rest of Russia; provincial Russia/the capitals) informs Klyuev's cultural geography, they argue, which may also be presented as a set of "historico-cultural zones," created by the poet's employment of toponyms and "ethnonyms" (the White Sea Coast, Olonia, the Russian north; medieval Russia; the Old Believer zone; the all-Russian-Orthodox zone; the Slavic zone; the Slavic and Finno-Ugric zone; the Great Steppe and Tatar-Mongol zone; the Caucasus; the Byzantine and early Christian zone; the biblical zone; ancient Greece and Rome; ancient Egypt; the Indo-Iranian zone; the Muslim East; Indochina; Africa; western Europe; the Americas; and finally Australia [a zone comprising but one allusion in the entire corpus of Klyuev's poetry]).[70] These distinctions effectively chart the extent and distribution of Klyuev's geographical references, in their appropriate historico-cultural context, although naturally some are open to interrogation (for example, does Klyuev's Umbria really belong with *ancient* Greece and Rome; should Kargopol' be counted as a "holy place," but not a "town"; is it correct to add Vyatka and Perm' to Klyuev's "Russian north"?). Without a doubt, the careful scholarship of Yatskevich and her pupils not only illuminates much in Klyuev's poetry, but also provides vital material for future scholars. However, like all such projects, it also has certain limitations: first of all, it is synchronic, treating all of Klyuev's poetry as a single, unitary text. Second, it reduces the dynamic relations between clashing elements to binary oppositions, or else ignores them altogether (citing fragments of texts to illustrate points can be very misleading when the overall contexts are, first of all, that of the entire poem, then, possibly, the cycle, and then usually the collection—in these contexts, the interplay of referents will seem quite different). Third, it tends to give equal weight to every allusion (while it has been argued here that, for example, Kargopol' and Nice are not equally rich in symbolic potential). Fourth, it cannot take account of allusions which are implied without being expressly named (such as the oaks of Mamre in "El' mne podala lapu," discussed above). For Yatskevich, as for a significant number of other scholarly readers of Klyuev, the poet's mytho-geographical realization of Russia is, first and foremost, an anachronistic but very powerful re-sacralization. It is, for example, in this light that she and other similarly inclined readers see the poet's lines from *Pogorel'shchina,* discussed in chapter 6:

> Нерукотворную Россию
> Я, песнопевец Николай,
> Свидетельствую, братья, вам! (684)
>
> To a Russia not-made-by-human-hands,
> I, Nikolai the singer of songs,
> Testify before you, brothers!

However, while such a reading is clearly legitimate, it may seem inadequate if it neglects the self-conscious, modernist elements which might be argued to inform it *simultaneously.* If such plurality is accepted, then the multiple planes of time and place encountered within Klyuev's works no longer require a reductive, unitary reading. Moreover, the playful elements in the later work, and the marked preoccupation with stylization are then more easily incorporated into an overall account of the poet's work (it should be borne in mind that, in *Pesn' o Velikoi Materi,* Feodorovsky Gorodok in Tsarskoe Selo shares with the wooden church of the opening lines equal status as an artistic model, as will be demonstrated in chapter 6).

What is perhaps most telling of all in the project to describe Klyuev's cultural geography, however, is the simple fact that it begins with onomastics—Klyuev's toponyms, of which there are such extensive catalogues, are the most striking signs of his "historico-cultural zones."[71]

One other elaborate and very scholarly attempt to read Klyuev's "cultural geography" should be mentioned here, rather different in character from that of his Vologda readers, and less predicated upon geography per se: the Petrozavodsk scholar Elena Markova's work on Klyuev, drawing primarily on the concept of the poet's work as a sophisticated elaboration of the cultural encounter between Russian and Finno-Ugric elements. In a series of articles and then in a book, Markova examines and elucidates many features of this encounter, again providing a sophisticated and largely unitary account of Klyuev's mythopoetics. She describes the "concentration" of Klyuev's north, the notion of nature as a temple, the poet's concept of the "trans-Onega" region, and many other features examined here, and joins a number of other scholars in remarking that "universality, eternity is Klyuev's time."[72] She and Lyudmila Kiseleva, who leads a group of scholars and students working on Klyuev at Kiev University, have in general provided the most sophisticated readings of Klyuev's mythopoetic system in terms of its popular and Orthodox referents (both have, for example, written very informatively on Klyuev's employment of the language, thematics, and onomastics of iconography).[73]

It is worth noting that of the three bodies of scholarship briefly described above, one has been produced in a major and traditional cultural centre of the Russian north, and another has been produced in the capital of Karelia. Only Kiseleva, working in Kiev, is outside of the (expansive and regularly reimagined) core region of Klyuev's own poetic mythology.

Place thus continues to play a significant role in the reading of Klyuev, as may also be seen in the active memorialization of the poet in his native region. There, in Vytegra, a museum devoted to the poet has been established as an affiliate of the local *kraevedcheskii muzei* ("museum of local studies," incorporating local history, art, natural history, and contemporary culture). The director and curators of this museum have been extremely active, not only in the memorialization of Klyuev—beginning when the poet was of dubious status in the eyes of Soviet power, national and local—but also in the promotion of scholarship and study of him: annual symposia take place in Vytegra, and a series of almanacs, partly or wholly devoted to the poet, have emerged from there in recent years; even schools now pay particular attention to the relationship between Klyuev and his local region, and mark that association in the display cases of their museums. There is nothing at all remarkable (although much that is truly admirable) in the emergence of such readings and even appropriations of the poet, but there is a certain irony in their concreteness, which may be contrasted with the abstract and frequently mythologized cultural geography and history within the poet's work. As has already been noted, Vytegra barely occurs by name in his work, his home villages are never mentioned, and his autobiographical texts frequently move his birth and upbringing hundreds of kilometers away from them.

Klyuev is expressly not a poet of his own native region, at least as that might be understood within the Anglophone tradition—as a very clearly defined, geographically very specific region. The briefest of comparisons with such authors as John Clare and Thomas Hardy should suffice to reinforce that point. The works of both authors are imbued with a sense of dramatic and potentially catastrophic transformation of landscape and culture, analogous to the mature Klyuev, but they are also very tied to a specific and clearly defined (albeit, in Hardy, renamed) region. Clare, in particular, provides a useful parallel to Klyuev—for example, his treatment of the fauna of his native area is in marked contrast to Klyuev's—while Hardy's historical proximity to Klyuev makes the comparison of Russian poet and British author, especially in the overall context of European modernism, potentially useful. Such comparisons may also help to illuminate, at least speculatively, differences in national cultural context—it could be argued that the cult of specific and concrete provincial places, closely observed, is not only more characteristic of the Anglophone tradition than the Russian, but also more (and differently) elaborated in the modern period by the very different socioeconomic circumstances of the English-speaking world and Russia. This distinction, furthermore, serves as a reminder that the Russian readers of Klyuev today approach his poetry, produced less than a hundred years ago, with a very clear sense of great cultural distance between it and them, predicated not so much upon the immanent qualities of the texts as upon the historical processes which have transformed Russia, and especially rural Russia—many would argue to the great detriment of the latter. Of course, those processes, in turn, effect particular readings of the texts (and produce particular kinds of readers).

On the other hand, Klyuev *is* very much a poet of his home region as he renders and mythologizes it—as will be seen, in his final poem he designates himself "singer of the Olonian peasant house"; and the Russian north as described and populated by him, from the peasant house itself to the toponymic catalogues so frequently encountered in his verse, has a clear, although abstract, identity, while many aspects of his poetic practice can in fact be associated with features local to the Vytegra region.

Partly because of these paradoxes, the contemporary location of Klyuev is an especially contested issue, with many of his students insisting on the distinctive qualities of the poet not only as author but also as prophet and seer. Their insistence is partly in response to those who challenge Klyuev's authority and, especially, authenticity, and partly in response to those who simply ignore him. For all the expansion of scholarship in recent years, Klyuev remains, as has been remarked, a relatively unread poet. This fact illuminates yet another problem of time and place: Klyuev is frequently identified as one of the "new-peasant poets," and he certainly expressed considerable affinity for several of the other authors usually united under that label. Yet Klyuev's poetics and autobiography distinguish him very markedly from Esenin, Klychkov, and the others, while it is from them, not him, that a line of descent for modern Russian ruralism might be charted. In other words, having no successors, Klyuev becomes much more difficult not only to place but also to read. However, it is not this isolation, nor the fate of the Russian countryside, which most potential readers would cite as the principal obstruction between themselves and the poet, but his language. Here, too, a popular conception is that Klyuev's language draws very strongly upon the dialectal specifics of the Russian north, with the supposedly anachronistic remnants of older forms and so on.[74] It is certainly true that local and regional forms are encountered in Klyuev's work, but it is also surely true that they are not the only, nor even perhaps the principal causes of difficulty in the comprehension of the poet's language (still less, it might be added, of his poetics in general). The relationship of his poetic language to the dialects of his home region has yet to be explored in full.[75] However, a cursory examination of the glossaries provided in academic editions of Klyuev's poetry will indicate that his poetry draws on an extremely wide range of linguistic sources (for example, the specific and arcane terminology of particular arts and crafts is frequently encountered—as his treatments of iconography illustrate well). It is hoped that the work of the Vologda group will provide further enlightenment in this area, but it seems likely that general conclusions on language would be similar to those attempted here on time and space, which emphasize both the integrity of certain reiterated patterns and the syncretic, often unstable nature of larger units.

Another significant analogue to the issues examined in these pages is provided by the actual physical spaces inhabited by the poet: it seems that not only (although most famously) in Leningrad but also in Vytegra before that and even Siberia afterward, the poet surrounded himself with artifacts expressive of an archaic, rural, vernacular culture, and of an ancient ecclesiastical tradition. The accounts of his Leningrad room are particularly familiar, and are supported by photographs. This re-creation of a specific but syncretic space—which may be seen as a product of the encounter of artist, collector, student, cultural provocateur, modernist, and northerner of peasant origins—is a very concrete demonstration of the multiple sources and plural values of Klyuev's activities as a mature cultural figure. It is also telling that, notwithstanding the high regard in which his judgment was held, he seems to have made a number of egregious errors in the identification of artifacts within his collection, as his correspondence from Siberia was to reveal (*Sd* 344, 374, 613, 625).

Other elaborations of time and space in Klyuev's life and work are equally telling. His own progress from village to provincial town, and on to capital cities articulates the cultural demography of modern Russia, while his dismissal of the middle, small-town stage from much of his poetry anticipates the ideological and mythologizing concentration on the opposites of rural Russia and "center" in the later twentieth century. His collecting of artifacts associated with old and rural Russia, in order to create mythological spaces within a modern urban environment, anticipates some of the elements of apartment-centered life for the postwar Russian intelligentsia, while also making a particular cultural statement which has analogues and opposites in the behavior of other modernists.

Similar conclusions may be reached if these issues are addressed in terms of sources: Klyuev's time and place, and Klyuev's re-creation of time and place cannot be imagined without the documented history of the poet himself, or without the documented, and tragic, history of his native land

and native region, nor yet can they be imagined without the many intermediate elements which render them possible—from the polemics of the Denisovs and Avvakum to the travelogues of Sluchevsky and Prishvin, the works of Mel'nikov-Pechersky (a not infrequent referent for the poet), and the anthropological studies of Sergei Maksimov, who wrote extensively on two of Klyuev's favorite topics: the Russian north and Russian bread.[76] All of these authors and books, along with many other cultural actors and objects, not only facilitate but also constitute essential features of Klyuev's own complex textual universe.

No examination of time and place would be complete without some concluding remarks on the future location of the poet. It has been a supposition throughout the preceding pages that Klyuev is both an interesting and a worthwhile poet, but it has also been frequently suggested that he is relatively little read, and all too often misread. In fact, Klyuev might have much to offer the reader of the future, with his local but universalist thematic, his alternative visions of human love, his frequent defense of the cultural remnants of the past and the current vestiges of the natural world. The story of the poet and his texts most certainly articulates key elements in the history of his own country, while those texts themselves may yet appeal, as the poet himself predicted, to the reader of the twenty-first century. The following chapters examine in detail exemplary tests representing the major genres in which Klyuev worked, in order to explicate further the specifics of Klyuev's practice in different literary contexts, while also hoping to suggest ways in which the poet and his work can be reintegrated into the history of Russian letters and, at the same time, made accessible to the reader of today.

Chapter Three

Texts of Fraternity: Klyuev's Early Collection *Bratskie pesni,* Transformation of the Lyric, Popular-Religious Motifs

ALTHOUGH PRE-SOVIET and thereby exempt from the more acute ideological problems which beset the composition, recording, preservation, and distribution of Klyuev's later works, the collection *Bratskie pesni* (*Fraternal Songs*) provides ample illustrations of textual instabilities—aesthetic, material, ideological, and editorial. Moreover, *Bratskie pesni,* as a work centered on the notion and claimed form of songs of popular, collective, and alternative religious spirituality, marks a very important stage in Klyuev's early maturity: it is a product both of his engagement with a very specific politico-cultural program and of the fascination with popular religious movements which marked Russian culture in the age of symbolism; it is marked both by an orientation toward collective folk culture and by a highly self-conscious "literariness"; it is also the first address to and exploration of homosexuality in the poet's oeuvre. Although a single episode in his career, it shares many themes with important later works, and it provides abundant illustrations of the ways in which Klyuev's work positioned him as uniquely qualified to express the "people's" point of view, but as that "people" and viewpoint were imagined and even constructed by the educated classes.

Bratskie pesni is also the effective starting point in Klyuev's work for the construction of a large, complex, and predictably unstable exploration of popular religion, including not only Russian sectarianism but also the Old Belief. This matrix is one of the key features of Klyuev's aesthetic and social program, and it also provides some of the principal statements of homoeroticism in his poetry. Exploring both *Bratskie pesni* and its successor works therefore permits not only an examination of exemplary features of the poet's lyric works of the 1910s but also an exploration of one of the most significant (and disputed) aspects of his cultural identity.

The collection well illustrates the material instabilities that are characteristic of Klyuev's books of poetry. The title "Bratskie pesni" is borne by no less than four quite different, although interrelated, publications in the year 1912. First and foremost, it is the title of Klyuev's collection *Bratskie pesni: Kniga 2,* which, as the appended numeral suggests, was his second published collection, following *Sosen perezvon.* The numeral also suggests that the reader should bear in mind the importance of sequence—this is the poet's second book of poems, and should be read as such. Indeed, for the poetry of the opening decades of the twentieth century, collections may often be seen as key markers of stages in the organic (and/or thematic) development of a poet, while within collections cycles of poems often make an even more forceful statement of literary-autobiographical or thematic organization.[1] However, the suggestion of chronological sequence made in this case by the subtitle of *Bratskie pesni* is belied (in characteristic fashion) by Klyuev's own prefatory remarks, which indicate, among other things, that most of the poems published here in fact *predate* those published in his first collection. They appear here rather than there, it is claimed, for formal (and implicitly thematic) reasons, since earlier "they were not recorded by me, but were transmitted orally or in written form without my intervention," and only now have they been "restored from the words or notes of others" (*Sd* 419). This evident, albeit implicit, contradiction between sequence and theme is rendered yet more paradoxical by evidence which suggests that, on the whole, Klyuev's claims are not in fact true. Of the thirty-two poems in the collection, fifteen appear to have been composed in 1912, three in 1911, and eight in 1910—in other words, about half the poems date from *after* the composition of *Sosen perezvon,* and most of the rest are contemporaneous with the latest poems in that first collection.[2] Meanwhile, the explicit contradiction between, on the one hand, the literary claim to authorship and, on the other, the association with folkoric transmission and supposedly semi-folkloric composition is one of the core problems for any reading of the collection, and of Klyuev's life and works in general.

Moreover, the book title *Bratskie pesni* designates not only this quite substantial collection but also another collection of brochure dimensions, published in the very same year and containing only nine lyrics, all but one of which are also to be found in the larger version. This second publication, *Bratskie pesni: Pesni golgofskikh khristian* (*Fraternal Songs: Songs of the Golgotha Christians*) appeared as a supplement to *Novaya zemlya* (*New Land*), the journal with which Klyuev was most intimately associated at the time, and which had also published the larger *Bratskie pesni* in the very same year. The ideological program of *Novaya zemlya* contributed much to the very notion of the "fraternal song."

Also in 1912 a cycle, consisting of three poems which appear in both the large and small editions of *Bratskie pesni,* was published in *Novaya zemlya* under the title "Bratskie pesni." And in addition to the two collections and the three-poem cycle, a single poem under the title "Bratskaya pesnya" ("Fraternal Song") was published in *Novaya zemlya* during the same year. That poem, which begins "Poruchil klyuchi ot ada" ("The keys of hell were handed," 152–53), appears in the large *Bratskie pesni* with the same title, but in the small edition without a title. In 1913 Klyuev published in *Narodnyi zhurnal* (*Popular Journal*) a poem beginning "Pravda li drugi, chto na svete" ("Is it true friends, that on the earth"), under the title "Bratskaya pesnya: (Iz pesen 'Brat'ev-pakharei')" ("Fraternal Song: [From the Songs of the 'Plowmen Brethren']"). This poem does not appear in either of the *Bratskie pesni* collections, nor, indeed, in any of Klyuev's subsequent collections, although it was republished a year later, without that title.[3]

Klyuev's final contribution to this destabilization of denomination comes in the two-volume *Pesnoslov* (1919), which is divided into eight separately titled sections. Of these the first four, it will be recalled, reproduce the titles of his first four collections—"Sosen perezvon," "Bratskie pesni," "Lesnye byli," and "Mirskie dumy"—although the *contents* of these four sections correspond only partially to the contents of the first four separately published collections themselves. "Bratskie pesni" in *Pesnoslov* contains twenty-nine poems, of which eleven do not appear in either version of the collection *Bratskie pesni.* In the *Pesnoslov* "Bratskie pesni" there are also modifications to the titles and contents of some of the poems which had appeared earlier in the two books entitled *Bratskie pesni.* And while only eighteen of the poems in the large *Bratskie pesni* go into the section bearing the same title in *Pesnoslov,* nine more poems from that book are transferred in *Pesnoslov* to the section "Sosen perezvon," one poem goes to the section "Lesnye byli," and another to the fifth section, "Pesni iz Zaonezh'ya." Three poems in the large-edition *Bratskie pesni* do not appear in *Pesnoslov* at all; the poem from the small-edition *Bratskie pesni* which was excluded from the large edition is also absent from *Pesnoslov.* Lastly, one poem from the large book, entitled "Valentine Brikhnichevoi" ("To Valentina Brikhnicheva") and beginning "Zareveyut nagornye sklony" ("Evening colors the mountain sides red"), only *appears* to be absent from the "Bratskie pesni" section in *Pesnoslov:* in fact, the poem is included, but without that title and otherwise unchanged except for a more felicitous opening line, "Dremny pleski vechernego zvona" ("Sleepy are the splashes of the evening bell").[4]

This abundant reiteration and even confusion of titles might perhaps indicate the poet's relative carelessness, but his correspondence on publications of his poetry suggests—not surprisingly—otherwise.[5] It indicates, too, a measure of fluidity in his representation of the generic status of particular poems. It may also be partly the result of editorial intervention by others, for which there is some evidence in his publications of the 1910s. Without a doubt, it demonstrates the significance for the poet of the concept of the *bratskaya pesnya,* which, as will be seen, combines the spiritual, ideological, sexual, and aesthetic, at times in a programmatic manner. In any case, it is both expressive and representative of the problems of textual instability in the age of modernism.

The fraternal songs themselves mark the beginning of Klyuev's singular preoccupation with images and forms associated with sectarian collectivity, viewed from both inside and outside the world of sectarianism, as generally imagined in early twentieth-century Russia, and as recast by the poet himself. The very emergence of the fraternal song as a type in Klyuev's work also illustrates yet another important paradox in his professional biography—and a paradox that has echoes in many areas of twentieth-century Russian writing. On the one hand, these songs respond to a perceived need and an expressed ideological program associated with a journal and a grouping that were keen to find a "peasant-prophet" who would fit their own view of the state of Russia and of its potential for reinvigoration. It was much in Klyuev's interest to be such a figure, and for a short time he was: the fraternal songs can be seen, to a certain extent, as having been written "to order," to suit the needs of Brikhnichev and his Golgotha Christians, and to further the ambitions of the young poet. On the other hand, the combination of the particular features which, as will be argued, characterize the "core" poems of this type introduces into Klyuev's work a very significant line of poetic development. That line outlasts by many years his association with the Golgotha Christians. Indeed, it is through these fraternal songs and their later progeny that one of the most important and contradictory themes in Klyuev's personal lyrical universe gains its first powerful statement: his homoeroticism. That feature is far distant from the popular and collective ideology apparently promoted by the Golgotha Christians. Hence, in Klyuev's own creative biography, the fraternal songs foreground and render yet more problematic the polarities of authenticity and fabrication, between which move so many discussions of the poet and his work. Moreover, discussions of these polarities not only articulate differing points of view on the poetic identity, achievement, talent, and even honesty of Klyuev but also clearly rehearse arguments central to any discussion of Russian national cultural identity (debates over the "popular," the authentically national, the nature of "elite culture," and so on). Once again, encountering the now-marginalized Klyuev can take the reader (and certainly takes those who write on Klyuev) directly into the central combat zones of Russian cultural polemics.

Thus, the exemplary story of the title *Bratskie pesni* and its meaning does not end with Klyuev's own final employment of the term. In order to understand the profile of Klyuev as a poet today, it is important to consider not only what and when he himself published, but also his posthumous publishing history. All of the Soviet editions of the poet, beginning with Bazanov's *Stikhotvoreniya i poemy* of 1977 for the *malaya seriya* (small series) of the Biblioteka poeta (Poet's Library) and concluding with Azadovsky's *Stikhotvoreniya: Poemy* of 1991, present a highly selective—and usually, as is all too predictable, ideologically restricted—version of Klyuev. They also pay scant attention to the (admittedly unstable) distinctions the poet himself made in dividing his works up to the late 1910s into collections, nor, as is equally predictable, do they make clear the distinctions essentially imposed upon him by publishing circumstances from the later 1920s until the end of his life. There was one noble but minor exception at the very end of the Soviet period: the 1990 publication by the publishing house Stolitsa of a photoreprint of Klyuev's fifth major collection, *Mednyi kit.*[6] In other words, except for this reprint, no posthumous publication of Klyuev in Russia during the Soviet period presented the poet in a way which reflected him and his work as both appeared in his own lifetime. And, needless to say, original editions of Klyuev were great rarities after the 1930s. In recent years, reprints of other Klyuev collections have appeared, but many problems remain for the reader who aspires to an "ideal" order in which to read the poet.

In the West there were two substantial editions of Klyuev, both published before the earliest Soviet posthumous collections: the misleadingly named *Polnoe sobranie sochinenii* (*Full Collected Works*) of 1954, and *Sochineniya* (*Works*) of 1969. The former, edited by Boris Filippov, contains 359 poems; the latter, edited by Filippov and Gleb Struve, contains 427, making it by far the largest collection of Klyuev's poetry published until 1999. *Sochineniya* states that, like its predecessor, it contains all of Klyuev's poetic works known at the time of publication to the editors. There it is explained that *Polnoe sobranie sochinenii,* although compiled on similar principles, was produced when the editor had access to a smaller corpus of Klyuev's published works (1:509). Moreover, as *Sochineniya* notes, its predecessor omitted a few known lines *po soobrazheniyam moral'nym* (on moral grounds), at the behest of the publisher. Both collections take *Pesnoslov* as the poet's own definitive statement of his oeuvre up to 1919, and use various ad hoc distinctions for all other poems. Thus volume 1 of each edition uses the same eight divisions as Klyuev's *Pesnoslov,* beginning with "Sosen perezvon" and concluding with "Krasnyi ryk." Consequently, as in *Pesnoslov,* the second section of the first volume in each collection is entitled "Bratskie pesni." In *Polnoe sobranie sochinenii* this section reproduces the twenty-nine poems of the analogous section in *Pesnoslov,* whereas in *Sochineniya* the same section includes not only those twenty-nine poems but also the three poems which Klyuev included in the large-edition *Bratskie pesni,* but did *not* include *anywhere* in *Pesnoslov* ("Kostra stepnogo vzvivy," "Put' nadmirnyi sovershaya," and "Ty ne plach', moya kasatka" ["Completing your celestial circuit," "Weep not, my swallow," and "The leaps of a steppe bonfire"], 127–28, 117, 130–31), and, as two separate and independent poems,

"Valentine Brikhnichevoi" and "Dremny pleski vechernego zvona," which, as noted above, differ from one another only in title (or absence thereof) and first line.

In other words, *Sochineniya,* for thirty years by far the largest edition of Klyuev, widely used not only abroad but also by scholarly readers in the Soviet Union, even though it was effectively a banned book, produced yet another, now posthumous, version of Klyuev's own classification. The editors note that of all the early sections of *Pesnoslov,* "Bratskie pesni" differs most from its book original, and they suggest that Klyuev, publishing *Pesnoslov* in 1919, might have wished to dilute the religious tone prevalent in the book *Bratskie pesni* (1:522). Perhaps the poems omitted from *Pesnoslov* altogether were indeed victims of self-censorship: "Kostra stepnogo vzvivy" presents a sinister vision of Russia's future, in which the speaker is ready for what appears to be a warrior-monk's exploit; in "Put' nadmirnyi sovershaya" the speaker calls upon the addressee, "Queen, Angel, Maiden, Spirit, and Bird," to grant him spiritual union and save him from the Serpent; while in "Ty ne plach', moya kasatka" an unnamed speaker foretells winter sleep and spring rebirth. Yet many of the poems which Klyuev did include in the *Pesnoslov* "Bratskie pesni" are every bit as mystical. Even if the decision to include these three poems in the *Sochineniya* "Bratskie pesni" is seen as an attempt to face the problems which circumscribed domestic authorial intention throughout the Soviet period, and to resolve those problems by giving an author posthumous foreign liberty, a further instability has been introduced into the already complex fabric of Klyuev's oeuvre by this editorial fiat. Moreover, the tension between the perceived polarities of authenticity and fabrication, far from being resolved, is revealed upon close examination as heightened (if somewhat concealed) by such editorial intervention—where, the informed reader may wonder, is the "real Klyuev"?

With the publication in 1999 of by far the fullest edition of Klyuev's verse to date, *Serdtse edinoroga* (*Heart of the Unicorn*), edited by Viktor Garnin, with an introduction by Aleksandr Mikhailov, many of the most aggravating problems facing Klyuev's readers were resolved (although the consequences of those problems remain, even after their resolution—most accessible versions of Klyuev's work are still marked by them). Here, at long last, were almost all of the poet's extant works, accompanied by learned apparatus and a very informed introduction. *Serdtse edinoroga* takes account of the new publications of the glasnost period and beyond, and is free of the inevitable textual omissions and misreadings of earlier posthumous editions.[7] It is a latter-day descendant of the famous Soviet Biblioteka poeta, in which Klyuev had only been represented, it will be recalled, by a volume in the "small series" (that is, the series with the least claims to scholarly authority). The "large series" of Biblioteka poeta provided a major, in some cases *the major* source of twentieth-century poets' works for the Soviet reader. Its volumes usually presented poets' work in chronological order of composition, with variants and revisions noted and sometimes cited. Such is the case with *Serdtse edinoroga.* Hence, by using this volume, a particularly dutiful reader could conceivably read Klyuev's poetry from beginning to end in something like the order of its composition (although such a reader would, it is true, often encounter later, revised versions of poems, rather than the original of the first date of composition, since the "author's last known wishes" determine which version of a poem is presented). However, what that reader most certainly could not do is read Klyuev *by collections*—since these very significant markers of a poetic career were largely ignored by the editorial practices of the Biblioteka poeta series, followed by *Serdtse edinoroga.* And given the great rarity of Klyuev's original editions, noted above, only a reader with access to exceptional academic or private libraries (or perhaps to both) will have any chance of understanding Klyuev's poetry in terms of the major collections he himself put together.

As has been noted, it is clear that during the modernist period, a book of poetry (*sbornik*) was a major landmark in an author's career—a brief look at the review pages of literary periodicals is sufficient to prove this (and Klyuev's own reputation was very significantly affected by the reception of his major collections). It is also abundantly clear that large collections of poetry were not only repositories of selected verse but were also integral books in their own right, often composed by thematic principles, sometimes containing narratives related to the experiences of a central lyrical "I." The aesthetic and intellectual interests of the period, in conjunction with the material circumstances of book-making and of book-reading, produce many and diverse examples of such key books. The *sborniki* (and often, later, the authors' own revised, collected works) of, among others, Bryusov, Bal'mont, Blok, Bely, and even Tsvetaeva and Pasternak illustrate both the diversity and the centrality of the book of poetry for this period. Klyuev is no exception: *Sosen perezvon, Bratskie pesni, Lesnye byli, Mirskie dumy, Mednyi kit, Pesnoslov, L'vinyi khleb,* and (with some qualifications) *Izba i pole* are analogous in compositional principles and significance as literary statements to the books of other major poets of Russian modernism. For these reasons, it is highly desirable to examine not just the poems contained in Klyuev's three major versions of *Bratskie pesni* but those versions themselves—even their physical shape. And it is highly regrettable that very few readers indeed have the opportunity to do so.[8]

The big *Bratskie pesni* of 1912 is over eighty pages long. It opens with the brief author's note, quoted above, claiming that the poems which follow were mostly written before *Sosen perezvon* and have been widely disseminated in oral form. After this very strong (but rather misleading) statement comes a lengthy preface by Valentin Sventsitsky, at that time an ideologue of the Golgotha Christians, and subsequently an Orthodox priest (he died in prison in Siberia in 1931).[9] Sventsitsky calls Klyuev's poems "a prophetic hymn to Golgotha," seeing them not as verse but as a "new religious revelation," where the poet becomes a prophet. Klyuev, he claims, has expressed the new world which can be reached by the warrior of Christ, who understands the meaning of this latter-day Golgotha.[10] Sventsitsky's excited promotion of Klyuev's poetry is followed by the poems themselves, each poem beginning on a new page. As always in Klyuev's collections, the order of the poems is of great significance. It is most definitely not in the chronological order of composition (as is also characteristic of Klyuev—although by no means of all of his contemporaries: contrast, for example, Tsvetaeva). The first poem is "Bratskaya pesnya" (with "Poruchil klyuchi ot ada" as its first line) and the last is "Pesn' pokhoda" ("Campaign Song," 153–54), in the variant beginning with the line "Iisusa krest krovavyi" ("The bloody cross of Jesus"). Space does not permit a lengthy examination of the interrelationship of the poems as ordered in the collection, but the opening sequence may serve as an example of the whole: the militant, collective, and prophetic opening poem is followed and contrasted by "Osenyus' mogil'noyu ikonkoi" ("I shall cross myself with a sepulcher icon," 95), in which the single and isolated lyrical "I" declares his intention to wander among the people, collecting *pevuchie skazan'ya* (sung tales) to bring to the addressee, who is *krovavyi i svyatoi* (bloody and holy) but remembered among the people. The third poem is "Kak zvezde, proletnoi tuchke" ("As for a star, for a passing cloud," 107), in which the speaker appears to assert the need for individual suffering, not collective action, as a means of access to holy writ. The fourth poem, "On pridet! On pridet! I sodrognutsya gory" ("He shall come! He shall come! And mountains shall shudder," 156–57), moves back from the individual to the collective and prophetic, announcing the millenarian coming of the *Prishelets-tsar'* (Stranger-king) who will elevate the speaker and his female addressee—*sestra* (sister)—for their *podvig lyubvi* (exploit of love). The fifth poem, "V Moem rayu obitel' est'" ("In My paradise is a cloister," 144–45), describes the heavenly sanctuary accessible only to those who have borne "Golgotha's cross." This opening sequence thus announces the dominant religious and mystical themes of the collection (both collective and individual), in part through a series of contrasts, frequently established by successive poems. Other major themes emerge in the second half of the book, introduced almost halfway through the thirty-two poems by one of Klyuev's earliest works "'Bezotvetnym rabom . . .'" ("'As a silent slave . . . ,'" 79), first published in the almanac *Volny* (*Waves*) in 1905. After this poem, a series of lyrics provide allegories of individual fate, often colored by natural or rural features.

The poems of this edition are followed by eight pages of publisher's announcements—in itself an unremarkable fact for the period, although their nature is rather distinct: the works of Brikhnichev, Sventsitsky, and Klyuev as published by *Novaya zemlya* are advertised, and then extracts from seven reviews of Klyuev's *Sosen perezvon* are presented, presumably to shore up the ideological significance of the work of the Golgotha Christians (by associating that work with a poetic *sbornik*, it should be noted). Finally, the works of the three Golgotha authors (Brikhnichev, Sventsitsky, and Klyuev) are again announced and promoted.

Every element in the composition of this edition of *Bratskie pesni* is intriguing, and many are both partly characteristic of the age in general and simultaneously unique to Klyuev in their specifics. The organization of the poetry itself is very clear; the poet's somewhat contradictory claims about the poems foreground one of the major paradoxes of his work; the ideological positioning of the poetry is made abundantly evident by prefatory and final pages, but is—again characteristically—somewhat belied by the poems themselves.

The small *Bratskie pesni* of 1912, baldly subtitled *Pesni golgofskikh khristian,* is a mere fourteen pages long and has no prefatory or concluding material. The poems are numbered from one to nine, and follow one another without page breaks. "O, pospeshite, brat'ya k nam" ("O, hurry to us, brothers," 158–59) opens the collection, and the only works to have titles, "Pesn' pokhoda," and "Pesn' utesheniya" ("Song of Consolation," 175–76), conclude it—on a particularly militant note. The collection is thematically very integral, as will be demonstrated at greater length below.

Pesnoslov, produced at the very beginning of the Soviet period, presents a rather different set of textological problems, as was suggested in chapter 2. While especial caution should be exercised in examining as an integral and complete work a collection so buffeted by publishing circumstances, it is clear that it is, *mutatis mutandis,* analogous to the collected works prepared by some of the symbolists: the poet reviewed and revised his earlier work, using the titles of previous collections for sections of volume 1 of *Pesnoslov,* but placing different poems under the old headings. Hence the new version of "Bratskie pesni" presented here. Again, there is no space for detailed analysis of the editorial changes nor of the order of poems, but it is worth noting that, of the eighteen poems from the large *Bratskie pesni* preserved in the *Pesnoslov* section of fraternal songs, only five are among the first sixteen poems of the new version, while the last thirteen poems of the section are all from the large *Bratskie pesni* (but in a different order). A new three-poem cycle, "Radel'nye pesni" ("Songs of Ecstasy"), has been created from poems previously published separately and apart, and this cycle is followed by the long poem beginning "Pod ivushkoi zelenoi" ("Under a green willow"), which appears here under the title "Usladnyi stikh" ("Poem of Praise," 154–55), and by "Pesn' pokhoda," which concludes *Pesnoslov*'s "Bratskie pesni," thereby reinforcing overall thematic similarity with the ending of the two previous versions. The opening of *Pesnoslov*'s fraternal songs, is, however, quite different from earlier versions: it consists of two poems describing powerful individual (and distinctly heterodox) mystical experiences: "Ya byl v dukhe v den' voskresnyi" ("I was in the spirit on the Lord's day," 110–11) and "Begstvo" ("Escape," 142–43), the first line of which announces stridently "Ya bezhal v prostor lugov" ("I fled to the meadows' space"). Overall, in the first half of the *Pesnoslov* version, individual mystical experience predominates, sometimes in association with the natural world. Thus the movement from the individual to the collective voices characteristic of earlier versions of *Bratskie pesni* is even more marked in this later revision, while the contrast between the concluding poems of "Bratskie pesni" and the opening poems of the next section of *Pesnoslov*, "Lesnye byli," is especially clear.

To summarize, a return to the original publications of Klyuev's fraternal songs is both enlightening and predictably disorienting. Each major version is different, each speaks of the poet's status as a canonical modernist, and of his unique place within modernism, and each reminds the reader of his special relationship to prominent ideological questions and to material circumstances (Klyuev's own financial and social situation was quite different, after all, from that of most of the poets of modernism, thereby making his relationship with publishers and reviewers very different).

It is to be hoped that the pages devoted here to the exposition of this example of labyrinthine textual complexity, albeit expressive of a certain frustration experienced during any attempt at textual codification, will not be seen merely as the literal-minded lament of a reductive and obsessive researcher. On the contrary, it is expected (and feared) that the problems outlined will be familiar to anyone who has attempted to produce a conclusive statement of what and when any poet of this period actually wrote. Such problems are partially the result of a general tendency among such poets toward provisional contextualization of individual poetic utterances—poets of the modernist period often wrote and rewrote individual works, and situated and resituated those individual works in larger compositions. They are also the result of the proliferation of publishing opportunities in the period, often provided by small and short-lived journals and publishing houses. They are, furthermore, an inevitable consequence of the intersection of a poet's career with the Soviet period in Russian history. In Klyuev's own case, publishing opportunities in the early 1910s, and publishing obstacles in the later years of the decade have contributed specific features to this process. Klyuev's repeated remaking of his *bratskie pesni* is also very clearly in parallel with his repeated remakings in his later autobiographical statements of his own origins and cultural formation—as is frequently the case, Klyuev's practice as a poet finds an almost exact analogue in his constructions of his own persona.

The very title "fraternal song" is, moreover, problematic for reasons which extend well beyond the bibliographic. As the word *pesnya* and Klyuev's prefatory remarks remind the reader, the fraternal song suggests a genre associated with collective, oral transmission and performance.[11] As has been seen, the larger book of *Bratskie pesni* contained a long preface by V. Sventsitsky promoting Klyuev as a prophet and preacher, in whose songs there was both an echo of the songs of earlier Christian martyrs and the joyful voice of a newly liberated earth. The reception of both the fraternal songs and of Sventsitsky's view of them can be illustrated quite easily, since the collections were widely reviewed—fifteen reviews are attested in 1912, with metropolitan and provincial organs represented.[12] Although Sventsitsky's comments were widely criticized, Klyuev's preface was generally accepted at face value, and the sectarian and popular origins of the songs were assumed by reviewers, who included the poets Nikolai Gumilev, for *Apollon* (*Apollo*), Valerii Bryusov, for *Russkaya mysl'* (*Russian Thought*), Vladimir Narbut, for *Rodnaya strana* (*Homeland*), and Lyubov' Stolitsa, for *Novoe vino* (*New Wine*). Gumilev, for example, accepted Klyuev's association of the songs with collective creativity and, citing Klyuev's preface, added, "That is exactly how examples of popular art are indeed created, somewhere in the forest, on the road, where there is neither the possibility nor the will to write down, to refine a work, and where a clumsy ending may be added to a successful stanza, where not only grammar, but also meter may be ignored."[13] The anonymous reviewer in *Strannik* (*The Wanderer*) also accepted Klyuev's association of his poems with popular transmission, as did M. Chunosov in his review for *Novoe slovo* (*New Word*), although Narbut's perceptive review totally ignored the sectarian element in the collection, while praising the more lyrical features and—as did several other reviewers—dismissing Sventsitsky's views.[14] Extracts from the poems themselves were often cited to illustrate their proximity to popular forms and thematics. The widespread fascination with sectarianism and its songs, against the background of which both Klyuev's poems and such interpretations must be read, will be discussed below, and other authors who had written poetry and prose using sectarian motifs will be enumerated. But it is worthwhile here to compare the reception of Klyuev's work with that accorded to a prominent predecessor. Gumilev, who wrote enthusiastically of *Bratskie pesni,* had also greeted Klyuev's first collection, *Sosen perezvon,* very positively, in an earlier "Letter on Russian Poetry." There he also examined the eighth volume of Bal'mont's collected works, containing *Zelenyi vertograd* (*Green Garden*), a collection which Bal'mont had originally published in 1909. That work was, as Gumilev remarked, "inspired . . . by the songs and tales of *khlysty.*" He continued, "Many poems are simply fakes. Their authentic religious aroma has, of course, been completely dissipated in Bal'mont's work."[15] Although he granted some of the poems stanzas which convey the naivete or slyness characteristic of sectarian songs, he then cited a stanza (from "Po blagodati" ["By Grace"]) rather more characteristic of Bal'mont than of sectarians:

Мы не по закону,	Not by law,
Мы не по благодати.	And not by grace.
Озарив икону,	We'll light the icon lamp,
Ляжем на кровати.	And go to bed together.

Bal'mont's works were inauthentic, whereas Klyuev's songs, for Gumilev, seem to prove that the Olonian poet was a "prophet of a new force, of popular [*narodnaya*] culture," and their intermittent clumsiness was proof of their popular origins.[16] And indeed, once Klyuev's fraternal songs are set beside such examples of playful literary eroticism, loosely based on popular assumptions about sectarianism, it becomes clear why *Bratskie pesni* and their author, newly emerged from the people, were so received.

Moreover, as the briefest examination of some of the fraternal songs themselves shows, within the poems, the *imagined* audience and performers are primarily sectarian: in short, what is evoked is the secretive world of religious sects, with their mysteries which so fascinated the turn-of-the-century Russian reader. At the same time, context and content both make abundantly clear the contemporary sociopolitical tendency implicit, and sometimes explicit, in Klyuev's fraternal project. That is, on the one hand, these are sectarian songs of the people; and on the other hand, they are hymns for a new movement with a social agenda expressed in religious terms, and that movement is willing to promote Klyuev as its prophet and bard. Within this framework, too, the status of the fraternal songs is problematic, inviting further polar discussion.

How then are Klyuev's fraternal songs to be understood, and what do they have in common with songs actually sung by religious groups? Klyuev's own answer was that they *were indeed sung by religious groups*—that, at least, was what he remarked to Blok in a letter of early spring 1912:

> *New Land* is offering to publish a book of my poems in the spirit of "The Song to the Brethren"—in no. 7/8 of *New Land.* All the poems should be of that kind—the journal offers 300 rubles for that and asks for an immediate response, as they need to print in the newspapers that my book will be a supplement to the journal. They write so persuasively, with the heading "Hasten to do good," that I am embarrassed to reply with an unjustified refusal. Perhaps the *New Land* people really believe that my songs are an "echo of the

> singing on the Mount of Olives." I really do not know what to do. My letters are being distributed around Moscow; at Old Believer gatherings they sing my poems "The keys of hell were handed" and "Beneath the green willow."[17]

But even Klyuev's own remarks are far from clear. And, as Azadovsky points out, at the time of this letter, Klyuev in fact had relatively few religious hymnlike poems written—certainly not enough for a whole book—even if some of them really were being sung at Moscow Old Believer gatherings.[18]

For the sake of the following discussion, a "fraternal song" is taken to mean something approximating to a poem that articulates a collective point of view, with a religious tonality and martyrological thematics, at times colored also by sociopolitical preoccupations, and written in a language and meter which are at the very least stylized versions of folklore. Of the poems at one time or another placed under the general heading "Bratskie pesni" by Klyuev himself—there are over forty—only fourteen actually may be argued to fit that definition. The remaining poems, while sharing some of these features, are not clearly distinguished from the poems of *Sosen perezvon* or *Lesnye byli*—the collections either side of *Bratskie pesni*—and do not display the combination of elements listed above. Many are poems with a religious, even apocalyptic or martyrological coloring, but spoken in a conventional first-person voice and almost entirely without signs of folkloric stylization (and most of the poems added to the "Bratskie pesni" section of *Pesnoslov* could be described thus). Hence, numerically predominant in the large collection *Bratskie pesni* are such lyrical (and rather derivative) works as the following:

Позабыл, что в руках: — Сердце, шляпа иль трость? Зреет в Отчих садах Виноградная гроздь.	I have forgotten what is in my hands: A heart, a hat, or a cane? In the gardens of the Lord Grape bunches ripen.
Впереди крик: «нельзя», Позади: «воротись». И тиха лишь стезя, Уходящая ввысь.	Ahead the cry: "don't," Behind: "return." All that is quiet is the path Leading upwards.
Не по ней ли идти? Может быть, не греша, На лазурном пути Станет птицей душа. (132)	Shouldn't I follow it? Maybe, if no sin is committed, On the azure path The soul will become a bird.

The lyrical, individual (and rather trite) mysticism of the poem has little in common with the core fraternal poems, while its literary, derivative nature is indicated by its symbolist lexicon (*stezya, lazurnyi*). The speaker's somewhat ill-defined aspirations are expressed in a purely conventional poetic language and a standard literary meter (anapestic dimeter) and rhyme scheme (crossed masculine rhymes). Many poems in the large versions of *Bratskie pesni* are similar to this one, "Pozabyl, chto v rukakh," providing a background against which the core poems stand out, and with which they may be very clearly contrasted.

Although the fourteen poems fulfilling all the above requirements of fraternal songs form the core of the collection, even within this group great diversity may be observed, as well as many elements which are very distinct from the characteristics enumerated above (of particular importance is a secondary, homoerotic association for the notion of fraternity, often implied or even stated). The poems are (in the order in which they appear in the big collection *Bratskie pesni*): "Bratskaya pesnya" (with the first line "Poruchil klyuchi ot ada"); "On pridet! On pridet! I sodrognutsya gory"; "V Moem rayu obitel' est'"; "Akh vy, drugi — p olyubovnye sobrat'ya" ("Oh, friends, brothers amicable," 177); "O, pospeshite, brat'ya, k nam" ("O, hurry to us, brothers," 158–59); the two-poem cycle "Na kreste" ("On the Cross," 180–81); "Ty vzoidi, vzoidi, Nevechernii Svet" ("Arise, arise light of no evening known," 178–79); "Mne skazali — Sveta vek ne vidat'" ("They told me—I should not see the Light for an age," 177–78); "Brachnaya pesnya" ("Wedding Song," 133–34); "Polunoshchnitsa" ("Midnight Service," 159–60); "Vechernyaya pesnya" ("Pod ivushkoi zelenoi" [later published as "Usladnyi stikh"]); and "Pesn' pokhoda." In addition to these thirteen poems, the final poem of the brochure version of *Bratskie pesni,* "Pesn' utesheniya," is also considered by theme and poetics a "core" poem, although it does not appear either in the large collection or anywhere in *Pesnoslov.*

Lest it be thought that the the criteria elaborated above and used here to identify these "core" fraternal songs are arbitrarily imposed, it should be noted that they have led (quite independently) to the identification of a group of poems which the poet himself seem to have seen as core to his recurrent versions of the fraternal songs. Of the nine poems that comprise the smaller, brochure collection of 1912—a publication which seems to be clearly programmatic in intent (*Songs of the Golgotha Christians* is, after all, its subtitle)—eight are among the "core" poems identified above.[19] Meanwhile, the somewhat reduced version of "Bratskie pesni" provided in *Pesnoslov* includes all but one of the fourteen poems identified above. In other words, these poems do indeed seem to form the core of the poet's fraternal songs, around which accretions and removals of other poems take place. As is often the case, when examining Klyuev's oeuvre, change, variation, and central continuity are all visibly attested, with attendant problems and contradictions. It should also be noted that Klyuev's reviewers also tended to quote those "core" works more than any others in their comments on

Bratskie pesni—comments which, as has been said, often dwelt on popular and religious features.

Lastly, however, it should be added not only that these poems appear in a different order in each version of *Bratskie pesni,* and, in the case of the large collection and *Pesnoslov,* in the company of different poems, but also that there are modifications both to text and to title in later versions. Most notably, "Akh vy, drugi — polyubovnye sobrat'ya," "Mne skazali — Sveta vek ne vidat'," and "Ty vzoidi, vzoidi, Nevechernii Svet" are united in the new cycle "Radel'nye pesni," while "Vechernyaya pesnya" has become "Usladnyi stikh."[20]

Thus, an examination of the many versions of what Klyuev called "bratskie pesni" clearly underlines the mobility and mutability of the organizing structures imposed upon individual poems, first by the poet himself, and later by others. These structures, it may be argued, are fundamental to generating meaning, and their mutability means that the same poem will be read quite differently in a different context. At the same time, a careful survey of all the poems Klyuev associated at one time or another with the idea of a fraternal song identifies a core group of works that was not as subject to change and reorganization (although still marked by instabilities). By briefly examining each of those core poems, by illustrating their principal characteristics, and by establishing the criteria by which they may be compared with their literary and popular models, it will be possible to identify the key criteria, formal and thematic, which made the concept of the "fraternal song" so important for the poet, and, it would seem, for many of his contemporary readers.

"Bratskaya pesnya" ("Poruchil klyuchi ot ada"), one of the poems being sung by Old Believers, according to Klyuev's letter to Blok cited above, opens the large *Bratskie pesni* of 1912, is the second poem of the 1912 brochure version (but without a title), and is the twenty-first poem in the *Pesnoslov* section. It is clearly a definitive fraternal song, having appeared initially in the Golgotha Christians' journal *Novaya zemlya.* In that first publication the poem had three epigraphs: the first was St. Paul's famous "O death, where is thy sting? O grave, where is thy victory?" from 1 Corinthians 15:55 (somewhat disingenuously attributed simply to "Paul of Tarsus"), the second "from the Prophet Zechariah" (in fact, part of Zechariah 9:16), and the third "from popular [*narodnye*] songs" (although in a suspiciously literary trochaic tetrameter). These epigraphs were removed in subsequent publications, although the verse was reused as an epigraph to Klyuev's 1919 article "Samotsvetnaya krov'" ("Gemstone Blood," *Sd* 141). There are significant differences between the various published versions of this poem, and in particular between the publications in the two *Bratskie pesni* of 1912 and the *Pesnoslov* version, which has three fewer stanzas. The editors of *Sochineniya,* who restore the cut stanzas and publish the original version, but without epigraphs, assert that the cuts were made "mainly for reasons of censorship" (1:524). The final three stanzas of the poem in its 1912 version provide abundant evidence to motivate its apparent popularity with the Golgotha Christians, if not with practicing Old Believers:

Крест целящий, крест разящий,
Нам водитель и завет.
Брат на гноище лежащий,
Подымись, Христос грядет!

Он не в нищенском хитоне,
И не с терном вкруг чела . . .
На рассветном небосклоне
Плещут ангелов крыла.

Их заоблачные гимны
Как прибой морей звучат . . .
Звякнул ключ гостеприимный
У предвечных рая врат.

The cross that cures, the cross that strikes
Is our guide and covenant.
Brother lying on detritus,
Arise, Christ is coming!

He is clad not in a poor man's cloak,
And has no thorns around his brow . . .
At the dawn's horizon
Wings of angels splash.

Their celestial hymns
Sound like the tide of seas . . .
The welcoming key has sounded
At the everlasting gates of paradise.

A self-consciously programmatic theme, and a literary lexicon and meter (trochaic tetrameter) mark this poem. Less clear, however, is the story of the poem's rewriting—one might question the confident commentary of *Sochineniya.* The first two stanzas quoted above were omitted in *Pesnoslov,* and whereas the other omitted stanza has a clearly triumphalist, "muscular Christian" note ("My — soratniki Khristovy,/Preispodnei klyuchari" ["We are Christ's fellow soldiers/Stewards of the gates of hell"]), these two are little distinguished from those beside them in ideological proclamation.

Meanwhile, the final lines of the original version are, in fact, far more triumphalist than those in *Pesnoslov*, where that triumphalist note is heard once more in the variant "Nashi bitvennye gimny/Burevetrami zvuchat" ("Our battle hymns/Sound like storm winds"). Again, individual editorial decisions may be read as personal (many readers will see aesthetic improvement in them) or as imposed, and there can be no absolute clarity. The apparatus to *Serdtse edinoroga* suggests, moreover, that the poet created yet other manuscript versions of this poem (853).

Furthermore, while this poem may confidently be identified as a key fraternal song (and was by the poet himself), it should also be noted that it has much in common with another group of Klyuev's triumphalist songs of quite different thematics and context—his most pro-Soviet works of the immediate postrevolutionary period and of the 1920s. This last group, like the fraternal songs, may, of course, be argued to share a common original impulse—a perceived "social commission" (*sotsial'nyi zakaz*), to use the Soviet-period term, that is to say, both groups were written partially to fulfill a perceived demand and to serve as programmatic statements intended to promote the poet—another paradoxical moment of continuity in the poet's oeuvre.

"On pridet! On pridet! I sodrognutsya gory" is the fourth poem in the large *Bratskie pesni,* the sixth in the brochure, and the twenty-third in the *Pesnoslov* section. It consists of six stanzas of anapestic tetrameter. The first three describe the drama of the Second Coming, with attendant apocalyptic detail and an element of political retribution:

> Он затопчет, как сор, вероломства законы,
> Духом уст поразит исполинов-бойцов,
> Даст державу простым, и презренным короны,
> Чтобы царством владели во веки веков.
>
> He shall trample, like filth, the laws of betrayal,
> With a breath from his lips shall strike down warrior-giants,
> And shall give power to the simple, crowns to the scorned,
> That they should rule the kingdom for ever and ever.

The elevated lexicon and obvious quotations of the sacred, together with the politico-apocalyptic thematics, make the poem a key statement of collective, sectarian expectation, reminding the reader of the widespread perception at the time that in Russian religious dissent lay the potential, and perhaps even the model, for radical social action. But the final three stanzas turn radically away from these programmatic and general preoccupations: the speaker addresses his "sister" and announces the prospect of their individual salvation at the final hour:

Содрогаясь, мы внемлем Судьи приговору:
«Истребися», «Воскресни», «Восстань и живи» . . .
Кто-то шепчет тебе: «к серафимов собору
Вы причислены оба — за подвиг любви»

Trembling we will hear the Judge's verdict:
"Be destroyed," "Resurrect," "Arise and live" . . .
Someone will whisper to you: "You are both to be numbered
Among the host of seraphim for the exploit of love"

The nature of the "exploit of love" is left unexplained, and the radical reorientation of the poem in its final three stanzas, while very characteristic of Klyuev's mature poetics in general, seems to undermine its initial statement of an apparently collective view, just as the standard literary meter and rhyme scheme militate against a reading of sectarian "authenticity." Moreover, the poem was first published with the title "Sestre" ("To a Sister"), although in book publications Klyuev removed that title, which was redolent of the individual and personal (854). Notwithstanding the mixture of contrasting elements and contradictory indicators, this poem, as will be seen below, was to be cited as an example of Klyuev's plagiarism of the popular in a violent quarrel that broke out between the poet and his erstwhile patrons shortly after the publication of his books of *Bratskie pesni.* Again, the poem is somewhat different in *Pesnoslov,* and there are also later manuscript variants (854).

"V Moem rayu obitel' est'" is the fifth poem in the large *Bratskie pesni,* coming immediately after "On pridet! On pridet! I sodrognutsya gory." It does not appear in the brochure version, and is the twenty-second poem in the *Pesnoslov* section (immediately after "Bratskaya pesnya"). One of Klyuev's first publications in *Novaya zemlya,* it is in iambic tetrameter (the most widespread of all metrical forms in Russian) and, like "Bratskaya pesnya," highly programmatic. The lyrical speaker of the poem is, apparently, divine (hence the capitalized possessive pronoun), and speaks of the welcome He will afford to the elected:

За непреклонные врата	Past the unbending gates
Лишь тот из смертных проникает,	Pass only those among mortals
На ком голгофского креста	On whom gleams the elevated seal
Печать высокая сияет.	of Golgotha's cross.

In this stanza the combination of the word *pechat'* (seal) with "Golgotha's cross" is of particular note, since it indicates the association of the program of the "Golgotha Christians" with popular sectarianism—*pechat',* as will be seen below, is the term for castration among the *skoptsy.* Unlike some of the other highly programmatic "fraternal" works, there appear to be no variants of this poem.

"Akh vy, drugi — polyubovnye sobrat'ya" is the sixth poem in the large *Bratskie pesni,* immediately following "V Moem rayu obitel' est'." It is the third poem in the brochure version of the collection, and the twenty-fifth poem in the *Pesnoslov* version, where it is the first poem of the new cycle "Radel'nye pesni" (the title of which refers to the *radeniya* or ecstatic rites of sectarians). The poem celebrates the mystical union of brothers with brothers and with the divine (with homoerotic overtones, as the punning opening line suggests—a startling and contradictory combination of the sociopolitical with the provocatively personal). It concludes:

Разделяют с нами брашна серафимы,
Осеняют нас крылами легче дыма,

Сотворяют с нами знамение-чудо,
Возлагают наши душеньки на блюдо.

Дух возносят серафимы к Саваофу,
Телеса на Иисусову Голгофу.

Мы в раю вкушаем ягод грозди,
На земле же терпим крест и гвозди.

Перебиты наши голени и ребра . . .
Ей, гряди ко стаду, Пастырь добрый!

Аминь

Seraphim share victuals with us
Shade us with wings lighter than smoke,

Create with us a wonder-sign,
Place our souls upon a dish.

Seraphim raise spirits to the Lord of Hosts,
Bodies to Jesus's Golgotha.

In paradise we taste clusters of berries,
On the earth we suffer cross and nails.

Our shins and ribs are shattered . . .
Oh, come to your flock, good Shepherd!

Amen

It is characteristic that the stylization promoted by the elevated diction (the Church Slavonic *brashna* and *telesa,* here translated as "victuals" and "bodies") and folkloric gestures (the noun combination *znamenie-chudo*, here translated as "wonder-sign") is undercut by the somewhat grotesque line "Place our souls upon a dish."

"O, pospeshite, brat'ya, k nam," is the eighth poem in the large *Bratskie pesni,* the first poem in the brochure, and the twentieth poem in the *Pesnoslov* section. The poem is a call to fraternal worship in the sanctuary of nature, again with homoerotic overtones. Its language and meter are unproblematic and primarily "literary":

О, поспешите, братья, к нам,
В наш чудный храм, где зори — свечи,
Где предалтарный фимиам —
Туманы дремлющих поречий!
. . .
Служить Заутреню любви,
Вкусить кровей, живого хлеба . . .
Кто жив, души не очерстви
Для горних труб и зовов неба!
. . .
Доверясь радужным ладьям,
Мы поплывем, минуя мысы . . .
О, поспешите, братья, к нам
В нетленный сад, под кипарисы!

O hasten, brethren, to us,
To our wondrous temple, where dawns are candles,
Where altar incense is
The mist of sleeping riverbank!
. . .
Serving the day's Prime of love,
Tasting blood and living bread.
Whoever lives, do not let your soul go stale
For celestial trumpets and calls of heaven!
. . .
Trusting to the rainbow vessels,
We shall sail past capes . . .

O hasten, brethren, to us,
To the eternal garden, beneath cypress trees!

Here the syncretism which characterizes every period of Klyuev's poetry is evident in the combination of collective voice, homoerotic undertones, master-image of nature as place of worship, and compressed cultural topography (from the implied northern forests—*dymnye dubravy* [smoky oak groves]—of the opening stanzas to the cypress trees of the last). The specifically sectarian coloring is provided, among other ways, by the key motifs of brother, vessel, and garden—the last two being characteristic terms for sectarian groups, frequently encountered in their folklore.

The two-poem cycle "Na kreste" ("On the Cross") provides the tenth and eleventh poems of the large *Bratskie pesni,* and the eighteenth and nineteenth poems of the *Pesnoslov* section, with variants. It is not found in the brochure. In the cycle, the speaker seems to describe his own crucifixion in the form of a sylvan Christ, as the first stanzas of each poem suggest:

Лестница златая
Прянула с небес.
Вижу, умирая,
Райских кринов лес . . .
. . .
Гвоздяные ноют раны,
Жалят терний чело.
Чу! провеяло в тумане
Серафимское крыло . . .

A golden staircase
Has leapt from the heavens.
As I die, I see
A forest of heavenly tree crowns . . .
. . .
Nail wounds ache
Thorns pierce my brow!
Oh! In the mist
A seraphim's wing fluttered past . . .

In these two poems, it is thematics rather than language or meter which is primary in dictating membership in the core group of fraternal songs. It is significant that the *Pesnoslov* variants of this cycle reduce the "fraternal" and local elements in the first poem. Line five reads "V kushchakh dukhov kliry"—instead of "V kushchakh brat'ya-dukhi" ("In the foliage are the choirs of spirits"; "In the foliage are the spirit-brethren"); while lines seven and eight read “Khmel’ vina i mirry/Vetrom doneslo” instead of “Ladan cheremukhi/S vetrom doneslo” (“The wind has brought/Intoxication from wine and myrrh”; “With the wind has come/Bird-cherry incense”). But, in a paradox which discourages reading only “self-censorship” into the changes, the second poem in the *Pesnoslov* variant concludes with the lines “Gde ty, svetlaya otchizna —/Golubinyi Nazaret” (“Where are you, bright homeland—/Dove Nazareth?”), where *golubinyi* carries clear Russian popular associations, while the final line in the original version has the more canonical, biblical conclusion “Moi Favor i Nazaret?” (“My Mount Tabor and Nazareth?”). In other words, the final line in the *Pesnoslov* version links the sylvan Christ to the folk cosmology of the *Golubinaya kniga* (*Book of Depth*), although the context also suggests an association with *golubi* (doves), while the first version of the poem merely has two standard Christian referents—Mt. Tabor, the place traditionally identified with Christ’s transfiguration, and Nazareth.[21]

In the large *Bratskie pesni,* “Na kreste” is followed immediately by “Ty vzoidi, vzoidi, Nevechernii Svet,” which sustains from beginning to end the stylization observed intermittently in other poems, summoning and welcoming the *Nevechernii Svet* (Light of no evening known) as guarantor of human (fraternal) joy:

Ты взойди, взойди, Невечерний Свет,
С земнородными положи завет!
. . .
Без Тебя, Отец, вождь, невеста, друг,
Не найти тропы на животный луг.

Arise, arise Light of no evening known,
With the earth-born set down a covenant . . .
. . .
Without You, Father, leader, bride, and friend,
The path to life’s meadowland may never be found.

“Mne skazali — Sveta vek ne vidat’ ” is the twentieth poem in the large *Bratskie pesni,* where it forms the second part of the two-poem cycle “Pesnya pro sud’bu” (“Song About Fate”). The first poem of the cycle is “Iz-za lesa, iz-za temnogo” (“From out the forest, the dark forest,” 160–61), which elsewhere appears alone under that title. The latter poem, in the form of a stylized folk narrative, relates the three choices of a generic *dobryi molodets* (good swain)—to become a plowman, a factory worker (*sic*), or to gain eternal life. “Mne skazali — Sveta vek ne vidat’ ” is not included in the brochure version of *Bratskie pesni,* while in *Pesnoslov* it is the twenty-sixth poem in the section, and the second in the newly formed cycle “Radel’nye pesni.” In a trochaic meter and with folkloric stylistic markers (the short-form adjective of *strela zubchata* [saw-toothed arrow]; the suffix of *voditsa* [water]), it seems a fairly unremarkable allegory of love, in which the speaker tells of his unintended violence to a swan, except for the framing first and last couplets, the first with its apparent statement of epiphany, and the last with its startling revelation of the "fraternal" erotic meaning of the allegory:

Мне сказали — Света век не видать,
Белый Светик и поныне во глазах.

Я возьму каленовострую стрелу,
На полете звонкоперой накажу:

«Не кровавь, стрела зубчата острия,
Ни о зверя, ни о малого червя».
. . .
Вдоль по речке лебедь белая плывет,
Выше берега головушку несет,

Выше леса крылья взмахивает,
На себя водицу всплескивает.

Угодила звонкоперая стрела
В жилу смертную лебяжьего крыла. —

Дрогнул берег, зашаталися леса,
Прокатилися по взгорьям голоса:

«Ныне, други, сочетался с братом брат:
С белой яблоней — зеленый виноград!»

I was told, I'd not see the Light for an eternity,
But the Bright Light is yet in my eyes.

I shall take a sharp-forged arrow,
As it flies I shall tell that feather-sounding arrow:

"Do not dip your saw-toothed blade
In the blood of beast nor of humble worm."
. . .
Along the river swims a white pen-swan,
Carrying her head above the bank,

Flapping her wings above the woods,
Splashing water on herself.

The feather-sounding arrow has hit
A mortal vein in the swan's wing.

The bank shook, the woods were rocked,
Across the hillocks sounded voices:

"Now friends, brother is joined with brother:
With the white apple tree—the green vine!"

The stylized folkloric elements which are beginning to appear in Klyuev's poetry at this time are combined here both with very traditional lyric elements (the allegory itself, and the female swan as principal metaphor) and with the startling religious and homoerotic frame.[22] The final lines, giving the union of *brother with brother* the mythic status of the union of natural opposites—(northern) apple blossom in bloom; (southern) grapevine—are particularly striking, since they redirect the gender motifs of the poem, previously structured on the opposition of male human and female swan. The combination of such diverse and recognizably dissonant elements, and the radical redirecting near the end of the poem of what appears at one point to be a familiar and homogeneous poetic statement, are becoming characteristic elements of Klyuev's poetics during the period of the composition of *Bratskie pesni,* and will be, *mutatis mutandis,* abiding elements of his works for the remainder of his life. In the specific case of this poem, such combinations simultaneously announce and subvert the "fraternal" features of the poem, and give the thematic redirection toward sexuality especial force.

"Brachnaya pesnya" is the twenty-second poem in the large *Bratskie pesni* and the ninth in the *Pesnoslov* section. It is absent from the brochure. The poem—its title apparently a punning combination of "wedding song" and "mating song" (as of birds)—celebrates the mystical union of brothers, with homoerotic and even sadomasochistic overtones. The poem opens and concludes with a chorus:

Белому брату
Хлеб и вино новое
Уготованы.
Помолюсь закату,
Надем рубище суровое,
И приду на брак непозванный.

For a white brother
Bread and new wine
Are prepared.
I shall pray to the sunrise,
I shall put on a plain shirt,
And shall come uninvited to the wedding.

The central section, also metrically irregular but trochee-based, seems to be spoken in the voice of a second, younger "brother":

Ты узнай меня, Братец,
Не отринь меня, одноотчий,
Дай узреть Зари Твоей багрянец,
Покажи мне Солнце после Ночи,
Я пришел к Тебе без боязни,
Молоденький и бледный как былинка,
Укажи мне после тела казни
В Отчие обители тропинку. . . .

Acknowledge me, my Brother,
Do not reject me, we are of one father,
Let me see the scarlet of Your Dawn,
Show me the Sun after Night,
I have come to You without fear
Young and pale like a blade of grass,
Show me after the body's punishment
The way to the Father's cloisters.

"Polunoshchnitsa" is the twenty-fifth poem in the large *Bratskie pesni*, the seventh (but in a very different variant) in the brochure, and the third in the *Pesnoslov* section. In the first and third publications the poem consists of a summons to midnight service, followed by the reply of the congregation. In the brochure it lacks the first fifteen lines, containing the metrically irregular summons, leaving only the voices of the congregation, celebrating the opportunity to enter a sinless communion with a somewhat pagan divinity. The penultimate stanza of the poem in all versions celebrates with particular enthusiasm:

Наша нива — тверди круг,
Колосится звездной рожью,
И лежит вселенский плуг
У Господнего подножья.

Our meadow is the circle of the firmament,
Ripening with starry rye,
And the universe's plow
Lies at the feet of the Lord.

"Vechernyaya pesnya" is the twenty-eighth poem in the large *Bratskie pesni.* It appears fifth in the brochure, but without a title, and, as "Usladnyi stikh," it is the twenty-eighth and penultimate member of the "Bratskie pesni" section of *Pesnoslov.* This, according to Klyuev, in his letter to Blok, quoted above, is one of the two poems being sung by Moscow Old Believers. The *Pesnoslov* version of the poem not only changes the title but also omits one couplet. The editors of *Sochineniya* assert baldly that this omission was made for reasons of censorship (1:525). The couplet omitted in *Pesnoslov* reads:

Ныне, братики, нас гонят и бесчестят,
Тем Уму Христову приневестят.

Now, brothers, we are persecuted and dishonored,
And thus we will be betrothed to the Mind of Christ.

As so often, the interpretation of editorial changes is highly charged with extra-textual meaning, and also highly speculative (no such remarks are made in the more sober *Serdtse edinoroga,* which notes a manuscript where the poem is entitled "Radel'naya pesnya" [854]). In any case, the poem is, as Klyuev's own remarks in his letter indicate, programmatic for an understanding of the "fraternal song" in general. Based on trochaic pentameter (characteristically, fulfilled more in the second half of the poem), it celebrates, in a sustained first-person plural, the collective joys of the brotherhood. With slight homoerotic overtones and with marked folkloric stylization (especially in the opening stanzas), the lyrical speakers welcome the realm of light:

Под ивушкой зеленой,
На муравчатом подножьи травном,
Где ветер-братик нас в уста целует,
Где соловушко-свирель поет-жалкует,
Соберемся-ка мы, други-братолюбцы,
Тихомудрой, тесною семейкой
Всяк с своей душевною жилейкой.
. . .
Да еще мы, братики, воспомним,
Дух утробу брашном сладостным накормим,

Как мы, духи, человечью плоть прияли,
Световязами, ловцами в мире стали,
Как рыбачили в водах Генисарета,
Где, Ты, — Альфа и Омега, Отче Света?
. . .
Мы восплещем, други, возликуем,
Заодно с соловкой пожалкуем,
С вешней ивой росно прослезимся,
В серафимский зрак преобразимся.
. . .
Мы восплещем зарными крылами.
Над кручиными, всерусскими полями,
Вдунем в борозды заплаканные нови
Дух живой всепобеждающей Любови,
И в награду, друженьки, за это
Вознесут нас крылья в лоно Света.

Under the green willow tree,
At its ant-run, grassy foot,
Where brother wind kisses our lips,
Where the nightingale pipe sings its complaint,
Let us gather, friends, brother-lovers,
As a peaceful, tight-knit family,
Each with his own spiritual pipe.
. . .
And moreover, dear brothers, let us remember,
Feeding our spirit hunger with sweet victuals,
How we, spirits, took on human flesh,
Became weavers of light, fishers in the world,
How we fished in the waters of the Sea of Galilee:
Where are You—Alpha and Omega, Father of Light?
. . .
We shall arise, friends, we shall rejoice,
Together with the nightingale we'll sing,
With the vernal willow we'll weep dew,
And be transformed into a seraphim eye.
. . .
We will flash our dawn wings
Above the sad all-Russian fields,
We will breathe into the tear-stained furrows of fresh soil
The spirit of all-conquering Love,

And as a reward, dear friends, for that
Wings will raise us to the bosom of the Light.

The juxtaposition of folkloric stylization, militant Christianity, fraternal homoeroticism, biblical, and apparently political references renders this hymn the quintessential *bratskaya pesnya.* Whether it was sung by Muscovite Old Believers is, of course, another matter altogether—but that the poet's claims seemed plausible at the time is evident, and telling.

The final poem (number thirty-two) in the large *Bratskie pesni* is entitled "Pesn' pokhoda." With the same title it appears as the penultimate (eighth) poem in the brochure, and the twenty-ninth and last poem of the "Bratskie pesni" section of *Pesnoslov.* The poem first appeared as "Pesn' brat'yam" ("Hymn to the Brothers") in *Novaya zemlya.* The *Pesnoslov* version differs considerably from earlier publications, omitting the first stanza, the penultimate stanza, and the final, separate couplet, which was preceded by two lines of ellipsis. A reader seeking the "true version" among posthumous editions may be a little confused, as in so many cases: *Polnoe sobranie sochinenii* reprints the *Pesnoslov* version; *Sochineniya* reprints the original version, but without the final lines (in other words, creating a new, posthumous version); Azadovsky, in his 1991 edition, *Stikhotvoreniya: Poemy,* provides the *Pesnoslov* version, as does *Serdtse edinoroga,* with somewhat confusing apparatus (853–54). Once again, textual instability is generated by a number of different but related factors: the poet's editorial practices; the context of his publication, republication (and nonrepublication—the poem's last appearance in print during his lifetime was in *Pesnoslov*) of the poem; and the editorial practices and constraints of posthumous publications. The editors of *Polnoe sobranie sochinenii,* it will be recalled, relied primarily on *Pesnoslov,* and did not have access to the same range of sources as the editors of *Sochineniya,* while editors in the Soviet Union worked both with similar and with other constraints. Meanwhile, the editors of *Sochineniya* were at pains to identify and restore "censored" or self-censored passages. Later Russian editions have continued to follow strictly the "author's last published version" rule, sometimes with annotation, sometimes without.

All of this editorial complexity cannot obscure the simplicity, even naivete, of the poem itself. It is in the most trite of meters for literary appropriations of folklore, trochaic tetrameter, with an entirely standard rhyme scheme (crossed, alternating masculine and feminine), but with a lexicon that is largely bereft of folkloric stylization. In contrast to most of the other lyrics examined here, it is relatively homogeneous, its general fields of reference being predictable for what Bazanov sees as a propaganda poem for the Golgotha Christians—the Bible and the liturgy; and the militant martyrology of politicized Christianity.[23]

*Иисуса крест кровавый —
*Наше знамя, меч и щит,
*Зверь из бездны семиглавый
*Перед ним не устоит.

Братья-воины, дерзайте
Встречу вражеским полкам!
Пеплом кос не посыпайте,
Жены, матери, по нам.

Наши груди — гор уступы,
Адаманты — рамена.
Под смоковничные купы
Соберутся племена.
. . .
В светлом лагере победы,
Как рассветный ветер гор,
Сокрушившего все беды,
Воспоет небесный хор, —

Херувимы, Серафимы . . .
И, как с другом дорогим,
Жизни Царь Дориносимый
Вечерять воссядет с ним. —
. . .
Гробовой избегнув клети,
Сопричастники живым,
Мы убийц своих приветим
Целованием святым:

*«Мир вам, странники-собратья,
*И, в блажентсве равный пай,
*Муки нашего распятья
*Вам открыли светлый рай.»

И враги, дрожа, тоскуя,
К нам на груди припадут . . .
Аллилуя, аллилуя —
Камни гор возопиют.

* . . . .
* . . . .

The bloody cross of Jesus
Is our banner, sword, and shield,
The seven-headed beast from Hell
Will not resist its power.

Warrior brothers, dare
To meet the enemy regiments!
Wives and mothers do not powder
Your tresses with ash for us.

Our chests are the spurs of mountains
Adamantine are our shoulders.
Beneath groves of fig trees
The tribes will assemble.
. . .
In the bright camp of victory,
Like the mountains' dawn wind,
A celestial choir will sing to
Him who crushed all ills,

Cherubim, Seraphim . . .
And, as with a friend beloved,
Life's King in majesty
Will sit down to dine with him.
. . .
Escaping the grave's containment,
Sharing with the living,
We shall greet our own destroyers
With a holy kiss.

"Peace be with you, brother-wanderers,
And in bliss an equal share,
The torments of our crucifixion
Have opened bright paradise for you."

And our enemies, trembling, yearning,
Shall fall upon our breasts . . .
Alleluia, alleluia,
Mountain stones shall cry out.

. . . .
. . . .

*Аллилуя, аллилуя —	Alleluia, alleluia,
*Сонмы сил возопиют . . .	Hosts of forces shall cry out.

(Lines marked with an asterisk are omitted in *Pesnoslov.*)

Here the characteristic clashing registers and referents are absent, as is the specific national and regional color (the *smokovnichnye kupy* are the clearest indication of that absence—fig trees would find the climate of northern Russian somewhat inclement). The poem is, indeed, programmatic, and consistently stylized.

One fraternal song, as defined above, remains, "Pesn' utesheniya," which was first published in a 1912 book by Iona Brikhnichev, and then as the ninth and last work in the brochure version of *Bratskie pesni.* It did not appear either in the large book version or anywhere in *Pesnoslov.* Indeed, it seems that Klyuev did not publish this poem again after its 1912 appearances (857). It is written in a fully sustained trochaic tetrameter, and, like "Pesn' pokhoda," is stylistically homogeneous. The opening and closing lines illustrate well its somewhat martial theme and tone:

Что вы, други, приуныли,	Why, friends, are you downcast,
Закручинились о чем,	What are you grieving over,
О безвестной ли могиле	About the unknown tomb
Аль о рае золотом?	Or about golden paradise?
О житейском хлебе-соли, —	About everyday plenty,
Изобильном животе,	Abundant life,
Аль от мук гвоздиной боли	Or from the torments of nail wounds
На невидимом кресте?	On an invisible cross?
. . .	. . .
Расплесните перья крылий,	Spread the feathers of your wings,
Просияйте молоньей —	Shine forth like lightning—
Красотой затмите зори,	With beauty eclipse the dawns,
Славу звезд, луны чертог,	The stars' glory, the palace of the moon,
Как бывало на Фаворе	As it was on Mount Tabor
У Христовых чистых ног.	At the pure feet of Christ.

These, then, are the fourteen core fraternal songs, according to the definition given earlier. In the large collection and in the *Pesnoslov* section they are, of course, surrounded by other works, some of them quite different in tone, and even as a core group they show great variety in manner and content (and indeed quality), while they often demonstrate individually the same instabilities which mark the very use of the term "Bratskie pesni" and the status of the various collections so entitled. As is characteristic for

Klyuev's work as a whole, they are contradictory in their genesis and in their status as finished works. They may, on the one hand, be regarded as an "organic" or "natural" development from the early poetry of social protest and individual lyricism, while, on the other hand, they are clearly programmatic poems, apparently written with a particular body of sponsors in mind (the "Golgotha Christians"). They were widely taken as authentic popular hymns (even by the poet himself, if his remark to Blok is to be taken literally), while they are also marked by a very literary and self-conscious preoccupation, shared by many Russian modernists, with the "elemental" and even erotic qualities hidden in the most elusive corners of the Russian national identity. They speak, at the very least, for an imagined sectarian collective, and they also articulate the poet's own sexuality (indeed, they seem to be among the first clear poetic markers of Klyuev's consciousness of his own sexual orientation). Such contradictions are at the heart of Klyuev's poetic oeuvre and his own identity as an author. And these contradictions are also reflected in and compounded by the reception and subsequent fate of his poetry.

In the symbolist period new collections of poetry were actively, widely, and quickly reviewed, and often—even if the authors in question were relatively unknown—the reviewers were established authors and arbiters of taste, as has been seen. Hence, the reception by literary Russia of Klyuev's large collection *Bratskie pesni* was easy to gauge in the discussion above. It is equally easy to see how the relationship of Klyuev's fraternal songs to their supposed popular models was understood. The reactions of Gumilev, among others, have already been noted. Like other reviewers, who praised *Bratskie pesni*, it was, above all, *authenticity* that he saw in the collection. Aleksandr Izmailov, at the time a prominent author and critic, gave another telling endorsement in the newspaper *Birzhevye vedomosti* (*Stock Market News*): "Give a few of his songs to an expert in Russian sectarianism and he will positively identify them as a product of sectarian lyricism and he will be, in his way, quite correct."[24]

In many ways, Klyuev's "fraternal" episode anticipates both his "patriotic" period, which produced his "Mirskie dumy," and his "revolutionary" enthusiasms, which occupied him intermittently from 1917 until the early 1920s. In that last period political passion and, perhaps, opportunism coincided with the general mood and with personal, misplaced religious expectation to produce a Christological version of Leninism. His patriotic poems and his later "revolutionary" works, expressing that odd (but not unique) ideological medley, were to provoke a diversity of responses. The revolutionary episode would conclude with the revelation by Trotsky of Klyuev's "duplicity." And here, too, the fraternal episode anticipates in a minor key, and with far less serious consequences for the poet, its revolutionary successor. At the end of 1912 Klyuev quarreled with his erstwhile sponsor Iona Brikhnichev, who had been promoting him as bearing within himself a "true Golgothan Christ."[25] In the aftermath of this break (its cause remains obscure), Brikhnichev wrote a pamphlet entitled *Novyi Khlestakov: Pravda o Nikolae Klyueve* (*The New Khlestakov: The Truth About Nikolai Klyuev*). Klyuev, as the title indicates, was accused—not for the first or last time—of insincerity and fraud. The fragments published from Brikhnichev's pamphlet (which he sent to Bryusov and Gorodetsky) indicate that its author now found Klyuev greedy, untruthful, and manipulative. But the primary accusation was that the poet was a *plagiarist*.

> In August 1909, in the Cossack village [*stanitsa*] of Sleptsovskaya in the Caucasus, I heard the hymn "He will come, He will come, and the mountains will tremble."
>
> *Literally* the very thing which was included in *Fraternal Songs*. The sectarians of "New Israel" were singing this hymn. It created a stunning impression on me then. I wanted to record it, but they would not let me.
>
> And in August of 1911 Klyuev read us a series of songs, including "He will come," and said that *these were not his songs but were recorded by him in Ryazan' guberniya*. In March 1912 Klyuev published this hymn *under his own signature*. And then included it in *Fraternal Songs*. [emphases in original][26]

The skeptic would wonder why Brikhnichev had waited so long to make such an accusation, while the cynic would doubt that in 1912 anyone could remember accurately a song heard in 1909, especially since it had been impossible to record it at that time. Meanwhile, the careful reader would note not only that the poem has a very literary form (anapestic dimeter, alternating feminine and masculine rhymes), but also that the "hymnlike" first three stanzas are followed by four individualized, "lyrical" stanzas, in which the speaker addresses his "sister" and predicts their eternal salvation. But more interesting than the ad hominem accusations or their rebuttal is the preoccupation with authenticity evident even in Brikhnichev's indictment. Here it is naive and confused, but it is evident in more sophisticated form in many other reactions. This preoccupation reiterates one of the major themes in the perception of Klyuev and the reception of his work. Meanwhile Brikhnichev's narrative of events suggests, like Klyuev's preface to the larger collection *Bratskie pesni,* that the poet himself made contradictory claims about the origin of his "songs." Brikhnichev's story finds some confirmation, as Azadovsky points out, in a remark Klyuev made to Esenin in a letter of 1915: "I visited your *guberniya,* lived with flagellants in Dan'kovsky county, very good and interesting people, I returned from them with fraternal songs" (*Sd* 238).[27] Klyuev here seems to suggest that the poems he had published as his own fraternal songs were taken from the sectarians whom he had met while staying, in 1911, with one Grigorii Eremin, a sectarian resident of the village of Gremyachka in Dan'kovsky county (although the exact phrasing of his remark, *ot nikh ya vynes bratskie pesni,* is ambiguous—does he mean *his own* fraternal songs, or just *some* fraternal songs; does he mean that he brought back the *idea* of fraternal songs, or the texts themselves?). Yet even this remark conceals as much as it reveals, for Klyuev went to Gremyachka to visit Leonid Semenov (Semenov-Tyan-Shansky), who had abandoned his life as a man of letters and Petersburg *intelligent* in order to "go to the people." In other words, if Klyuev's claim to have brought his fraternal songs back from the country is taken at face value, it should also be noted that his route to the Ryazan' sectarians (and, therefore, to his songs) was not direct, but via literary St. Petersburg.[28]

And what of the sectarian songs themselves? The general enthusiasm for the Old Belief, and the specific fascination with Russian sectarianism had led, by the 1910s, to many investigations of the hidden and intriguing culture of religion outside the established church. Already a generation before Russian modernism, such works as Dobrotvorsky's *Lyudi bozh'i* (*God's People,* 1869) and Reutsky's *Lyudi bozh'i i skoptsy* (*God's People and Castrati,* 1872) had helped to introduce sectarians to the reading public, at roughly the same time as Leskov and Mel'nikov were treating mainstream Old Believers in their fiction, and Mel'nikov was also writing on sectarians.[29] Although the works of Dobrotvorsky and Reutsky were products of state-sponsored, even official hostility (which also left its mark on Leskov and Mel'nikov), they provided documentary accounts of the history and contemporary activities of sectarians, drawing on evidence presented in court cases when sectarians had been prosecuted. Reutsky suggested a genealogy for the *khlysty* and the *skoptsy* (the latter descended in part from the former) which traced the sects back to the late seventeenth century, and to a blending of schismatic—Old Believer—and imported, schismatic, Protestant belief. Reutsky also quotes both startling accounts of enforced castrations in nineteenth-century Moscow and, copiously, sectarian songs. The first foreign account of Russian sectarianism is said to have been *Études sur la situation intérieure, la vie nationale et les institutions rurales de la Russie* by Baron Auguste de Haxtausen (Hanover, 1847), and it was he who seems to have first associated flagellants with sexual promiscuity (i.e., their commission of the infamous *sval'nyi grekh* [group sin] during religious ecstasies).[30] In the second half of the nineteenth century, treatments tended to modulate between hostility and enthralled interest, with an admixture of prurient fascination with the more extreme supposed sexual practices of sects. Almost all authors seem to have quoted sectarian songs, sometimes at length. Interest in sectarian songs even arose abroad: a collection of *khlyst* songs was published with brief commentary in Austria in 1885.[31]

By the first decade of the twentieth century, interest in and at least passing familiarity with sectarians as well as the Old Belief was widespread—hence, for example, Rozanov's essay "Poezdka k khlystam" ("Trip to the Flagellants") of 1904–05, generally considered one of the best treatments of the subject, and frequent allusions in the poetry and fiction of the period, from Blok and Bely to Kuzmin.[32] Bal'mont's collection *Zelenyi vertograd* of 1909, it will be recalled, is based on sectarian motifs as mediated through the general literary preoccupations of the period, while Kuzmin's *Osennie ozera* (*Autumn Lakes,* 1912) contains stylizations of *dukhovnye stikhi* (spiritual verses). Kuzmin's literary/cultural fascination with the Old Belief provides several interesting parallels and contrasts with those of Klyuev.[33] Meanwhile, Mel'nikov's Old Believers and sectarians in the novels *V lesakh* (*In the Woods*) and *Na gorakh* (*In the Mountains*) had their somewhat distant fictional descendants in those of Merezhkovsky (*Antikhrist: Petr i Aleksei* [*The Antichrist: Peter and Aleksei*], the third part of his "trilogy") and of Bely in his *Serebryannyi golub'* (*Silver Dove*). The fascination with the Old Belief and Russian sectarianism was partially predicated upon and fed by the myths of sexual promiscuity and ritual murder among the *khlysty* and *skoptsy,* while the notion of the popular, "elemental," potentially revolutionary spirit of these groups also attracted authors. It is also characteristic that Old Believers and sectarians, although radically different in many ways, were and still are often run together in the popular imagination, not least because the established church expressed similar hostility both to the "priestless" Old Believers and to the more radical sectarians.

Characteristic, too, of much of this interest was the paradoxical combination of exoticism and national observation: the Old Believers and sectarians were at one and the same time seen as fascinatingly but dangerously alien (even to the extent of practicing outrageous acts of mass sexual intercourse and cannibalism) and as quintessentially and archaically *Russian.* Hence they formed a very powerful, flexible, and even contradictory means of depicting the national self—both one's own and alien—thereby collapsing in certain ways the traditional Russian opposition of *svoi* (the possessive pronoun meaning one's own, analogous to the Latin *suus*) and *chuzhoi* (not one's own, another's, alien). Their alienness could also be recovered, however, in another familiar Russian dichotomy—between people and intelligentsia, for Russian dissenters were almost exclusively of the *narod.* But even here, as the individual examples of Kuzmin, Rozanov, Semenov, and others suggest, the dichotomy could be dismantled in alluringly transgressive ways—not all Old Believers were remote from the mainstream of Russian society; the sectarians could be visited and even joined by members of the intelligentsia. Moreover, by the later decades of the nineteenth century, some Old Believers and many descendants of Old Believers, latterly converted to Orthodoxy, had become very prominent in Russian society, as the great merchant families—many of whom came from the old faith—achieved financial and cultural prominence in society, thus giving yet another, contradictory, dimension to the image and meaning of alternative popular religion for Russian modernism.

Needless to say, a preoccupation with the "exotic" content of Russian heresies and heretical communities was more common than scientific study, but folklorists, for example, did study Russian sects, and in 1912, the very year of Klyuev's *Bratskie pesni,* a collection of over seven hundred sectarian songs was published: Rozhdestvensky and Uspensky's *Pesni russkikh sektantov-mistikov* (*Songs of Russian Mystic Sectarians*), which draws upon both published and unpublished sources.[34] While prolonged scholarly investigation would be required to establish in detail the relationship between actual sectarian songs, as sung in the early twentieth century, and Klyuev's *bratskie pesni,* the songs from that collection provide a sufficiently large sample of sectarian folk poetry to permit the reader to reach some general conclusions. At the same time, it must be assumed that most of Klyuev's readers did not have such materials in mind or to hand when they read and judged his fraternal songs. They were more attuned to the familiar fictional treatments, to the images of Old Believer and sectarian culture propagated in the poetry of the symbolists and their near contemporaries, and to the widespread stereotypes outlined above. What Klyuev himself knew and had at his disposal at the time—and where it came from (personal encounters, native knowledge, reading, or a combination of such diverse sources)—is almost certain to remain unclear.

A cursory examination of the songs quoted by Reutsky and his successors suggests—not surprisingly—that the distance between Klyuev's poems and the songs of the sectarians themselves is considerable, although many features of those songs are certainly reminiscent of Klyuev's poetry, even if the context is quite different. Sectarian songs are often narrative, blending biblical and recent events, and sometimes citing historical figures (sectarians or their enemies) and actual toponyms. In some, an individual speaker (frequently female) addresses the divinity or sings of love for Him. Many summon the Almighty or call for His blessing. Often they make the familiar sectarian associations of godliness, purity, and *radenie* (ecstatic worship). The songs vary considerably in length, and some consist of well over one hundred lines. Rozhdestvensky and Uspensky, who see no clear distinction between flagellant and castrati works, caution that the songs frequently combine quite heterogeneous elements, while dividing them into the following thematic categories: songs about historical sectarian figures; songs addressed to unnamed leaders of their society; songs about sectarian society as a whole (descriptions of the sectarian "vessel" or garden, accounts of persecutions, calls for mortification of the flesh, and so on); ritual songs (various stages of the *radenie*); events from the Gospels, and so on, narrated as sectarian commentaries; and mixed songs.[35] Although Rozhdestvensky and Uspensky speak of the lexical obscurity of many of the songs, the glossary they provide consists largely of explanations of proper nouns and commentaries on the specific usage of common words (*belyi, znamya, krug, sad* [white, banner, circle, garden]). There are few genuine archaisms in their songs (as they point out, many are of recent origin), and even folk usages are relatively familiar and unproblematic. There seems to be little evidence of dialect in most of the songs (none of which, it should be added, seems to have been recorded in northern Russia), and, of course, there are few genuinely "literary" stylistic markers.

Much here recalls Klyuev's fraternal songs, and sometimes his mature poetics as a whole: for example, the blending of the biblical with the modern, and the widespread mixing of abstract and concrete in general; the accessibility of the divinity to personal address; and the preoccupation with describing the society of brethren, its practices, and its relationship to the rest of society. Formal features are also shared between these songs and Klyuev's poems: the former, marking their relatively recent origins, usually rhyme and often employ literary meters or variants thereof (in contrast to most Russian folk poetry); many contain elements of dialogue or, at least, direct speech, like some of Klyuev's fraternal songs (exchanges between speaker and Savior, for example); and while there are no hints of the eroticism of popular perception, nor, of course, any homoeroticism, the image of Christ the awaited bridegroom is frequent, and the ecstatic nature of *radenie* is frequently emphasized. As Rozhdestvensky and Uspensky emphasize, the language of sectarian songs is allegorical and pictorial (*obraznyi*)—for example, the sectarian world is often depicted as a vessel or as a garden with trees (sometimes cypress trees, as in Klyuev's "O, pospeshite, brat'ya, k nam").

At the same time the language, point of view, overall structure, frequent narrative and historical elements, and above all, stylistic and thematic homogeneity all distinguish the sectarian songs very clearly from Klyuev's works. And, of course, his fraternal songs have their own, very specific, sexual agenda.

Brief quotation of songs from Rozhdestvensky and Uspensky's collection will illustrate some of these points. The twenty-ninth song in the collection, about the founder of the *skoptsy* Kondratii Selivanov, begins thus:

От белой зари, от белой зари
От Восток-страны, от Иркутския
Выкатало к нам красно солнышко,

Красно солнышко, сударь батюшко,
Сударь батюшко, искупитель свет,
Ты Сион, гора превысокая!

From white dawn, from white dawn
From Eastern land, from Irkutsk land
There came to us a fine sun
A fine sun, a master and father,
Master and father, bright redeemer,
You, Zion, mighty mountain!

This song is characteristic of the narrative works, conveying in partly allegorical terms the actual story of Andrei/Kondratii Ivanov/Selivanov (died 1832).

Garden imagery, characteristic of sectarian models of religion, and the use of direct speech are both exemplified by the opening of the 203rd song:

На Сионских на горах	On Zion mountains
Стоял царский вертоград,	There stood a royal garden,
Плодовитый дерев сад.	A fruitful orchard garden
А кто этот сад садил,	And the man who planted it,
Тому Дух Святой сходил,	To him descended the Holy Ghost,
Большую радость сотворил,	Brought great joy,
«Христос воскрес» говорил.	Said, "Christ is risen.
«Во истину» — повторил.	"Risen indeed," repeated.

Christ is summoned during flagellant *radenie* in the 428th song, here reproduced in its entirety:

Хлыщу, хлыщу,	I lash, I lash,
Христа ищу.	I seek Christ.
Сниде к нам, Христе,	O Christ, come down to us,
Со седьмаго небесе,	From seventh heaven,
Походи с нами, Христе,	Walk with us, O Christ,
Во святом кругу,	In sacred circle,
Сокати с небеси,	Descend from heaven,
Сударь Дух Святой.	Lord Holy Ghost.

The "most important flagellant prayer," essential to any *radenie,* is reproduced in a number of variants. Below is the first variant (song 365):

Дай нам, Господи,	Give us, O Lord,
К нам Иисуса Христа,	Give to us Jesus Christ,

Дай нам, сударь, Сына Божия	Give us, master, the Son of God
И помилуй, сударь, нас.	And have mercy on us, master.
С нами Дух сударь Святый.	With us is the Holy Ghost master.
Господь, помилуй, сударь, нас.	Lord, have mercy, master, upon us.
Пресвятая Богородица,	Most holy Mother of God,
Упроси, мой свет, об нас	Beg, my light, for us
Света Сына твоего,	Your Bright Son,
Бога нашего святого.	Our holy God.
Свет тобой спасен,	Light saved by you,
Государь души нашей.	Lord of our soul
Без тебя, мой свет,	Without you, my light,
Много грешных на земле,	There are many sinners on the earth,
На сырой земле — на матушке	On the wet mother earth,
На сударыне кормилице.	Our mistress and provider.

A final example is provided by a song (no. 435) said to be sung by the "sisters" of a sect alone during *radenie:*

Девство сохранили,	We've preserved our virginity,
Венцы не уронили;	Not dropped our crowns;
У Бога живого	We've lived under the protection
Жили под покровом,	Of the living God,
Под всем верным словом:	According to the all-true word:
Евангелие читали,	We've read the gospel,
Радели на круге,	Danced ecstatic circles,
Были верны слуги;	Been loyal servants,
О душах тужили,	Grieved for our souls,
Чины заслужили;	Deserved our orders;
Берегли все дело;	Protected our cause;
У нас птица пела,	The bird sang for us,
Юность утешала,	Consoled our youth,
В небо поспешала;	Hastened to heaven;
Юность духом пела,	Youth sang in spirit,
В царство захотела;	Desired the kingdom
Богом занялася;	Heeded God,
В крылах поднялася;	Was raised on wings;
Пела, веселилась,	Sang, rejoiced,
В чистоте явилась . . .	Appeared in purity.

While similarities and differences between Klyuev's works and the folk originals, as outlined above, are evident, perhaps the most striking (if entirely predictable) distinction is an overall one: in the sectarian songs the *functional* predominates—they convey information pertinent to the faith of the singer, they serve a clear spiritual purpose as prayers and hymns, they celebrate a collective moment of religious ecstasy. In Klyuev's poems these functions become aesthetic echoes, and the relatively monolithic combination of form and function evident in the folk works is broken. At the same time, Klyuev's own fraternal songs do claim a functional element, as the very title *Bratskie pesni* implies, as Klyuev himself stated in his letter to Blok and in his prefatory remarks to the large collection, and as the relationship between the poet and the Golgotha Christians very evidently demonstrates. However, that functional element does not predominate over the aesthetic—which may help to explain the break with the Golgothans. On the other hand, it is easy to understand why so many readers chose to privilege the "authentic" element in Klyuev's fraternal songs, when those works are placed beside the poems of Bal'mont and Kuzmin, which were also products of that general early twentieth-century fascination with sectarianism and the Old Belief. Bal'mont's works are characterized by a monolithic lyric stylization, clearly suggested by *Slova potseluinye* (*Words to Kiss by*), the subtitle of his *Zelenyi vertograd,* from which an egregiously aestheticized piece of erotica has already been quoted. Elsewhere in Bal'mont's collection, some of the terminology and motifs of sectarianism are employed, but in a purely aestheticized (and sometimes lyric-erotic) context:

Отчего душа болит, а уму не говорит?
  Я люблю. Я люблю.
Отчего огонь в крови, хоть зови, хоть не зови?
  Я люблю. Я люблю.
Отчего на небесах звезды ясные в венцах?
  Я люблю. Я люблю . . .[36]

Why does my soul ache, but speak not to my mind?
  I love. I love.
Why is my blood on fire, whether you summon me or not?
  I love. I love.
Why are the clear stars in the heavens wearing crowns?
  I love. I love . . .

Kuzmin and Klyuev perhaps have more in common in their use of motifs and forms from popular religious poetry. Some of Kuzmin's "spiritual verses" in *Osennie ozera* are expressly folkloric in manner while being largely without stylization, but unlike Klyuev's fraternal songs, Kuzmin's works are aesthetically integral—without the fractures which so mark many of Klyuev's most interesting works. Kuzmin's "Stikh o pustyne" ("Poem

About the Wilderness") describes the lyrical speaker's aspiration to solitary contemplation in a manner which is thematically reminiscent of Klyuev, but stylistically quite different.[37]

Я младой, я бедный юнош,	I'm young, I'm a poor youth,
Я Бога боюся,	I fear God,
Я пойду да во пустыню	I shall go even into the wilderness
Богу помолюся.	I shall pray to God.
Молодое мое тело	With fasting I shall tire
Постом утрудити,	My young body,
Мои глазоньки пресветлы	With tears I shall shroud
Слезами затмити.	My bright eyes.
. . .	. . .
Не взыщу я питей пьяных,	I shall not seek for strong drink,
Друзей прелюбезных.	Nor for loving friends.
Дерева, вы деревочки,	Trees, my dear trees,
Мои братцы милы,	You are my kind brothers,
А береза белоножка	And white-limbed birch
Дорога сестрица.	Dear sister.
О, прекрасная пустыня,	O fine wilderness,
Мати всеблагая,	Mother bountiful,
Приими свое ты чадо	Accept me your child
В свои сладкие недра!	Into your sweet bosom!

With time, the tendency to perceive Klyuev's fraternal songs as simply an outgrowth of the folkloric model became refined among his readers. Boris Filippov's long essays introducing the two Western collections (1953 and 1969)—essays which were undoubtedly as influential in promoting a certain view of the poet in his homeland as in the West—suggest that Klyuev's *khlystovshchina* (imitation of the flagellant sect) should be seen in combination with the religio-philosophical currents of the first two decades of the century. In effect, Filippov presents a sophisticated model of Klyuev's conceptual eclecticism, although he does not interrogate the literary material in which it is embedded, preferring to remark apropos of *Bratskie pesni* that many of the poems "directly echo *khlyst* compositions" (1:21). In the apparatus to the 1969 edition, Filippov's commentaries on individual poems, both from *Bratskie pesni* and from other parts of Klyuev's oeuvre, reinforce this position (1:521–22, 541, 545–46, 550–51, 553, 561, 565). Emmanuel Rais, author of another extended essay on the poet in that edition, although troubled by Klyuev's readiness to combine Old Believer and flagellant materials, takes the sectarian elements as evidence of authentic *khlystovstvo* (membership of a flagellant sect), while emphasizing the complexity of Klyuev's aesthetics and worldview. Rais's approach also implies that the emergence of such materials in Klyuev's oeuvre coincides with the poet freeing himself from the early symbolist influences which produced the most derivative verse of his early years—an implication which produces key insights for the narrative of Klyuev's poetic career (1:69, 75). However, neither author writes at length about *Bratskie pesni* specifically.

In Russia, among the scholars who worked for many years on Klyuev, Vasilii Bazanov alone seems to have devoted serious attention to the fraternal songs themselves. His posthumously published book includes a chapter on *Bratskie pesni* and the Golgotha Christians. For Bazanov, constrained by his time and place of writing, they are largely works of propaganda, inspired by the Golgotha Christians, and all too many are distinguished by their poor quality.[38] Azadovsky provides a fuller account of Klyuev's role in the Golgotha Christian movement, while also reminding his readers of that movement's place within the general religio-social tendencies of the time and of its relationship to the activities of one of the major intellectual centers of the period, the Petersburg Religio-Philosophical Society. As for *Bratskie pesni,* Azadovsky is—characteristically—inclined to read the poems partly as works of striking originality and partly as works of *stilizatsiya* (stylization). This last term is often applied by those hostile to Klyuev, who see in his work a fatally literary imitation of the "outer form" of the popular, but Azadovsky is more cautious.[39] His judgment is intriguing: "The striking, gifted, and original poet and the crafty man of popular learning and stylizer grew more and more within him and came closer and closer to one another. It was as if Klyuev was turning into an actor, playing himself. One may think that in this is one of his unexplained 'mysteries.' "[40] It is equally interesting that this view of the poet, from Azadovsky's book of 1990, is not entirely at one with the rather more critical and even hostile view evident in his 1993 preface to the poet's autobiographical "The Loon's Fate," discussed in chapter 4, yet is repeated verbatim in the new version of his biography of the poet, published in 2002. Klyuev's identity, literary and personal, continues to challenge his students.

Since the beginning of the 1990s two American scholars have written on Klyuev. John Ogden's doctoral dissertation explores the fraternal songs, and analyzes in some detail the history of relations between the popular and the literary, thus providing a background to the reception of Klyuev's works.[41] Ronald Vroon devotes two articles to the issues explored here with regard to *Bratskie pesni:* in one he attempts to place Klyuev on a spectrum running from stylization to popular by comparing Klyuev's use of garden imagery to that of other "new-peasant" poets and to the symbolists; in the other he reads Klyuev's use of "sacred speech" against the background of the poet's interest in and relationship to both sectarianism and the Old Belief.[42] Vroon, removed from the ideological immediacy of the implied debate which seems to pervade discussions by all native Russophone scholars and which is also (and abundantly) evident in more popular treatments of Klyuev in his homeland, provides a series of suggestive, although inevitably tentative, conclusions: Klyuev's use of language does differ from the symbolists and from the other "new-peasant" poets, and is closer to the language of popular religious poetry than is the case with his contemporaries; Klyuev's apparent claims to affiliation both with mainstream Old Belief and with sectarianism are inherently contradictory, but not necessarily evidence of purely stylized literary borrowing; on the contrary, Klyuev was evidently very sympathetic to aspects of both the Old Believer and *khlyst* worldviews, and shared the hostility of Russia's religious dissenters for many aspects of established society and of modernity. Several authors have emphasized the similarities between some of the fraternal songs and exemplary sectarian folk poetry (Filippov and Vroon cite particular examples), although Ogden's observation that Klyuev's folk-related poetry *may begin with quotation, only to move rapidly away from the source* is worth bearing in mind.[43] But most authors who have looked at *Bratskie pesni* have, of necessity, encountered broader issues of the sort already explored in these pages. And everyone writing on the subject (as on Klyuev in general) has encountered the problem of perspective.

Indeed, a multiple perspective is demanded by these and many other of Klyuev's works: they must be seen as both popular and literary, functional and aesthetic, original as poetry and close to collective origins. Any examination of them also illuminates the inherent contradictions and instabilities which are characteristic of those many works of Russian literature which self-consciously modulate between the oral and the literary. Here, as elsewhere in Klyuev's oeuvre, the physical instabilities of textuality intersect with the conceptual instabilities of aesthetics.

Equally important for the history of the reception of Klyuev's fraternal songs is the fact that publications of and about the culture of Russian sectarians and, to a large extent, the Old Belief itself came more or less to an end in the second decade of the twentieth century. For obvious reasons, publications of religious folklore in general, and sectarian songs in particular, not to mention studies of such materials or works of art inspired by them, were very limited until the end of the Soviet period. Consequently, just as the image of Klyuev the sectarian peasant poet was predicated initially on early twentieth-century cultural fashion, so it has been predicated latterly on the cultural remoteness of that fashion and on the virtual extinction of the source of the fashion. Meanwhile, the main lines of early twentieth-century Russian modernism were one of the major preoccupations of Russian philological scholarship in the later Soviet period. Although traced only cautiously in print, they were meticulously studied by the best postwar scholars, whose own activities were of great cultural and political import as acts of intellectual resistance and integrity. Hence, it became increasingly difficult to accept Klyuev, a poet whose place in Russian modernism was predicated upon his appeal to a worldview (and indeed, to a world) quite remote from modernism itself. Partly for that reason, the bipolar reception of the fraternal songs and many similar works has been sustained to the present day. The questions of "authenticity," "originality," and the genuinely popular remain as ideologically tense as they were when Klyuev was first embraced and then rejected by the leader of the Golgotha Christians. The objections raised eventually by the embittered Brikhnichev and the stories told by him and by Klyuev speak to the emblematic significance of the authentically popular in high culture—one of the recurrent contradictions of Russian culture as a whole in the last two centuries. Only once it has been identified and assimilated by high culture can the popular voice speak and be acknowledged, but once that assimilation has taken place, the voice, of course, can no longer be regarded as collective or even popular.

Hence, the conceptual contradictions and polarities which mark both the initial reception of Klyuev and, indeed, the poet's own making and remaking of himself continue not only to dominate discussions but also to construct poetic texts as contextually and conceptually unstable. Meanwhile, the relationship between concepts and material circumstances, so important for an understanding of the creation, preservation, partial destruction, and limited distribution of Klyuev's oeuvre is also relevant to an understanding of the situation of the poet as a published author today. For example, it is true that the print-runs of the few editions of Klyuev prepared in Russia in the last thirty years have been (for that country, at least) relatively small; that several important editions were produced by houses rather distant from the main centers of Russian publishing; and that many of Klyuev's poems were not republished in Russia between the early 1920s and the very end of the twentieth century, while many recent publications have come in journals which most readers would only be able to locate in major academic libraries.

At first glance, this account would seem to be typical of the publishing history of many major Russian modernist poets in the late Soviet period: limited and inaccessible publication (in other words, an author could be described in official sources as "published," while remaining very hard for the average reader actually to read). But such observations overlook one simple fact, which distinguishes Klyuev from many of his confrères: whereas, during the "book boom" of the 1970s and 1980s, almost all new editions of authors who might be considered "problematic" for official Soviet cultural policy sold out immediately after (or even before) publication, and could be obtained subsequently only with great difficulty, at least three late-Soviet editions of Klyuev did not sell out quickly. They are *Izbrannoe*, a "popular" edition produced in 1981 by Bazanov and Shevtsova on the basis of their earlier academic edition, which could still be found for sale in book shops in the mid-1990s; the Kunyaevs' *Stikhotvoreniya i poemy* of 1986 (published in Archangel); and Stanislav Kunyaev's small edition of the same name, published in 1991 in the series "Twentieth Century: Poet and Time" by the publishing house Molodaya gvardiya (Moscow). By the early 1990s there was no rarity value in editions of previously problematic authors, so the 1991 edition would hold far less attraction for the Russian reader, and in the early 1990s book distribution was very uneven (hence the largely regional availability of Subbotin and Kostin's *Pesnoslov* [Petrozavodsk, 1990]), so the fate of Kunyaev's edition of 1991 is no surprise. But the widespread availability of the 1981 *Izbrannoe* many years later testifies to a very important fact: Klyuev has a disproportionately large number of scholarly readers, but attracts few of the (many) general readers of Russian poetry. In other words, by the late twentieth century he had become more *physically* than *conceptually* accessible to the reader of Russian verse.

The fraternal songs form part of an episode in Klyuev's professional biography, largely restricted to the early 1910s, but some of their features are to be found again and again in his later poetry, in his prose, and in his "created lives," while other aspects of his later life and work share typological similarities with the fraternal episode. His next collection, *Lesnye byli* of 1913, containing works more or less contemporaneous with *Bratskie pesni,* is oriented more to the peasant world in general, and to Klyuev's mythologization of that world. There is little or no trace of the homoerotic aspects of the "fraternal" in *Lesnye byli,* while the collective voice of *Bratskie pesni* is also largely absent. Indeed, the peasant-oriented poems here often have a female lyrical speaker (for example, "Posadskaya" ["Settlement Song," 164–66]). The title "Lesnye byli" does, however, share the instability of designation noted for "Bratskie pesni": the collection of that name is radically different from the section so called in *Pesnoslov.* In that new version of "Lesnye byli" religious and mystical motifs are largely representative of the supposed dualities of Russian popular beliefs—Christian and simultaneously "pagan." In Klyuev's next collection, *Mirskie dumy* (1916), the popular, collective voice is heard again, sometimes in the totally new context of the patriotic hymns. "Besednyi naigrysh, stikh dobropisnyi" ("Conversational Folk Tune, a Sound Verse," 273–78) confirms the compositional associations between Klyuev's popular "civic" verse and sectarian thematics. The opening section of the poem alludes to the current war and contains the much-quoted reference to the "zheleznoe tsarstvo/So Vil'gel'mishchem, tsarishchem poganym" ("iron kingdom/With Wilhelm-giant, godless emperor"), but it is preceded by an epigraph supposedly drawn from a secret sectarian scroll. It is not the only poem in *Mirskie dumy* with a sectarian epigraph: "Skrytnyi stikh" ("Secret

Verse," 205–8) is prefaced by lines "from the songs of Olonian *skrytniki* [secret sectarians]." The sectarian features, however, are largely superficial, for "Skrytnyi stikh" is a narrative poem, describing in somewhat obscure terms the assembly of a brotherhood to lament the appearance of a modern, industrial evil (the poem runs together Klyuev's patriotic and anti-urban themes). It was also the occasion of a letter to his editor, Viktor Mirolyubov, setting out a sort of artistic credo (characteristically odd in language and even punctuation), and claiming that the obscure terms in the poem were all authentic and northern:

> It was composed under the unbearable pressure of those images and words with which the countryside is full at the moment. To recast those images and words so that they would fit those who know the people superficially and have no idea of the inner content of "forbidden" [*zarochnye*], "secret" [*potainye*], "absolving" [*otpusknye*] words of everyday popular sorcery (I should say, popular fakirism), with which the people speak heart and soul—to recast them would be a sin. And therefore in this piece, wherever harmony and the power of the word demanded it, I left untouched genuinely popular words and images, which I ask not to be taken as purely Olonian, as they (words, dialect) are firmly entrenched, as I know from experience, in all of northern Russia and Siberia. A certain density of images and of words such as those mentioned above, which may, on first glance, seem a misuse of them—was produced in what I wrote quite freely, according to the same secret instructions and laws, according to which, for example, are created Indian temples, which present, for the refined taste of the European (which in fact is not derived from the depths of nature), an insane abundance and chaos of sculptures of gods, tigers, women, elephants, many-winged and many-visaged creatures. (*Sd* 217)

This commentary illustrates how tied was Klyuev's interest in the sectarian worldview (at least as he—and others—constructed it) to the rest of his aesthetic program and practice: the secret, mysterious density of language and imagery is emphasized, with very marked words used to designate secrecy and sorcery, yet it is associated not only with a very local and specific culture but also with certain cultural universals, albeit supposedly inaccessible to refined European taste. Indeed, the relationship between the "secret," "hidden" culture of the Russian north and the Orient (particularly India) was to be an abiding theme in his work from this time on, with an implied parallel between Russian popular religion and the spiritual world of the East.

Among the poems from the collections *Lesnye byli* and *Mirskie dumy* which migrate to the section "Pesni iz Zaonezh'ya" in *Pesnoslov*, "Sizyi golub'" was associated with the songs of the *skoptsy* by the editors of *Sochineniya*, while they claimed that "Stikh o pravednoi dushe" recalled spiritual verses and "Proslavlenie milostyni" the religious songs of beggars ("Grey Dove," "Poem about a Righteous Soul," "Praise of Alms," 187–88, 229–30, 222–23; 1:541, 542).

It is *Pesnoslov* itself which provides the next major account of Klyuev's poetry, and its reformation of earlier designations has already been mentioned. The three sections which comprise its second volume, "Serdtse edinoroga" ("Heart of the Unicorn"), "Dolina edinoroga" ("Valley of the Unicorn"), and "Krasnyi ryk" ("Red Roar"), do not correspond in title, nor, for the most part, in contents, to earlier collections, but they do sustain the thematic interest in popular religion observed earlier in the 1910s. Many poems present a syncretic view of peasant practice and belief, combining canonical Christian motifs with mythologized elements and places of peasant activity:

В дымовище сгинул бес,
Печь, как старица, вздохнула;
За окном бугор и лес
Зорька в сыту окунула.

Там, минуючи зарю,
Ширь безвестных плоскогорий,
Одолеть судьбу-змею
Скачет пламенный Егорий.

На задворки вышел Влас
С вербой, в венчике сусальном . . .
Золотой, воскресный час,
Просиявший в безначальном.

The devil vanished into the chimney,
The stove sighed like an old nun;
Beyond the window dawn plunged
Hill and woods into honey water.

There, bypassing dawn,
Expanses of unknown plateaus,
In order to overcome the dragon fate,
Gallops flame-bright St. George.

Into the backyard came Vlas
With a pussy willow and a tinsel halo,
The golden resurrection hour,
Shining in that which has no beginning.

Many features of this poem ("Brodit temen' po izbe" ["Darkness wanders round the house"], 240–41; in the cycle "Izbyanye pesni"), from lexicon to meter, proclaim its literary stylization of popular religion and mark its distance from the "fraternal songs." However, while such is probably the predominant presentation of the "spiritual" in these sections of *Pesnoslov,* sectarian motifs and forms associated with the earlier fraternal poems resurface here, sometimes beside a growing number of references to the Old Belief.

The revolutionary period and Klyuev's association with Ivanov-Razumnik's "Scythians" make aspects of schismatic and sectarian belief and practice once more directly apposite. In "Dolina edinoroga" a series of poems, several striking for their homoeroticism, recast earlier sectarian motifs, this time with a strong admixture of explicit *skoptsy* references. As is so often the case, the location of such works within the overall section is noteworthy. "Dolina edinoroga" contains a number of Klyuev's most explicitly programmatic statements on the superiority of the country to the town, and of nature to man. "Olenii gusak sladkozvuchnee Glinki" ("The innards of deer sound sweeter than Glinka," 318–19), which itself precedes his polemical and programmatic poems to Esenin, is one example. Another is "Trud" ("Labor," 386–87), which opens:

> Свить сенный воз мудрее, чем создать
> «Войну и мир» иль Шиллера балладу.
>
> To tie together a cart of hay is finer than to create
> *War and Peace* or a Schiller ballad.

That this is a paradoxical—because *literary*—attack on literature need hardly be stated—the punning use of *mudree* (meaning both "wise" and "difficult") in the very first line provides an emblem of that paradox. There is further obvious literary play in those opening lines—as Azadovsky points out, the author of *War and Peace* himself would certainly have agreed with Klyuev's relative evaluation of agricultural and literary labor.[44] This very programmatic poem precedes, in "Dolina edinoroga," three of the most strikng poems to reiterate—in characteristic contrast—aspects of the original fraternal songs: "Gromovye, vladychnye shagi," "Dva yunoshi ko mne prishli," and "Brat'ya, eto korni zhizni" ("Thunderous, masterful steps," "Two young men came to me," "Brothers, these are the roots of life," 323–25, 366–67). In these poems, and others such as "Budet brachnaya noch', sovershenie tain," "O skopchestvo — venets, zolotoglavyi grad," and some of the eight poems of the cycle "Spas" ("There will be a wedding night, the completion of mysteries," "O castrati sect—the crown, the gold-headed city," "Savior"; 351, 333, 341–51), evidently sectarian themes, motifs, language, and images are used in conjunction with a more individual voice than in the original fraternal songs (the speaker is often the agent, even the progenitor, of spirituality), but share the latter's homoerotic and even sadomasochistic moments. As is so often the case in Klyuev's poetry of this period and subsequently, the language of revelations (and of Revelation) is not only employed, but also redirected toward specific themes quite alien to the sectarian context. The final lines of "O skopchestvo—venets, zolotglavyi grad" illustrate well the conjunction of sectarianism, cultural eclecticism, programmatic literary polemics, discursive fragmentation, and even playfulness that are all typical of the poet:

О скопчество — арап на пламенном коне,
Гадательный узор о незакатном дне,
Когда безудный муж, как отблеск маргарит,
Стокрылых сыновей и ангелов родит!
Когда колдунью-Страсть с владыкою-Блудом
Мы в воз потерь и бед одрами запряжем,
Чтоб время-ломовик об них сломало кнут . . .

Пусть критики меня невеждой назовут.

O castrate sect—Negro on a flaming steed,
Clairvoyant pattern of the endless day,
When an unsexed man shall give birth, like pearl to light,
To hundred-winged sons and angels!
When we shall harness to the heavy cart of losses and misfortunes
The sorceress Passion and the monarch Fornication,
That time the drayman should break his whip on them . . .

Now let the critics call me ignorant.

The final line, standing alone and presenting a radical change in direction (simultaneously deflating all of the preceding material and willfully recognizing and therefore authorizing its *literary* nature), suggests not only poetic distance from the fraternal songs of 1912 but also the extent to which the cultural models provided by sectarianism are, nonetheless, embedded in Klyuev's later oeuvre: outsider and initiate; popular and learned; apocryphal yet canonical; allegorical and literal; sexual and spiritual; collective but individual; hierarch and heretic.

For these reasons, only the most literal reading, it might be argued, would identify fabrication without authenticity here. Hence, there is only superficial contradiction in the presence beside such sectarian elements of abundant Old Believer motifs, which themselves are often to be found in similar disjunctive contexts:

Где рай финифтяный и Сирин
Поет на ветке расписной,
Где Пушкин говором просвирен
Питает дух высокий свой,

Где Мей яровчатый, Никитин,
Велесов первенец — Кольцов,
Туда бреду я, ликом скрытен,
Под ношей варварских стихов.

Когда сложу свою вязанку
Сосновых слов, медвежьих дум?
«К костру готовьтесь спозаранку!» —
Гремел мой прадед — Аввакум.

Сгореть в метельном Пустозерске
Или в чернилах утонуть?
Словопоклонник богомерзкий,
Не знаю я, где орлий путь. (340–41)

Where paradise is folk enamel, and Sirin
Sings upon a painted branch,
Where Pushkin feeds his elevated spirit
With the speech of bakers of communion bread,

Where abide sycamore Mei, Nikitin,
Kol'tsov—firstborn of Veles,
There go I, visage concealed,
Beneath a burden of barbarous verse.

When shall I set down my bundle
Of pine words, bear thoughts?
"Prepare for the stake at first light!"—
Roared my ancestor—Avvakum.

Burn in snowy Pustozersk
Or drown in ink?

God-loathed word-worshipper
I know not where lies the eagle path.

In this poem, also from "Dolina edinoroga," folk beliefs and mythology (the bird Sirin, the ancient Slavic god Veles, protector of cattle) meet literary patrimony (Mei, Nikitin, Kol'tsov); literary identity—caught between ink and authenticity—meets claimed descent from the greatest of the Old Believers, the archpriest Avvakum. But perhaps the key reference is to Pushkin's recommendation to listen to the speech of the Moscow women who baked communion bread (890). In this allusion, high culture turns to the popular; profane to the sacred (yet not to the Old Belief of Avvakum, but to established religion, it should be noted) for its model.

Also associated with sectarian motifs and preoccupations are the images of Rasputin found in Klyuev's work (suggestive as analogue and opposite to the poet himself). The following stanza from "Na ushcherbe krasnye dni" ("Red days are fading," from "Krasnyi ryk," 414–15), quoted in chapter 2, makes the association explicit in a reference to *Bratskie pesni* as the poet's "songs of ecstasy":

Не мой ли «Сосен перезвон»
И *радельных песен свирели*
Затаили Распутинских икон
Сладкий морок, резьбу и синели?
[emphasis added]

Was it perhaps my "Peal of the Pines"
And the *pipes of my songs of ecstasy*
That hid the sweet darkness, carving and blue
Of the icons of Rasputin?

For these reasons, the intermittent association of Lenin and the revolution with the Old Belief (most evident in the first two poems of the Lenin cycle, 377–78, 399–400) should come as no more of a surprise to Klyuev's readers than it was a source of delight to his Bolshevik critics.

Crucial to the poetic geography of the later Klyuev are the Vyg monastic communities of Old Believers, and their leading writers. Vyg provides a literal midpoint between Onega, beside which the poet was born, and the White Sea coast (from which the founders of the Vyg community came), where his later autobiographical statements locate his birth, while Vyg's identity as a center of learning within which intellectuals *from the people* flourished is of equal significance in Klyuev's deployment of it as a model. Also significant for Klyuev is the fact that the Vyg writers were, as one scholar puts it, conservative in faith, but alert to innovation in literature.[45]

And, of course, the appeal of the Vyg writers as polemicists, defiant of established power, is as obvious as in the case of Avvakum.

Some of the themes first expressed in the fraternal songs are also to be seen, much transformed, in Klyuev's prose and his long poems—for example, "Gagar'ya sud'bina" has much to say (some of it very misleading) about Klyuev's engagement with sectarianism, and it is in that autobiographical narrative that he claims to have sung a sectarian hymn of his own composition to Leo Tolstoy, whom he visited as a very young man, while Rasputin and sectarianism play quite a prominent role in *Pesn' o Velikoi Materi.*[46] It should be noted that in "Gagar'ya sud'bina" (composed in the early 1920s), Klyuev's remarks on and claims about sectarianism and sectarian songs invite the very discussions of authenticity, fabrication, and even, potentially, plagiarism which were occasioned by the fraternal songs themselves in the early 1910s.

In the later lyric verse there are also striking evocations of the earlier sectarian motifs, for example in "Drevnii novgorodskii veter" ("Ancient wind of Novgorod," 494–95), where a characteristically eclectic world includes an allusion to sectarian ritual:

Бобры за постройкой плотины,
Куницы на слежке тетерьей
И синие прошвы от лыж
К мированице — келье пустынной,
Где Ярые Очи — зырянский Исус
С радельной рубахой на грядке —
Вот мое сердце и знанье, и путь!

Beavers building their dam,
Martens pursuing black grouse,
And blue streaks from skis
To the maker of myrrh, to the hermit cell,
Where the Icon of Fierce Eyes is a Komi Jesus
In a sectarian shirt at work in the vegetable patch—
That is my heart, and knowledge, and path!

Meanwhile, the typically provocative first line of "Kto za chto, a ya za dvoperst'e," written in 1928, reiterates the polemic importance of the Old Belief, both in content and as a rhetorical model ("Men may support what they wish, but I am for making the sign of the cross with two fingers"; 541–42). The role of sectarianism and the Old Belief in providing models of cultural genealogy for the poet himself and analogues for contemporary events (a very characteristic collapsing of the personal and the social into one) is stated with great force in a striking poem from the early 1920s which evokes not only relatively modern schisms but also the heretical Strigol'nik sect of medieval Russia:

От иконы Бориса и Глеба,
От стригольничьего Шестокрыла
Моя песенная потреба,
Стихов валунная сила.

Кости мои от Маргарита,
Кровь — от костра Аввакума.
Узорнее аксамита
Моя золотая дума:

Чтобы Русь, как серьга, повисла
В моем цареградском ухе . . .
Притекают отары-числа
К пастуху — дырявой разрухе.

И разруха пасет отары
Татарским лихим кнутом,
Оттого на Руси пожары
И заплакан родимый дом.
. . .
И желанна великая треба,
Чтоб во прахе бериллы и шелк
Пред иконой Бориса и Глеба
Окаянный поверг Святополк! (511–12)

From the icon of Boris and Gleb
From the Strigol'nik *Six Wings*
Comes my song sacrifice,
The boulder power of my verse.

My bones are from Chrysostom's Pearl,
My blood from Avvakum's fire.
More elaborate than ancient velvet
Is my golden thought:

May old Russia hang like an earring
In my Constantinopolitan ear . . .
Flocks of days gather round their
Shepherd—tattered destruction.

And destruction tends the herds
With a wild Tatar whip,
Hence old Russia burns
And the family home is mourned.
. . .
A great rite is needed,
That before the icon of Boris and Gleb
In ashes, beryls and silk
Be laid down by cursed Svyatopolk!

The poem begins and ends with the first saints of the Russian church, Boris and Gleb, murdered by their brother, "cursed Svyatopolk." Their icon is associated with the poet's own literary identity (it is one of the sources of his song) while, by implication, the events to which it refers provide an analogue for contemporary Russia. But the poet's identity is also predicated on the heretical Strigol'nik sect of fourteenth-century Novgorod and their use of the Jewish astronomical tables, the *Six Wings;* on a popular collection of the writings of John Chrysostom; and on the fire where Avvakum was burned at the stake.

Thus a certain thematic continuity with the early songs of fraternity survives, forming an interesting contrast both with the characteristic eclectic material referents of the 1920s (objets d'art, sacred and otherwise, are as common in Klyuev's poetry of this period as they appear to have been in his otherwise impoverished living quarters) and with the orientation toward Old Russian culture. That culture is, by definition, high and ecclesiastical ("official"), whereas most of his sectarian references, and even his allusions to the Old Belief, notwithstanding the relative antiquity of his Old Believer heroes, are popular and contemporary in tenor. Of course, such achronological syncretism is itself characteristic of sectarian hymns.

Beyond such specific features, it should not be forgotten that Klyuev's poetry in general and the history of that poetry (its suppression, preservation, transmission, publication, and reception) illustrate and demonstrate the paradoxical, syncretic cultural combinations and the nonlinear but apocalyptic time which "Ot ikony Borisa i Gleba" clearly (or, at times, obscurely) elaborates. Hence Klyuev's work may be said to embody in microcosm aspects of Russian culture and society which continue to fascinate and frustrate both Russian and foreign commentators. It is no surprise that, at the very end of the twentieth century, in and after the collapse of Soviet power, there emerged a renewed and very diversely expressed interest in Russian popular religion, Russian sectarianism, the Old Belief, and associated phenomena. Individual studies of Klyuev express such interests, as the work of Ronald Vroon in the United States, discussed above, and Elena Yukhimenko in Russia, among others, illustrate. As was noted in chapter 1, Yukhimenko, a learned student of the Old Belief, provides a sober and convincing account of the relationship between Klyuev's worldview and that branch of Russian popular religion.[47] As she observes, the Old Belief clearly offers a powerful cultural model for the later Klyuev. To understand its relevance to the poet, especially in the Soviet period, it is essential to recall that the Old Belief was both popular and learned, very local and yet very widespread, often quite close to established religion, yet also persecuted by the establishment. Its relationship to time, its view of the present as apocalyptic, and its preoccupation with pre-Petrine culture also provide very important analogues and models for Klyuev. Sectarianism is less evident in the later Klyuev, but is very important, beyond the "fraternal" episode, not least for facilitating the exploration of a complex sexual discourse—an aspect of Klyuev's life and work which has yet to be addressed fully by scholarship.

Meanwhile, general studies provide the intellectual contexts for local readings of a single poet. In Russia recent years have seen a flood of publications devoted to sectarianism and the Old Belief, from editions of major texts to new scholarly and popular studies, while Western scholars have also shown greatly increased interest in these matters.[48] Among these many and diverse publications, Aleksandr Etkind's *Khlyst: Sekty, literatura, i revolyutsiya* (*Flagellant: Sects, Literature, and Revolution*), a work of nearly seven hundred pages devoted to "the discourse about sects in Russia at the turn of the century," deserves special mention.[49] Etkind surveys and unifies the subject under thematic and personal headings (from the scandalous to the philological, and from Prishvin to Tsvetaeva), and, of course, devotes a subchapter of eleven pages to Klyuev. And yet again, both the disputed life of the poet's texts and the disputed texts of the poet's life shape Etkind's initial presentation of the poet, contrasted, perhaps somewhat erroneously, with the symbolist Dobrolyubov in the opening sentences: "The paths of Klyuev and Dobrolyubov are opposites. One left the high culture of the Symbolists for sectarians; the other, on the contrary, joined the ranks of professional poets from the sectarians."[50] As has been shown, it might be more accurate to say that Klyuev came to sectarianism already a professional poet. In fact, however, Etkind's treatment of Klyuev's "sectarianism" is more cautious than these initial remarks might suggest, and does not neglect the "strategic" convenience of Klyuev's claims and projections, nor the cultural eclecticism which militates against any narrowly sectarian reading of Klyuev's use of motifs from the *skoptsy* and the *khlysty*. However, there remains a powerful and engaging irony in the very existence of Etkind's book and similar studies: they themselves not only explore Russia's preoccupation with sectarianism at the turn of the century but also adumbrate the return of that preoccupation at the century's end.

On the other hand, Klyuev himself, so anchored in his time and place, fits paradoxically into ours, while his fraternal songs prove both a single brief episode in his poetic career and an early exemplar of some of the most recurrent features of his oeuvre and of the material textuality of that oeuvre. These poems seem a perfect fit for the preoccupations with popular religion and mysterious, collective spirituality that were prominent in the early years of the twentieth century, but, at the same time, they articulate a relationship between the popular and high culture that was, if not unique to Klyuev, certainly different from the modernist standard. Moreover, and equally paradoxically, they enable an exploration of alternative sexuality that is very different from the genteel, voyeuristic eroticism of other authors on the subject. Reiterations even of the designation "bratskaya pesnya" indicate the fundamental importance of the concept in the poet's work, while the many variants associated with that concept are highly suggestive of the instabilities which mark so many aspects of his verse and life.

Chapter Four

Prose of Identity and the Identity of Prose: "Gagar'ya sud'bina"—Klyuev's Prose, Questions of Genre, Problems of Autobiography

MANY OF THE PROBLEMS of textuality, identity, and reception illuminated by an examination of the fraternal songs recur when Klyuev's most extensive autobiography is explored. "Gagar'ya sud'bina" ("The Loon's Fate") was summarized in chapter 1, where it was also noted that it was extensively quoted long before it was published—a phenomenon quite characteristic of the later Soviet period, when problematic material often edged its way into print piecemeal.[1] Indeed, the publishing history of Klyuev's oeuvre provides an especially striking example of that phenomenon in Bazanov's long article on the *poema Pogorel'shchina,* "Poema o drevnem Vyge" ("A Narrative Poem About Ancient Vyg")—an article which was published in 1979, eight years *before Pogorel'shchina* itself appeared in print in the Soviet Union.[2] The overall characteristics both of publishing and of scholarly debate in the early 1990s (a period distinguished by instability, unpredictability, and intense polemics, even by the standards of modern Russia) are also well illustrated within the Klyuev bibliography and in particular by "Gagar'ya sud'bina." Having awaited publication so long, that text emerged not once, but twice within two years, on the pages of different literary journals, edited by different scholars. Moreover, the editor of the second publication, Konstantin Azadovsky, pointedly criticized in his apparatus the first publication, edited by Aleksandr Mikhailov.[3] Indeed, the story of the emergence into print of "Gagar'ya sud'bina" echoes, in its revelation of contextual problems of textuality, the facts of its composition seventy years before. Like so many of Klyuev's works, "Gagar'ya sud'bina" invites interrogation and poses many problems of definition and interpretation at various levels of textuality, from the most material to the most conceptually abstract. Problematic in its very material status, it is also unstable in form and genre, and promotes rather than elides the instabilities in the poet's identity explored in chapter 1. In the intersections of these problems and instabilities it rehearses many of the same general and specific cultural issues as the fraternal songs. Hence, the answer to the simple question "What is 'Gagar'ya sud'bina'?" will be multiple and complex.

Its material status illustrates these difficulties in the most elementary way. The text is published from a manuscript not in the poet's own hand, but in that of his close associate, Nikolai Arkhipov, who recorded a considerable amount of material dictated or related by the poet. There is no known manuscript in the poet's own hand. While the activities of an amanuensis are of great significance in intellectual biographies from many ages and cultures, the Soviet period of Russian literature gave the work of the writer's recording companion a special meaning, and it was often endowed subsequently with qualities of moral and political heroism by succeeding generations of readers. When writing and publishing became difficult, composition and recording also changed character, so that not only did authors compose and record their works "for the drawer," as noted in chapter 2, but, as intimate performance became a significant means of literary dissemination, the author's special auditors themselves often played a very significant role in the recording of his work. In these phenomena, as in others, the material circumstances of twentieth-century Russian literary production echo preindustrial, indeed medieval, culture, while retaining many of the signs of general European modernity.

"Gagar'ya sud'bina" was composed at the very beginning of the period when oral composition and transmission were becoming quite common, even typical. The 1920s and 1930s were generating, as indicated earlier, a new form of "pre-Gutenberg" literature. The circumstances of the composition and recording of the text thus not only place it into a very large category of such works composed in the Soviet period but also diminish its putative stability as a finished work of Klyuev himself. These facts not only serve to caution against any purely documentary treatment of the work but also reiterate the close association between material circumstances and aesthetics which is such an important aspect of Soviet-period Russian literature.

Moreover, the literal problems of authorship find parallels in other issues raised by the work. For example, and as is typical of the poet's prose in general, it poses a series of problems to the reader, from accessibility to interpretation. Indeed, Klyuev's prose, only collected in 2003, and in some cases published only once before that, forms an intriguing and challenging conglomeration of genres and forms, many of them code-transgressive in ways specific to Klyuev or else general for his period. While the challenges of his verse have yet to be met in full by scholarly readers, the challenges of his prose have barely been recognized. The reception of Klyuev as poet—both by his contemporaries and by posthumous readers—has already been sketched and may now be resumed very briefly: in and immediately after the symbolist period his verse was read widely and discussed even more; for most of the Soviet period, it was studied cautiously at home, occasionally abroad, and was generally inaccessible; in recent years it has been studied and debated intensively, but little read. The reception of his prose is yet simpler to relate and requires no chronological specifics: barely studied, barely read, barely known.[4]

The corpus of Klyuev's prose is, in fact, quite extensive, and very diverse. The earliest examples are "letters" from the village, with a clear ideological agenda, written for publication in Mirolyubov's journals. "V chernye dni: (Iz pis'ma krest'yanina)" ("In Dark Days: [From a Peasant's Letter]," *Sd* 103–4) was published, unsigned, in *Nash zhurnal* (*Our Journal*) in 1908. Another article, written in the village for the educated urban readership and employing the characteristic stance of the informed man of the people, "S rodnogo berega" ("From the Native Shore," *Sd* 105–10), was quoted in detail by Aleksandr Blok in his article "Stikhiya i kul'tura" ("Element and Culture") of 1908, but was not published in full until 1975.[5] Between 1910 and 1917 Klyuev appears to have published another five pieces of prose—two reviews, a response to Artsybashev's "Zapiski o Tolstom" ("Notes on Tolstoy"), the essay "Plenniki goroda" ("Captives of the City"), and the prose poem "Za stolom Ego" ("At His Table," *Sd* 111–16). The reviews and the response to Artsybashev, while indicative of Klyuev's cultural and ideological interests, are occasional pieces. "Plenniki goroda" is a very poetic attack on the city, as a place of alienation, written for the Golgotha Christians, whose program and interests were described in chapter 3. The one-page "Za stolom Ego" blends verse and prose, political and personal mythology in a manner characteristic of much of the later prose, and uses narrative forms encountered often in his later poetry: individual address (to an unnamed "sister," apparently martyred); description of a mystical vision (of "His table," offered freely to the visionary and the martyr-addressee).

Between 1919 and 1923 Klyuev is said to have published twenty-nine pieces of prose, all but one of them appearing in the local newspaper in Vytegra, and some subsequently republished in Moscow organs. The range of these pieces is striking: some are short (often eccentric) notes on local theatrical productions; others provide satirical commentary on local problems (one is even based on complaints about the noise made by a local night watchman).[6] The longer pieces are less easily categorized, often combining an elevated revolutionary, even military, rhetoric with apocalyptic notes and with the ecclesiastical language encountered in his poetry of the time. Their ideology is utopian, with enthusiastic support for the new regime, soon tempered by alarm at the fate of the peasant community and culture from which the author's own utopian vision is drawn. "Krasnyi kon'" ("Red Steed," *Sd* 118–19) of 1919 uses imagery and language reminiscent of the flagellants and of the Golgotha Christians to announce the arrival of a new time. Meanwhile, "Krasnyi nabat" ("Red Alarm," *Sd* 128–32), also from 1919, is a highly rhetorical call to arms, full of religious imagery, which summons its readers to defend the new republic from the massed forces of greed and capital.[7] "Sorok dva gvozdya" ("Forty-two Nails," *Sd* 136–41) and "Samotsvetnaya krov'" (*Sd* 141–44), both from 1919 and also employing highly rhetorical forms and religious language, criticize the new state's attacks on religion, which is depicted as an institution of the people, and, in the latter, as a partially aesthetic phenomenon.[8]

As can be seen, the prose of this period allows one to speak of a protean quality in Klyuev's literary and intellectual activities, and an original, even eccentric (although by no means unique) view of the times. Klyuev, it will be recalled, was expelled from the Bolshevik Party in 1920 for "religious convictions . . . in full contradiction of the materialist ideology of the party."[9] It is hardly surprising, then, that after 1920 he ceased to be an unequivocally welcome figure in the Bolshevik institutions of Vytegra, although he enjoyed the support of two editors of the local newspaper (Aleksandr Bogdanov, editor from March 1919 to May 1921; and Arkhipov, who became editor in September 1922 and whom Klyuev followed to Petrograd in summer 1923).[10] Partially as a result of Klyuev's situation after his expulsion, another problem in examining his prose emerges: most of the short pieces from the early 1920s listed under Klyuev's name in the standard bibliography were published either pseudonymously or anonymously in the Vytegra paper. Klyuev's authorship is attested by documentation in only one case. The other attributions were made in the 1980s by two Klyuev scholars: one attribution by Konstantin Azadovsky, the rest by Sergei Subbotin, using word-frequency profiles of Klyuev's prose and verse of the period. Thus, even if these attributions are accepted (and the argument for them is strong), other problems remain: on the one hand, the anonymous pieces provide evidence of greater versatility and flexibility on the part of the author; on the other hand, their anonymous or pseudonymous publication not only places them in a separate category from the earlier and very evidently and acknowledged "Klyuevan" works, with their poetic language and apocalyptic or millenarian expectations, but also strongly suggests that they self-consciously elaborate a different and somewhat separate *literary identity* for their author. Again, external circumstances and internal literary features are entangled in cause and effect; and again, Klyuev's textual strategies echo his "life-creating" practices. As a consequence, it might be argued that when the poet writes satirically, but anonymously, of the illicit cutting of flour from the local mill (a bread-and-butter piece of local Russian journalism anywhere), he is trying on for size another literary identity altogether.[11] Of course, it may also be that the primary motivation for writing such quotidian pieces was financial. Further irony comes from the inversion that produces the anonymous short notes accompanying publication in 1919 of selections from the verse of Esenin, Shiryaevets, Kirillov, and the poet described below:

> A clairvoyant poet of the people, fixing upon himself the astonished attention of all of his great contemporaries.

> The son of Olonian forests, who has struck Russian literature with verbal thunder. Workers' and peasants' power did not fail to honor the Red Bard, publishing his writings alongside the immortal works of Lev Tolstoy, Gogol, etcetera. (*Sd* 153)[12]

In fact, this anonymous and rather flattering characterization of the poet Klyuev seems to be the work of none other than Klyuev himself.

Of the signed pieces, "Sorok dva gvozdya" is of particular interest. The first part is built around two extended and elaborate metaphors, linked together in the first sentence of the piece: "The night-soil removers cleaned the latrine and let out such a vile smell that not only could I not open a window—it was out of the question to breathe in my cell" (*Sd* 136). The vile smell (which has polluted all the country and turned the minds of the people to evil) eventually turns out to be the antireligious propaganda represented by the speech of an orator whom the narrator encounters mocking the abundance of nails from Christ's cross found in Russian churches and elsewhere: he counts forty-two, including four he has seen in Jerusalem. The cell of the opening sentence is the monastic residence of the narrator (and an image sometimes used by the lyrical speaker of Klyuev's late poetry to represent his urban residence), who elaborates on his monkish identity later:

> My legs have been made heavy by the thousand-bow rule of the Solovetsky monastery, and my body fettered [*telesa verizhnye*]: I carried nine-pound fetters on my shoulders [*rama*] until the Red Year; I wore them in Petersburg, and in them I drank tea with all manner of spirit-struggling [*dukhoboinye*] writers and scholars. (*Sd* 138)

Through these elaborate metaphors the narrator mocks and parodies vulgar antireligious propaganda, and defends the religious faith and appurtenances of the people as representative of the national Christology. The piece contains eight lines of Klyuev's own verse, and a large number of quotations and distortions of the scriptures, culminating in a succession of biblical quotations near the end. The blending of politics, cultural mythology, original self-portrait, and highly idiosyncratic views will be familiar to any reader of Klyuev's verse.[13] The accumulation of quotation from religious sources, also familiar, is mixed with highly particular and contemporary commentary and a starkly transgressive, although at times also playful, humor (the elaborate metaphor of the smell is both) in a manner reminiscent of Klyuev's fondness for heterogeneous combinations. The monk theme, elaborated at some length, directly echoes elements in Klyuev's created autobiographies explored earlier, just as the flagellant references in other of his signed prose pieces echo motifs from the poetry also examined elsewhere in these pages. The stylistic eclecticism (archaisms, contemporary usage, popular language, and so on) elaborates the same heady blend of elements. In the passage quoted above a number of archaisms stand out. For example, the poet not only uses the plural for a singular meaning in the phrase *telesa verizhnye* but also uses an archaic plural form, while, at the same time, he makes the plural of the archaic *ramo* (shoulder) not *ramena,* as it should be, but what appears to be his own newly modernized *rama.* In short, "Sorok dva gvozdya" is characterized by a formal and generic fluidity which contributes to the generation of elusive and even apparently contradictory meanings. The reactions of his Vytegra readers of 1919 are unknown, but provide ample grounds for enthralling speculation (not least when his own repeated characterization of his hometown as deeply provincial and even ignorant is recalled).

Sergei Subbotin enumerates at some length characteristic stylistic features of the Vytegra prose, partly in order to support his attributions of the anonymous and pseudonymous pieces. He points to the rhythmical organization, derived in part from the use of anaphora and (sometimes partial) syntactic parallelism; he also notes the use of amplification, based upon the accumulation of similar elements (synonyms, epithets, comparisons, and so on) and partly upon the accumulation of quotations, especially from scripture. Subbotin further notes Klyuev's tendency to elevated generalization and abstraction, even when the matter under discussion is concrete and specific, leading to ornamentality which is functionally close to poetic discourse. These observations lead Subbotin to reinforce an association made implicitly and explicitly by Klyuev himself throughout his mature oeuvre: the reiteration here of many of the themes and devices of Old Russian literature, and, for Subbotin, an especial proximity to the "weaving of words" familiar in works of the fourteenth and fifteenth centuries, as well as to the more common analogue for Klyuev from the seventeenth century—the archpriest Avvakum.[14] Supporting his argument with reference to leading scholars of medieval Russia (first and foremost to Dmitrii Likhachev), Subbotin concludes: "Klyuev succeeded as no other twentieth-century Russian writer in producing a lively incarnation of the centuries-long traditions of the literature of medieval Russia."[15] With allowances for overstatement, it must be said that Subbotin's case is well-argued and clearly substantiated by the prose itself. Moreover, not only did Klyuev repeatedly identify himself with those traditions in his programmatic statements in verse, prose, and literary conversation, but the very content of some of the Vytegra prose invites the comparison, as is evident from the monkish persona who narrates "Sorok dva gvozdya."

Here too lies an entanglement of aesthetics and material circumstances: Klyuev self-consciously adopts stylistic features, themes, and material familiar to preindustrial ages, while functioning in a cultural situation which itself has created circumstances that many would see as "medieval" (from the pre-Gutenberg status of belles lettres to the despotic marshaling of culture and society—although to characterize, as does popular parlance, the Soviet version of the latter as "medieval" is perhaps to do an injustice to the Middle Ages). And here again, Klyuev, while an exceptional and even peripheral figure (what could be more peripheral than his Vytegra-published pieces?), also rehearses a salient feature of Russian culture in the twentieth century. Not for nothing did so many Russian studies of medieval culture seem to have such contemporary resonance; and not for nothing, in the post-Soviet period, has the subject of Old Russian literature after the end of Old Russia emerged as an acknowledged area of scholarly discourse in the publications of medievalists themselves.[16]

For these and other reasons, the generic identification of Klyuev's prose is problematic. As Subbotin notes, some of his theater reviews have very little in common with the type (again, one may speculate on how they were received in 1920s Vytegra). The longer pieces, like so much of his verse, are also slippery in form and substance, not only in the very obvious modulation from prose to verse (sometimes original, sometimes quoted) but also in language, point of view, and tone. Given such slippage, it is important, before turning to "Gagar'ya sud'bina" and its sibling texts, to examine briefly other Klyuev texts which not only demonstrate similar generic fluidity but also indicate aesthetic and other proximities to the prose already examined.

First, Klyuev, like most authors of his period, was a very active correspondent, and the last twenty-five years have seen the publication of many of his letters. His correspondence with Blok has already been discussed, and, as it will be recalled, Blok not only cited Klyuev's letters in his own articles but also quoted an article Klyuev himself wrote in the form of a letter. The correspondence with Blok, although early, is, in general, clearly more than a private or even professional literary correspondence, since Klyuev not only asserts himself but also propagates a broad social agenda in a way that shaped his emergence as an author. While some of his letters are relatively monolithic as exemplars of personal or professional correspondence, the explicit literary form of the Blok letters is elaborated again with several later correspondents, by no means all of them professional authors themselves. This phenomenon is most remarkable in his letters from Siberia, quoted in the opening chapter: the poet, in extremis, composes elusive and contradictory literary epistles. The poet also writes quite remarkably confessional pieces, culminating in the prolonged "Ochishchenie serdtsa" ("Cleansing of the Heart," *Sd* 361–67), dated December 30, 1934–April 30, 1935, and sent to Khristoforova-Sadomova.[17] Here the epistolary form is not so much transcended as abrogated, while the text itself blends the highly personal in content and address with the spiritually general, both abstract and concrete. It will be recalled that the letters from Siberia have also been characterized as close in form to certain medieval genres, reinforcing the generic parallels with Klyuev's prose and supporting the contradictory impressions of, on the one hand, overall textual integration (within the poet's work) and, on the other hand, dislocation (in chronology and form).

Second, Klyuev's own oral discourse—whether public and performance-oriented, or notionally private and to a single interlocutor—often bore many characteristics which invite comparison with the finished texts of his prose and verse. Compositions which may have been recorded in some form by the poet himself but have subsequently been lost, yet are known from accounts of oral performances, include the tale of Evstafii the Cat and Stepanidka the Mouse, which, as Azadovsky notes, is attested by several memoirists.[18] There were also oral tales which Klyuev seems to have performed for one interlocutor only, of which a striking example is his life history as told to Khristoforova-Sadomova and discussed in the opening chapter.

Then, third, there is the material recorded by Arkhipov, and preserved in the archives of the Pushkin House in Petersburg. Extracts have been widely quoted by scholars familiar with the archive. Among the most interesting pieces are those associated with Esenin, especially the lengthy "Besovskaya basnya pro Esenina" ("Diabolical Fable About Esenin," *Sd* 63–66), previously published by Mikhailov, among others.[19] Eighty-five such items recorded by Arkhipov, and including the "Diabolical Tale," are included in *Slovesnoe drevo,* in its second section, "Notes Recorded in Various Years: About the Poet Himself and Time, the Classics and His Contemporaries" (*Sd* 51–76), apparently in the order in which they were recorded on twenty-five pages of manuscript (presumably from the so-called *chernaya tetrad'* [black notebook] maintained by Arkhipov). These items, like the other examples listed here, are clearly worked as literary texts, but were presumably performed for a single auditor (and amanuensis). Again, the boundaries between genres and between the private and the public are repeatedly crossed.

Fourth, a special place and even a tentatively separate genre designation has been accorded to a body of Klyuev narratives published in the 1990s: the poet's dreams (*Sd* 79–100). Two of the most prominent contemporary Klyuev scholars, Konstantin Azadovsky and Aleksandr Mikhailov, published and discussed these narratives (in many cases, the same narratives, and in the same year), noting their association with his oeuvre in general, and with his allegories of Russia in particular.[20] Few readers will be surprised to learn that the manner of transmission raises problems. One set of dreams was recorded between the early 1930s and 1967 by Khristoforova-Sadomova, apparently in her own words, and possibly closer to 1967 than to the time of Klyuev's presumed relation of them. For the other set, quite clearly expressed in language typical of Klyuev, two slightly different versions of recording and transmission exist. According to Azadovsky, the dreams were recorded by Klyuev and then copied by Nikolai Arkhipov into his own notebooks; according to Mikhailov, they were recorded by Arkhipov from Klyuev's relation at the time of the initial account (in the early 1920s). There appears to be no known dream manuscript in the poet's own hand. Like his correspondence and other texts and near-texts on the periphery of his literary oeuvre, these recorded dreams have much in common—language, imagery, thematics, and so on—with his acknowledged belles lettres. In turn, his prose, in particular, and his poetry frequently narrate or allude to dreams, visions, and hallucinations. Here too the general, the popular, and the specific coincide: the Russian fascination with dreams and their interpretation is well attested and constant (familiar dream books circulated very widely in manuscript throughout the Soviet period, and reappeared in print as soon as Soviet power loosened its grasp, while new dream books were also created in the twentieth century). The interpretation of dreams played a particularly prominent role in popular soothsaying, and the marked role assigned to them in Klyuev's work has a social and ideological feature. The symbolist fascination with the occult and links to it through unconscious or nonrational elements are equally well known, while Klyuev himself, a product of all of the above circumstances, was also personally much preoccupied with his dreams. Hence their problematic textualization and proximity to some of his other, more "public" texts.

Finally, beyond these examples of discourse, public and private, lie aspects of Klyuev's creation and re-creation of himself which, although not textual in nature, are open to reading as texts. Among these, the manner of his dress was frequently commented upon, while the decoration of his room in 1920s Leningrad has already been discussed. To the latter example should be added the textual "cell" inhabited by the narrator of "Sorok dva gvozdya" in 1919 Vytegra, as well as the icon-collecting exile in 1930s Siberia—one a figure from published prose, the other attested in the poet's private correspondence. As ever, identities clash and intersect, while texts and textualities provide associations across periods and boundaries of form.

"Gagar'ya sud'bina" and the other prose pieces comparable to it, as the body of works most explicitly predicated upon elucidating the poet's identity (and most elusive in that project), must then be regarded in these multiple and fluid contexts. It will be recalled from the discussion in chapter 1 that Klyuev composed a series of autobiographical narratives in the Soviet period: two short pieces were published in the early 1920s; two longer pieces from the same period (of which one is "Gagar'ya sud'bina") remained unpublished until recently; and two other short autobiographical accounts were also published posthumously. The circumstances which gave rise to these diverse texts are characteristically mixed. First, they are functions of Klyuev's own construction and reconstruction of his literary identity, to be understood beside many of his other activities in the period, as explored in the opening chapter. Second, two of them seem to be specifically products of the demand for potted autobiographies which was a characteristic of early Soviet literature, and all of them, as has been noted, should be seen against the background of the somewhat formulaic autobiographies typically produced by writers in answer to that demand. Klyuev's works, of course, at best fulfill only partially the formulaic requirements of the genre (even his account of repeated imprisonment during the imperial period is, in its details, far from the standard). Third, while the autobiographical works certainly draw on and suggest many of the same literary models as other Klyuev texts (ranging from the Bible and Old Russian and ecclesiastical literature to contemporary authors), they are more marked by an orientation toward the oral than any of Klyuev's other prose. Subbotin, in the analysis of Klyuev's Vytegra prose discussed above, explicitly excludes from his discussion folkloric features (*fol'klorizm*) and those works or parts of works oriented toward "folkloric *skaz*," on the grounds that these are subjects which require separate treatment.[21] His caution is characteristic of scholars approaching the problem of the relationship between Klyuev's work and folklore, which, as the examination of the fraternal songs in chapter 3 has already shown, is indeed complex and problematic. Moreover, the general questions of relations between modern literary texts and folklore, even where the former seem explicitly to emulate or to be modeled on the latter, are extremely difficult in Russian culture, and any answers to them, however tentative, are inevitably loaded with ideological as well as methodological assumptions of a highly provocative kind. As must be evident, this is one of the reasons for the intensity and not infrequent savagery of the debates provoked by Klyuev throughout his career and posthumously. Thus, to examine the textual nature of "Gagar'ya sud'bina" is to enter an area of much-disputed territory.

So far only the disputes over Klyuev's mythmaking have been discussed. As is characteristic for the poet's entire oeuvre, these disputes may be linked to the more or less literally textual issues explored below.

It will be recalled that "Gagar'ya sud'bina" was recorded by Nikolai Arkhipov in the early 1920s, and was finally published from a manuscript in his hand by Aleksandr Mikhailov in 1992 and by Konstantin Azadovsky in 1993. But the two scholars, whose views diverge on so many points, even differ over the nature of the transcription from which the narrative is published, just as they differ on Klyuev's dream texts. According to Mikhailov, throughout the 1920s Arkhipov "recorded [*zapisyval*] Klyuev's poems, recollections, dreams, pronouncements of various kinds, and, finally, autobiographical stories."[22] For Azadovsky, the text of "Gagar'ya sud'bina" was "noted down (or rather *copied*) by Arkhipov."[23] In other words—as in the case of Klyuev's dream narratives—the material status of the text is under dispute: is it a record of an oral account given by Klyuev to Arkhipov, or is it a copy by Arkhipov of an account *written by Klyuev himself*? It must be presumed that there can be no definitive answer to this question, the very existence of which illustrates yet again the encounter between historical circumstances and artistic practice: the nature of the recording, preservation, and long nonpublication of the text preclude clarification, while its form and content also place it in an ill-defined area between public and private, conventionally literary and oral. Azadovsky's publication is accompanied by an illustration of the first page of the narrative and by his comments, supported by the illustration, that the transcription is "externally stylized in an Old Russian manner: every chapter opens with a red Cyrillic capital letter."[24] Arkhipov's amateur stylization of the manuscript is thus associated both with one of the multiple literary identities of the text and with Klyuev's own antiquarian interests (among them, manuscript books).

It is no surprise that the dispute over Klyuev's life, examined at some length in the opening chapter, also divides Mikhailov and Azadovsky in their treatment of "Gagar'ya sud'bina." For the former, although "Gagar'ya sud'bina" may seem not like a "reliable, but rather an invented description by the author of the events of his life," it is nonetheless an autobiography: "it is the autobiography of his spiritual life, which is the most important thing for a creative personality."[25] Moreover, while Mikhailov acknowledges that much of the contents of Klyuev's autobiographies may not be confirmed, he does tend to give some credence to claims such as the poet's literal descent from Avvakum and other (aesthetically and ideologically convenient) forebears. Azadovsky, on the other hand, prefaces his publication of "Gagar'ya sud'bina" with his most detailed and critical deconstruction of the "myth" of Klyuev, neglecting the question of genre to address largely biographical issues. His article and his critical apparatus to "Gagar'ya sud'bina" are, nonetheless, works of exemplary scholarship and seem to represent one of his most cogent statements on the identity of the poet and the meaning of his work. At the end of the prefatory article, Azadovsky remarks that he had published part of "Gagar'ya sud'bina" in an article of 1987, where he noted that he would publish it in full soon, and had published other parts of it in his book of 1990. He criticizes Mikhailov for publishing the text in full himself (and, Azadovsky asserts, inaccurately) in 1992, concluding his article with the following remarks:

> However, the text should be published again. . . . Our principal aim, as previously, is to provide a scholarly interpretation, based on documents, of the

confused question of Klyuev's biography. Cultural history is, ultimately, built from facts. They must be separated from mystifications, imitations, and plagiarism![26]

In other words, once more both text and context raise related questions of authenticity, ownership, and genre. And the question of ownership is raised not only by the initial circumstances of composition but also—explicitly—in the scholarly context of the work's eventual full publications. Indeed, it is intriguing to note that the 1990s scholarly arguments around Klyuev and Klyuev scholarship echo in striking ways the debates around the poet during his life. Azadovsky uses his publication of "Gagar'ya sud'bina" to raise again the issues of Klyuev's "plagiarism," which first arose in Brikhnichev's apparently naive pamphlet, but which, as Azadovsky points out here and elsewhere, recurred at later points in the poet's career.[27] Azadovsky's own ambivalence on this issue is evident.[28] However, the immediate target of his remarks on plagiarism at the end of his article, quoted above, seems to be the contemporary scholar with whom he polemicizes. As ever, dizzying spirals of association across times, places, and forms of discourse seem to accompany any reading of Nikolai Klyuev.

Tat'yana Ponomareva, the only other scholar to have written at any length on "Gagar'ya sud'bina," is more circumspect in her treatment. In her book on Klyuev's prose (published with a tiny print run—in this case three hundred—and thus, like several other major publications discussed in these pages, essentially inaccessible to all but the most resolute of nonspecialists), she devotes twelve pages to it. She places it within the informal cycle of Klyuev's autobiographical prose, noting the motifs it shares with and develops from other pieces; she reads the text partly against the models of hagiographic and neo-hagiographic literature, and notes such stylistic features as the recurrence of metrical phrases and the emulation of oral narration.[29] Her approach eschews, to all intents and purposes, the polarities generated by discussions of veracity and authenticity, thereby delineating a quite different and, it might be argued, more promising outline for future discussion both of the autobiographical texts and of Klyuev's various forms of life-construction in general. But she, too, confronts the interpretive spirals which any reading of Klyuev seem to generate: according to her, there are signs of the "hagiographic genre," Klyuev repeatedly employs triadic construction, and often resorts to abstraction; yet the text also makes ample use of concrete, everyday detail, is modeled to a significant degree on modernist forms, and has a clear programmatic direction in its treatment of such episodes as the visit to Tolstoy. And Ponomareva remarks, too, the dual status of Klyuev's autobiographical prose—"notes" for one's intimates, like the memoirs of the eighteenth century; but also fragments of an unfinished literary project, presumably intended for publication, and having much in common with other Russian literary memoirs of the twentieth century.[30]

Such spirals are evident everywhere in the form and content of "Gagar'ya sud'bina" itself. Its episodic narrative (the piece is divided into ten relatively short and separate sections) has already been described and its opening lines cited in chapter 1. The summary of its contents provided there is worth reviewing here. According to "Gagar'ya sud'bina," Klyuev's birth was unusual and combined Christian and pagan elements ("baptized" by a peasant woman, in a vat used for making bread). He learned to read from ancient prayer books, saw visions as an adolescent, and had miraculous dreams after his beloved mother's death. Twice he lived on the Solovetsky Islands, and there he enjoyed the status of a respected and much-visited hermit and ascetic. But on the advice of an elder who came to see him and talked of Eastern religions, he turned to sectarianism and became a "Christ" (i.e., a flagellant). He spent two years as the psalmist of a sectarian "Vessel" (i.e., group) in Samara, before escaping on the eve of the ritual castration planned for him by the group. Then he went to the Caucasus, where he was taken captive by a band of swarthy youths, who took their pleasure of him by turns. His memories of his lover Ali, whose heart he broke when he left, remain fond to this day. Traveling all over Russia, he eventually came to Moscow, made the acquaintance of men of letters, but disliked city life and educated company. He fled, via St. Petersburg (this is 1911–12) to his home region. There his mother foresaw and prepared for her death, which he continues to lament. None of his works is worth a single song of hers. As a youth, in the company of a group of *skoptsy,* he visited Tolstoy at Yasnaya Polyana. For refusing to serve in the military, Klyuev was imprisoned. In all he was imprisoned three times, on one occasion attracting the favors of the murderer Dubov. The guards, resenting his humility and silence, beat him mercilessly. During a pilgrimage in the far north, the young Klyuev encountered Grigorii Rasputin, whom he later visited on Gorokhovaya Street in St. Petersburg. Klyuev was taken to read his poetry before the empress. He also visited the empress's sister, Elizaveta Feodorovna, in Moscow. Such were the twists and turns of his life.

Closer examination will confirm the intriguing complexity of this narrative, a complexity announced in its very title, which signals several features of the work as a whole. Both noun (*sud'bina*—fate) and possessive adjective (*gagar'ya*—of the loon) are suggestive of the directions the text will take. *Sud'bina* (instead of the standard *sud'ba* for "fate") is a very evident marker of an orientation toward folk narrative, and is usually encountered in a context where the fate described is difficult or painful (*gor'kaya sud'bina* [literally, "bitter fate"] is a familiar combination). Meanwhile the loon ("diver" in British English) is ubiquitously regarded as a quintessential image of northern nature and life. The two species encountered in European Russia are the red-throated loon and the black-throated loon (*Gavia stellata* and *Gavia arctica,* or Russian *Krasnozobaya gagara* and *Chernozobaya gagara,* respectively). While *Gavia immer* (the common loon or great-northern diver), the species most commonly encountered in North America, is famed for its tremolo and yodel-like calls, generally considered enchanting sounds of northern wilderness, the two species of northern Russia are known for their "moaning, piercing cries."[31] Loons figure prominently in legend and lore throughout northern Europe and North America, often being associated with the spirit world, and sometimes seen as heralds, most often of weather. In the words of Edward Armstrong, in *The Folklore of Birds,* "throughout circumpolar Eurasia the diver is associated with shamanism."[32] In many cultures it is forbidden to kill a loon, although they are also often encountered as talismans. To a Russian of today the loon is likely to be seen as a herald of fate—a northern equivalent of the cuckoo.[33] Thus, the loon of the title joins Klyuev's extensive repertoire of rather literary representatives of northern ecology, but carries with it associations with folklore and the popular culture of omens and portents. Indeed, it is one of the most common of the ninety-eight avian visitors to his poetry.[34] However, the particular significance of the loon in this work is not explored until the opening lines of the eighth section:

> The gray loon is the queen of water birds. The gray loon's feather is enchanted: tuft fitting tight to tuft, at the very end of the feather is a pipe [*pishchik*]. . . . The loon can never be caught alive, and only he who knows how waters ferment in the earth's mixing bowl, and what yeast has been placed in that bowl, can find the loon beneath the poisoned root where it meets its death. At the hour of death the water bird surrenders to the fortunate [*talannyi chelovek*] its enchanted pipe, its singing gray feather.
>
> Great Onega is the loon's chalice, its water pasture, and its place of last resort [*zaplyv smertnyi*]. (*Sd* 38–39)

Research has yet to reveal the source of Klyuev's loon legend. While elements in it may well be drawn directly from northern folklore, it is equally likely that the entire story is the poet's own elaboration, based upon the fact of the loon's prominence in that folklore. The passage is typical of Klyuev's programmatic statements about himself and his art: the origins of art are in ancient, pagan magic and special skills, tied to the elements and to the natural world in general. It is also characteristic for Klyuev to depict human practices with which he sympathizes by analogy to nature, but here the natural world itself is—in an interesting reversal—implicitly compared to one of the poet's abiding images of the center of the peasant world: the baking of bread. Reversal, magic, and skill are also implicit in the term used for the "pipe" which the bird uses for its music and which, also by implication, the poet has acquired: *pishchik,* in its primary meaning, is a pipe "used for *luring birds*" (*Oxford Russian Dictionary;* the entry in Dal' supports this definition). But the core figure here is the poet—unmentioned, but assumed. He, it is implied, has secret knowledge of the earth which is a mark of his good fortune (*talan*). The northern loon (vaguely described here as "gray"—the principal color on the neck of both species encountered in European Russia) is also by implication associated with the familiar legends of the fire bird, which may illuminate an entire room by dropping a single feather. As for the magical powers of the bird, here too it remains unclear whether actual northern legends and beliefs are being described. The language is markedly folkloric in places, yet the rhetorical structure of the passage is highly literary. The final line links the central loon image to the tour of sacred places of the Onega region which follows (and where popular and Old Russian versions of Christianity predominate). Moreover, this passage, like so much of Klyuev's prose and verse, makes a gesture which is typical of many texts of Russian modernism: not only does the author claim a special and secret, hieratic, knowledge, but he also requires his reader to be an initiate. The language, imagery, and referents form a particular and marked code which the reader must know if he is to be able to read with any sort of confidence or competence. In the case of Klyuev the demands are exceptional. Few Russian authors can have used such diverse vocabulary, and few so many and so diverse allusions. Moreover, the syntactic structure of his prose (and, a fortiori, his verse), tending to syllepsis, anaphora, and other devices of omission, compression, and, simultaneously, repetition, compel the reader, even after lexicographic research, to pause long over many phrases. For many modern Russian readers the results are rebarbative. Hence the common reaction that he is "impossible to read." All the more so if the reader is unsympathetic to the blending of peasant and modernist worldview which is such a significant part of the overall result. Moreover, as can be seen in "Gagar'ya sud'bina," an orientation to orality and to performance does not reduce the difficulty of his work, but rather produces a quality which the sympathetic reader or listener may equate either with spells and incantations or with a highly literary "weaving of words," but which the unsympathetic reader may find "unreadable," even "unbearable."

The programmatic claims and diverse stylistic gestures of the loon passage are reiterated throughout "Gagar'ya sud'bina." The moral and spiritual superiority of the peasant and natural worlds is asserted repeatedly, and the author consistently claims a secret knowledge of the texts of these worlds (literal and metaphorical), although they are represented by very literary blends, some unique to the poet himself, some representative of the views of "high culture" in general. Examples include, in the first section, the blending of Christian and pagan ritual, and the recounting of the author's dreams and visions; in the second section, the combination of detailed narrative of his time on Solovki with accounts of Eastern religions and flagellant practice he encountered; in the third section, his claims to knowledge of the secret, holy Russian church, hidden from the hierarchy and from modernity in the dwellings of the peasantry; in the fifth section, the account of the special qualities of his mother's songs and the divine signs at her death; in the sixth section, the account of the meeting with Tolstoy, when the young poet started to sing a flagellant hymn of his own composition; in the seventh section, the description of the spiritual topography of the north. It is equally characteristic that this section concludes, in a wrenching move to the specific and contemporary, with an account of an encounter with Rasputin, who reveals special powers. He—simultaneously a parallel and antonym to Klyuev—is further discussed in the eighth section, only for the poet's own powers to be proved superior here and again in the final section, where Klyuev performs before members of the imperial family.

While the tone of "Gagar'ya sud'bina" is not particularly gloomy, it is also worth noting that the associations implicit in the title (the loon as a bird of omen, later revealed to be associated through its death with magic and song and, it may be inferred, with the narrator's own gifts; the suggestion of doom in the word *sud'bina*) are sustained by its contents: the world described is in the pre-Soviet past, irretrievably lost; the imperial family were massacred, Rasputin brutally murdered; Ali's broken heart led him to suicide; Klyuev's mother is dead; even then "iron tentacles" were threatening the pastoral world; Moscow is a city of erstwhile beauty, and so on. As with so many of Klyuev's autobiographical narratives and claims, the unstated context for this text is loss.

Beside these markers run others characteristic of another important strain in Klyuev's aesthetics and ideology: hostility to "official" society and to urban, educated culture. These are evident in the description of the lifeless literati in the fourth section, in the portrait of Tolstoy as a *grand seigneur;* in the implied criticism of Rasputin for his assimilation to official ecclesiastical and court culture; and in the treatment of the imperial court itself in the final section. By implication, "Gagar'ya sud'bina" rejects the very "high culture" upon which the possibility of reading the text is predicated—another characteristic gesture for the period, made with especial savagery by Klyuev and legitimized by his emergence from "the people," on whose behalf he has suffered imprisonment, as described in the sixth section. Beside this gesture, contradictory in itself, stands another, greater contradiction: the narrative of the author's sexual epiphany, facilitated by his capture by a band of Caucasian youths (and reiterated in prison narratives of the seventh section):

For about four days these people took my love, each time claiming me from one another. In farewell they gave me about one hundred rubles in money, a cashmere shirt with a forged silver belt, and boots. They also placed in a bag various sweet things for me.

The cliff which hid the burning spring had been smashed. Before me there opened a whole world of hitherto vague feelings and henceforth understood, beautiful pathways. In prison, at an overnight stop, in a monastery or in an elegant salon I console myself with the image of Ali, who was like a young, aromatic cypress tree. Later I learned that he had searched for me all over the Caucasus and southern Russia and had shot himself out of despair. (*Sd* 35)

Contradictions in identity and in textuality are thus implicitly associated with an assertion of a kind of sexuality highly unusual for a "peasant poet," albeit unremarkable for a Russian modernist. Moreover, the assertion is made in a form which combines the conventional ("Orientalism" linked to homosexuality) with the highly unconventional (the initiate as himself the object of an undying and eventually fatal passion). That "Gagar'ya sud'bina" combines programmatic statements about literary identity and mythologization of the origins of the poet's gift with a rather elaborate statement of sexual awakening seems to provide highly significant markers in the construction of identity, although the scholars (all Russian) who have heretofore discussed this work have chosen to elide the question of sexuality altogether.

It is evident that the episodic structure and folkloric lexicon—both markers of orality, and indicating the *skaz* orientation of "Gagar'ya sud'bina"—are themselves combined with, and even opposed by, some of the rhetorical features identified by Subbotin as characteristic of the prose which looks to Old Russian literature (that is, essentially, to archaic, "high," ecclesiastical culture) for its model. Extended parallels and stylistic accumulation abound, as the passages quoted above illustrate. Further illustration is provided by the opening lines of the fourth and fifth sections (marked by preoccupations with time and space that have already been explored in chapter 2):

Life on the country roads of Russia, beneath the tinkling of robins, beneath the mosquito buzz of the stars, was ever more stubbornly and ominously threatened by stone tentacles. And the inevitable was accomplished. The expanses of Mosdok, the pine lips of the White Sea coast spat me out into Moscow. With ten kopecks in my pocket I measured in bast-shoe steps the streets of that city of erstwhile beauty. (*Sd* 35) . . .

Life in my native nesting places, beneath Olonia's bast stars, gave me songs, composed holy dreams, untroubled, like the earth itself. (*Sd* 36)

Parallels ("Life on the country roads . . . ," "Life in my native nesting places . . ."), reiterations ("beneath the tinkling of robins, beneath the mosquito buzz of the stars . . .") with a parallel in the next section ("beneath Olonia's bast stars"), and contrasts ("stubbornly and ominously threatened by stone tentacles," "composed holy dreams, untroubled, the earth itself") are very evident in the rhetorical structures of the two openings. The familiar movement between general and abstract, abstract and concrete is evident throughout, achieving as its principal effect the association between the totality of Russia (especially rural Russia, Klyuev's *la Russie profonde*) and the individual poet. The threat to that Russia from "stone tentacles" (that is, from urban civilization) is significant first and foremost because it dispatches the poet himself to the city—and, by ironic implication, into literature. Meanwhile, Ossetia, in the Caucasus, and the White Sea coast in the far north seem to conspire in a striking geographic union to "spit him out" into Moscow (a characteristically jarring image). But in Moscow the poet retains his general peasant characteristics (bast shoes). The *petit pays* of the fourth section is invoked to give the poet his songs, which are then associated with a universal ("like the earth itself").

The seventh section opens as follows, echoing the opening of the sections cited above, with evident "ornamental" accumulation, as well as the rhetorical devices already noted elsewhere:

> Like the Russian high roads, like the many-sailed, barge-traveled Volga, like the homeless clouds in the clear autumn sky—so are known to me prison and the beggar's pouch, metal bars in a brick wall, iron teeth, the profane scolding of the prison convoy. I have wept over many a blackened one-kopeck coin, many a loaf of bread given for the repose, for the salvation of the "poor young unfortunate." (*Sd* 38)

In every way, "Gagar'ya sud'bina" is mixed text, and the mixture is often one of contrasts or contradictions. This is evident even in matters of veracity, which, as has been seen, have ranged readers of many of Klyuev's works against one another, and which are especially provoked by this text. The final episode described in "Gagar'ya sud'bina" is the poet's visit to Grand Princess Elizaveta Feodorovna, which, it is claimed, was a more sympathetic experience than his appearance at the imperial court before the empress herself:

> In Moscow, too, I was a royal guest—of the Empress's sister, Elizaveta Feodorovna. There it was easier to breathe, and minds were more radiant . . . Nesterov, my favorite artist, and Vasnetsov would visit the Princess on Ordynka street, without any ceremony. Kind and simple was Elizaveta Feodo-

rovna, she asked me about my mother, what her name was and did she like my songs. From refined writers I have yet to hear such questions. (*Sd* 42)

As Azadovsky points out, Klyuev did indeed read his poetry before the grand princess in 1916, and of the two famous artists Nesterov was certainly present at the reading. But, the scholar notes, Klyuev's assertion that he "was a guest of" (*gostil*) the grand princess is an "evident exaggeration."[35] Here too, even in documentary terms, are characteristically contradictory gestures: on the one hand, the poet *did* meet and read before the grand princess (a detail which must have seemed all the more remarkable, if not incredible, at the time of narration—early 1920s—than at the time of the event itself); on the other hand, the circumstances were apparently quite different from those described. But equally characteristic is the programmatic aesthetic assertion occasioned by this narrative: Nesterov is the poet's "favorite artist." The superficially naive tone of the account of Klyuev's contact with the imperial family introduces a significant marker not only of his aesthetics but also of one of his artistic models—the Russian arts and crafts movement, associated, for example, with Savva Mamontov and his country house at Abramtsevo. Moreover, this self-conscious marker of artistic genealogy provides yet another of the text's inversions. Nesterov and Vasnetsov represent, among other things, the high-cultural appropriation (and reinvigoration) of native ancient and folkloric traditions. Such an appropriation not only contributed to the emergence of Russian avant-garde art at the turn of the century but also facilitated the emergence of artists such as Klyuev himself "from the people."[36] Furthermore, Klyuev's description of his Moscow visit to the empress's sister immediately follows his remarks on Tsarskoe Selo, where he states that the only things he liked were the food and the Cathedral of St. Feodor (Feodorovsky sobor), built between 1909 and 1912 at the behest of the imperial family and to the design of Vladimir Pokrovsky. The cathedral is one of the finest examples of late *style russe,* has ties to the arts and crafts movement itself, and is the object of Klyuev's praise again in *Pesn' o Velikoi Materi,* as will be seen in chapter 6. Moreover, on Ordynka Street the poet would have found the Martha and Mary Convent of Mercy, founded by the grand princess whom he claims to have visited, and built, like the Cathedral of St. Feodor, in a late version of the neo-Russian architectural style; the frescoes in the main church, itself designed by Aleksei Shchusev, were painted by Nesterov. Again, apparently casual narrative movement in fact produces the reiteration of significant and programmatic aesthetic information, which itself provides a suggestive model for the text itself (high-cultural, with a popular, ancient, native orientation). That movement also creates a significant contrast between artists: Pokrovsky, Nesterov, and Vasnetsov all belong unambiguously to high art and even to the artistic establishment; Klyuev self-consciously positions himself outside those spheres, while placing his work in parallel with the efforts of those artists. Thus here, as elsewhere, "Gagar'ya sud'bina" presents itself as popular, spontaneous, and naive, while also reminding the reader that the popular, spontaneous, and naive are themselves artistically cultivated and appropriated devices. The diglossia which has been identified as a characteristic feature of Klyuev's style—literary or social—thus has its analogues in his use of referents and cultural models.

Any discussion of the imperial family in "Gagar'ya sud'bina" must also address Klyuev's claims that he read to the empress and her daughters in Tsarskoe Selo—the episode with which the warm welcome provided by the grand princess is contrasted in this final section of the narrative. It is well known that Esenin did read to them, and Azadovsky concludes with blunt irony that Klyuev has here confused himself with his fellow new-peasant poet (whom he had helped to establish at Feodorovsky Gorodok in 1916 as a hospital orderly, thereby saving him from military service at the front).[37] However, even this conclusion is not uniformly accepted. Karokhin, in his book on Esenin and Klyuev, citing the memoirs of the singer Yurii Morfessi, suggests that Esenin *and Klyuev* may have read to the imperial family on one occasion.[38] Not only is this episode itself still a matter of conjecture and dispute, but it is also part of an intriguing series of treatments of the Romanovs. In one of Klyuev's earliest prose works, "S rodnogo berega," the ruling dynasty is treated with savage contempt (*Sd* 107), when the author writes from the point of view of a peasant hostile to official structures; here in "Gagar'ya sud'bina," composed in the early 1920s, the view of the imperial family is ambiguous; but, as will be seen in chapter 6, by the time of *Pesn' o Velikoi Materi,* Klyuev seems explicitly sympathetic to the martyred emperor and his family, and implicitly regretful for his earlier hostility. Thus these and other allusions to the Romanovs form part of a self-conscious and ongoing reassessment of the poet's own past, and that of his country.

"Gagar'ya sud'bina" itself must be seen as an internally contradictory text, which seems to deny its reader (as it also denies its narrator) any firm ground. It is also an externally contradictory text, as is especially evident in the dual contexts of its composition and of its publication, already outlined. While very clearly a "literary" text, treated heretofore as a text for a reader, "Gagar'ya sud'bina" was, as far as it is possible to tell, originally a *performed* text, presumably directed not first and foremost at a general or ideal imagined readership, but at a specific auditor: Nikolai Arkhipov. Thus although in appearance a finished piece, it has close genre ties to the stories Klyuev told to individual interlocutors throughout his life. Moreover, circumstances and intrinsic qualities combine to require any commentary on it not only to be provisional but also to resist any absolute claims of textual authority and ownership. Just as the text as a literary object is characterized by multiple forms of "contamination" (among textual hierarchies and genres as discussed above), so too the text as a document cannot be authoritatively established as Klyuev's alone—there is no way of telling if Arkhipov as recording "scribe" intervened between Klyuev and the text. Nor should this problem be thought purely a phenomenon of an enforced restriction to private performance, although that circumstance was, as has been suggested, highly productive of textual instability in the Soviet period. It was also related to a fluidity of boundaries between different forms of discourse which characterized Klyuev's entire career, and was itself a marker of the age. Hence, for example, the Vytegra newspaper published in 1919 his "Medvezh'ya tsifir'" ("Bear's Calculation") with the subtitle "The approximately restored speech [*slovo*] made by the poet Nikolai Klyuev at the Vytegra Red Army Club 'Freedom' before the play 'We Shall Conquer'" (153). The issues of ownership and authority which the context of the composition of "Gagar'ya sud'bina" raise are reiterated in the publications of 1992 and 1993, when two scholars seem separately to lay claim to the text and in one case to legitimize and in the other to undermine the text's authority. Azadovsky's open dispute with Mikhailov over the former's publication and the two scholars' very different views of the text itself are predicated upon the very special circumstances of late Soviet philological scholarship, in which intense, even savage, ideological and similar debates were conducted at several removes from their original ground.

It was a commonplace of the 1970s and early 1980s that the most interesting material in literary publications was often "in the fine print" (*melkim shriftom*)—that is, in the detailed scholarly apparatus to texts. In other words, statements which would have been impossible to make openly, in separate publications, could be made in the discrete and discreet form of notes to another text. The reader long trained in the arts of deciphering such information would then construct a notional original text out of the fragments.

Thus, here too, multiple reversals may be observed: the marginalia become the substance of a text; the editor becomes the writer; the reader becomes the editor. Of course, these displacements are very reminiscent of the displacements compelled of and by Klyuev's own texts of the 1920s and 1930s, and help to explain the passion which very evidently surrounds new Klyuev publications in recent years. "Gagar'ya sud'bina," however, was published in the immediate post-Soviet period, when previously subterranean currents had reached the earth's surface, and hence the especially odd and evident juxtapositions of its dual appearance in 1992 and again in 1993.

It has yet to reach a wide audience, even a wide scholarly audience, but its fate and possible appeal in the twenty-first century provide ample grounds for speculation.

Chapter Five

Poetry of Destruction and the Destruction of Poetry: Klyuev's Late Lyric Poetry and the "Razrukha" Cycle

KLYUEV'S LATE LYRIC POETRY not only addresses directly both the personal circumstances of the poet himself and the general circumstances of Russian society of the time, but is also very much shaped, and even mutilated, by those circumstances. Its reception, too, is determined by the situation in which the poet found himself and by the context in which it was first widely read—long after its composition, and, indeed, long after the death of the author. Particularly illustrative of these points is the cycle "Razrukha" ("Destruction"), although many other later lyric works fulfill the same and similar paradigms.

"Gagar'ya sud'bina," as has been seen, marks the beginning of the period when not only for Klyuev but also for many Russian authors (and perhaps for most *major* Russian authors) "pre-Gutenberg" conditions shaped the composition and transmission of their work, and totalitarian attention shaped the course and often the ending of their lives. For some authors not only publishing but also writing became very difficult. Klyuev, too, suffered a period of agraphia. According to the dates in *Serdtse edinoroga,* the poet, it will be recalled, wrote no lyric poems between 1922 and July 30, 1925, the date of "Ne budu pisat' ot serdtsa" (522–23), nor are there any *poemy* from this two-and-a-half-year period. Thus the end of his Vytegra years marks a clear and decisive break in his career. Klyuev's travails in the later 1920s and the 1930s have already been outlined: his *poema Derevnya,* published in 1927, and his collection *Izba i pole,* published the next year and containing only two previously uncollected poems, mark, to all intents and purposes, the far boundary of his life as published author. Between 1928 and Klyuev's death in 1937 only four publications of his verse are recorded.[1] Of these, two are publications of "Matros" (1918; "Sailor," 388–89), and a third consists of the four-poem cycle"Stikhi iz kolkhoza" (1932; "Verses from a Collective Farm," 583–87), his last attempt to win favor with secular authority.

But Klyuev's estrangement from the printed word had begun earlier. The appearance in print of new work by the poet was very rare after his extensive publications of 1922 and 1923 (the collections *L'vinyi khleb* and *Lenin,* and the *poemy Chetvertyi Rim* and *Mat'-Subbota*).

The consequences of Klyuev's divorce from the printing press have already been outlined, and it should be emphasized again that they were fundamental not only in shaping that late poetic output but also in determining its survival and transmission (or otherwise), and in its contextualization when eventually published. In other words, not only does totalitarianism inevitably transform the thematics of poetry and the psychology of composition, but it also transforms the very physical substance of verse, which becomes quite different as a direct result of the sociopolitical environment. In these circumstances poetry also becomes even more different from prose than in more "normal" conditions, since the possibilities of performance and oral transmission (through memorization) still available to it—however dangerous—give it dimensions of existence largely denied to prose. Meanwhile, the individual poetic utterance may well become more isolated from the overall body of a poet's work, and the subsequent retrieval of individual lyrics becomes even more difficult than the recovery of extant but unpublished works of prose.

Even today the full profile of the poet's output in the years between his move from Vytegra to Leningrad in 1923 and his death in 1937 is not entirely clear. The fact that the vast majority of his new works in that period existed only in manuscript or typescript not only during his lifetime but also until the late 1960s (and a significant minority beyond that decade) guarantees that at least some have been lost forever, while others exist in multiple, sometimes unreliable, versions. Moreover, as a poet who continued to work but whose professional existence lay largely outside the boundaries of the world of printed literature, Klyuev operated within literary parameters that were quite different from those of most modern writers in the first world. The distinguishing criteria of "finished/unfinished" and "public/private," for example, have far less clarity in these new circumstances. On the other hand, it is clear that despite the pressures applied upon him or created for him by political circumstances, he continued to compose very actively. Approximately seventy lyrics from the period 1923–37 have now been published; and the majority of his *poemy,* finished and unfinished, also come from this period (*Zaozer'e, Derevnya,* and *Plach o Sergee Esenine,* 1926; *Solovki,* 1926–28; *Pogorel'shchina,* 1928; *Kain,* 1929; *Pesn' o Velikoi Materi,* 1931; *Kreml',* 1934). In other words, Klyuev is known to have composed about eighty more or less separate poetic works in this period, and some of them (including not only the *poemy* but also many of the 1930s lyrics) are long. While neither volume nor length is a measure of quality (and, indeed, opinions vary about the quality of the later works), the very fact of Klyuev's continued functioning as a poet in these conditions must, in and of itself, be counted an act of cultural defiance. The prominence of *poemy* and similar works in this period, however, warns the observer not to draw a strict and exclusive distinction between poets who published and poets who did not and could not publish: his oeuvre shows the same tendency to long, narrative works in this period as that of many "published" poets.

Klyuev's poetic career after he left Vytegra also fulfills another paradigm of the time: while most of his works were clearly "unpublishable," it is obvious that a number of his pieces were expressly "for publication." These include the four "Stikhi iz kolkhoza" mentioned above, "Bogatyrka" of 1925, "Leningrad," "Zastol'naya," "Segodnya prazdnestvo u domen," and "Ya kuznets Vavila," all of 1926, and "Yunost'" of 1927 ("The Giant Girl," "Leningrad," "Song for the Table," "Today the blast furnaces are celebrating," "I am Vavila, the blacksmith," "Youth"; 523–24, 529–33, 540–41). In the last-named poem the speaker, evidently a Young Pioneer, celebrates the beauty of his uniform. These poems illustrate an irony characteristic of the period: that which was intended expressly for publication *thereby* invites accusations of "inauthenticity," on the grounds that only what could *not* be published could possibly be the *authentic* voice of the poet. Indeed, from this period until the middle of the 1980s, a very significant reversal of categories conventional in the modern "first world" haunts Russian high culture: the published word is always under threat of conviction for impoverishment, servility, and dishonesty; the unpublished (and, increasingly, the *unrecorded, merely spoken*) word becomes validated as authentic and primary—at least, when and where opinions are exercised freely. Nor do the ironies of this reversal of hierarchies end here: when Klyuev was discussed again in print within the Soviet Union, in the 1960s and 1970s, it was his late *published* poems that were appropriated by Russia-based authors, who themselves were often obliged to modify radically their intellectual positions in order to publish their scholarship and criticism. They, of course, seized on Klyuev's ideologically "safe" works so as to justify and promote him at home. Meanwhile scholars publishing outside the Soviet Union largely dismissed those works. Thus the former writers published, quoted, and often praised with remarkable enthusiasm Klyuev's small body of "pro-Soviet" works, apparently ignoring almost all his other poetry of the period, while the latter actively sought and published the Klyuev who was unpublishable at home. Both activities had, of course, their own obvious and even justifiable contextual logic, although they produced very particular images of the poet.

Finally, in the post-Soviet period it has become easier to survey the totality of an author's output in its historical and aesthetic range without resorting to such radical gestures, but it must be said that the tools for analyzing and discussing the "court poetry" of the Soviet period, especially that produced by authors who were not first and foremost court poets, have yet to be brought into general use, while sober assessment of the previously unpublished work is often difficult. The discomforting (but, common sense suggests, not unsurprising) fact that some poets seem to have produced what is by most standards "good poetry" while writing "to order" or to protect themselves is the clearest indication of the need for renewed consideration of this issue, not least because it is vital to an understanding of the psychological environment of Stalinism. The phenomena of worthwhile court poetry and the problems attendant upon it are widespread, yet attract attention only rarely and in the most extreme cases, such as that of Mandelstam.[2] Another striking example, but without the canonical impact today of Mandelstam's Stalin poem, is Zabolotosky's "Goriiskaya simfoniya" ("Gori Symphony") celebrating Stalin's birthplace—a work that was ignored publicly both in the Soviet Union and outside it for the second half of the twentieth century, but for the high quality of which an uncomfortably powerful case might be made. Few would be willing to make such claims for Klyuev's propaganda lyrics of the 1920s (although the later, longer, and more complex *Kreml'*, finally published in 2006, is a somewhat different case), but they are an integral part of his professional activities in those years, and provide a significant context within which to read the bleaker, even apocalyptic works on the fate of Russia which he was composing at the same time.[3] Of the latter, an early and striking example is the lyric "Nasha sobachka u vorot otlayala" ("Our dog has done its barking at the gates," 536–37), which—as Azadovsky puts it, "by some miracle"—*was* published in the very year of its composition: 1926.[4] Equally significant is the (admittedly limited) evidence of Klyuev's attitudes to his "publishable" work. As his correspondence with Yar-Kravchenko indicates, Klyuev's late *Kreml'*, written in Siberia (in extremis), and, it must be assumed, intended by the poet—with undue but understandable optimism—to save his life and to bring him back to European Russia, seems to evoke from Klyuev exactly the same professional and proprietary feelings as politically dangerous works from the early 1930s which he expressly forbade his correspondent to circulate (*Sd* 317–18).[5]

Here, as in so many other aspects of his creative biography, the individual and the general coincide: Klyuev showed himself capable throughout his career of occupying contradictory positions, sometimes simultaneously; moreover, the Soviet period demanded of its citizens in general, and its artists in particular, the ability dramatically to make and remake themselves not only according to chronology but also according to the contemporaneous, often contradictory, demands of complex social situations. Klyuev's "masks" and "created biographies"—themselves to a degree products of the cultural environment of the symbolist period, and to a degree the result of his personal situation and character—were, in one sense, a perfect fit for the new age. In another sense they were, of course, a dangerous provocation of that age.

Thus Klyuev could in 1926 write (but not publish) "Ne budu pet' kooperatsiyu" ("I will not sing praises to cooperatives," 527–29), an aesthetic manifesto with a characteristically provocative opening line, while also writing and publishing as "Novye pesni" ("New Songs") the four poems of 1926 listed above, works which praised none other than the cooperative structures of Soviet society. Hence too, in 1926 he could write (and publish) both "Nasha sobachka u vorot otlayala" and "Leningrad" (one of the "New Songs"). Bleak indeed is the picture of the present painted by the former:

Наша собачка у ворот отлаяла,
Замело пургою башмачок Светланы,
А давно ли нянюшка ворожила-баяла
Поваренкой вычерпать поморья-океаны.

А давно ли Россия избою куталась, —
В подголовнике бисеры, шелка багдадские,
Кичкою кичилась, тулупом тулупилась,
Слушая акафисты да бунучки казацкие?
. . .
Хороша была Настенька у купца Чапурина,
За ресницей рыбица глотала глубь глубокую
Аль опоена, аль окурена,
Только сгибла краса волоокая.

Налетела на хоромы преукрашены
Птица мертвая — поганый вран,
Оттого от Пинеги до Кашина
Вьюгой разоткался Настин сарафан.

У матерой матери Мамелфы Тимофеевны
Сказка-печень вспорота и сосцы откушены,
Люди обезлюдены, звери обеззверены . . .
Глядь, березка ранняя мерит серьги Лушины!
. . .
За оконцем Настенька в пяльцы душу впялила —
Вышить небывалое кровью да огнем . . .
Наша корнаухая у ворот отлаяла
На гаданье нянино с вещим башмачком.

Our dog has done its barking at the gates,
The blizzard has swept away Svetlana's shoe,
Was it so long ago that the nanny worked her magic,
Drawing up oceans with a ladle.

Was it long ago that Russia sheltered in a peasant house—
In the headrest beads and Baghdad silks,
Strutting its headdress, wrapped in its fleece coat,
Listening to hymns of praise and Cossack pennants flapping?
. . .
Beautiful was the merchant Chapurin's daughter Nasten'ka,
Behind her lashes a fish swallowed mighty deeps,
Either made drunk or smoked out,
But the ox-eyed beauty is gone.

The bird of death—the cursed raven,
Has landed on the painted mansion,
Thus from Pinega to Kashin
The snowstorm has rent Nastya's dress.

The strong mother Mamelfa Timofeevna's
Folk-tale liver is ripped up and her nipples are bitten off,
People are unpeopled, beasts less than bestial . . .
Look, the early birch tree is trying on Lusha's earrings!
. . .
Beyond the window Nasten'ka has woven her soul into the lace
frame—
Weaving the incredible in blood and fire . . .
Our crop-eared dog has done its barking at the gates
At the nanny's fortune-telling with the prophetic shoe.

But the tone of "Leningrad" could hardly be more optimistic:

В излуке Балтийского моря,
Где невские волны шумят,
С косматыми тучами споря,
Стоит богатырь — Ленинград.
. . .
Когда же заря молодая
Багряное вздует горно —
Великое Первое Мая
В рабочее стукнет окно.

Взвалив себе на спину трубы,
На площади выйдет завод.
За ним Комсомол краснозубый —
Республики пламенный мед.

At a bend in the Baltic Sea,
Where the waves of the Neva roar,
Quarreling with the rough-edged clouds,
Stands the mighty Leningrad
. . .
When the young dawn
Lights up the scarlet furnace—
The great First of May
Will knock on the worker's window.

Hoisting on its shoulders trumpets,
Out on to the squares comes the factory,
Followed by the red-toothed Komsomol—
The republic's red honey.

It is possible to reiterate the "authentic/inauthentic" opposition, so often the center of polemics over Klyuev, and to note that only "Nasha sobachka u vorot otlayala" is full of gestures characteristic of the poet in general: diverse and obvious literary allusions (Zhukovsky's "Svetlana," Mel'nikov's Nasten'ka, and so on); geographic universality (from Baghdad to Pinega); very visible and audible patterning, sometimes close to cacophony or pleonasm ("U *mat*eroi *mat*eri *Mame*lfy Ti*mo*feevny"). However, "Leningrad" is also typical of Klyuev, for whom end-stopped lines and regular meter are especially characteristic of his stylized songlike narratives, and also increasingly typical of all of his lyrics from the mid-1920s on. Nonetheless, "Leningrad" and its brethren—programmatic poems apparently intended to indicate "good will" on the part of the poet—are isolated works in Klyuev's 1920s oeuvre, and have as analogues in the 1930s only the four "Stikhi iz kolkhoza" poems and *Kreml'*—the last a product of desperate exile, but, in fact, a work far more typical of Klyuev's poetics than some of the earlier out-and-out propaganda works.

The majority of Klyuev's late works are preoccupied with the fate of the country, with the nature of his poetry itself, and with that most traditional of lyric topics—individual love. When they combine two or three of these themes in one poem—as they often do—the effects are especially striking. Not only are the civic and the traditionally lyric united in a strikingly transgressive coupling, but the lyric theme itself is once again explicitly "transgressive," in that the love is homosexual. Prior to this period, homoerotic themes were evident intermittently, first in the "fraternal" and related poems of *Bratskie pesni,* then in later sectarian lyrics and in more conventional love poems, as well as in isolated, individual lines. In the most striking of such pieces the combination of popular, folkloric elements with "transgressive" symbolist eroticism seemed to authorize the homosexual thematics. Now, in the late poems, the new state of poetic production, in which established boundaries between public and private have disappeared, but in which the prospects of traditional publication are limited indeed, seems to permit a new form of sexual openness. In other words, the Stalinist cultural situation seems to contribute to the frank articulation of homosexuality—another circumstance not without irony. It should be recalled, however, that the "authorization" was, at best, very partial—limited to the poet and his intimates, for Klyuev's homosexuality contributed to his arrest in 1934, and thus to his early death. Klyuev himself, however, seems not to have observed these limits and divisions, even if they were significant in producing his late love poetry, for according to Gronsky, he actively sought the publication of "O chem shumyat sedye kedry."[6] Of course, biographical circumstances also help to explain the foregrounding of homosexual love in these late poems—above all, Klyuev's profound (and pained) affection for Anatolii Yar-Kravchenko, with whom so many of the late poems, lyric and narrative, are associated. Nonetheless, it is significant that the exclamation of vitality so characteristic of the late poetry can explicitly combine the personal and the public, often in tones that are expressly *civic,* as in the final lines of "Po zhizni raduites' so mnoi" ("Through life delight with me," 591–92):

Уймись, поджарый надоеда, —
Не остудят метели деда,
Лишь стойло б клевером цвело,
У рябки лоснилось крыло
И конь бы радовался сбруе,
Как песне непомерный Клюев! —
Он жив, олонецкий ведун,
Весь от снегов и вьюжных струн
Скуластой тундровой луной
Глядится в яхонт заревой!

Calm down, scrawny bore—
Snowstorms will not chill the old man,
As long as the stall flowers with clover
The speckled hen's wing shines,
And the horse delights in its harness,
Like the boundless Klyuev in song!—
He lives, the seer of Olonia,
All from snows and blizzard strings
Like a bone-faced tundra moon
He peers into dawn's amber!

These lines assert the continued life of the poet and "Olonian seer" and conclude with him looking into "dawn's amber" with what may seem a note of general optimism (morning, new dawn, and so on). However, amber—an image encountered frequently in Klyuev's late work—is unambiguously and without exception associated with the lyric and the personal: it stands everywhere for the beloved's eyes. In other words, the speaker's poetic vitality is asserted in programmatic terms (explicitly traditional—northern Russia; poet as seer, and so on; implicitly a-Soviet or even anti-Soviet), but this public discourse of literature and society is associated with the barely encoded reference to the beloved with which the poem ends. The association is perhaps even more striking when the master theme is not love, but betrayal (by far the most productive theme and, apparently, inspiration in Klyuev's late non-narrative works). One of the longest and best exemplars of that association is "Povest' skorbi" ("Tale of Woe," 1933). This work, nearly two hundred lines long, was finally published in 1990.[7] In *Serdtse edinoroga* it is included among Klyuev's *poemy,* and, indeed, it is longer than some of its neighbors (696–701). A twelve-line epigraph from an "ancient prison song" appears to lament the betrayal of the speaker by his (male) beloved, and provides the title for the poem itself:

Над домом вечного позора
Стоят два ангела с крестом,
И часовые для дозора —
Внизу с заряженным ружьем!
Как ангел тихий, непорочный,
И ты мне верен был шесть лет,
Но вот пробил наш час урочный, —
Нарушен клятвенный обет!
Тебе простить вину такую
Я хотел бы, но не смог,
И повесть скорби роковую
Угрюмо слушает острог.

Above the house of endless shame
Stand two angels with a cross
And sentries for patrol
Below with loaded rifles!
Chaste like a quiet angel,
You were faithful to me for six years,
But now our appointed hour has struck—
Broken is the sworn oath!
I would like to forgive you

What you've done to me, but can't,
And now the prison gloomily attends
The fateful tale of woe.

While some of Klyuev's epigraphs have only a tangential bearing on the poems which they preface, this one introduces many of the primary features of "Povest' skorbi": it interweaves highly personal thematics with civic implications (the speaker and addressee are, after all, *prisoners*); it combines high and low (the literary and the folkloric); and it crosses the conventional with the transgressive (lament of betrayed lover, homosexuality). The epigraph also shares with the poem the most common meter of the late poetry: iambic tetrameter. The poem itself opens with a condemnation of the faithless lover:

Ты не поверил до конца
В Пречистый Лик, в зарок кольца
С крестом московских патриархов,
И вот колтун с собачьей пархой,
Твои ночные завсегдатаи,
Сулят Оксану в темном гае.

You did not believe to the end
In the Pure Visage, the pledge of the ring
With the cross of Moscow patriarchs,
And now knotted hair and ailing skin
Your nighttime constant visitors,
Promise Oksana in a dark grove.

The collapsing of personal faith into confessional faith, and the association of personal betrayal with anathema, provide striking examples of the solipsistic union of poet and country, individual and collective recurrent in the late lyrics. Expressly "civic" motifs provide the background for this betrayal in the stanza which begins at the twenty-fourth line:

Моя родимая земля
Расшита кровяной синелью,
И к дьявольскому рукоделью
Любимый приложил персты,
Сорвав влюбленности цветы
И дружбы сумеречный розан!

My native land
Is embroidered like bloody chenille,

And my beloved put his fingers
To the devil's handiwork
Plucking the flowers of love
And the dusky rose of friendship!

In the following two stanzas (lines 38–46), the speaker articulates the composition of his "tale of woe" with typically syncretic metaphors for the making of poetry, and then describes a moment of piety:

Поблеклым вереском да воском
Я расшиваю повесть скорби, —
Лазорь и шелк уснули в торбе,
Им не пойти стихом вприсядку.
Я теплю синюю лампадку
Пред образом из Белозерья, —
По чудотворному поверью,
Он ослепил орду татар. . . .

With faded heather and with wax
I embroider this tale of woe—
Azure and silk have fallen asleep in the bag
They will not come out to dance in verse.
I heat the blue icon lamp
Before the icon from Belozer'e—
According to a miraculous belief
It blinded a Tatar horde. . . .

Here the speaker "embroiders" his tale—a characteristic and telling figure for the actions of the poet (and a reference to familiar northern crafts)—but azure and silk, vivid colors and materials equally typical of Klyuev, will not *dance* in his verse. The running-together of the motif of popular craftsmanship with vivid, if conventional, images of wealth and color, and also with the figure of—presumably popular—dancing provides an elaborate and multivalent representation of the author's own art. It is equally telling that this quatrain is followed by a description of the speaker's veneration of a wonder-working icon, presumably from the Belozersky Monastery, one of the great monasteries of the Russian north (in fact, the identity of this icon is unclear—it seems that it is *not* one of the famous icons associated with the resistance to the Tatars). This quatrain, however, concludes—indeed, is graphically represented as being broken off—with an ellipsis and is immediately followed by the beginning of a highly lyrical narrative of the now lost love, in which the characters of lover and beloved are identified quite unambiguously:

Жил дед и Анатолий Яр —
Лосенок, что пришел напиться
К ручью лесному, морок длится
Седьмой поземок и весну. . . .

There lived Grandfather and Anatolii Yar—
An elk calf, come to drink his fill
At a forest stream, the illusion lasts
For seven blizzards and a spring. . . .

In short, even within the first quarter of the poem, referent, tone, and theme have changed again and again, although (in contrast to some of the late poems) the disjunction is not so powerful as to lead the reader to question whether any integral meaning can be salvaged from the fragments. Like the majority of the late lyrics, these changes in direction are contained within a very conventional meter and a relatively standard rhyme scheme (compound metrical forms are less common in these late works than earlier), although the strophic structure of this poem is somewhat irregular. And while Klyuev's language always demands close attention (and often a dictionary), and here is certainly lexically and stylistically diverse, this poem, again like many of the later works, is more linguistically accessible than much of his earlier poetry.

When the making of the "tale of woe" is described again, at and after line 98, yet another association is added to the master image of sewing:

Но скорби повесть нижет вновь
За порванною нитью — муза.
С душистой земляникой кузов
Мои стихи теперь — опенки
Без самоцветного лосенка,
Что в сердце искупал копытца!

But once again the Muse is threading
The tale of woe on the broken thread.
A basket with fragrant wild strawberries—
My poems now are agaric mushrooms
Without the jewel-precious elk calf
That bathed his hooves in my heart!

The marked reiteration—even some rhymes and syntax are repeated (*chto v serdtse iskupal kopytsa*—compare *chto prishel napit'sya*)—emphasizes the novel elements: the Muse; the fact that now the speaker's poems appear to be (bright-red, poisonous) agaric mushrooms, not wild strawberries. The combination of imagery from the natural world with highly and conventionally literary figures such as the Muse is also very typical. Nor are the literary references restricted to the general. In the penultimate stanza of the poem a specific (and rather startling) literary analogue for the situation of speaker and addressee is suddenly elaborated:

От невской пасмурной волны
И от иглы адмиралтейской
Питаться повестью злодейской
Тебе, как Дантесу, не внове:
Взгляни, росинка свежей крови
Горит и на твоей перчатке!
С судьбою не играют в прятки —
Я умираю, не кляня,
Прости, Владычица, меня!
Я твой в рубахе пестрядинной,
Поэт посконный и овинный,
Но Пушкину сродни звездой,
Убит любимою рукой
И дружбой в ранах не обвязан!

From the Neva's gloomy waves
And from the Admiralty needle
It's nothing new for you, like d'Anthès,
To feed upon an evil tale:
Look down, a drop of fresh blood
Burns on your glove too!
You can't play hide-and-seek with fate,
I die, without a curse,
Forgive me, Queen of Heaven!
I'm yours in my coarse peasant shirt,
A poet of hemp and of the barn,
But linked by the stars to Pushkin,
Killed by a loving hand
And not bandaged by friendship in his wounds!

Again, run together are the grief at personal betrayal and the assertion of cultural and poetic identity (the "hempen" poet), while the association of the speaker's fate with that of Pushkin, killed by George d'Anthès in a duel, is rich with implications—savage for the addressee, not unflattering for the speaker. Moreover, here and in the final stanza emerges another theme recurrent in the late poetry—the anticipated death of the poet. Another late poem, thematically close to "Povest' skorbi," is entitled "Iz predsmertnykh pesen" ("From Songs Written Before Death," 612–13), while Klyuev's last known poem, although unrelated to the personal themes of these works, explicitly and movingly prefigures his death. And here, as elsewhere, the poet's own death is tied not only to the experience of personal betrayal but also to the grand themes that equally preoccupy him in these late works—national crisis and disaster; and confessional loyalty ("Forgive me, Queen of Heaven"—it should be noted that the confessional tenor of Klyuev's late work, and of his correspondence, is generally Orthodox rather than schismatic or sectarian).

No discussion, however brief, of "Povest' skorbi" would be complete without allusion to its physical location. The poem was published twice: in 1990 by Konstantin Azadovsky, who based his publication on typescript copies in the archives of Nikolai Arkhipov and Ivanov-Razumnik; and in 1991 by Aleksandr Mikhailov, from the Ivanov-Razumnik archive. The provenance of the text is entirely characteristic of Klyuev's late works, although, somewhat unusually, it seems to present no significant textological problems (the two publications are more or less exactly the same). Equally characteristic is the fact that both publications were in relatively minor periodicals, where, a decade later, only a specialist would be likely to find them. Klyuev's late poetry continues to be as unlucky as its author. Even *Serdtse edinoroga* seems to misplace the poem—designating it a *poema,* and providing very limited commentary.

While in Klyuev's *poemy*—all written in the Soviet period, and many in his "pre-Gutenberg" years—it is public discourse and grand historical themes which tend to predominate (although the longest, *Pesn' o Velikoi Materi,* is, as will be seen, also highly personal), the late lyrics are mostly presented as occasioned by personal themes, whether they be love and betrayal, meditations on aging and death, or individual addresses. These occasions, and the poems associated with them, may be seen, among other things, as further expressions of the compositional context of the late works: love, especially homosexual love, romantic betrayal, personal isolation and imminent death, and friendship all become far more than conventional lyric themes in the Stalinist situation, while the collapsing of subject and audience into one (that is to say, those whom one addresses and about whom one writes are also one's primary, perhaps one's only, audience and readership) provides an added compositional impulse as well as another example of the disintegration of standard contextual boundaries. In addition to the numerous poems to Yar-Kravchenko, announced and unannounced, there are also lyrics addressed to the poet Pavel Vasil'ev and the singer Nadezhda Obukhova. Klyuev clearly felt some sympathy with Vasil'ev, although he was later to hold him partially responsible for his 1934 arrest, to judge from a letter of October 1935 (*Sd* 371, 385). The poetic address to Vasil'ev, "Ya chelovek, rozhdennyi ne v boyakh" ("I am a man born not in battle," 615–18), elaborates both that sympathy and, again, Klyuev's own poetic creed—as ever, not without contradictions. The poem to Obukhova, "Bayukalo tebya raiskoe drevo" ("The tree of heaven sang you lullabies"), is even more interesting, and may be included among the late masterpieces (618–19). Klyuev's abiding syncretism is marked by the very subject—a poem addressed to and about a great Russian operatic singer. Formally somewhat unusual among the late works, it nonetheless shares the general tendency to combine the very specific and personal with the general and civic. It is quoted here in full:

Баюкало тебя райское древо
Птицей самоцветной — девой,
Ублажала ты песней царя Давида,
Он же гуслями вторил взрыдам.
Таково пресладостно пелось в роще,
Где ручей поцелуями ропщет,
Виноградье да яхонты-дули! . . .
И проснулась ты в русском июле:
«Что за край, лесная округа?»
Отвечают: «Кострома да Калуга!»
Протерла ты глазыньки рукавом кисейным,
Видишь — яблоня в плату златовейном!
Поплакала с сестрицей, пожурилась
Да и пошла белицей на клирос.
Таяла, как свеченька, полыхая веждой,
И прослыла в людях Обуховой Надеждой.
А мы, холуи, зенки пялим, —
Не видим, что Сирин в бархатной зале,
Что сердце райское под белым тюлем
Обожжено грозовым июлем,
Лесными пожарами, гладом да мором,
Кручинится по синим небесным озерам —
То Любашей в «Царской невесте»,
То Марфой в огненном благовестье.
А мы, холуи, зенки пялим! —

Не видим крыл в заревом опале,
Не слышим гуслей царя Давида
За дымом да слезами горькой панихиды!
Пропой нам, сестрица, кого погребаем
В Костромском да Рязанском крае?
Ответствует нам краса Любаша:
«Это русская долюшка наша, —
    Голова на коле
    Косынка в пекле,
    Перстенек на Хвалынском дне».
        Аминь.

The tree of heaven sang you lullabies
A jewel bird—a maiden,
You pleased King David with song,
He answered wails with his psaltery.
Such was the sweet singing in the grove,
Where the stream murmurs kisses,
Grapevines and amber-pipes! . . .
And you woke up in a Russian July:
"What country is this, forest land?"
They answered, "Kostroma and Kaluga!"
You wiped your eyes with a muslin sleeve,
And saw—an apple tree in a gold-trimmed scarf!
You cried with your sister, joked
And went off like a novice to the church choir.
Melted, like a candle, blazing eyelids,
And became known among men as Nadezhda Obukhova.
And we, lackeys, stare, eyes wide open—
Can't see, that Sirin is in the velvet hall,
That a heart from heaven beneath white tulle
Has been singed by stormy July,
By forest fires, hunger and plague,
Yearns for the blue celestial lakes—
As Lyubasha in "The Tsar's Bride,"
Or as Marfa in fiery Angelus.
And we, lackies, stare, eyes wide open!—
Don't see wings in the dawn's opal,
Don't hear the psaltery of King David
Behind the smoke and tears of a bitter funeral mass!
Sing us, sister, the name of the departed
In the lands of Kostroma and Ryazan'.

Lovely Lyubasha answers us:
"It is our Russian fate—
  Head on a stake
  Scarf on fire,
  Ring on the bottom of the Caspian Sea."
    Amen.

Like so many other Klyuev poems, it opens with a conceit—the addressee had a charmed, mythological past and, one day, found herself transported to Russia. This conceit is gradually abandoned in order to elaborate the present in which the addressee and the country find themselves. The poem also shares with many other Klyuev works an interest in quotation and in the identification of particular historical or cultural figures—here characters from Rimsky-Korsakov's *The Tsar's Bride* and Mussorgsky's *Khovanshchina,* and roles played by the addressee. Nor, indeed, are those figures merely adjuncts to the description of the addressee, since they enable reference to one of Klyuev's master-figures (the self-immolation of Old Believers, which provides the culminating scene of *Khovanshchina*—hence Marfa is "in fiery Angelus") and also reiterate the related theme of Russia's destruction, as the quotation in the final lines provides an answer to the request "Sing us, sister, the name of the departed."

The story of this poem's publication is different from that of "Povest' skorbi," but provides another textological paradigm for the late Klyuev. It appears as one of thirty-seven late lyrics published for the first time in *Sochineniya,* copied from Soviet archives by the British Slavist Gordon McVay.[8] This was the first significant publication of Klyuev's post-1928 poetry. Only very gradually did the poems published there make their way into print in the Soviet Union. The Obukhova poem was luckier than most other late works, appearing, for example, in the Biblioteka poeta edition of 1977, *Stikhotvoreniya i poemy* of 1986, *Zaveshchanie* of 1988, *Pesnoslov* of 1990, *Stikhotvoreniya i poemy* of 1991, and *Stikhotvoreniya: Poemy* of the same year. However, only in 1988 was it published from the fair copy. The draft version of the poem, published first in *Sochineniya,* which, it will be recalled, served as the standard edition of Klyuev for over thirty years, has eight significant variants from that fair copy, several of which seem to stem from problems with transcribing the manuscript. There are also numerous differences in punctuation. The intervening publications between *Sochineniya* and the appearance of the final version seem to correct the most obvious misreadings of the former, but all appear to be based upon the same (evidently less than final) text as *Sochineniya* itself. Such textual problems were, of course, part and parcel of the later Soviet period, when works were often published without the participation of their authors. Many authors of the 1960s and 1970s lost touch with their own works as the latter entered the sea of samizdat, and could conveniently claim that they had no role in publication when those works eventually emerged abroad. Other authors were long dead when their works saw the light of day, in the West or in the Soviet Union. And in Klyuev's case, problems generated by misreadings and textological errors compound other difficulties. His late poetry is, in and of itself, marked by syntactical breaks, linguistic irregularities, and radical discontinuities of narrative, image, and tone, so that distinguishing clearly between immanent poetics and traces of physical circumstances often becomes well-nigh impossible. In other words, the extra-textual problems of transmission can very easily pass for intra-textual problems of Klyuev's own poetics.

Thematic discontinuity (although accompanied usually by formal continuity) marks most of Klyuev's mature poetry, but is especially striking in the late lyrics. Although not marked by compression, these works are elusive in their associative coherence in a manner which, *mutatis mutandis,* may recall the late lyrics of Mandelstam, whose literary situation bears some resemblance to Klyuev's last fifteen years. "Bayukalo tebya" is all the more striking as a double exception—it is thematically integral, but not metrically homogeneous.

There are many examples of the intermingling of immanent and contextual problems in the late works. The cycle "O chem shumyat sedye kedry" ("What the Gray Cedars Talk of," 551–70) provides one example—is it, as Klyuev seems to describe it, a *poema,* or is it, as successive editors have indicated when publishing parts of it, a cycle of lyric poems?[9] While answering that question might seem largely an "academic" matter, the diverse ways in which the components of "O chem" have been published is a substantive issue in tracing the reception and understanding of the late Klyuev: six poems were first published in *Sochineniya,* with significant textual problems, and with no indication of their interrelationship (suggesting, since the source of those publications was Klyuev's own archive, that their compositional history may be individual and separate—and, indeed, Klyuev sent parts of the cycle separately to Yar-Kravchenko in various letters); three were published as "From the Cycle 'What the Gray Cedars Talk of'" in the Biblioteka poeta *Stikhotvoreniya i poemy* of 1977; one appeared under the same heading in *Izbrannoe* (1981); eight works of a numbered *thirteen* from the "Cycle" were published in *Stikhotvoreniya i poemy* of 1986, where the thirteenth is "Klevetnikam iskusstva," a poem that has no relationship to "O chem" whatsoever; seven of twelve from the "Cycle" appeared in Subbotin's *Pesnoslov,* but with a note in the critical apparatus that a letter of the poet's calling the work a *poema* had been found, but too late to move these extracts to the *poemy* section of that volume. No parts appear in Kunyaev's *Stikho-*

tvoreniya i poemy of 1991, nor in Azadovsky's collection of the same year. Finally, Mikhailov, in his little-known *Stikhotvoreniya i poemy* (Stavropol', 1992) published the entire work—as the last member of the *poemy* section of his edition—but broke it down into *thirteen* parts, dividing what is published elsewhere as a single poem into two (splitting off the second half of "Nedoumenno ne kori" ["Do not rebuke in astonishment"] into a new work, beginning at "Sbezhala temnaya voda" ["Dark water ran off"]). Nor should it be forgotten that *O chem shumyat sedye kedry* was also the title of a collection of thirty-three lyrics, compiled by Klyuev in 1933 and intended for publication by the Writers' Publishing House in Leningrad (Izdatel'stvo pisatelei v Leningrade). In 1978, from the sixty-page manuscript of that collection, Azadovsky published in the provincial journal *Baikal* five lyrics, four of which are also part of the cycle of the same name.[10] Azadovsky's treatment of these archival materials was the subject of polemical remarks by Subbotin, in his review of the Kunyaevs' 1986 *Stikhotvoreniya i poemy*.[11] That review illuminates many of the archival and archivo-political problems of these publications.

Thus "O chem shumyat sedye kedry," which exemplifies and condenses many of the late Klyuev's favorite themes and devices into a single, if discontinuous, whole and which, according to one account, played some role in the poet's arrest, is nowhere published without problems, even though parts of it appeared in print as long ago as the late 1960s.[12] The fate of "Stikhi iz kolkhoza," a polar opposite to "O chem," but composed the same year, is, in its way, just as revealing. That cycle of four poems, written, it may be presumed, with extra-literary intentions, but important in the profile of Klyuev's poetry in the 1930s, seems only to have been republished in full once: in *Sochineniya* (as "Stikhi o kolkhoze"), until its appearance in *Serdtse edinoroga*. The Biblioteka poeta *Stikhotvoreniya i poemy* of 1977 has three of the four poems; *Izbrannoe* of 1981 has one. As was typical of editorial treatment in the 1960s, 1970s, and 1980s of potentially embarrassing court poetry by poets trying to win breathing space or favor, later Soviet editions de-Sovietized Klyuev to the extent of excluding this work of socialist realism altogether, yet without representing the rest of his late output with anything approaching thoroughness (whereas scholars, as was noted above, had earlier quoted with enthusiasm "pro-Soviet" works of the poet).

Of course, editors, relying on different archives, come to different conclusions and work under different constraints. However, editorial selection and the exercise of individual preferences have especially significant consequences in cases where no statements of poetic intent and conception have been made in print by the poet himself, nor has a full, collected works-type edition been prepared subsequently. For example, while the limited number of poems dated after 1923 in the Biblioteka poeta edition of

1977 (20 out of 221 lyric poems in the collection) is to be explained largely by political constraints, it is Azadovsky's stated reservations about the late poetry that presumably led him to include only 18 poems written after 1923 in his *Stikhotvoreniya: Poemy* (which totals 153 lyrics, and which shows no signs of Soviet-period editorial constraints). Forty-nine of the 419 lyrics in *Sochineniya* are from that period—that edition publishes all of Klyuev's works known to its editors, while 26 of 152 in Subbotin's *Pesnoslov,* compiled in the late Soviet period, are dated after 1923. Only in 1999, with the publication of *Serdtse edinoroga,* could a reader curious about Klyuev's later poetry find an up-to-date, more or less complete statement of the poet's entire output, with 68 of its 510 lyrics dated after 1923.

Moreover, not only are there omissions in every publication, but there are also a number of "phantom" appearances. Mikhailov's thirteenth part to "O chem shumyat sedye kedry" is one such. *Sochineniya* publishes others. The following four lines are published as "a fragment from the unpublished hymn-*poema* 'City of White Flowers'" (2:238):

> Будет трактор, упырь железный,
> Кровь сосать из земли.
> Край былинный мой, край болезный,
> До чего тебя довели!
>
> The tractor, an iron vampire,
> Will suck the blood from the earth.
> My land of legends, land of sickness,
> What have they done to you!

Its provenance is from the memoirs of V. Zavalishin, who mistakenly associates the four lines ("not the best four, it seems") with *Pogorel'shchina* (2:382). *Sochineniya* even assigns the same status (as a full and independent work of poetry) to a vulgar aside Esenin attributed to Klyuev around 1916 (2:221).

A more telling indicator of poetics, time, and place is provided by the publications of "Ya leto zoril na Vyatke" ("I waited out summer on the Vyatka"). In *Sochineniya* (2:288–89), as in a 1987 publication by Stanislav Kunyaev in the journal *Druzhba narodov,* this poem consists of twenty-four lines, mostly celebrating the archaic charm of the Vyatka area (where, it will be recalled, Klyuev spent his summers from 1929 to 1932).[13] The opening is distinctly pastoral:

> Я лето зорил на Вятке,
> Жених в хороводе пихт,

Любя по лосьей повадке
Поречье, где воздух тих,
Где челн из цельной осины
Веет каменным веком, смолой:
Еще водятся исполины
В нашей стране родной!

I waited out summer on the Vyatka,
A bridegroom in a dance of firs,
Loving, as elk are wont to,
The riverbanks, where the air is quiet,
Where a boat from a whole aspen tree
Breathes the stone age, breathes resin:
There are still giants roaming
In our homeland!

And in this version, only the final stanza sounds a cautionary note:

Полюдье же лаптем железным
Попирает горбыль кедрачам.
Ой, тошнехонько дедам болезным
Приобыкнуть татаркским харчам!

Tribute collectors with a peasant shoe of iron
Stamp out lumber in cedar groves!
Oh, old sickly men find it nauseating
To get used to Tatar food!

However, in 1988, Azadovsky in the Riga journal *Rodnik,* and after him Subbotin in his *Pesnoslov,* published "Ya leto zoril na Vyatke" as a poem of *forty* lines, the final sixteen comprising a text which *Sochineniya* and Kunyaev had published as an independent and separate work, beginning with the line "Oi, krovavo berezyn'ke v busakh" ("Oh, it is bloody for the birch in beads," 2:294).[14] It is possible that, at some stage, Klyuev had conceived of two separate and very different poems, but if so, the combination of the two into a single work transforms both: as the speaker, in a radical change of direction (albeit typical for the later Klyuev), moves from pastoral Vyatka to a narrative of his return to Moscow, colored by his caution and anxiety in the capital:

Ой, кроваво березыньке в бусах
Удавиться зеленой косой . . .

Так на Вятке, в цветущих чарусах,
Пил я солнце и пихтовый зной.
И вернулся в Москву черемисом,
Весь медовый, как липовый шмель,
Но в Пушторге ощеренным рысям
Не кажусь я, как ворог, досель.
Вдруг повеет на них ароматом
Пьяных трав, приворотных корней! . . .
За лобатым кремлевским закатом
Не дописана хартия дней.
Будут ночи рысиной оглядки,
Победителен рог ветровой,
Но раскосое лето на Вятке
Нудит душу татарской уздой!!

Oh, it is fearful for the birch in beads
To be strangled by a green tress . . .
So on the Vyatka, in flowering marshlands,
I drank the sun and the heat of firs.
And returned to Moscow like a Komi,
All honeyed, as a lime-tree bumblebee,
But I'm not showing myself for the moment,
Like a foe, to the frenzied lynxes in the Fur Market.
Just in case they catch a breath
Of the heady grasses, love-potion roots! . . .
Behind the heavy-skulled Kremlin sunset
The charter of days is unfinished.
There will be nights of lynx caution,
Victorious is the wind horn,
But the slant-eyed summer on the Vyatka
Eats at the soul like a Tatar bridle!

Azadovsky publishes his text from a copy made by Arkhipov, and notes that the poem was included in the unpublished collection *O chem shumyat sedye kedry*. He explains that the *Sochineniya* texts (which have a number of serious misreadings) and Kunyaev's publications are based on drafts in the Moscow archive of Klyuev. But for thirty years, from the publication of *Sochineniya* in 1969 to the publication of *Serdtse edinoroga* in 1999, it was these phantom texts that were most readily accessible to readers. Given the archival circumstances this is fully understandable, but again, Klyuev's critical change of thematic direction in mid-poem (begun in the final stanza of the poem as published in *Sochineniya* and by Kunyaev) is lost, and with it the problematic integrity of his Vyatka/Moscow dichotomy. Equally, if the last sixteen lines of the poem are seen only as a separate poem, with a sinister if obscure commentary on Moscow in the early 1930s, the contrasting context of antiquity and the exotic (the non-Russian element in the cultural and economic life of the Vyatka area is emphasized) is lost.

Other major works among the late lyrics have suffered similar fates—partial, fragmentary publication, distorting not only the shape of the final version but also its reception. Examples include "Mne revolyutsiya ne mat'" ("The revolution is not mother to me," 577–78) and the poem entitled "Moemu drugu Antoliyu Yaru," which begins "Prodrogli lipy do kostei" ("To my friend Anatolii Yar; The limes are soaked to the skin," 607–9). The latter may easily be confused with another poem of the same title(!), beginning "Ne veryu, chto chitat' bez slez" ("I do not believe that you will read without tears," 609–11).[15]

While *Serdtse edinoroga* has clarified many of these problems, and produced a more reliable and complete corpus of Klyuev's poetry, it should not be thought that the issues identified and discussed above, any more than the multiple versions of *Bratskie pesni,* are simply the preserve of editors and particularly obsessive researchers. First, these multiple, partial, and fragmentary versions of Klyuev's verse have not simply ceased to exist (both in physical form and in readers' own concepts of the poet) with the emergence of better editions. Second, and more importantly, they are expressive of a cultural situation which is itself, because of historical circumstance and intellectual development, very productive of multiple, fragmentary versions of texts, in which the divisions familiar in other parts of the world ("draft," "final version," "authorized version," "pirated text," and so on) do not apply, or do not apply to the same degree. Anyone who has ever published in Russia, or who has ever looked at the Russian Internet (or even, for that matter, at the bookstalls outside major metro stations in the capital), will have seen abundant evidence that what is described here in the rather specific circumstances of the publishing history of Klyuev's poetry exemplifies very widespread phenomena, obtaining, *mutatis mutandis,* in the present as well as in the Soviet period.

As far as Klyuev's work is concerned, material circumstances and immanent features of the late poetry itself (discontinuity, obscurity, tendency to narrative or thematic incoherence) unite to present a fragmented, difficult, and provisional body of works. Various archives (Klyuev's own, those of Arkhipov and Ivanov-Razumnik) contribute to these processes by preserving—and distorting—versions of his late poetry, as has already been mentioned. However, the most extraordinary role in the preservation of the late poetry was played by the archive of the organization responsible for the destruction of the poet himself. As was noted in chapter 1, very little was known of the last years of Klyuev's life until quite recently, and before the late 1980s the only significant published source for Klyuev's 1930s poetry was *Sochineniya*. It has also been noted that the last years of Soviet power saw the publication of studies and texts drawing on materials in private and state archives which had long been inaccessible. Among the latter, the most remarkable sources turned out to be the archives of the KGB itself. Much of what is known of Klyuev's life (and death) in Siberia is drawn from his Tomsk file, explored in some detail by Pichurin, as described in chapter 1. But his Moscow KGB file, compiled at the time of his arrest, conviction, and dispatch to Siberia in 1934, provided even more remarkable literary evidence. In 1989 the author Vitalii Shentalinsky was able to obtain the files on a series of very prominent writers held by the Soviet security organs in their headquarters in Lubyanka Square. Among them was the file on Klyuev. Not only did that file contain a transcript of the poet's interrogation (in which, as has been seen, Klyuev was remarkably steadfast in his pronouncements, and also remarkably true to his "created lives") but also, as appendices, previously unknown poems. The most exciting find was a manuscript of *Pesn' o Velikoi Materi*—Klyuev's massive *poema* of the early 1930s, long thought lost. That work is discussed in chapter 6. But another discovery was a cycle of lyrics entitled "Razrukha" ("Destruction"), opening with "Pesnya Gamayuna" ("Song of Gamayun" [a prophetic bird]). During interrogation Klyuev is recorded as referring to these lyrics as statements, among other things, of his opinion that "the policy of industrialization is destroying the foundation and beauty of Russian national [*narodnaya*] life, moreover that destruction is accompanied by the suffering and death of millions of Russians."[16] Referring to the cycle as "unfinished," he suggested that his fellow-poet and friend Pavel Vasil'ev had taken it from his room during Klyuev's absence.[17] Not only, then, is the cycle an "arrested text" in more than one sense, but it may also, perhaps even as a stolen text, have provided one of the pretexts for its author's own arrest. That Klyuev defended it as his *authentic* word in such desperate conditions only adds to its significance.

"Razrukha" was first published by Shentalinsky in his 1989 article on Klyuev's Moscow KGB dossier. A corrected text was published by Subbotin in his *Pesnoslov* of 1990, and, in that version, it appears in Stanislav Kunyaev's edition, *Stikhotvoreniya i poemy* of 1991. Shentalinsky notes that only the first poem in the cycle is in manuscript, with the remaining ones in an OGPU typescript. His publication divides the cycle into four poems: "Pesnya Gamayuna," "Ot Lache-ozera do Vyga," "Est' demony chumy, prokazy i kholery," and "Skripit iudina osina" ("From Lake Lache to Vyg," "There are demons of plague, leprosy, and cholera," "Judas's aspen creaks"). Subbotin's text of the cycle consists, however, of only three poems—he publishes "Skripit iudina osina" as a continuation of "Est' demony chumy, prokazy i kholery," noting that "the parts of the cycle published in *Ogonek* under the numbers III and IV (in full correspondence to the KGB typescript, where the numbering of texts in the cycle is in the hand of an unknown party) in fact represent a single text: part IV is a direct continuation of part III."[18] The Soviet security organs, it would seem, must be numbered among the poet's earliest intrusive editors. Nearly sixty years on, Subbotin finds himself obliged to reconstruct passages evidently misconstrued by these careless editors.

A further problem arises when the cycle is set beside the other major work discovered in this dark archive, *Pesn' o Velikoi Materi.* That work, discussed in the following chapter, turns out to contain in toto the first poem of the "Razrukha" cycle. In *Pesn'* it is presented as the song of a *ptitsa roshch tsesarskikh* (bird from the imperial glades, 764) at a gathering of religious elders and mystics, while in "Razrukha" it is the song of a traditional Slavic bird of ill omen. In other words, the same poem serves two different functions in two different works, neither of which is textually complete. The editors of *Serdtse edinoroga* resolve the problem by presenting the second and third poems of the KGB's cycle as "Iz tsikla 'Razrukha'" ("From the Cycle 'Destruction,'" 624–31), leaving the song to the imperial bird in *Pesn'* (764–65). But even that decision only serves to foreground the fluid and provisional status of these texts.

"Razrukha" was appended to the record of Klyuev's interrogation for February 15, 1934, as proof of his guilt "in the composition and distribution of counter-revolutionary literary works."[19] Composed in 1934, it is the last known verse by Klyuev prior to his Moscow arrest (his last "free" poetry). It has none of the personal themes associated with Yar-Kravchenko which are so prominent in his poetry of 1932 and 1933. However, the cycle shares certain elementary features with much of the other late poetry: various forms of reiteration (thematic and rhetorical) are prominent, as are their familiar formal opposites in the late works—semantic discontinuity and obscurity; the meter is iambic (mostly iambic tetrameter, the favored measure of the late lyrics), and the poems are long—"Pesnya Gamayuna" is the shortest at 36 lines, while "Ot Lache-ozera do Vyga" is over 100 lines long and "Est' demony chumy . . ." is over 150 lines long. "Pesnya Gamayuna" introduces the major themes of the cycle: the arrival of ill-omened news; the loss of traditional Russia, and destruction of hearth and home; the present as plague; a catalogue of disasters tied to places expressive of the physical and cultural geography of the Russian empire; the destruction of the Russian north. "Ot Lache-ozera do Vyga," the most complex and elusive of the three poems, charts a metaphorical journey across that physical and cultural geography, encountering past and present, documented and visionary horrors. "Est' demony chumy, prokazy i kholery" links its catalogue of plagues to a lament for Russian towns and rivers afflicted by the present, and concludes with an elaborate description of Stalinist Moscow.

"Pesnya Gamayuna," in its first line, announces the arrival of *vesti gor'kie* (bitter news) about a series of natural disasters, described in the following lines: the Aral Sea is drying up; cranes are rare in the Ukraine; the grasses of the Mozdok steppe no longer sing; underground wheels creak beneath the Sarov monastery; the blue Volga is growing shallow; evil men are burning the trees of Kerzhenets; and the meadows of Suzdal' are rotting. Most of the poem is devoted to the enumeration of these various disasters, while three times the news "Chto bol'she net rodnoi zemli" ("That the native land is no more") is stated, the final reiteration providing the last line of the poem. Not for the first time, Klyuev provides a poetic and cultural topography of Russia, in which the religious and the natural are combined, with the places named representing all points of the compass, and central Russia too. Of those places, Sarov (in the east of European Russia) is the site of the famous monastery of which St. Serafim was a member. The monastery, a place of natural sylvan beauty, was one of the most popular pilgrimage destinations in the late imperial period. At the time of the composition of "Razrukha" it had, of course, been closed for less than ten years. The area around the Kerzhenets River (also to the east; earlier associated by Klyuev with the Bolshevik leader in the first poem of the "Lenin" cycle) was one of the major centers of the Old Belief, made especially famous by Mel'nikov's novels. Suzdal' (north-central Russia) is one of the ancient cities of Kievan Rus'. The Ukraine (the west), the Aral Sea (far southeast), and the Mozdok steppe (south) represent not only geographical boundary areas for Russia and its culture but also the extent and natural diversity of the Russian empire and its successor state. In each case ecological disaster (to use an anachronistically modern term), implicitly or explicitly associated with the activities of man, is illustrated in a bleak catalogue. The poem ends with lines on the fate of the north proper (until that point absent from the poem's gazetteer):

И Север — лебедь ледяной —	And the North—an icy swan—
Истек бездомною волной,	Has bled to death with homeless wave,
Оповещая корабли,	Informing ships
Что больше нет родной земли!	That the native land is no more!

As in other cases among the late works, this poem is not only modeled on prophecy (not least in its tendency to obscurity) but quite literally *is* prophecy. Such prophetic works have attracted commentary, and it has already been noted that Klyuev described himself in an (anonymous) gloss of 1919 as a "clairvoyant poet," while the term "prophet" was applied to him from the earliest commentaries, such as those of Sventsitsky at the time of *Bratskie pesni.*[20] The mystic, popular, apocalyptic elements which "Pesnya Gamayuna" draws upon form a significant part of Klyuev's cultural battery, and once again represent the intermingling of features of Russian modernism (especially symbolism) with the popular. While the poem primarily describes the consequences of Soviet policy, as criticized by the poet at his subsequent interrogation(!), it cannot be denied that its "prophecy" has indeed proved clairvoyant: the problems of the Aral Sea were revealed in the last decades of the twentieth century; dams and industry have transformed the Volga, and complaints abound of its new shallowness; the general ecological problems of Russia are well known. Shentalinsky even notes that "underground wheels" at Sarov could be interpreted to mean the secret nuclear weapons plant Arzamas 16, which was located in the city previously associated with Serafim, the early nineteenth-century ascetic canonized at the beginning of the twentieth century.[21] However, prophetic discourse, even after the event, conveniently invites diverse interpretations, so Lyudmila Kalinina, writing ecstatically that Klyuev was "a genuine talent and indeed always a clairvoyant," appears to see these lines as designating a reaction to the country's rejection of the path of St. Serafim.[22] It is also striking that the third poem in the cycle speaks prophetically of *vesti chernye, skakun iz Karabakha* (black news, a fast steed from Karabakh), and it is even more striking that these "prophecies" were first published—and straight from their place of arrest—during the radical and chaotic transformation of the Soviet Union in the late 1980s, when the conflict in Nagorno-Karabakh was a frequent source of "black news." Turning to the other major text from that archive, at least two authors see the employment in *Pesn' o Velikoi Materi* of the apocalyptic motif of the "star Wormwood," from Revelation 8:11, as a prophecy of the nuclear disaster of 1986 ("Tut nispala polynnaya zvezda" ["Here fell the star wormwood"]).[23] As was widely pointed out at the time of the disaster, *chernobyl'* is a species of wormwood. Perhaps, however, it says as much about Russia today that one might attempt to interpret Klyuev's poetry as literal prophecy as it does about Russia in the 1930s that Klyuev described the state of the country in such apocalyptic terms. Once again, the literary time of modern Russia reveals itself as far from linear—Klyuev's prophecy-modeled lines of the 1930s become literary facts in the late 1980s, when their prophetic content already seems literally fulfilled. It must be said, however, that energetic attempts to promote this *veshchii* (prophetic) Klyuev do not seem to have drawn more readers to the poet, perhaps because late twentieth-century Russia found ample and equally bleak prophetic words in rather more accessible forms.

Among the poems of the early 1930s which are close to "Pesnya Gamayuna" in the treatment of ecological indicators of national crisis is "Komu by skazku rasskazat'" ("To whom should I tell my tale," 597–99). Here the speaker enumerates a series of such signs which he wishes to avoid hearing (sunsets do not bathe like "a pack of foxes" [*stadom lis*] in the Ob' River; the banks of the Pechora are pierced by piles; no elk trails mark the tundra, and so on). And other late poems are as prophetic after the fact as "Razrukha." Most striking is "Iz predsmertnykh pesen" ("From Songs Written Before Death," 612–13), beginning with the line "Zmeya zmeyu tseluet v zhalo" ("A snake kisses a snake on the sting"), in which the speaker anticipates his own final years.

> За что отель покинул вымя
> И теплый пах, в каком Нарыме
> Найдет он деда с грудью турьей?!
>
> Why has the calf abandoned the udder
> And the warm groin, in what Narym
> Will he find his grandfather with the aurochs chest?!

The composition of this poem predates by a year Klyuev's exile to Kolpashevo, at that time in the Narym administrative region. Again, however, the reference to his future place of exile is first and foremost a poetic statement of the present—in what bleak place will the beloved find the abandoned speaker, the poem asks, in order to emphasize the betrayal which is the speaker's current lot. Nonetheless, the title—"From Songs Written Before Death"—certainly contributes to the prophetic aura of the poem, which was only published in the 1990s. In these and similar poems, however, the ecological and prophetic elements are interwoven, as can be seen, not only with national and cultural themes but also and strikingly with the personal, whereas "Razrukha" has no traditional lyric themes such as love and betrayal.

It should also be noted that neither the prophetic nor the apocalyptic are new in Klyuev's work of the 1930s. For example, *L'vinyi khleb* is much marked by the apocalyptic (not least in its final poem, "Pole useyannoe kostyami" ["A field sown with bones," 472]). Among later exemplars, "Nasha sobachka u vorot otlayala" of the mid-1920s has already been mentioned, although the mixture of apocalyptic and redemptive signs in "Nasha russkaya pravda zagibla" of the same period is, perhaps, more characteristic of Klyuev's treatment of the fate of Russia in those years. A similar mixture of elements may be observed in "Ot ikony Borisa i Gleba," discussed in chapter 3. There, it will be recalled, Klyuev, as a preface to a portrait of a sinister and catastrophe-struck contemporary Russia, traces for himself a sort of cultural genealogy: the icon of Boris and Gleb, the writings (*Shestokryl*) of the Strigol'nik sect, an anthology of the writings of John Chrysostom (*Margarit*), and the martyrdom of Avvakum, all of which explain and authorize the speaker's vision.

Over a decade later, and in extremis, Klyuev remained true to this claimed genealogy, and again associated it with his view of the catastrophic fate of modern Russia. During his 1934 interrogation, according to the transcript, the poet expressly claimed descent from the archpriest Avvakum and went on to state that his view that the Bolshevik Revolution had been catastrophic for the country was expressed in the poems of the "Razrukha" cycle.[24] Like so many of Klyuev's own literary works, the transcript too is a text of obviously mixed rhetorical and mythological descent. And like so many transcripts of interrogations, it also raises black-ironic questions of authenticity (who was the actual author, under what circumstances, and to what extent was it written to order, or in collaboration with editorial assistants of a very specific kind?). Like much of his poetry, the transcript's clashing stylistic registers may be contrasted with a strikingly stable self-portrait (descended from Avvakum), which seems to authorize the quotations from "Razrukha":

> My views on Soviet reality and my relationship to the policies of the Communist Party and to Soviet power are determined by my reactionary religio-philosophic outlook.
>
> *Descended from an ancient Old Believer family, going back through my mother's line to the Archpriest Avvakum, I was brought up on the Old Russian culture of Korsun, Kiev, and Novgorod, I nurtured in myself a love for ancient, pre-Petrine Russia [Rus'], whose singer I am.*
>
> The building of socialism undertaken during the dictatorship of the proletariat in the USSR has definitively destroyed my dream of Ancient Russia. Hence my hostile relationship to the policies of the Communist Party and to Soviet Power . . .
>
> My view that the October Revolution cast the country into an abyss of suffering and disasters, and made it the most unhappy in the world, I expressed in the poem "There are demons of plague, leprosy, and cholera." [emphasis added]

It is impossible to read this transcript without reflecting that perhaps the most consistent feature of Russian intellectual life in the late twentieth century was irony, and for good reason, for an ironist, armed with a sense of the overall contours of modern Russian cultural history, could not resist pointing out that it was in the Lubyanka that the created lives and poetic creation of Klyuev achieved their most striking unity. That ironist would also revel in the facts that led, as has been noted, to Klyuev's description of Russia in the 1930s being published in the 1980s and read as newly fulfilled prophecy.

The second poem in "Razrukha," "Ot Lache-ozera do Vyga," describes a metaphorical journey, with overtones of pilgrimage, across a Russia scarred by ecological and political catastrophes that are associated with the diabolical. In the opening lines the speaker charts a specific journey he has undertaken, accompanied by sinister omens and signs:

> От Лаче-озера до Выга
> Бродяжил я тропой опасной,
> В прогалах брезжил саван красный,
> Кочевья леших и чертей.
>
> From Lake Lache to Vyg
> I wandered by a dangerous path,
> In glades there flashed a red shroud,
> The wanderings of forest spirits and devils.

Lake Lache (or Lacha), just south of Kargopol', and the source of the Onega River, is mentioned in the late twelfth-century *Slovo Daniila Zatochnika* (*Address of Daniil the Exile*) and is traditionally identified as the place of exile of Daniil himself. The multiple problems of that text and the related *Molenie* (supplication)—identity of the author, genre status of the texts, relationship to high-literary traditions and to folklore, and so on—find echoes in the work of Klyuev himself. Moreover, Klyuev's own letters (especially his early correspondence with Blok and, in a quite different tone, his letters from exile) reproduce some of the stylistic features—but not the humor—of Daniil Zatochnik, who himself figures occasionally in Klyuev's earlier writings. Indeed, Lake Lache is discussed in Klyuev's correspondence with Blok, and is also mentioned twice in the mid-1910s lyric "Sgotovit' dedu krup, pomoch' rasvesit' seti" ("Prepare the old man some groats, help him hang up his net," 251–52).[25] Much later, Klyuev, in his *zayavlenie* (statement) of 1932 to the directorate of the Writers' Union, written to defend himself after the attacks on *Derevnya,* and to plead for material support, lists Daniil Zatochnik among his artistic models and associates ("from Daniil the Exile to Pososhkov, Fet, Surikov, Borodin, Vrubel', and the youngest in the Father's tent, Esenin," *Sd* 407).

The destination of the first line of "Ot Lache-ozera do Vyga" is the famous Old Believer communities on and near the Vyg River (the Danilovo community for men; Leksa for women), which feature often in Klyuev's works, as do Vyg's greatest authors, the Denisov brothers Simeon and Andrei. Thus, in the opening lines of this poem, geography, history, and culture are (characteristically) conflated in the trope of wandering from Lache to Vyg *by a dangerous path;* that is to say, traveling from the twelfth to the eighteenth century, from the status of literary exile and supplicant to schismatic polemicist, but also traveling physically a relatively short distance across the Russian north. The last point contrasts not only with the metaphorical associations (great historical and cultural distance) of this opening line but also with the more typical toponymic self-definitions of Klyuev's verse, which play on geographical *extent* to reinforce cultural *expanse,* and which are exemplified at other points in this poem. For once, here is a journey which could conceivably be undertaken on foot, just as the speaker claims to have done—from the southern tip of Lake Lache to the site of the Vyg community would be approximately 250 kilometers, as the crow flies. Of course, the physical journey would most certainly be arduous and even dangerous, and would be a great deal longer than 250 kilometers. The dangers of the metaphorical journey are equally clear, and are elaborated throughout the poem. The implications of religious wandering in the opening line are realized, indirectly, in line eighteen, when the Denisovs' "book" is described as a *strannich'ya kisa* (wanderer's or pilgrim's bag), and in the various visions and signs of divine intervention encountered in the metaphorical narrative of the poem as a whole. Such play between the concrete and the metaphorical provides an unbroken thread throughout the poem.

The poem also elaborates a series of chronological oppositions, which are suggested in somewhat paradoxical fashion by the opening line. The fundamental opposition is between the Stalinist present, described in apocalyptic terms several times in the poem, and the integral, continuous time of previous Russian history, mythologized in characteristic images of ancient beverages, the Russian peasant hut, and so on. Within this framework Lake Lache and Vyg, although chronologically distant from one another, are mythologically as close as they are geographically. However, they also serve as approximate boundary markers in cultural time: Daniil Zatochnik representing the early flowering of Old Russian literature, and the Vyg community its very furthest extension into modern times.

The toponymic announcement of the opening line is distinguished from everything that follows by the absence of rhyme—it and the poem's final line are the only unrhymed lines in the entire work, which, for the most part, consists of irregularly alternating couplets of masculine and feminine rhymes (there are also four lines of crossed rhyme, the fourth line of which also forms a rhyming couplet with the next line).

The remaining one hundred lines of the poem elaborate on the initial themes, employing many of the features familiar in Klyuev's poetry in general and his late works in particular (semantic flexibility and sometimes interrupted syntax, parallelism, reiteration, rapid and sudden passage between the concrete and specific and the general, allusion to distant past and to present, blending of fictional and evidently factual, association between lyrical speaker and nation) to facilitate the description of the journey announced in the opening line in both metaphorical and partially literal terms.

Klyuev's late works do not, on the whole, observe clear strophic divisions, nor do they contain simple thematic or semantic breaks. On the contrary, the changes in direction often seem unpredictable, and may occur in the middle of periods (themselves often of some length—one in "Ot Lacheozera do Vyga" is sixteen lines long, another fourteen, a third, containing such a change of direction, is twelve lines long). Although the poem is characteristically elusive in structure, it may nonetheless be divided somewhat provisionally into eight sections of uneven length as follows. The first section (lines one to ten) describes the speaker's journey from Lache to Vyg. On the journey he saw diabolical signs, and noted nature's torment. He compares himself to a wounded elk, but concludes that he had "shown death his hooves" (*smerti pokazav kopyta;* that is, escaped death). The elk is a recurrent image for the lyrical "I" in the late poetry, usually associated with love and abandonment. Relocated from its usual romantic setting in Klyuev's verse, the animal here enables the assertion of survival. The second section of the poem (lines eleven to thirty) begins with an elaborate simile for the trans-Onega region, and then narrows to a description of Danilovo, where the Denisov brothers prepared their *Pomorskie otvety* like a honey drink for the ages. A long period addresses that book: a wanderer's bag where "synodal fox" and "she-beaver from the depths" (*sinodal'naya lisa, bobrikha poddonnaya*) fight; a book which Rome and Alexandria, Bombay and Paris will read; which murmurs like a village swallow over crucified Russia, and which, like a reed, looks into the depths of the water to prophesy (the country's?) fate—not plague carts, but aspic in the shade of birches, with a magic ladle(!). In the third section (lines thirty to forty-seven), the journey trope is resumed: the red shroud of the opening lines reappears, and oils the path to "tormented lakes" (*isterzannye ozera*), where the speaker casts his glance into their waters and catches a "fresh whitefish, bony as death" (*kostlyavyi, kak smert', sig*). Here the text is corrupt, but Subbotin, relying on apparent allusions to Isaiah 1:6, reconstructs as follows: the whitefish (now apparently a man) is partially eaten by other fish and his flesh is rotting, but he mouths a prayer.[26] The speaker addresses him, asking him where he is from and what he needs. To which the addressee replies in the most enigmatic lines of this enigmatic poem:

«Я ж украинец Опанас . . .	"I am the Ukrainian Opanas . . .
Добей зозулю, чоловиче! . . .»	Finish off the Cuckoo, man! . . ."

This transformation of the fish/man into a specific and apparently fictional Ukrainian who calls for the extermination of a bird of omen concludes the third section of the poem.[27] The unexpected appearance of the Ukrainian Opanas (Afanasii in Russian) also recalls the equally sudden emergence of what appears to be a generic Ukrainian near the end of "Pesnya Gamayuna," in the line "Zamolk Grit'sko na Ukraine" ("Gritsko [Grisha in Russian] has fallen silent in the Ukraine," 765). Klyuev's Opanas might be seen as echoing the protagonist of Eduard Bagritsky's civil war narrative *Duma pro Opanasa* (*Lay of Opanas,* 1926). Bagritsky's Opanas is a bloodthirsty Ukrainian who eventually falls victim to the Bolsheviks. Bagritsky reworked the story into the libretto for an opera in the early 1930s, that reworking coinciding approximately with the composition of "Razrukha." The name could also be read as an allusion to Apanas, the father of Vasil' in Dovzhenko's film *Zemlya* (*Earth*) of 1930. That Opanas initially opposes collectivization, but then is convinced of its merits by Vasil', only to see his son murdered by kulaks. The implications of either association (or both), combined with the silence of Opanas in "Pesnya Gamayuna," and his strange situation and instructions in "Ot Lache-ozera do Vyga," are rich indeed.

The fourth section of the poem (lines forty-eight to fifty-seven) describes the speaker's vision, also caught by his "fishing," and qualified as a "sinister catch" (*ulov zloveshchii*): nature, in a neo-liturgical scene, provides a background against which angels collect a thousand souls from the waters. In the fifth section (lines fifty-eight to sixty-six), the speaker returns to the Vyg River (here in the alternative form "Vygo") to lament the loss of the Old Believer community, which is identified with Kitezh, the island that sank of its own will beneath the waters of Lake Svetloyar to avoid the Tatars—a story that had great currency among Old Believers, for whom it was an important spiritual model. The historical Vyg had, of course, been closed by the imperial authorities in the middle of the nineteenth century. Kitezh is a frequent referent in Klyuev's work (for example, the lyric "Rus'-Kitezh" of 1918 or 1919 ["Old Russia-Kitezh," 410–11]), and provides yet another illustration of the multiple perspectives in which Klyuev's poetry may be seen: on the one hand, Kitezh and related images figure frequently in Russian folklore, not least among the Old Believers; on the other hand, the legend had gained new prominence in the early years of the twentieth century, especially through Rimsky-Korsakov's famous opera *The Legend of the Invisible City of Kitezh and the Maid Fevroniya* (premiered 1907) and Prishvin's essay "U sten grada nevidimogo (Svetloe ozero)" ("At the Walls of the Unseen City [Lake Svetloyar]," 1909).[28] Klyuev attended a performance of the opera in 1915.[29] "Kitezh" does not appear in his verse before that date, a fact which suggests that, at least in this case, the path was from high culture to the popular. The sixth section of "Ot Lache-ozera do Vyga" (lines sixty-seven to eighty-seven) seems to begin in mid-period, as the object of description changes from Vyg to the White Sea Canal (*belmorskii smert'-kanal* [White Sea death-canal/channel]), the great and much-eulogized Stalinist project which was in fact completed, in the summer of 1933, largely by forced labor. Three specific and, again, presumably fictional participants in its construction are mentioned, introducing lines on "Great Russia," which was soaked beneath a red shower, and has hidden its tears in the canal. In the second part of the description, the canal is seen as a "monument to great pain" and a "heavenly broom" (*pamyatnik velikoi boli, metla nebesnaya*) for those who refused to remain loyal to peasant Russia. The seventh section (lines eighty-eight to ninety-nine) address Russia in a long exclamation—it would have been better to have remained true to its rural and magical self than to have a sluice of blood and way of lice from the White Sea coast to Ararat. This exclamation is interrupted for five lines by a parenthesis apropos of the Turkic word for "pancake," enabling a very characteristic, but apparently casual, universalization of a domestic image:

Россия! Лучше б в курной саже,
С тресковым пузырьком в прорубе,
Но в хвойной непроглядной шубе,
Бортняжный мед в кудесной речи
И блинный хоровод у печи,
По Азии же блин — чурек,
Чтоб насыщался человек
Свирелью, родиной, овином
И звездным выгоном лосиным, —
У звезд рога в тяжелом злате, —
Чем крови шлюз и вошьи гати
От Арарата до Поморья.

Russia! It would be better in the peasant stove soot,
With cod bubbles in the ice hole,
But in magnificent pine-tree furs,
There is wild honey in the sorcerer's speech
And a pancake dance around the stove,
In Asia pancake is "churek,"
So that man can satisfy himself
With pipes, homeland, barn
And the star meadow of elks—
The stars have horns in heavy gold—
Than to have a sluice of blood and lice embankments
From Ararat to the White Sea coast.

The final five lines of the poem comprise the eighth section, in which flax blooms and St. George appears, but wolves are heard howling, and the opening is reiterated, with considerable geographical expansion (providing the first line with a clear thematic rhyme, in the absence of any linguistic rhyme):

Я брел проклятою тропой	I wandered down a cursed path
От Дона мертвого до Лаче.	From the dead Don to Lache.

While the divisions proposed here—and, indeed, some of the readings—should be regarded as provisional and cautious, it is clear that the poem is both dense and expansive in the manner of the best late works. The motifs of pilgrimage and popular revelation are embedded in appropriate cultural referents (Vyg, Lache, the works of the Old Belief) but are linked, partly through simple geographical association, to an image of contemporary Stalinism drawn from the very same part of northern Russia as Vyg and Lache themselves—the White Sea Canal project.[30] In a poem built around poles and parallels, it is significant that the northern section of the canal follows the course of the northern Vyg River, while the southern section runs roughly parallel to the southern Vyg River—Stalinist construction has been imposed upon the ancient physical and cultural geography of the north (the rivers gave their name to the Old Believer community). Meanwhile, the notions of exile, schism, and apocalyptic thought which underlie the figures of Daniil Zatochnik, the Denisov brothers, Vyg, and Old Believer writings are realized anew in the situation and visions of the speaker in contemporary Russia. A spiritual wanderer and outcast (and Klyuev himself was literally both in the early 1930s), the speaker encounters not only familiar and even conventional signs of evil but also unique visions of ill omen, and ties them to a specific and historical moment—the digging of the White Sea Canal, which, in the lines that follow, is itself then metaphorically filled with Russia's tears. Throughout the poem geographical expansion and contraction alternate—neighbors Vyg and Lache are followed by Rome, Alexandria, Paris, and Bombay; the relatively short and domestic distance of "Lache to Vyg" contrasts with the national north-south axes of "from Ararat to the White Sea Coast" and "from the dead Don to Lache." At the same time, these points of expansion and contraction are themselves interrelated: Vyg, Lache, and places on or near the White Sea Canal express the contrasting past and present of the Russian north; Rome, Alexandria, Paris, and Bombay are significant points on a macrocosmic cultural and spiritual map to match the Russian microcosmic map sketched elsewhere in the poem; while the metaphorical expressions to designate Russia in its imperial entirety (Ararat to the White Sea coast, the Don to Lache) are also loosely expressive of the specific, if monumental, project of Stalin's canal. Historical personages (Neofit, the addressee of the *Pomorskie otvety,* Andrei and Simeon Denisov) and a possibly historical personage (Daniil Zatochnik) are paired with specific but apparently fictional characters, the Ukrainian fish/man Opanas and the diggers of the canal—Akimusha, Prov from the Vetluga River (near Nizhnii Novgorod), and old Fekla. Other master-pairs underlie the poem's thematics. Among the foremost is the contrasting pairing of the *miloe nedavnee* (pleasant recent past) of an historico-mythological Russia—evoked in those words in line sixty, and implied throughout the poem—with the newly sinister present. An equally significant pair, at the core of so much of Klyuev's work, is provided by nature and culture. Nature interprets culture throughout the poem (pines moan, aspens are in blood to their waists, the lakes provide the strange creature of ill omen, weeping heather lights candles, and so on). Nature is also a recurrent vehicle in similes of man's activities, and sometimes vice versa (the speaker wanders like an elk, the trans-Onega region is embroidered with seagulls like a scarf, hierarch and heresiarch argue like fox and beaver, the latter's book murmurs like a swallow, and so on). Finally, although here largely by implication, nature is also the victim of modern man's activities—a theme explicit elsewhere in the cycle and evident throughout Klyuev's mature work.

To say that the poem is, at times, obscure would be an understatement. The few attempts to interpret it so far have been tentative, and even Klyuev's best editor hesitates before its textological problems: Subbotin concludes that line seventy-five, "Ot tachki, zastupa i gorstki" ("From wheelbarrow, spade, and handful") is "probably" a corruption in the typescript.[31] Again, material textuality and the matter of the text intersect. And no reading should forget that the poem, like so much of Klyuev's later work, was never published by the poet, and is probably best considered unfinished.

The third and last poem of the "Razrukha" cycle, "Est' demony chumy, prokazy i kholery," opens with a deviation to iambic hexameter from the iambic tetrameter of the first two poems, returning to the shorter measure only at line forty-six (and in the middle of a couplet, so that *glasnitsakh* [eye sockets] in the six-foot line forty-five rhymes with *orlitsa* [female eagle] in the four-foot line which follows). However, as a whole the poem is far more continuous and less resistant to interpretation than "Ot Lache-ozera do Vyga." The opening thirteen lines catalogue diabolical diseases and plagues from scrofula to syphilis with a descriptive verve that is almost grotesque. The following six lines explain that opening: the year 1918 (perhaps a startling substitute for 1917, but according to one of the rare commentators on this cycle, chosen because it was the beginning of the Gulag and the Red Terror) visited upon Russia a diabolical plague.[32]

Images of the diabolical and of plagues have already occurred in Klyuev's poetry, and in similar contexts to the opening of "Est' demony chumy, prokazy i kholery." "Nerushimaya stena" ("Indestructible wall," 542–43) of the mid-1920s inveighs against the order to dress the "horned lords of life" in the "pearls of verse" (*rogatykh khozyaev zhizni . . . odet' v zhemchuga stikhov*). Two poems of the early 1930s use intriguing and obscure images of the Devil's ball to describe contemporary Russia: "Rossiya byla glukha, khroma" ("Russia was deaf, lame," 599–601) and "Khozyain sada smugl i v rozhkakh" ("The owner of the garden is dark-skinned and horned," 603–4). Beyond the general diabolical and epidemical imagery, both poems share specific elements with "Razrukha": the "tear of St. Serafim," the destruction of the home in "Rossiya byla . . . ," the crow and mourning nature, and the cutting of trees, for example. But while each of these poems has polemical intentions, they are all quite different in overall shape from the "Razrukha" cycle, which mixes its allegorical descriptions in prophetic manner with abundant allusions to specific features of the present.

Line twenty of "Est' demony chumy, prokazy i kholery" opens a catalogue of the lamenting towns and rivers of Russia. The catalogue, sixty-two lines in total, begins with Novgorod the Great and Vladimir, ancient northern cities of Rus', expanding gradually in geographic and cultural terms through Kolomna, Ryazan', the Oka, Kasimov (where the cross outshines the proud minaret), and Murom to the Volga, Zhiguli, Karabakh, the Irtysh, and the Enisei. After the first appearance of the refrain *Plach', russkaya zemlya* (Weep, Russian land), the lament returns to central, ancient Russia with Chernigov and Kursk, the choice of which, like several other elements in the poem, echoes *Slovo o polku Igoreve,* and finally to Kiev and Yaroslavl'.[33] Many of the places are evoked in terms of familiar cultural associations, now derelict: the frescoes of Theophanes the Greek in Novgorod (to him the judgment of executioner and mob are vile); Kiev, to which pilgrims no longer come to see the *pesnotsvetnyi rai* (song-colored paradise) of the Caves Monastery. Other lines speak of ecological loss: the Irtysh and Enisei rivers lament the present, knocking on the ocean's door like beggars, gloomy from misfortune, lashed by whips, and robbed of the sables which once decorated the shoulders of their shores. This catalogue of lamenting toponyms is at least distantly reminiscent of such classic catalogue laments as those of the chorus in Aeschylus's *Persae.* However, it is colored not by the exotic (as are the Persian place names in the Greek chorus, for example) but by the familiar. Yet that familiar is most definitely not the banal of characteristic modernist and postmodernist catalogue verse (from Whitman's *Song of Myself* to Sokovnin's *predmetniki* [lists]). Again, Klyuev's poetics locate him between rather than within traditions.

The catalogue ends with a definitive summary:

Вы умерли, святые грады,	You've died, holy cities,
Без фимиама и лампады	Without incense and icon lamp
До нестареющих пролетий.	Until the spring that grows not old.

There follows a thirteen-line address to Moscow, rather different in character from the catalogue which preceded it. That city is presented as an heir to the Byzantine tradition, echoing, as Subbotin sees it, the "third Rome" notion of Moscow's messianic role.[34] This address concludes with a line consisting entirely of the names of the emperors Vespasian and Constantine, and is followed by the most complex part of the poem, a passage of some forty lines interweaving themes and images associated with suicide, Stalin and Stalinism, and the betrayal of traditional cultural values. The passage begins with the line "Skripit iudina osina," which, it will be recalled, was the point at which Klyuev's interrogators appear to have created a separate, fourth, member of the "Razrukha" cycle. In this passage, Klyuev's tendency to asyndeton and parataxis is particularly evident, and, combined with characteristically long periods, makes some lines prophetically obscure. But in addition to the literary models of ancient prophecy and lament (mediated in part through Old Russian literary forms), there emerges a series of evident, sometimes announced, allusions to specific modern Russian poets—from Pushkin through Nekrasov to Mayakovsky. Such combinations of polar literary elements (old and new; sacred and profane; general and specific) exemplify the poetic polarities of the cycle and the late poetry as a whole. In the opening lines of this section, the subject seems to change, unannounced, from the aspen on which Judas is traditionally thought to have hanged himself, to the raven, with its sinister announcement of the present.[35]

Скрипит иудина осина
И плещет вороном зобатым,
Доволен лакомством богатым,
О ржавый череп чистя нос,
Он трубит в темь: колхоз, колхоз!

The aspen of Judas creaks
And flaps like a full-cropped raven,
Happy with its rich morsel,
Cleaning its nose against a rusty skull,
It trumpets into the darkness: "kolkhoz, kolkhoz"!

The suicide theme, announced in the first line of the passage, with its reference to the death of Judas, is reiterated first in the "bodies of suicides" (*samoubits tela*) which wash to the mouth of hell in a wave across the air, and then in the specific figure of the suicide Mayakovsky:

Злодей, чья флейта — позвоночник,
Булыжник уличный — построчник.

The evildoer, whose flute was a backbone,
And the paving stones of streets his theme.

Mayakovsky is associated with the destruction of popular traditions in the lines that follow, and is, by implication, contrasted with Nekrasov and with

Pushkin—allusions to them precede and follow, respectively, the lines on Mayakovsky. Immediately after the aspen and the raven, images of devilry and plague, first encountered in the opening of the poem, return as the devil emerges in a "scarlet shroud" (*bagrovyi savan,* echoing the "red shroud" of the second poem in the cycle, just as the paths beneath the black thicket here recall distantly that poem's allusion to mysterious actions beneath Sarov). The source and identity of the diabolical are explained in lines which begin with Nekrasov and end with what turns out (but only, as is characteristic, in glosses to the original lines provided later in the poem) to be a description of the Moscow Kremlin:

Не для некрасовского Власа
Роятся в притче эфиопы —
Под черной зарослью есть тропы,
Бетонным связаны узлом —
Там сатаны заезжий дом.

Not for Nekrasov's Vlas
The Ethiopians in the tale rush round—
Beneath the dark thicket run paths,
Linked with a concrete knot—
There is the house where Satan stops in.

Nekrasov's "Vlas," it will be recalled, describes a penitent peasant whose early life had been avaricious but who falls ill, sees an apocalyptic vision which includes "Ethiopians of black visage," repents, builds a church, and spends the rest of his life as a penniless wanderer. Thus, the startlingly precise reference to Nekrasov's hero both redirects the allusive pattern of the poem toward the specific and intensifies and reiterates its general thematics: Nekrasov, the gentleman-poet writing of the peasantry, is to be compared and contrasted with Klyuev the "peasant-poet" writing on behalf of the peasantry, and about the ravages of the ruling elite; Vlas the penitent kulak *avant la lettre* is a polar opposite of and yet also brother to Klyuev, raging against modern diabolical authority and labeled by his enemies a "kulak poet"; both Vlas and Klyuev's lyrical speaker in the second poem of the cycle are *stranniki* (wanderers); the diabolical visions of Vlas and those of the cycle are associated and are both calls for repentance; and Vlas represents, in a high-literary appropriation, the popular Russian principles, the destruction of which is the main subject of Klyuev's cycle.

The following lines appear to describe, indirectly, the flight across Moscow of a diabolical figure "drunk with blood" (*ot krovi p'yanyi*), trembling at the cross on the Dormition Cathedral, and heading to the dwelling of "the sinister cat" (*zloveshchii kot*—the clearest allusion to the bewhiskered leader himself). Here, again in mid-period, another change of focus turns the poem from this description of the diabolical resident of the Moscow Kremlin to a digression in which the lyrical speaker of the poem, who seems to describe his own poem as a means to grant voice to the souls of the victims (with the "cuckoo gully" [*log kukushii*] echoing the mysterious line "'Dobei zozulyu, Cholovoche'" of the second poem in the cycle). As before, the rudimentary narrative is disorientingly anchored in asyndeton:

> Но в боль берестяному свитку
> Перо, омокнутое в лаву,
> Я погружу его в дубраву,
> Чтоб листопадом в лог кукуший
> Стучались в стих убитых души. . . .
>
> But to the pain of the birch-bark scroll
> I'll dip my pen, soaked in lava,
> Into the oak grove,
> So that, like autumn in the cuckoo grove,
> The souls of the dead may strike into verse. . . .

After this digression, the description of the modern hell (*betonnyi cherep* [concrete skull]), ready to accept the bodies of suicides, returns and introduces another jolt to the specific—the polemical address to the suicide Mayakovsky, quoted above. In the final thirteen lines of the poem the major themes are summarized, as Moscow, an "inconsolable widow" (*neutishimaya vdova*), is seen sitting on a garbage dump, while Judas's aspen creaks (again). The speaker asks who will provide salvation—East ("Porfirnyi Brama na vostoke" ["Purple Brahma in the East"]) or West (Rome)—only to conclude with two lines of negation, without a final rhyme, but with a final ellipsis:

> Нет русских городов-невест
> В запястьях и рублях мидийских. . . .
>
> There are no Russian bride-towns
> In bracelets and Medean rubles. . . .

In fact, the question about salvation, asked by the speaker in the preceding lines, to which first rhetorical questions and then negation provide answers, is a barely encoded allusion to Pushkin's famous "Prorok" ("Prophet"), with its image of a fiery coal inserted by a six-winged seraph into the poet/prophet's body. Klyuev's speaker asks:

Но кто целящей головней	But who with a healing fiery log
Спалит бетонные отеки . . .	Will burn off the concrete swellings . . .

Pushkin's poet and prophet, violently reconstructed by the seraph, is told in the final lines of "Prorok" to walk across seas and lands and to burn with his words the hearts of men (*Glagolom zhgi serdtsa lyudei*). Klyuev domesticates the fiery coal, transforming it into a burning log, and renders contemporary his own previous images of plague, asking who will burn off the *concrete* swellings of flesh; but the shallow-buried allusion to Pushkin also and most tellingly provides an intermediate genealogical point between ancient prophecy and "Razrukha," and between the popular images of wandering seer and the high-cultural models of visionary which are implicit here, and explicit earlier in the cycle, in the position of the lyrical speaker.

It seems likely that the "Razrukha" cycle marks—and, to a certain degree, even produces—a chronological end point in Klyuev's career: it was one of the very last works composed before his arrest, and played some role in his conviction and exile (hence, presumably, its preservation in his file, as evidence). The apocalyptic time which the cycle sees arriving for Russia had certainly arrived for the poet himself. The careful reader of the nearly three hundred lines of this *arrested* cycle will not be surprised that Klyuev had, as noted above, entitled another poem of the period "Iz predsmertnykh pesen" ("From Songs Written before Death"). Not only was the poet quite literally ill (he had heart problems), but many of his late poems seem not only to foretell but also to invite his death. Yet again Klyuev is seen to combine established conventions (self-consciously "last" poems, and so on) with features of the new literary environment of the Soviet period—poetry as last testament; poetry as arrest warrant and even death warrant.

However, the arrest of Klyuev and his texts in 1934 did not lead directly and immediately to his death. He was granted some three years more, albeit in Siberian exile. The texts so far published from his life there are mostly epistolary (some of them remarkable in and of themselves), but one lyric poem is known: "Est' dve strany: odna — Bol'nitsa" ("There are two countries—one the Hospital"), and the *poema Kreml'*. While the survival of two poems (one a plea for clemency) does not encourage the reader of Klyuev to think grandly in terms of poems "after death," as has at least one reader of the late Mandelstam, "Est' dve strany . . ." is certainly a remarkable and self-consciously final poem.[36] It is about last things, and is a defiant statement of the poet's position.

Есть две страны: одна — Больница,
Другая — Кладбище, меж них
Печальных сосен вереница,
Угрюмых пихт и верб седых!

Блуждая пасмурной опушкой,
Я обронил свою клюку,
И заунывною кукушкой
Стучусь в окно к гробовщику:

«Ку-ку! Откройте двери, люди!»
«Будь проклят, полунощный пес!
Куда ты в глиняном сосуде
Несешь зарю апрельских роз?!

Весна погибла, в космы сосен
Вплетает вьюга седину . . .»
Но слыша скрежет ткацких кросен,
Тянусь к зловещему окну

И вижу: тетушка Могила
Ткет желтый саван, и челнок,
Мелькая птицей чернокрылой,
Рождает ткань, как мерность строк.

В вершинах пляска ветродуев,
Под хрип волчицыной трубы
Читаю нити: «Н. А. Клюев, —
Певец олонецкой избы!»

Я умер! Господи, ужели?!
Но где же койка добрый врач?
И слышу: «В розовом апреле
Оборван твой предсмертный плач!

Вот почему в кувшине розы,
И сам ты — мальчик в синем льне! . . .
Скрипят житейские обозы
В далекой бренной стороне.

К ним нет возвратного проселка,
Там мрак, изгнание, Нарым.
Не бойся савана и волка, —
За ними с лютней серафим!»

«Приди, дитя мое, приди!» —
Запела лютня неземная,

И сердце птичкой из груди
Перепорхнуло в кущи рая.

И первой песенкой моей,
Где брачной чашею лилея,
Была: «Люблю тебя, Рассея,
Страна грачиных озимей!»

И ангел вторил: «Буди, буди!
Благословен родной овсень!
Его, как розаны в сосуде,
Блюдет Христос на Оный День!»

There are two countries—one the Hospital,
The other—the Cemetery, between them
Runs a row of sad fir trees,
Gloomy firs, and gray willows!

Wandering in the shadowy glade,
I dropped my walking stick,
And like a dreary cuckoo
Knock at the coffin-maker's window:

"Cuckoo! People, open up the door!"
"Be damned, midnight cur!
To whom are you carrying a clay bowl
With the dawn of April roses?!

Spring has perished, and into the pines' mane
The snowstorm weaves gray hair . . ."
But, hearing the rattle of a weaver's loom,
I lean towards the sinister window

And see: old aunt Tomb
Weaving a yellow shroud, and the shuttle,
Flashing like a black-winged bird,
Gives birth to fabric, like the rhythm of verse.

In the heights above dance the winds
To the wheezing of the she-wolf chimney,
I read the words sewn in the shroud: "N. A. Klyuev,
The singer of the Olonian peasant house!"

I've died? Lord, surely not?!
But where's the sickbed, good doctor?
And I hear, "In rosy April
Your last lamentation was cut off!

That's why there are roses in the pitcher,
And you are a boy in blue flax! . . .
Life's carts rattle by
In a distant, mortal land.

No way leads back to them,
There all is darkness, exile, Siberia.
Don't fear the shroud and the wolf,
After them comes a seraph with a lute."

"Come, my child, come!"
Sang the unearthly lute,
And my heart sprang like a bird
From my chest into the groves of heaven.

And my first song,
When the lily was a wedding chalice,
Was "I love you, simple Russia,
Country of rook-covered winter crops!"

And the angel answered, "Be it so, be it so!
Blessed is the native rite of spring!
It, like roses in the vessel,
Is watched by Christ for Judgment Day!"

Written in the late Klyuev's ubiquitous iambic tetrameter, "Est' dve strany" recalls parts of "Razrukha" in describing an ominous and prophetic vision, and shares some specific motifs with that cycle (speaker as wanderer; cuckoo; shroud), but differs from it in being explicitly individual and self-consciously metapoetic in attempting to define the poet's literary position and legacy. Again Klyuev's prophecy was partly fulfilled: he quite correctly anticipated his (indeed, tragically predictable) death in exile, but erred in chronology, for he died not in April, but, as has been noted, in October 1937. The overall vision of the poem has something of the quality of Klyuev's narratives of his dreams, but differs from them, as from the apocalyptic visions of "Razrukha," in its conclusion, which offers resurrection for the poet and acceptance of his view of Rasseya (peasant Russia). It is also consistent with much of his late work in its employment of conventional (rather than schismatic or sectarian) religious motifs—Klyuev's late letters in particular seem to articulate a more "established" version of Orthodoxy, although he continued to acknowledge Avvakum as his "ancestor." Here, however, those elements of established Orthodoxy are married to popular, "pagan" elements: Christ watches over the native *ovsen'* (first day of spring) until Judgment Day.[37] The poem concludes, then, with the poet posthumously integrating pagan and Christian under the emblem of Rasseya. Pichurin has noted that it opens with a description of the actual landscape of Klyuev's surroundings in Tomsk—a characteristic opening in the anecdotal and physical, but which is followed by a quite otherworldly vision, located, however, quite conventionally in a cemetery.[38] Again, the progression from concrete to abstract generates much of the poem's movement. The identification of the poet as "singer of the Olonian *izba*" and lover of peasant Russia is unambiguous, but more intriguing is the association of the shuttle weaving the funeral shroud for that singer with the production of poetic lines: in the fifth stanza, old Aunt Tomb is weaving a yellow shroud, and the shuttle, flashing like a black-winged bird, "rozhdaet tkan', kak mernost' strok" ("gives birth to fabric, like the rhythm of verse"). That the weaving of a shroud should be associated with the generation of the rhythm of poetic lines is redolent not only of Klyuev's ambiguous and often polar imagery, but also of the intersection of historical time and poetic persona: Klyuev's own lines were, indeed, his funeral shroud. This stanza introduces the central section of the poem, and is itself preceded by a cacophonous stanza which foregrounds the texture, if not the measure, of the verse:

Весна погибла, в космы сосен
Вплетает вьюга седину . . .»
Но слыша скрежет ткацких кросен,
Тянусь к зловещему окну

***V**e**s**na pogibla, v ko**s**my **s**o**s**en*
***V**pletaet **v**'yuga **s**edinu . . ."*
*No **s**ly**sh**a **sk**rezhet t**k**ats**k**ikh **k**rosen,*
*Tyanus' **k** zlove**shch**emu o**k**nu*

Whether "Est' dve strany: odna—Bol'nitsa" was the very last of Klyuev's lyrics or not (and it probably was), it is certainly a very appropriate and emotionally charged final statement. Unlike much of his 1930s work, it is continuous and forms an integral whole. Like much of his late work, it is closely associated with last things in the individual sense (the poet's anticipated death) and the universal (Onyi Den'—Judgment Day). And like all of his published late work, it testifies to the destruction of poetry and exemplifies the impulse to describe that destruction *in poetry*.

Chapter Six

Mother Song: *Pesn' o Velikoi Materi* and Other *Poemy*

THE STORY OF *Pesn' o Velikoi Materi* (*Hymn of the Great Mother*), by far the longest of Klyuev's works, is remarkable: the poet worked on it for several years and seems to have considered it his most important project; it was long thought to have disappeared, along with the poet himself, after his Siberian exile, providing yet more testimony to the ravages of Stalinism. During the glasnost period, the poem's discovery in a KGB archive offered a striking illustration both of the fate of "arrested" literary texts and of the remapping of cultural history in the aftermath of totalitarianism; while its reception illuminated many of the problems in posthumous readings of the poet. *Pesn'* has yet to receive widespread scholarly treatment, but no account of Klyuev and the textual issues raised by his oeuvre can neglect such a significant work, and, indeed, arguments may be made for its right to join the first ranks of twentieth-century Russian *poemy*.

Klyuev, as has been noted, shared with many poets of the late modernist period a tendency toward long narrative and discursive poetry, and, like many of those poets, he expressed that tendency most clearly in the second half of his career. For his generation, whose early work and coming of age coincided with the late symbolist period, that second half of poetic maturity came (and often clashed) with the early years of Soviet power. Those years are, indeed, noteworthy for their *poemy*—beginning with Blok's *Dvenadtsat'* (*The Twelve*) and continuing with major works by Khlebnikov, Mayakovsky, Pasternak, Zabolotsky, the émigré Tsvetaeva, and many others. The inner workings of literary history and the general historical patterns of the time thus coincide to produce a particularly large body of significant *poemy*, many of them evidently and directly related to historical events of the early twentieth century. It is abundantly clear that Klyuev's work of this period shares the general tendency to narrative and discursive poetry, as the late lyrics examined in chapter 5 have already suggested, but that tendency is most clearly expressed in the ten extant or partially extant and published works which are generally classified as *poemy* (*Mat'-Subbota, Chetvertyi Rim, Zaozer'e, Plach o Sergee Esenine, Derevnya, Pogorel'shchina, Solovki, Kain, Pesn' o Velikoi Materi, Kreml'*). As with every other area of his output, these works present a series of problems for interpretation and even comprehension, partly as a result of their compositional history and general reception (or lack thereof). Moreover, their genre classification reveals relatively little about them, and, in several cases, barely helps distinguish them from other works by the poet which are not generally classified as *poemy,* but which share much with these ten. Furthermore, as has been seen, Klyuev himself seems to have classified as a *poema* what most readers would term a "lyric cycle" ("O chem shumyat sedye kedry"), while several members of the group of ten *poemy* to be discussed here do not exceed in length some of the longer works normally classified and universally listed in editions as lyric poems, and none of the ten is *unproblematically narrative.* Hence two of the most basic genre distinctions—length and narrative content—do not apply consistently to Klyuev's *poemy.* In fact, the body of works examined here as *poemy* could be more than doubled by the inclusion of such long poems as "Pesnya o Sokole i o trekh ptitsakh Bozhiikh" of 1909 ("Song About the Falcon and Three of God's Birds," 100–103), "Skrytnyi stikh" of 1914, "Besednyi naigrysh, stikh dobropisnyi" of 1915, "Mirskaya duma" of 1915, "Poddonnyi psalom" of 1916, "Belaya Indiya" of 1916 ("White India," 307–10), "Mednyi kit" of 1918, and by the inclusion of the numerous long late poems exemplified by "Povest' skorbi," examined in chapter 5. Nor is it in the least surprising that some of these "lyric" works have much in common—from thematics to imagery, from metrics to structure—with the *poemy.* For that matter, the same could be said of Klyuev's prose, and even of his dreams. Genre fluidity, then, is even more characteristic of Klyuev than it is of the period in which he worked.[1] Nonetheless, the ten works listed may be—at least loosely and provisionally—distinguished from those near neighbors: three of the ten (*Chetvertyi Rim, Mat'-Subbota, Plach o Sergee Esenine*), appearing as separate publications, were thus distinguished by the poet's own practice from other long works, while *Zaozer'e, Derevnya, Pogorel'shchina, Kain, Pesn' o Velikoi Materi,* and *Kreml'* are longer and more narrative-oriented than any of the long lyric poems.

As in every other area of Klyuev's work, circumstances of composition and transmission render any account of these *poemy* inevitably cautious and incomplete. Five of the ten were not published during the poet's lifetime, and of those five, two (*Kain* and *Pesn' o Velikoi Materi*) are evidently incomplete in the versions published to date, while a third (*Solovki*) may well be a fragment; and Klyuev himself expressed a desire—apparently unfulfilled—to rework *Kreml';* only *Pogorel'shchina,* of these five, seems relatively unproblematic as a material text. Moreover, the group of extant *poemy* is haunted by the shadows of other works. Klyuev's correspondence from Siberia suggests that, beyond the known and now published "Est' dve strany . . ." and *Kreml'*, he may have written other poems, but almost nothing is known of these phantoms, beyond a few remarks in his published correspondence. In a letter to Nikolai Golovanov of July 25, 1934, Klyuev mentions a "Povest' ob Alkonoste nezhdannom" ("Tale of the Unexpected Alkonost"), apparently addressed to the singer Antonina Nezhdanova, which he hoped to finish (*Sd* 326); on August 10, 1936, he wrote to V. N. Gorbacheva (wife of Sergei Klychkov) that he had written a *poema* and several lyric poems, but that they were now in "the cruel hands of others" (*v chuzhikh zhestokikh rukakh,* that is, they had been confiscated [*Sd* 379]); on December 22, 1936, he wrote to her that she should tell Pavel Vasil'ev that he had written four *poemy* (*Sd* 385–86). Even his relatively extensive (and optimistic) remarks to Ada Rudakova in his letter of March 2, 1935, are short on details: "The most astonishing thing of all is that my Slavic Muse does not abandon me. Her reed pipes are more picturesque and brighter than all previous pipes. I have written two big *poemy*—striking in their feelings and eastern beauty" (*Sd* 355). Garnin, in his commentary to this letter, identifies the two works as *Kreml'* and the *poema Narym,* begun in Kolpashevo according to the memoirs of Roman Mensky, but even that identification is dubious, since *Narym* is the only work Mensky records Klyuev as working on and it could equally well be an early version of *Kreml'* (*Sd* 617).[2] It is unlikely that much more will be learned of these phantoms, but what is known of them would seem to reinforce the impression, created by the extant Siberian works, that Klyuev remained able to function as a poet, even in these extreme circumstances. And the emphasis on the composition of *poemy* in those last, difficult years is both noteworthy and suggestive of a direction the poet's work was taking, of which the only extant landmark is *Kreml'*.

The earliest of the ten extant and published *poemy, Chetvertyi Rim* (*Fourth Rome,* 635–40) and *Mat'-Subbota* (*Mother Sabbath,* 640–49) were composed in Vytegra and published in 1922. Both are dedicated to Nikolai Arkhipov, and both present familiar elements of the mature poet's syncretic mythology (the peasant *izba* as a specific but also universal center; East and West united in Russian vernacular forms; established and popular religion combined; homoeroticism). *Mat'-Subbota,* through which the refrain "Angel prostykh chelovecheskikh del" ("Angel of simple human affairs") echoes, is built thematically around the process of bread-making—from harvest to oven—for which verse-making is given as a specific analogue:

Невозмутимы луга тишины —
Пастбище тайн и овчинной луны.
Там небеса, как полати, теплы,
Овцы — оладьи, ковриги — волы;
Пищным отарам вожак — помело,
Отчая кровля — печное чело.

Mother Song

Ангел простых человеческих дел
Хлебным теленьям дал тук и предел.

Судьям чернильным постылы стихи,
Где в запятых голосят петухи,
Бродят коровы по злачным тире,
Строки ж глазасты, как лисы в норе.
Что до того, если дедов кошель —
Луг, где Егорий играет в свирель,
Сивых, соловых, буланых, гнедых
Поят с ладоней соборы святых:
Фрол и Медост, Пантелеймон, Илья —
Чин избяной, луговая семья. (641)

Imperturbable are the meadows of quiet—
The pasture of secrets and of the sheepskin moon.
There the heavens are warm like a sleeping bench,
Sheep are the pancakes, peasant bread—oxen;
The leader of the food herds is the brush,
Paternal protection comes from the brow of the stove.

Angel of simple human affairs
Gave to the calving of bread both shortening and limit.

To inky judges cold are the poems
Where cockerels cry in the commas,
Cows wander over grassy dashes,
And lines are as wide-eyed as foxes in holes.
What does it matter if grandfather's bag
Is a meadow where St. George plays the pipes,
Where grays, dark and light bays, and duns,
Are fed from the hand by gatherings of saints:
Frol and Medost, Panteleimon, Elijah,
A peasant house order, a meadow family.

In *Chetvertyi Rim* such literary-programmatic elements are also evident and include not only the general but also the specific and even the polemic. The poem begins with a transparent attack on Esenin, with the very first lines negating Esenin's proud self-characterization in *Ispoved' khuligana* (*Confession of a Hooligan*) that "teper' on khodit v tsilindre/I lakirovannykh bashmakakh" ("now he walks round in a top hat/And polished shoes").[3] The speaker asserts his identity, predictably, in quite different terms:

Не хочу быть знаменитым поэтом
В цилиндре и лаковых башмаках,
Предстану миру в песню одетым,
С медвежьим солнцем в зрачках,
С потемками хвой в бородище,
Где в случке с рысью рычит лесовик!

I do not want to be a famous poet
In a top hat and patent-leather shoes,
I will appear to the world dressed in song,
With the bear sun in my eyes,
With the darkness of pines in my beard,
Where the badger roars mating with the lynx!

The attack on Esenin in *Chetvertyi Rim* has attracted considerable comment, and its place in the complex and prolonged "love-hate" professional and personal relations of the two poets is significant; but, as the remaining lines of the opening indicate, with their characteristic slippage away from the initial polemic to independent assertion of the poet himself, *Chetvertyi Rim* is more of a manifesto than an invitation to dispute. That manifesto, as the millenarian title suggests, is typically trans-cultural and universalist, but oriented on the imagined peasant universe:

«Для варки песен — всех стран Матрены,
Соединяйтесь!» — несется клич . . .
Котел бессмертен, в поморьях щаных
Зареет яхонт — Четвертый Рим:
Еще немного, и в новых странах
Мы желудь сердца Земле вручим.

"For the brewing of songs—Matrenas of the world,
Unite!" resounds the call . . .
The cauldron is immortal, on cabbage-soup north shores
Amber dawns—the Fourth Rome:
In just a little while, in new countries,
We'll hand the acorn of the heart to the Earth.

These two *poemy* of the early 1920s are followed by three written and published in the mid-1920s: *Plach o Sergee Esenine, Zaozer'e,* and *Derevnya* (649–67). While the two earliest *poemy* have much in common, these three differ radically from one another in almost every respect. *Plach o Sergee Esenine* (*Lament for Sergei Esenin*), written shortly after Esenin's suicide, is probably the most studied of Klyuev's *poemy.* It is also the most significant of Klyuev's contributions to the poetic "dialogue" with Esenin, continued by the former after the latter's death, and here marked by the incorporation of fragments of the younger poet's texts. Its manipulation of elements of the funeral liturgy and other textual models, its fragmentary narrative—of Esenin's life and death—and its apocalyptic tone have much in common with Klyuev's other later *poemy.*

Отцвела моя белая липа во саду,
Отзвенел соловьиный рассвет над речкой.
Вольготней бы на поклоне в Золотую Орду
Изведать ятагана с ханской насечкой!

Умереть бы тебе, как Михайле Тверскому,
Опочить по-мужицки — до рук борода! . . .
Не напрасно по брови родимому дому
Нахлобучили кровлю лихие года.

Неспроста у касаток не лепятся гнезда,
Не играет котенок веселым клубком . . .
С воза, сноп-недовязок, в пустые борозды
Ты упал, чтобы грудь испытать колесом.

Вот и хрустнули кости . . . По желтому жнивью
Бродит песня-вдовица — ненастью сестра . . .
Счастливее елка, что зимнею синью,
Окутана саваном, ждет топора.

Разумнее лодка, дырявые груди
Целящая корпией тины и трав . . .
О жертве вечерней иль новом Иуде
Шумит молочай у дорожных канав? (656)

My white lime tree has finished flowering in the garden,
The nightingale dawn has finished sounding over the river,
It would be easier to pay respects to the Golden Horde
And get to know a dagger cut for the khan!

You should have died like Michael of Tver',
Gone to sleep like a peasant, beard to your waist!
It was not in vain that the wild years
Pushed down a roof low on your native house.

There is a reason why swallows are not making nests,
And kittens don't play like happy balls . . .
From the cart, an unfinished sheaf of hay, you fell
Into empty furrows, to try your breast against the wheels.

And your bones snapped . . . Along the yellow stubble
Wanders a widow-song—sister to bad weather . . .
Happier is the fir which, in the blue winter air,
Wrapped in a shroud, awaits the axe.

Wiser is the boat, healing chests full of holes,
With lint of mud and grass . . .
Does the spurge in the ditches by the roads
Murmur of an evening victim or of a new Judas?

As the scholarly apparatus to *Serdtse edinoroga* points out (970), the opening lines of the passage quoted above draw upon Esenin's "Etoi grusti teper' ne rassypat'" ("This sadness cannot now be dissipated") of 1924.[4]

Meanwhile, *Zaozer'e* (*Beyond the Lake*) is the lightest and brightest of Klyuev's *poemy,* anticipating the northern pastoral elements of *Pesn' o Velikoi Materi.* The poem presents an Arcadian village year, beginning with the spring St. George's Day (23 April) and ending a year later with Easter and the next spring St. George's Day, as experienced and celebrated by "Otets Aleksei iz Zaozer'ya" ("Father Aleksei from beyond the lake"), the priest of a distant and idealized northern village. That village is characterized by a happy synthesis of nature and culture, and of pagan and Christian belief and practice. As other readers have pointed out, the principle of amalgamation extends even to the hero, for Father Aleksei's confessional status is unclear—apparently officiating in an Old Believer church, he seems nonetheless to be a servant of the established church (in fact, most Old Believers of the north were "priestless" anyway).[5] Indeed, by the mid-1920s the once-distinct markers of schismatic and/or sectarian culture are frequently encountered in Klyuev's work alongside unproblematically Orthodox features, which were themselves now beginning to function in his work (and to be seen by Soviet authorities) as signs of defiant spiritual and cultural opposition. Hence, in *Zaozer'e* the gentle nostalgia and idyllic integrity of village life, sacred and profane, form an especially harsh contrast with the historical context of the work's composition—the beginning of the Stalinist period:

Великие дни в деревне —
Журавиный плакучий звон,

Mother Song

По мертвой снежной царевне
Церквушка правит канон.

Лиловые павечерья,
И, как весточка об ином,
Потянет из Заозерья
Березовым ветерком.

Христос воскресе из мертвых,
Смертию смерть поправ,
И у елей в лапах простертых
Венки из белых купав.

В зеленчатом сарафане
Слушает звон сосна.
Скоро в лужицу на поляне
Обмокнет лапоток весна.

Запоют бубенцы по взгорью,
И как прежде в тысячах дней,
Молебном в уши Егорью
Задудит отец Алексей. (652–53)

Great days in the village—
The wailing peal of cranes,
The little church holds a service
For the dead snow-maiden.

Lilac late evenings,
And, like news from elsewhere,
Out from beyond the lake
Will come a breath of birch wind.

Christ has risen from the dead,
Conquering death through death,
And the fir trees hold in their extended boughs
Wreaths of white water lilies.

In a greenish peasant dress
The pine hears the peal.
Soon spring will wet its bast shoe
In a meadow puddle.

Bells will sing out on the hillock,
And as before in thousands of days,
Father Aleksei will pipe out
A service into St. George's ears.

These final stanzas, completing the cycle of the year in nature and in culture with the promise of imminent rebirth and even spiritual victory (explicit in Easter, implicit in the figure of St. George), emphasize that both regeneration and the cycle within which regeneration takes place are *eternal.* The conclusion acquires a special poignancy, even plangency, in publications where an editor has appended to the end of the poem its year of composition or of publication—1926, 1927, years which saw the further growth of political processes that would violently challenge any promise of rebirth or eternity in the spiritual realm (not to mention in the Russian village). Equally poignant is the relative proximity of this "Shepherd's Calendar" (albeit for a priest) to Klyuev's much earlier lyrics elaborating that favorite theme—the unity of peasant community and nature, of popular "pagan" and Christian spirituality. In each case, the world presented is part personal mythology, part popular ethnography, part anti-urban ideology, and always marked by a sense of Edenic loss. However, the work of the mid-1920s carries with it a sense of loss which is imminent or immediate and acute, not elegiacally remote (as in the work of the mid-1910s), and that loss is accompanied by a distinct frisson of present danger. Klyuev's remarks at a public reading of the poem in October 1927 (as recorded by Arkhipov) emphasize the pastoral and universal features of the *poema* and encourage a modern reader to speculate on the response of the poet's audience, listening to this poem almost exactly ten years after the Bolshevik coup:

> Through the formless visions of the present I lead you into the bright, enchanting world of Zaozer'e, where people and creatures pass the cycle of their earthly existence beneath the powerful and extensive inspiration of a being "with a perch splash in his eyes"—father Aleksei, the sort of man known also to the forests of Sarov, the dark oaks of Mesopotamia, and the underground shrines of Siam. (*Sd* 74)[6]

The last of Klyuev's poems to be published in his own lifetime, *Derevnya* (*The Village*), is contemporaneous in composition and publication with *Zaozer'e* but forms a distinct contrast with the latter in thematics, since its subject is essentially contemporary rather than self-consciously archaic. Thus it provides that very context of current events expressly excluded from *Zaozer'e.* Although short (well under two hundred lines in length), *Derevnya* ranges widely over Russian history and literature to provide a semi-apocalyptic vision of the present, colored by such favorite later motifs as the profanation of religion and ominous ecological problems:

Ты, Рассея, Рассея матка,
Чаровая, заклятая кадка!
Что там, кровь или жемчуга,
Иль лысого черта рога?
Рогатиной иль каноном
Открыть наговорный чан? . . .
Мы расстались с саровским звоном —
Утолением плача и ран.
Мы новгородскому Никите
Оголили трухлявый срам, —
Отчего же на белой раките
Не поют щеглы по утрам? (664–65)

Rasseya, Rasseya mother,
You enchanted, bewitched vat!
What is there, blood or pearls,
Or the horns of a bald devil?
Should the magic tub be opened
With a bear spear or a church service?
We parted with the Sarov peal—
The soothing of lamentation and wounds.
We exposed the crumbling shame
Of St. Nikita of Novgorod—
Why do no goldfinches sing
On the white willows in the morning?

Klyuev's "Rasseya," here and elsewhere in his later work, is both mother, ambivalently treated, and evil mother-in-law. Near the end of *Derevnya,* the speaker exclaims: "Ty Rasseya, Rasseya teshcha,/Nasolila ty likho vo shchi" ("You, Rasseya, mother-in law Rasseya,/You've put far too much salt in the soup," 667). "Rasseya" here also echoes Esenin's in the latter's famous *Moskva kabatskaya* (Tavern Moscow) poems—"Ty, Rasseya moya . . . Ras . . . seya . . ./Aziatskaya storona!" ("You, my Rasseya . . . Ras . . . seya/Asiatic land!").[7] Hence Klyuev's mother-Russia is (very characteristically) an amalgam of treatments—the conventional, other individual and specific treatments, and his own highly personal versions. *Derevnya* as a whole is also a characteristic amalgam. The referents provide the familiar spread of Russian cultural geography and history: Siberia and Kargopol'; the Volga, the Ob'; the Tatar horde, Kulikovo field, Yaroslavna, Vasilii Buslaev; Soviet agriculture, and Sovietized language ("Faktor,/Chto mashina . . . Ona toe . . ." ["The factor,/That the machine . . . It is, you know . . ."], 665), while the poem as a whole modulates between lament, prophecy, and polemic.

It is hardly surprising that published reactions to *Derevnya* were very hostile, nor that it was to be one of his last publications. In response to an invitation from the Writers' Union to engage in "self-criticism," Klyuev produced a robust, if somewhat tangential, defense of *Derevnya:*

> While admitting that in the work in question there is some obscurity, well calculated by me as an artist, and remoteness of images, essential for generating in the reader a multiplicity of comparisons and suppositions, I wholeheartedly assert that the *poema Derevnya* . . . is imbued to its deepest core with the pain of pipes, wailing in the red Russian wind. (*Sd* 406–7)

This defense serves as a further reminder of the proximity of Klyuev's later verse, at least in motifs and thematic structure, to popular prophecy and to other forms of nonliterary discourse for which structural integrity is not characteristic. Hence the tendency to blend past and present as a description of the future, and the frequent, sudden changes of tone or even referent which contribute to the difficulty of much of his work.

The remaining five extant *poemy* belong to the final period of Klyuev's literary existence, shaped by anxiously tended manuscripts and by intermittent oral performances (apparently in part to raise a subsistence income). The slightest of these four is *Solovki* (667–70), which may, as already noted, be classified as a *poema* only with qualifications. Apparently written from 1926 to 1928, the text as published (by Subbotin in 1989) is from a copy made by one Nikolai Kir'yanov, who in 1929 received from Klyuev a notebook containing *Zaozer'e, Derevnya,* and *Solovki.*[8] Subbotin argues convincingly that the text is genuine, and identifies among Klyuev's own manuscripts the draft for the final part of the published *Solovki.* However, the status of the text itself remains unclear: is it a finished work, or part of a larger (lost or never written) whole; is it an unfinished, but integral work; what is the significance of its inclusion in a manuscript book with two published *poemy;* and so on? The fact that its final twenty-four lines are also to be found in another late, unfinished *poema* (*Kain*) adds yet another problem to any discussion of its status (974–75). Not only are these problems typical for the late Klyuev, and for much of Russian literature beyond the parameters of the official in this period, but the poem, as it stands, is itself a product of many of the same problems (impossibility of publication; individualized dissemination; elision of the boundaries between private and public, draft and completed work; and so on). In any case, the composition of a manuscript book consisting of his pastoral *Zaozer'e,* the apocalyptic *Derevnya,* and the ambiguous *Solovki* is intriguing: a triptych of cultural narratives of the Russian village and the Russian north.

Solovki is tied thematically to the early claims made for and by Klyuev as an erstwhile ascetic resident of the Solovetsky Islands (and reiterated in his prose piece "Krasnyi kon'" of 1919); to his late preoccupation with the White Sea coast, which is encountered both in *Pesn' o Velikoi Materi* and also in some of his late recorded autobiographies; and to the trope, recurrent in his late work, of Russia abandoned by its saints and sacred symbols. Moreover, *Solovki* provides another occasion for that modified form of cataloguing (here of places and, principally, of saints) which is so characteristic of Klyuev's later poetry, and generally functions as a catalogue of catastrophe. The work also resembles other later *poemy* in its rhetorical ambiguity: beginning as an encomium to the far north's greatest monastic site, it continues with an allusion to the speaker's own years of natural and spiritual pupilage there, only to become first a lament for historical and fictional martyrs, and finally the song of St. Eleazar, founder of a famous community on Anzer Island. The song, although itself largely a lament, concludes with the apparent promise that, in the absence of human support, nature will provide a site for the Nativity. The movement between personal lyric and general civic themes is also typical of Klyuev's late poetics:

Распрекрасный остров Соловецкий,
Лебединый Секир-гора,
Где церквушка, рубленная клецки, —
Облачному ангелу сестра.
Где учился я по кожаной Триоди
Дум прибою, слов колоколам,
Величавой северной природе
Трепетно моляся по ночам . . .
Где впервые пономарь Авива
Мне поведал хвойным шепотком,
Как лепечет травка, плачет ива
Над осенним розовым Христом. (668)

Most beautiful Solovetsky Island,
Swanlike Hatchet Hill,
Where the church, of simple log rectangles,
Is sister to the celestial angel.
Where I studied by a leather-bound service book
The surf of thoughts, the bells of words,
Praying anxiously by night
To the majestic nature of the north . . .

Where first the sexton Aviva
Taught me in a whisper of evergreens
How grasses babble, willows weep
Above the autumn's pink Christ.

As noted in chapter 1, Klyuev's later references to the Solovetsky Islands, although in many ways similar to his earliest allusions to them as a famous site of northern monasticism and, implicitly or explicitly, as a site of popular resistance to authority, also require further, contextual reading: by the time of the composition of this *poema,* the monastery was closed and had been replaced by the first Soviet labor camp (where many intellectuals were incarcerated and some perished).

While the material status of *Solovki* is uncertain, there seems no doubt that another of the five late, posthumously published *poemy* has survived only in fragmentary form: *Kain* (*Cain*) was preserved in the same place as "Razrukha," examined in chapter 5—the archives of the KGB—and it presents many of the same problems as that cycle. As in the case of *Solovki,* the discovery of this incomplete text shed light on another manuscript, revealing that several previously unidentified pages of verse among the fragmentary survivals in the archive of Ivanov-Razumnik (most of which was destroyed during the Second World War) were part of the fair copy of *Kain.* Thus the published fragments represent a stage in Klyuev's work on a *poema* which he almost certainly finished, and which, in its complete form, is almost certainly lost forever. *Kain* also illustrates how Klyuev and his works provided weaponry in the especially acute ideological confrontations in Russia at the end of the twentieth century. It was published by the well-known (to many, "notorious") Stanislav Kunyaev. As noted in chapter 1, an extract appeared in the newspaper *Den'* in 1992, followed by a full publication of the extant parts (it is estimated that around five hundred lines have been lost) in *Nash sovremennik;* that publication was repeated in a collection of Kunyaev essays in 1995.[9] An ironist would note that Klyuev's luck in having at least fragments of his late works preserved for over fifty years by the Soviet secret police was matched by his luck in having those fragments published in organs of the Russian nationalist right, which were largely ignored or despised by the "philological elite" and, for that matter, by those large parts of the reading public that did not share the ideological premises of latter-day populist Russian nationalism. That ironist might add that there was only, at best, a partial fit between *Kain* and its places of publication. Nor does the work's "bad luck" end there: while the fragmentary *Solovki* and incomplete *Pesn' o Velikoi Materi* are included in the authoritative *Serdtse edinoroga, Kain* is not.

It seems that *Kain* was written during Klyuev's 1929 summer stay in the Vyatka region—the area where he spent a number of summers, and which was a major source of inspiration for his late works. The *poema,* as published, is divided into four parts, of which only the fourth appears complete. In the first, very fragmentary part, the speaker describes an October vision in which a diabolical figure tells him, the *zhguchii otprysk Avvakuma* (burning issue of Avvakum), that he is *ognem slovesnym opalen* (singed with the fire of words), but that nothing can be done without the friendship of Cain. Allusions to the fallen sites of Russian spirituality—Radonezh, Sarov, Diveevo—follow, and then comes a sinister picture of Stalinist Russia (lacunae in the text are indicated in the following passage by ellipses in parentheses):

На беду, на беду
Пятиконечную звезду
Я на мерлушнике нащупал —
Не то дворец, не то халупа
Чадила гарью человечьей,
Кому-то очередь для речи
Давал товарищ Гребешков
(. . .) у столов,
Так домовитый мудрый кот,
Крысиный усмирив народ
(. . .) лапкой мастерит
(. . .) буржуев
(. . .)
Ай, ай, и челюсти мои
(. . .)
Вонзали когти в клад заклятый.
И вот, усат, с брюшком седым
Зловещий кот владеет им.

For ill, for ill
I fingered the five-pointed star
On a sheepskin coat.
Somewhere between a palace and a hovel
It smelled of burnt human flesh,
Comrade Grebeshkov was giving
Someone the floor at a meeting
(. . .) by tables,
So the wise and thrifty cat,
After subduing the rat people
(. . .) with its paw makes
(. . .) bourgeois
(. . .)

Oh, oh, and my jaws
(. . .)
Pressed claws into the enchanted treasure
And there, bewhiskered, with gray belly
The evil cat is their owner.

The few extant lines of part 2 contrast a Pushkinian scene with its vulgar Soviet equivalent (Pushkin, as a measure of cultural integrity, has already been implied in the image of the scion of Avvakum scorched by the fire of words, which distantly but significantly echoes Pushkin's "Prorok"; and Pushkin figures in the same role elsewhere in Klyuev's late poetry). Part 3, more extensive, but still fragmentary, narrates the speaker's sinister dream of a decayed provincial town and of human butchery; enumerates further examples of the destruction of Russian culture, sacred and profane; apparently gives Cain's own account of his participation in the opening of sacred relics; provides a chorus elaborating Soviet acts in markedly Soviet language ("Kuda zapropastilas' skotina?" ["Where did the swine . . ."]); and laments the violation of nature and the flight of the saints, partly in the voice of an executed monk. Part 4 is the only complete section of the poem and probably provides a more or less reliable model for the preceding parts in its relatively seamless combination of past and present; personal (lyrical recollections of the speaker's pastoral youth) and general (history and fate of Russia). The lyrical recollections include memories of early (homosexual) love, while the history and fate of Russia is presented in a blending of pagan and Christian elements, and with the bloody present interwoven not only with the Arcadian past but also (and typically) with a somewhat ambiguous resurrection, as the final lines indicate:

Явился солнечно пригожий
К гагарьим заводям Христос,
Покинув кров, по мхам и хвоям,
К нему идут пастух и воин,
И рощи утренних берез.
Прядя дремучею ресницей,
Не могут кедры надивиться:
К реке, как в икрометье сомы,
С холстов текут людские сонмы —
Руси Крещение второе.
Ведут детей пчелиным роем,
Сребристей пены лен одежд . . .
Трепещет жаворонок вежд —
Вот-вот взовьется к небесам . . .

Mother Song

Проснись, Буй-Тур, иди к брегам!
Тебя сам милостник Никола
В кресчатой ризе ждет у мола.
Уж златокосая Моряна
Наречена святой Татьяной,
Она росистою звездою
Глядит в оконце слюдяное!
Восстань, о княже Гавриилe,
Пришел конец Сварожьей силе.
От мертвой сыти воев сонмы,
Сиянием креста ведомы,
Идут к родимой черемисе . . .
«Мой милый лебедь, пробудися!» —
Поет тростиночкой Татьяна —
«Я выплываю из тумана,
Чтоб на пиру вино живое,
Руси крещение второе,
Испить нам из единой чары! . .
Приди ко мне, мой лебедь ярый!»

Поэма покрывается пением венчального Ирмоса: «Святии мученицы, иже добре кровями червовь украсивши!»

A sunshine-bright comely Christ
Has appeared to the loon backwaters,
Abandoning their homes, through moss and pine,
To him come shepherd and soldier,
And groves of morning birches.
Flicking sleepy eyelids,
The cedars are astonished,
To the river, like catfish spawning,
Hosts of people flow from pictures—
A second Baptism of Russia.
They bring their children in swarms,
Their flaxen clothes are brighter silver than foam . . .
The lark of eyelids trembles—
Any moment an ascent to heaven . . .
Wake up, Fierce-Aurochs, come to the banks!
Almsgiver St. Nicholas himself
In cross-marked robes awaits you at the pier.
And golden-tressed Moryana
Is named St. Tat'yana,

> Like a dew-wet star
> She looks into the window of mica!
> Arise, o Prince Gabriel,
> The end has come for Svarog's power.
> Hosts of wails from dead meat,
> Led by the shining of the cross,
> Go to their native Mari land . . .
> "My darling swan, awake!"—
> Sings Tat'yana, like a reed—
> "I swim out of the mists,
> So that we might drink
> At the feast, the second baptism of Russia,
> The wine of life from a single goblet!
> Come to me, my fierce swan!"
>
> The poem concludes with the singing of the wedding hymn, "Holy martyr-women, who have decorated the church with their blood!"

This concluding passage is characteristic not only of *Kain* but of Klyuev's late oeuvre in general: it is, to say the least, obscure at times; it is very eclectic in its references (for example, the "Baptism of Russia" appears to be not only the "historical" event but also V. M. Vasnetsov's fresco of that name for the Cathedral of St. Vladimir in Kiev [1885–95]—an interesting marker of Klyuev's aesthetics); nature and culture are run together (Christ has appeared to the "loon backwaters," and the trees watch in astonishment this "second Baptism" of Russia); premodern elements, both pagan and Christian, emphasize the antiquity of the scene, while the context is apparently either modern or simply timeless in its apocalyptic blending of periods; and as a conclusion, the scene offers a disorienting mixture of pagan and Christian deities (some of them simultaneously pagan *and* Christian) in what seems to be the Second Coming, accompanied, as the author's prose note states, by the singing of the opening of a wedding hymn. It is also entirely characteristic that, as Eduard Meksh observes in the only substantial scholarly treatment of this poem, there is no such "wedding hymn."[10]

Kain, like "Razrukha," is a significant, albeit incomplete, artifact surviving the shipwreck of Klyuev's late works. As has been noted, other works seem to have been lost in their entirety, some perhaps as long and significant as those two. And even a provisional assessment of the survivors remains difficult. Their material textuality still presents problems; they are so colored by their post-composition history and by attempts to appropriate them to specific ideological positions of recent times that to see them first and foremost even in the modest context of the poet's own creative biography is difficult. To read them for the first time now, in the aftermath of the end of Soviet power, is to risk reading them as statements of the obvious—the cataclysm of twentieth-century Russian history. And, as has been seen in many other areas of Klyuev's work, any reading also risks endowing them with not only the stylistic and narrative manner of prophetic discourse but also the visionary power of prophecy itself. And to do that may well lead the interpreter a long way from the normal preoccupations of philology, and will certainly negate the metaphorical, stylized, literary manipulation of prophetic discourse which is at least as significant in these poems as any literal vatic claims. In part for these reasons, *Kain* has received virtually no scholarly attention yet, and one may speculate that it has not even had many readers. If and how it will be read in the coming decades is open to endless speculation, but its own future seems no more hopeful than was that of the country it surveyed in 1929. Perhaps future historians of Russian *poemy* will at least see it and its brethren as fascinating, if ruined, markers of a route of literary development which simply disappeared into the quicksand of Stalinism.

The fate of *Pogorel'shchina* (*Burnt Ruins,* 670–95) has been very different from that of *Kain.* Although, like the latter, it was not published in Klyuev's lifetime (despite an apparent publication agreement with *Krasnaya gazeta* [*The Red Gazette*]), it was well known in literary circles, since the poet seems to have read it often at his semi-public performances of the late 1920s and early 1930s; he himself evidently considered the work partly to blame for his arrest.[11] Indeed, one copy of the poem did find its way into the archives of the secret police.[12] But, unlike *Kain,* other copies of the text remained extant, and one, given to the Italian Slavist Ettore Lo Gatto, survived abroad.[13] From this copy the work was published posthumously, as the poet had requested, in the 1954 collection of Klyuev's work edited by Boris Filippov.[14] This publication, and its successor in *Sochineniya,* not only guaranteed that the poem received at least some attention in the West (it was even translated into English), but also that it became accessible, if only to a few, in the Soviet Union.[15] No doubt the existence of a published version abroad contributed to the appearance of Bazanov's article on *Pogorel'shchina* in *Russkaya literature* in 1979 (as discussed in chapter 4), seven years before fragments of the poem were published in *Stikhotvoreniya i poemy,* edited by the Kunyaevs, and eight years before the publication of a full version of the poem (from a more reliable manuscript than Lo Gatto's) in *Novyi mir.*[16] Subsequent publications refer to and use yet other manuscripts and typescripts (975–76).[17]

The relative abundance of typescript and manuscript copies of *Pogorel'shchina* indicates its central place in the poet's work of the late 1920s (its time of completion now seems certain, since one text is dated precisely—the Feast of the Protection of the Blessed Virgin Mary, 1928 [October 14, new style], 695). It is central, too, for any evaluation of Klyuev's *poemy:* it is his longest complete work (almost one thousand lines in all, and thus slightly longer than *Kreml'*); it shares thematic features both with the more pastoral *poemy* (*Mat'-Subbota, Zaozer'e*) and with the more apocalyptic later verse; it is polymetrical, yet dominated by the most common meter of the late verse (iambic tetrameter); and like so many of the later works, while it does have recurrent characters, motifs, and linked episodes, it lacks, as one commentator puts it, a "unified canvas of sequential events" (but here, in contrast to other exemplars, the work is undoubtedly complete, and the overall effect may be judged more definitively).[18]

The opening describes, in pastoral colors and with occasional dialectal forms, a northern fishing village, Sigovoi Lob (Whitefish Forehead), but contains the disorienting announcement from the narrator that "Tuda ne plyvu ya na pevchem vesle" ("I am not sailing there on my singing oar"). Not only does this line emphasize both the physical and, by implication, mythological inaccessibility of the location, but it also is redolent of the knowledge of loss which was only contextual in earlier accounts of the pastoral north.[19] The announcement that "porato basko zimoi v Sigovtse" ("it is very fine during winter in Sigovoi Lob"), which, in *porato basko,* has by far the most marked dialectal usage in the poem, precedes an enumeration of activities—in particular the popular crafts—and residents in the village. The links between cult, culture, nature, and the folk are ubiquitous. In the following passage, Old and New Testaments are characteristically blended, while the popular form "Onego" is preferred to the standard "Onega" for the name of the lake:

> У Прони скатерть синей Онега,
> По зыби едет луны телега,
> Кит-рыба плещет, и яро в нем
> Пророк Иона грозит крестом. (671)
>
> Pronya's tablecloth is bluer than Onega,
> Along its ripples runs the moon's cart,
> The whale-fish splashes, and within it
> The Prophet Jonah brandishes a cross.

Nature and religion (again, apparently a blend of Orthodoxy, Old Belief, and "paganism") are intertwined. For example, in the work of Pavel the icon-painter, St. George's steed is painted from a drake, St. Nicholas's chasuble from a maple, the Assumption from the feathers of doves, and the Crucifixion from a radish ("Raspyatie — s red'ki — kak gvozdi kresta,/Tak redechnyi sok opalyaet usta" ["The Crucifixion—from a radish—like the nails of the cross/Radish juice inflames the lips"], 672). As so often, here the associations are not literal, nor consistent, and certainly not representative of the popular consciousness. Instead, they are markedly synesthetic, recalling such programmatic pronouncements as "The innards of deer sound sweeter than Glinka," and they provide a startling mixture of abstract and very concrete associations, as the example of the radish, with its striking explanation and touch of eroticism, indicates. Equally praised is the potter Siliverst, who has made a head of Christ for the Lopsky Cemetery (a somewhat unusual artifact for a Russian cemetery—reinforcing the implications of Christian and "pagan" in the toponym: the *Lapp* Cemetery).

The celebration of the splendors of the village and its culture is suddenly interrupted by a song which tells of the fate of one Anastasiya Romanovna, who had forty suitors and forty *sarafans* but now lies dead, apparently violated and dishonored, a victim of urban corruption (perhaps a song about the first wife of Ivan the Terrible, supposedly poisoned by enemies at court?). The villagers provide various interpretations of the song, but Pavel the icon-painter then sees the worst of omens—St. George has galloped off his icon. There follows an address to saints and familiar icons, summoning their aid, but in vain:

> Гляньте, детушки, на стол —
> Змий хвостом ушицу смел,
> Адский пламень по углам:
> Не пришел Микола к нам! (678)
>
> Children, look at the table—
> The dragon has swept away the fish soup with his tail,
> A hellish fire leaps in the corners:
> St. Nicholas has not come to us!

Late winter—the poem follows a rough sequence of seasons in its narrative, while linear time is repeatedly disrupted in its symbolic structure—sees the arrival of the mythological (Slavic, pre-Christian) bird Sirin, who, in a characteristic synthesis of apparent opposites, sings "Kyrie Eleison" and then departs. This was the year when Pavel died, after painting an icon which depicted a magnificent church where sat on an emerald throne the traditional image of John the Baptist: "Kak grozd' v tochile vinograda/Useknovennaya glava" ("Like a bunch of grapes in a wine press/The Severed Head," 679). At that time the wood-carver Olekha saw two elders, Zosima and Savvatii (the names of the founders of the Solovetsky Monastery), who announced that they were abandoning their monastery, and who took him with them in their departure. Pronya the lacemaker dreamed that the village had been captured by a dragon, and she too, accompanied by the mythological Alkonost, left this earth. The new order now occupied her house:

А в горенке по самогонке
Тальянка гиблая орет —
Хозяев новых обиход. (681)

And in her living room
A feeble accordion cried for moonshine—
The custom of the new masters.

Siliverst and a companion built a monastic cell behind the cemetery and lived there in ascetic communion with nature and with God until they received a blunt epistle from Neil the elder, who lived on an ice pillar by Lake Onega: "Gotov'tes' k smerti" ("Prepare for death," 682). Witnessed and mourned by the local fauna, Siliverst and his fellow "brother" (mysteriously termed *svekor,* meaning "husband's father," that is, a *wife's* father-in-law), set light to the church and to themselves. They call upon Avvakum, who was burned at the stake, and Feodosii, whose order of the Old Belief engaged in such acts of self-immolation, to witness their deaths.

Now Great Sig is silent, but the narrator *pesnopisets Nikolai* (writer of songs Nikolai) bears witness to this *Nerukotvornaya Rossiya* (Russia not-made-by-human-hands, 684). The phrase is based upon the icon subject "Spas nerukotvornyi"—Savior Not-Made-by-Human-Hands (the image of Christ from a towel)—one of many icon motifs recalled in *Pogorel'shchina* (and in many other Klyuev poems). Nikolai's vision includes a catalogue of sites of Russian spiritual beauty and glory from Ustyug to Kostroma, and his declared intention is to withdraw from the world, and to bury his *korob pesennyi* (song box, 686) for a later generation to find.

In the autumn stoves yearn for bread, burbots have gone from the lakes, and hunger abounds. Pronya's dream has come true: Sigovets has been seized by a dragon, and parents eat their own children, while old women are buried alive and burned, to prevent the wolf from eating them. Thus died Great Sig in the year 1919 (another version of Klyuev's year of catastrophe—and contextually, for the death of rural Russia, rather *early*), its death linked to other evils. A Kasimov coachman's song is then interpolated, reiterating the loss of Russia, of individual places and people. Then *sosnovye kheruvimy* (pine cherubim, 690) appear, flying to the city to seek the daughter of Herod and to plead for mercy. They are met by a chorus of rejection, phrased in vulgar, bureaucratized, Sovietized Russian.

The final two parts of *Pogorel'shchina* take a characteristic turn away from the main narrative of the poem. The first of them is an elaborate narrative of the city of Lydda on the *Indiiskoe pomorie* (Indian coast, 692; the historical Lydda in Palestine, according to one commentator), magnificent and beautiful, but, for some reason, entirely without flowers.[20] The city is besieged by Saracens, and its citizenry appeal to the Virgin Mary. Her icon is disfigured, and where its paint is scattered in the sack of the city, flowers later grow in abundance. The final section of *Pogorel'shchina,* consisting of six six-line stanzas of trochaic trimeter (the only appearance of this meter in the poem), mixes yearning for the inaccessible Lydda with lament for contemporary, violated Russia and concludes with typical ambiguity:

Где ты, город-розан —	Where are you, rose-city—
Волжская береза,	Volga birch,
Лебединый крик	Swan cry,
И, ордой иссечен,	And, slashed by the Horde,
Осиянно вечен,	Eternal in hosannahs,
Материнский лик?!	Maternal visage?!
Цветик мой дитячий,	My child flower,
Над тобой поплачет	Over you will cry
Темень да Трезор!	Darkness and Dog!
Может, им под тыном	Perhaps, under the paling
И пахнет жасмином	They'll catch the scent of jasmine
От Саронских гор! (695)	From Sharon's hills!

Pogorel'shchina is a remarkable work, more varied yet more compact (despite its considerable length) than many of Klyuev's other long works. It combines vivid episodes from the life and death of its specific, fictional village and its inhabitants with extensive references to particular and general aspects of Russian culture, history, and geography, and with a mythic syncretism which creates an arena for the encounter of popular and high-cultural beliefs, established Orthodoxy, Old Belief, "paganism," legend, and poetic invention. Its language is dense and difficult (Klyuev provided Lo Gatto with a brief glossary; his later commentators have all followed suit), and its imagery frequently puzzling. However, *Pogorel'shchina* is by no means resistant to explication—as, it is hoped, the preceding account of its contents has illustrated. Indeed, it indicates more clearly than any of Klyuev's other *poemy* that one of the cultural projects implicit in Klyuev's oeuvre and persona could be realized: the marriage of the poetics of Russian modernism to the native and learned elements associated by Klyuev with the Russian village, the Russian north, and the Russian past. That marriage was, here and elsewhere in Klyuev's achievements, a remarkable but also a unique union. Although it may be compared with other phenomena of Russian modernism, it was distinct from most in that its only poetic offspring was Klyuev's own work, and there were no further heirs. Nor, for that matter, were there siblings—Klyuev stands alone among the "new-peasant poets," nowhere more clearly than in his *poemy*, which are quite unlike those of Esenin and the others.[21]

Although *Pogorel'shchina* was known in Klyuev's lifetime only in unpublished form—performed by the poet at readings, and read in manuscript by associates and intimates—it achieved a certain renown, as memoirs of those who heard him read it indicate. Indeed, the memoirists cited earlier often refer to the impression his reading of the poem made. Thus *Pogorel'shchina* achieved a semi-public status which seems representative of Klyuev's own situation in the late 1920s. Its export during his lifetime and its subsequent publication in the West in the 1950s ensured that it did not disappear completely from view. Although it existed, for most readers in Russia, in an alternative and inaccessible world, it was not entirely unknown, and did have its commentators. It simply belonged to that huge population of texts which formed "Russian literature abroad." Its return home in 1987 was thus one of the many markers of the early period of glasnost when every Soviet journal contained remarkable and thrilling revelations.

Far more remote than *Pogorel'shchina* was *Pesn' o Velikoi Materi.* Although it was known to have been one of Klyuev's major late works, the account of its fate provided by Ivanov-Razumnik in his *Pisatel'skie sud'by* remained for many years the accepted version of its fate:

> In exile Klyuev worked on finishing his best and largest work, the *poema Hymn of the Great Mother.* He sent the second part for safekeeping to his friend Nikolai Arkhipov, who was at that time a curator at the Museum of the Great Peterhof Palace; not knowing how to preserve the valuable manuscript, Arkhipov put it on top of one of the tall tiled stoves in one of the palace rooms. Soon after that he was arrested, and the Peterhof Palace was destroyed in the war in 1941.
>
> In my own archive I had a voluminous file—more than one hundred letters and more than fifty poems by Klyuev from the period 1933–37, including a copy of the first part of the *Hymn of the Great Mother.* That file, and my entire archive perished in Tsarskoe Selo [where the author had lived before the war] during the winter of 1941–42.[22]

Ivanov-Razumnik then provides the familiar and widely reproduced (but legendary) account of Klyuev's demise in Siberia, after his release: the poet left his place of exile with a "suitcase full of manuscripts," but "the suitcase disappeared without a trace, just as did, it must be assumed, the second and third parts of the *Hymn.*" Ivanov-Razumnik's account (written in 1942–43) of the loss of *Pesn'* was accepted as accurate, in broad terms, for some fifty years. Gradually, more information came to light about the nature and content of *Pesn'*, but these publications, mostly of the 1980s, provided somewhat conflicting accounts, and none disputed its loss.[23] Klyuev's letter to Gorbacheva of July 25, 1935, written in Tomsk (and published in 1988), confirmed Klyuev's own anxiety about the work: "The fate of my *poema, Hymn of the Great Mother,* pierces my heart. I composed it over six years. I collected Russian mysteries grain by grain" (*Sd* 370). At the time that letter was published, only tiny fragments of *Pesn'* had been found, and prospects for further discoveries must have seemed limited. Thus, above accounts of the persecuted Klyuev and the writings of his last years floated a spectral, lost work, described in contradictory terms by a small number of memoirists, and the subject of little more than qualified speculation on the part of scholarly commentators. The lost *Pesn'* served as one among many shadow monuments to the lost careers and lives of the Stalinist epoch. All that seemed to remain in the physical world were fragments, and there seemed little hope of any major archival find. Yet, quite contrary to expectations, a version of the entire work was found when the journalist Vitaly Shentalinsky gained access to the files of arrested intellectuals held in the central archives of the KGB. The discovery of a draft of the entire work in those archives, attached to the file compiled at the time of Klyuev's arrest in Moscow in 1934, must be considered the most significant event in the ongoing restoration of Klyuev's biography and oeuvre—a restoration which began in the West in the 1950s, was continued there in the 1960s, and then resumed in Russia in the 1980s.

Pesn' o Velikoi Materi was found with "Razrukha" and *Kain,* which have already been discussed. The last two are very important finds, and contribute much to an understanding of his later work, but *Pesn'* altogether transforms that understanding: here is the work on which he expended so much energy and time; here is by far his longest work (some four thousand lines); here is the ultimate "arrested" text in his story of arrested development. But here, too, is yet another illustration of the eccentricities of time and place in the story of Klyuev and his texts: *Pesn'* was lamented almost as soon as it and its author were presumed lost, and the lament was reiterated for fifty years; a few shards of evidence in memoirs and letters later allowed Klyuev scholars to speculate on its shape, and its loss was taken as another sign of the evils of the 1930s, when those evils could finally be discussed publicly; but then, quite suddenly, and at the end of the wave of "returns" in the glasnost period, a version of the text was found—incomplete and unfinished, but nevertheless one of the most striking literary discoveries in the vaults of the enemies of literature.[24]

Yet the reaction to this discovery was almost total silence. Little was written about the find, still less about the poem itself. The reasons for the silence are multiple and complex, and some will be familiar from earlier discussion of the poet's situation today: Klyuev remains a marginal figure for most readers of Russian poetry; Klyuev's most widely recognized scholar, Konstantin Azadovsky, is lukewarm on the poet's late work; it was not a Klyuev scholar but a journalist who gained access to the KGB file and published most of the poetry found there; Shentalinsky resisted invitations to tie this material evidence of the poet's martyrdom to the nationalist right and to its print organs, instead publishing extracts of *Pesn'* in the mainline "thin journal" *Ogonek* in 1991, and then the whole work in the equally mainline "thick journal" *Znamya* in the same year; and yet, for the readers (and writers) of those "mainline" publications, Klyuev lacked the appeal of many other martyred or persecuted authors. *Pesn'* was published not only when the reading public in general and even the scholarly public had grown tired of discoveries, returns, and reassessments but also when the entire enterprise of Russian literary scholarship was in shambles, and its future in doubt. For these and other reasons, *Pesn'*, on publication, received almost no commentary, and only in more recent years (and often in places far from the centers of metropolitan Russian culture) have scholars begun to publish serious analyses of it.[25]

Another set of problems dogs the version of *Pesn'* now available: it is very evidently a draft, "arrested" in every sense of the word, by the Soviet secret police, and so cannot be read in the same way as a finished work, published by the poet. Nor can it be read as a work which, although not published, was acknowledged as finished by the poet. In contrast, the poet seems to have given quite frequent readings of *Pogorel'shchina,* and typed copies were even sold, according to an informant of Azadovsky's.[26] This work's release to Lo Gatto in 1929 confirms the poet's intention that it be published eventually. *Pesn'*, as the poet's major project of the early 1930s, was conceived and written in quite different circumstances, and while Klyuev's correspondence makes his devotion to the work evident, it also emphasizes his caution. In May 1933 he wrote from Moscow to Yar-Kravchenko, apparently in reply to a letter from the latter accompanying a—badly—typed copy of *Pesn'* (*Sd* 297–98):

> I received your package with my *poema,* distorted and disfigured, of course, from the very first word: *Pesnya* [song] *o velikoi materi*—surely you know that *Pesn'* and not *pesnya* means something quite different, etc., etc., but the main thing is not that, but the destruction of the poem itself, the very thing that I have been full of these last years—now all my plans are destroyed—you have killed me and the *poema* in a barbaric and stupid way.
>
> Do you really not understand who, first and foremost, needs the work and

> for what purpose, and how many attempts have been made to extract it from me? What my open, sworn enemies have not achieved has been done and accomplished by you—my brother. You took so many oaths not to read or to show a single line . . . But evidently you have gone deaf and gone blind, and lost your mind as a result of your successes *on all* fronts! I cannot convey to you the horror and alarm which have seized me. I know full well that there can be no edition of my poetry, and that the prospect of publication is just an excuse for people to get their hands on my recent work, and there are you worrying about my fame! What do I need fame for! Come to your senses! Do not type a single line more of the *poema*. Burn everything! *As I did myself*—take back all the copies, whoever has them, and take no notice of any pleas. There cannot be any publications of them. (emphasis Klyuev's)

In other words, by 1933 the poet had decided that no copies of the poem whatsoever should be available to anyone, and had apparently acted to destroy existing copies. Thus the status of the text published from the KGB archive becomes especially problematic. Those problems are illustrated in microcosm by the fact that, in the letter quoted above, Klyuev refers to his work as *Pesn' o velikoi materi,* while the archival publication has *Pesn' o Velikoi Materi*—and Klyuev, as that same letter and many others show, was very attentive to every detail of the reproduction of his poems, so the lowercase of the 1933 title is unlikely to be an accident, and may well reflect a somewhat different thematic emphasis from the KGB text (which itself contains an alternative title—*Poslednyaya Rus'* [*The Last Old Russia*]). What stage, then, of his work on *Pesn'* is reflected in that text, and how reliable is it? In the transcript of his interrogation, he is recorded speculating that "Razrukha" and *Kain* were stolen, unfinished, from his desk—is this the case too with *Pesn',* and if so, stolen by whom and when?

Beyond these specific problems, as with the other two "arrested" works, a very general textological issue remains—how to treat the only extant version, if it is a draft? Any editor attempting to produce a detailed, academic edition of *Pesn'* will have to face this issue. Furthermore, the textological question implies another, even broader question: *how to read* such a work? What are the reader's "rules of engagement" with a text which seems to represent a stage in the author's work on a project—a stage which might have been superseded by versions now lost (this may be inferred from Klyuev's 1933 letter with its discussion of distributed typescripts)—especially when that project was not intentionally suspended or abandoned by the author, nor curtailed by illness or death? In other words, even now that a material text exists, shadows of other texts and possibilities are cast, obstructing any putative "natural" reading. While such problems and questions are far from unique to Russian literature of the Soviet period, they are especially characteristic of it, among modern literatures of industrial nations, and carry a special moral and political burden in that context.

The textological problems of *Pesn'*, and the attendant problems of hermeneutics, do not, however, explain directly its muted reception—after all, other texts with similar problems, from the same period, have received considerable attention. Some of them are among the most famous and accessible works of the period. Bulgakov's *Master i Margarita* was cited in chapter 2 to illustrate how the restrictive cultural environment of the 1930s not only provided extraordinary themes but also produced highly unusual narrative structures, partly because of multiple rewritings over a long period. Earlier versions of that novel have now been restored and published. Of course, the very different example of Bulgakov's prose serves as a reminder of another significant and elementary detail: Klyuev would have enjoyed more posthumous "luck" if he had been easier to read—*Pesn'* is a demanding text even for readers familiar with his language, imagery, and poetic structures, and, for a twentieth-century work in verse, it is very long. Moreover, as has been suggested in the previous chapters, there would be more Klyuev readers (and certainly more Klyuev admirers) if he fitted more neatly the paradigm of twentieth-century ruralism, which provides one of the most common approaches to him as a "new-peasant poet," but from which he is distinguished by such factors as his learning, albeit the learning of an autodidact; his universalism—Siam and India accompany Olonia in his verse; his proximity to modernism in poetic practice; the "spiritual," essentially apolitical nature of his nationalism, and the absence of ethnically exclusive attitudes—Klyuev is disappointing reading for the anti-Semitic right; and, perhaps above all, the shape of his biography and his character. Klyuev was an aesthete and a homosexual, with a strong dislike for the "hooliganism" of many of his confrères. Yet it is precisely that "hooliganism"—a usually alcoholic and willful blend of blasphemy and self-destructiveness, artistic and otherwise—which contributes a special and popular appeal to the image of Esenin and others. Moreover, it has been inherited, in a somewhat degraded form, by Esenin's successors (Rubtsov being an outstanding example). In other words, Klyuev does not quite "fit."

Hence, for reasons both local and general, *Pesn'* has remained a largely unread, if major, discovery of the late Soviet period. And, of course, no work can receive a broad critical evaluation if it is only read by a few supporters and enthusiasts, so it remains equally unjudged by the "philological elite," with the crucial exception of Azadovsky, who, in his 1990 book, damned what he knew with faint praise:

> In the *Hymn* there are variations and intensifications of motifs from *The Village* and *Burnt Ruins.* It is a hymn to the creative spirit of the Russian people,

> to that people's constructive genius. Remarkable are the lines which describe the construction of a wooden church. . . .
>
> However, as a work of art, the *Hymn of the Great Mother*—as far as may be judged from its individual [published] parts—is weaker than *Burnt Ruins*. The repetition of devices (composition, meter, rhythm, lexicon) and even their pronounced monotony, the unsuccessful "rhetorical" lines . . . all this supports the notion that, at the turn of the 1920s, Klyuev was far from successful in maintaining his previous artistic level.

Azadovsky's article on Klyuev for the "biographical dictionary" *Russkie pisateli 1800–1917* (*Russian Authors, 1800–1917*), published in 1992, gives very little attention to Klyuev's later work in general, and merely notes the 1991 publication of *Pesn'* in a final list of "other works."[27] And when Azadovsky published the revised version of his first Klyuev biography in 2002, including a considerable amount of material published since 1990, he repeated his original verdict on *Pesn'* verbatim.[28] This, then, is the verdict on *Pesn'* in the most authoritative books on the poet published to date.

Whether Russian letters have moved so far away from Klyuev's poetics that *Pesn'* will remain an untimely publication of semi-antiquarian interest, whether Azadovsky's dismissal of the work and its late brethren will become the canonical judgment, or whether *Pesn'* will move into a new focus and receive more positive and widespread readings remains, of course, to be seen.

The draft of *Pesn'* published by Shentalinsky is dated "1930" and "1931" (in the middle and at the end of the text, respectively; 979–80). At the point where the poem is dated "1930," the alternative title, *Poslednyaya Rus'*, occurs. The poem consists of three parts, of which the first two are simply entitled "Chast' pervaya" and "Chast' vtoraya" ("Part One," "Part Two"), while the last is called "Gnezdo tret'e" ("Third Nest"), leading the author of the most detailed commentary so far, Eduard Meksh, to choose to apply this designation also to the first two parts.[29] Given not only the application of the term to the last part in the draft but also the nonlinear nature of the poem, and the association of the word "nest" with one of the great projects of individual and national linguistic creativity—the *Interpretive Dictionary* of Vladimir Dal'—Meksh's choice seems appropriate and well justified, and is followed here. However, it should not be forgotten that the alternative title and the change from *chast'* to *gnezdo* are among many indications that the text under discussion is incomplete and unfinished. Since *Pesn'* is so little known, it is impossible to discuss it at all without providing a rather detailed account of its contents. It is thus unavoidable that discussion and summary are somewhat interwoven in the following pages.

The three "nests" are preceded by a short prologue. As published, the nests themselves are further divided into separate sections (sixteen, ten, and five, respectively), some of which are several hundred lines long, while others consist of just a few stanzas. Most sections are internally consistent in meter and form. Iambic tetrameter is the most common meter, with amphibrachic tetrameter, trochaic tetrameter, and trochaic trimeter also much in evidence. As Azadovsky remarks in the passage cited above, *Pesn'* bears some resemblance to *Derevnya* and *Pogorel'shchina* in thematics, and it is especially close to the latter in structure. It also shares a good number of motifs with the poet's "created lives," in particular the later ones, in its preoccupation with the White Sea coast and with the biography of the central hero (the son of a young and early-widowed mother and of an elderly father; early manifestations of talent; spiritual apprenticeship on Solovki; contact with the imperial court and with Rasputin). Indeed, the narrator/hero is unambiguously identified as "Nikolai Klyuev" and his mother as "Praskov'ya Klyueva," although their biographies are at times remote indeed from the documented lives of the poet and his mother. A mythical continuum from nature to culture, and from pagan, through Orthodox, to schismatic beliefs and practices is reiterated throughout the poem. The domestic tranquillity of both the heroine's and the hero's youth in the Russian north provides a familiar contrast both to the prophecies of doom heard later and to the modern and modernizing Russia encountered by the adult hero. National, popular art is celebrated early in the poem, while the "Third Nest" contains intriguing praise for a specific project of "neo-Russian" architecture. As ever, it is the range rather than the density of references which is striking (literary allusions to referents as diverse as Longfellow, Pushkin, and the Bible, plus a very wide range of historical, geographical, and cultural references). The linguistic fabric of *Pesn'* is equally varied, at times requiring considerable lexical dexterity even from a reader familiar with the poet's language in general, although it should be noted that the majority of the poem may be read with great ease. And, as is so common in Klyuev's work, *Pesn'* modulates unpredictably between the general and the specific, the public and the private, the historically anchored and the self-consciously timeless. Especially striking in such a long work with clear "epic" aspirations is the prominence of "lyrical" themes (including, at times, a lyric addressee—the speaker's young beloved), and of an intermittently present individualized speaker who is both narrator and *lyrical* hero. Finally, and in marked contrast to much of Klyuev's work, *Pesn'* combines sinister and ominously dark passages, such as are encountered in other late works, with frequent levity and even humor—qualities rarely encountered elsewhere in Klyuev's writing (although certainly attested in memoirs of the poet).

The prologue opens with a characteristic gesture, associating the poem and those who may have access to it with the purity of nature, and especially with the nature and culture of Lake Onega. But it ends with an equally familiar note of ill omen:

Mother Song

Ах, обожжен лик иконный
Гарью адских перепутий.
И славянских глаз затоны
Лось волшебный не замутит!
Ах, заколот вещий лебедь
На обед вороньей стае,
И хвостом ослиным в небе
Дьявол звезды выметает! (703)

Oh, the icon face is singed
By the fire of Hell's crossroads.
And the magic elk will not disturb
The backwaters of Slavic eyes!
Oh, the prophetic swan has been stabbed
For the crow flock's lunch,
And in the sky, with his ass's tail,
The devil sweeps away the stars!

The "First Nest" opens with a pastoral encomium to life on the White Sea coast, followed by a description of the construction of a wooden church by local craftsmen, led by one Akim Zyabletsov (as was *Zaozer'e,* the poem is confessionally vague, combining Orthodox and schismatic allusions with an admixture of popular "pagan survivals" throughout). The second section of the "First Nest" addresses directly a young beloved, partly in terms familiar from the love lyrics to Yar-Kravchenko, and provides as artistic models the pictorial skills of nature and of an ancient iconographer (*Pesn'* is especially syncretic in its treatment of artistry, celebrating not only painting but also architecture and popular crafts, and associating them all both with poetry and with natural processes). The third section introduces the speaker's recollections of his idyllic childhood on the White Sea coast, but concludes with the violence of the present—wolves have eaten the child's sugar horse, the window is broken, and childhood has been pecked apart by jackdaws (the avian population of this, as of other late poems, is abundant). The pastoral childhood is reiterated in the fourth section, where the everyday is endowed with magical—even, it might be said, "fairy-tale"—qualities (that is, "fairy-tale" in the literary sense—self-consciously stylized in a pseudo-popular manner). Among examples of the "fairy-tale" discourse is the conversation sustained by articles of clothing, no less. The fifth section is a lullaby sung by the speaker to his beloved, as the former prepares to narrate the biography of his mother. The sixth section consists of a single eighteen-line period, which comprises in its entirety an extended nature simile for the poetic re-creation of the image of the speaker's mother and of his own youth. The seventh section celebrates the idyllic domestic order of the narrator's boyhood—icons and creatures from pagan mythology watch over and decorate the house; the mother, now identified as Parasha (Praskov'ya), and father discuss the appropriate memorial for the boy's grandfather, recently departed. All is as it should be—ritual, art, family observances (and culturally diverse elements) are in harmony:

> Вспорхнув с лампады, алконосты
> Садились на печальный плат,
> И была горенка, как сад,
> Где белой яблоней под платом
> Благоухала жизнь богато. (714)

> Flitting from the icon lamps, Alkonosts
> Landed on the mourning head scarf,
> And the room was like a garden,
> Where—a white apple tree under a scarf—
> Life was richly fragrant.

The eighth section begins the story of Parasha's betrothal (characteristically, the narrative has moved forward and backward in time during the opening sections of this nest). In a scene distantly reminiscent of Pushkin's *Evgenii Onegin*, the pious eighteen-year-old, whose ideal suitors are drawn from the iconography of saints, seeks the identity of her future husband in a mirror, and, alarmed at the untutored result, decides to set off at once to see her friend Arina (again, "pagan" and Christian motifs are reiterated in happy combination). The ninth section describes her midwinter journey, accompanied by her mother, across the Russian north, marked by the signs of Old Believer piety and natural splendor. Mother and daughter stop to pray at a *skit* (a small monastic community), then continue their journey not without forebodings. The tenth section further describes the journey—Parasha's mother has an ill-omened dream; they ride past the church built by Akim in the first section of the nest—but the narrative then breaks off as the narrator laments his own disloyalty to his Old Believer origins, and observes his hellish situation in the present, far from the pious north. The eleventh section resumes the narrative of Parasha's journey: she arrives at the house of her friend Arina, where she is welcomed by the latter's widowed father, a whale-hunter, and where, at a *posidelki* (gathering of the young), she meets and dances with the enchanting Fedor, son of Kalistrat. To the accompaniment of verses stylized as folk song, the two dance. The twelfth section ties the principal dramatic knots of the story. An anxious Parasha decides to visit Father Nafanail, a schismatic hermit and runaway from the Solovetsky Monastery, who lives nearby. On her way through the snow to his cell, she encounters a wolf, but, in the spirit of her Old Believer forebears, she shows no fear and overcomes the threat, although she reaches the hermit's cell in considerable distress. There she is astonished to find Arina's father. Father Nafanail greets Parasha as a bride, then disappears, after prophesying calamity for Russia and the betrayal of ancient Russian values by Parasha's own future son (that is, the narrator of the *poema*). Arina's father confesses his love to the fevered Parasha, whom he carries home. The household, alarmed at Parasha's apparent sickness, summons a local shaman, so respected that even the local Orthodox priest courts his favor. The shaman's diagnosis is simple: the girl loves the boy; but the widower will kill the "beaver." In the fourteenth section Parasha explains her fate, as prophesied by Father Nafanail, to Arina: she will marry Arina's father. Arina should therefore marry Fedor, whom the narrative then encounters joyfully anticipating his union with Parasha. This section departs from the principal narrative, as the aging narrator addresses his sleeping (and young) beloved, and anticipates a distant future when his own verse may find an echo. The fifteenth section resumes the story of Parasha in spring (observation of the popular rural calendar is another feature *Pesn'* shares with other *poemy*). Now at home, and overwhelmed with religious yearning, she decides secretly to leave her parents and to undertake an individual pilgrimage to Constantinople(!). On the first night of her journey she has a vision of the Virgin Mary, who joins the poem's chorus of prophecy: Parasha's son will sing sweetly, but the "year of wrath" is near, ancient Russia is in its coffin. In the morning, lost in the vernal woods, Parasha falls into the lair of a bear, who locks her in his sleepy embrace. At that very moment Fedor, who is skiing through the woods(!), finds traces of Parasha. He comes to the rescue and saves Parasha, but perishes in single combat with the bear. The sixteenth and last section of this nest again abandons the story, as the narrator sings to his beloved a lullaby with somewhat sinister overtones.

The "Second Nest" opens with a quotation from the seventh section of the "First Nest"—the narrator's parents discussing the appropriate funeral monument for Parasha's father—but instead of resuming the narrative from that point, it rapidly moves to the narrator's own reflections on truth and poetics, providing an impassioned defense of his work, and repenting of his earlier errors:

> Неупиваемая чаша,
> Как ласточки звенящих лет,
> Я дал пред родиной обет
> Тебя в созвучья перелить,
> Из лосьих мыков выпрясть нить,
> Чтоб из нее сплести мережи!

Авось любовь, как ветер свежий,
Загонит в сети осетра,
Арабской черни, серебра,
Узорной яри, аксамита,
Чем сказка русская расшита!
Что критик и газетный плут,
Чихнув, архаикой зовут.
Но это было! Было! Было!
Порукой — лик нездешней силы —
Владимирская Божья Мать!
В ее очах Коринфа злать,
Мемфис и пурпур Финикии
Сквозят берестою России
И нежной просинью Вифезды
В глухом Семеновском уезде —
Кто Светлояра не видал,
Тому и схима — чертов бал!
Но это было! Было! Было —
Порукой образ тихокрылый
Из радонежеских лесов!
Его писал Андрей Рублев
Смиренной кисточкой из белки.
. . .
Но . . . многоточие — синицы,
Без журавля пусты страницы . . .
Увы . . . волшебный журавель
Издох в октябрьскую метель!
Его лодыжкою в запал
Я книжку «Ленина» намарал,
В ней мошкара и жуть болота.
От птичьей желчи и помета
Слезами отмываюсь я
И не сковать по мне гвоздя,
Чтобы повесить стыд на двери! . . . (751–52)

(The proposal for the lacuna is from Sergei Subbotin [979])

Undrainable goblet,
Like the swallows of the ringing years,
I gave an oath before my homeland
To pour you into melodies,
To spin a thread from elk paths,
To weave from it fish traps!

Mother Song

Perhaps love, like a fresh wind,
Will drive to the nets sturgeon,
Arabian niello, silver,
Patterned verdigris, velvet,
That all embroider Russian tales!
That critics and newspaper rogues
Sneeze at and call "archaisms."
But it's all true. True! True!
The guarantee—the face of unearthly power—
The Vladimir Virgin!
In her eyes is the gold of Corinth,
Memphis and Phoenician purple
Shine through Russian birch bark
And the tender blue of Bethesda's pool
Shines in distant Semenov county—
Whoever has not seen Lake Svetloyar
Sees even in monastic rule the Devil's ball!
But it's all true. True! True!
The guarantee—the quiet-winged image
From the woods of Radonezh!
It was painted by Andrei Rublev
With a humble brush of squirrel fur.

. . .

But . . . ellipses are chickadees,
Without a crane pages are empty . . .
Alas . . . the magic crane
Died in the October snowstorm!
With its foot bone as a fuse
I scrawled the book *Lenin*,
Full of midge swarms and swamp life.
With tears I wash off myself
Bird bile and droppings,
And there's no nail fit for me
To hang my shame upon the door! . . .

These lines, both highly individual and very characteristic of the late Klyuev, indicate the multiple directions taken by the narrator's own discourse in *Pesn'*. Russian nature, iconography, and the crafts of the ancient world are all cited to justify the poet's own artistic manner, and to reinforce his assertion of its validity and truth. Enemies are attacked (*kritik, gazetnyi plut*), and it is suggested that they lack the key secret knowledge (*kto Svetloyara ne vidal*) which will give access to spiritual enlightenment. Meanwhile, the narrator himself repents of his past errors (*knizhku . . . namaral*). If Subbotin's proposal for the lacuna is correct, and the book the author "scrawled" is his *Lenin,* then it is also worth noting that among the toponymic referents of this passage is *Semenovskii uezd* (county). The town of Semenov, not far from Nizhnii Novgorod, is some forty kilometers from Lake Svetloyar, and it is also the center of the Kerzhenets region, famous for its Old Believer settlements (and for the persecution of those Old Believers by the state). Klyuev's association of his artistic and ethical program with popular Russian spirituality and many of its famous provincial (and remote) sites is entirely characteristic. But it may also be recalled that in one of the most striking poems of Klyuev's Lenin cycle (and book), it is the *Bolshevik* leader who is explicitly associated with the Old Believers of this area ("Est' v Lenine Kerzhenskii dukh" ["Lenin has the spirit of Kerzhenets"], 377). Indeed, many of the associations made with Lenin in that poem of 1918 are also made in this passage, but in the aesthetic interests of the author, who is now *repenting* his association with Bolshevism. While this is not the place to explore in detail the interweaving and contrasting of patterns of reference between these two opposite points of Klyuev's oeuvre—his Lenin poems and his seditious and repentant *Pesn'*—the possibility that quite intricate allusions and reversals are buried here certainly reinforces the claims this passage makes for the value of some kind of secret (and sympathetic) communion with the poet's own interests. An ironist would conclude any such discussion, however, with the following commentary on the couplet "Whoever has not seen Lake Svetloyar / Sees even in monastic rule the Devil's ball!": to date, there is no evidence that Klyuev himself had actually seen Lake Svetloyar . . .

The passage discussed above is followed shortly by two lines displaying another characteristic feature—a strikingly obvious and specific poetic allusion (to the famous last poem of Derzhavin, "Reka vremen v svoem stremlen'i" ["The river of time in its course"]):

Мне скажут: жизнь — стальная пасть —
Крушит во прах народы, классы . . . (752)

They'll say: life is a jaw of iron,
It crushes to dust peoples, classes . . .

Like the preceding long defense of artistic method, this short and modified quotation (in the overall context of further aesthetic justification) is self-consciously anachronistic, replacing Derzhavin's *Narody, tsarstva i tsarei* with *narody, klassy* (Peoples, kingdoms, kings; peoples, classes), and placing the anachronistic *klassy* in the marked position at the end of the line. And like *Pesn'* as a whole, this opening section of the "Second Nest" moves quite unhesitatingly from a long and elaborate discussion of aesthetics in multiple contexts (eternal, syncretic, sacred, contemporary, and political) to the narrator's recollection of his mother's annual joyful dance on the occasion of her son's birth, only to conclude with a reiterated justification of the author's poetics, as descended from Memphis and from Svetloyar:

> Мои стихи не от перины
> И не от прели самоварной
> С грошовой выкладкой базарной,
> А от видения Мемфиса
> И золотого кипариса,
> Чьи ветви пестуют созвездья.
> В самосожженческом уезде
> Глядятся звезды в Светлояр, —
> От них мой сон и певчий дар! (755)

> My poetry comes not from the featherbed
> Nor from samovar mold
> With cheap market goods,
> But from a vision of Memphis
> And the golden cypress,
> Whose branches are cherished by constellations.
> In the county of self-immolants
> The stars look into Svetloyar,
> From them come my dreams and gift of song!

The movement between narrative and poetic program (with polemics); the combination of geographic and historical specificity with a contrary universalism; the elision of any boundaries between aesthetics, ethics, and, by implication, religion—all of these are very characteristic of *Pesn'*. Equally characteristic is the end-stopped iambic tetrameter, with sometimes approximate rhyme, while the relative simplicity of the language is common but not ubiquitous in the work (and certainly not common enough to make it an "easy read").

The second section of this nest opens with an enumeration of the narrator's reading in his youth (predictably, the list ranges from standards of the Orthodox Church and the Old Belief to esoteric and Oriental works of mysticism). The narrator's mother, now unambiguously identified as Praskov'ya Klyueva, is alarmed by the attention paid to her son by representatives of the world's religions and sects, eager to recruit him (Nestorians, the Dalai Lama, *skoptsy,* and so on), and she decides to send him to the Solovetsky Monastery. Guided by her own reading, which leads her to believe that "the wet mother earth" is suffering and that from Norway to China the "iron demon" is triumphing, she calls upon a diverse group of religious elders to gather at the Denisov Cross.

At the end of this section the text, as published by Shentalinksy, is dated "1930. Na Pokrov den'" ("1930. Feast of the Protection of the Blessed Virgin [October 14 by the secular calendar]"). This date is followed by a note stating that *Poslednyaya Rus'* (as it is called here) is not finished. Still to come are the gathering of elders; the death of the narrator's mother; her posthumous appearance to her stepdaughter Arina, with a warning of fearful danger; and Arina and her daughter Nastya at Parasha's grave (979).

The poem resumes with the third section of the "Second Nest," a thirteen-line evocation of the Denisov Cross, which stands at a crossroads where once two thousand people burned themselves to death. This section describes the gathering of elders summoned by Praskov'ya. It is predictably eclectic and exotic, and is equally predictable in its ominous anticipation of dark events for Russia. Makarii from the Altai leads the meeting, and tells of ecological and social catastrophe. Abaz from the Pamir speaks second, and his prophecy is diabolical. The third speaker is the *ptitsa roshch tsesarskikh* (bird from the imperial glades), whose song of evil omen is exactly the same as the first poem of the "Razrukha" cycle ("K nam vesti gor'kie prishli"). While the overall tone of this section is darkly prophetic, it is striking that there are moments of lightness and humor, in the Pushkinian tradition of self-conscious ironic deflating. The first is provided by the interpolation of the narrator's playful commentary, when he pauses at the end of his scene-setting to remark that he could easily confuse characters:

И ель смолистой едкой титькой
Поит Аленушку с Микиткой
(То бишь, Федюшу с Парасковьей.
К чему приводит цветословье!) (761)

And the fir nurses with its resinous
Bitter breast Alenushka and Mikita
(That is, Fedyusha and Praskov'ya.
There's the result of pretty wordplay!)

This is but one of a number of rather different voices with which the narrator (who is also, of course, the protagonist) speaks. The marked polyphony even within the overall narrative finds equivalents in the thematic, formal, and generic diversity of the work, as well as in the multiplication of story layers and chronologies.

The second light moment in this section is even more striking than the first: at the end of the gathering, just as the maid Elpateya has, at her own request, been turned by the "eternal gardener" into a "weeping poppy of the field," Parasha's voice is heard:

«Проснись, Николенька, кудель
Уже допрялася по спицу! . . .»
Гляжу, домашние все лица,
И в горенку от заряницы
Летят малиновки, касатки,
И сказка из сулейки сладкой
Меня поит цветистым суслом . . .
Готов наш ужин, крепко взгусло
В лесном чумазом котелке,
Но не лазурно на реке,
Пока не полноводно русло. (767)

"Awake, Nikolen'ka, the tow
Has spun right to the spoke! . . ."
Up I looked, familiar faces,
From the evening star, robins,
Swallows fly into our room,
And a tale from a sweet wine flagon
Nourishes me with a rich-colored mix . . .
Our dinner was ready, thick the blend
In the forest's grimy pot,
But no bright blue upon the river,
Until the channel's reached high water.

In other words, the entire preceding scene has been the narrator's youthful dream (which ends with a typical mixture of domestic comfort and natural order, interpenetrated and metaphorical). Exactly where the dream started remains unclear. Since the Solovetsky narrative will soon be continued, his mother's decision to send him to the monastery would seem to belong to the main story, whereas her summoning of the exotic elders may be the moment when the boy slips into his vision. The importance of dreams in Klyuev's work and life has already been noted, as has the presence of dreams in *Pesn'* itself. And prophetic visions play an especially prominent role in his later work. Also of significance here is the exemplary erosion of the boundary between sleep and awakening, reality and fantasy—eroded or demolished boundaries between different, even opposing, states, forms, and categories are as typical of *Pesn'* as the diversity of elements noted above (and are represented in the passage quoted by the elision of boundaries between home and nature, everyday description and metaphor). The representative significance of this slippage is further emphasized: by the fact that the prophetic visions are entirely justified and fulfilled in the poem's overall narrative and worldview (as if the gathering had actually taken place within the main story line); by the presence within this scene of the entire text of what appears elsewhere as a quite separate lyric poem; and finally by the surprising shifts from gravity to self-conscious levity.

The fifth section consists of an eight-stanza reiteration in irregular trochees of the relationship between the narrator and his young beloved, rendered in the style of a nursery fairy tale:

Жил да был медвежий дед,	Once there lived an old bear-man,
Самый вещий самоед,	The most prophetic Samoyed,
С ним серебряный лосенок,	With him lived a silver elk-calf,
От черемухи ребенок. (768)	Child of the bird cherry tree.

In this section the relationship in the narrated past between mother and youthful narrator, prominent in the preceding sections, finds a parallel in the relationship between narrator and beloved which belongs to the narrative present. Yet the modulation between different times and themes also has a characteristic counterpoint in the reiteration of the prophetic motif so prominent in the dream sequence—the narrator himself is, after all, *veshchii* (prophetic).

The sixth section of this nest is central and exemplary in its combination of levels of narrative and of thematics (and coming not long after the literal center of the text, it might well have ended up very close to the center of the finished work), although it is an exception in its compound, partially logaeoedic meter. It opens with the narrator lamenting the profanation of his "Byzantine treasure" and "bargeman's coarse shoe"—his song:

Ах, ты клад заклятый, огнепальный,
Стал ты шлюхой пьяной да охальной,
Ворон, пес ли — всяк тебя облает:
«В октябре родилось чучело, не в мае . . .» (769)

Oh, you enchanted, fiery treasure,
You have become a drunken, shameless whore,
Raven, dog—every creature will cry at you:
"Sloven, you were born in October, not May . . ."

From the individual, the lament thus moves to the national, describing and anticipating the fate of Russia in apocalyptic terms, including the "star Wormwood" of the Book of Revelation:

Тут ниспала полынная звезда, —
Стали воды и воздухи желчью,
Осмердили жизнь человечью.
Да и будет Русь безулыбной,
Стороной нептичной и нерыбной! (770–71)

Here fell the wormwood star—
Water and air became bile,
The life of man was befouled.
And Russia shall have no smile,
A land without birds and without fish!

Finally, the autobiographical narrative is resumed: Praskov'ya has decided to send her son to the Anzersky *skit* on the Solovetsky Islands. There the boy will be protected by the ancient saints of the community, and there the elders observe in secret the ancient, pre-Nikonian rites, earning themselves the acceptance of Old Believers—this is, in fact, a narrative sleight-of-hand that exemplifies the collapsing of confessional boundaries throughout the later poetry and demonstrates the individual peculiarities of Klyuev's mythology of the north (the Solovetsky Islands had ceased to be a stronghold of the Old Belief almost three hundred years before the presumed time of the narrative). The seventh section describes the boy's novitiate: his clairvoyant powers are recognized, and he is sent to one Father Savvatii (St. Savvatii was, as noted in chapter 5, one of the founders of the Solovetsky Monastery), with whom he observes the spiritual, almost liturgical, continuity between man and nature. Savvatii, however, joins the chorus of prophets of doom: he foretells disaster for Russia, abandoned by its impoverished saints and ignorant of its past.

The eighth section of this nest begins with an elaborate evocation of the sound of church bells (which, at the time of the composition of *Pesn'*, had recently been outlawed in the Soviet Union). Here again, nature and religious culture are one, as are the Christian and pagan beliefs of the north. The section concludes with six stanzas which blend a lullaby for the speaker's beloved with reflections on the speaker's own declining years (his aging is another recurrent, Pushkinian theme in *Pesn'*). In the ninth section the narrator describes his return home from Solovki. On his long journey he observes the desecration of nature (modern timber-cutting, signs of the onset of industrialization); he recalls his father, long dead in the northern ice floes, and the special chest which has been passed down from his self-immolant Old Believer ancestors. In a compressed family history the narrator even provides the etymology of his surname. In distant times a ship arrived in this land:

По ранне-синим половодьям,
К семужьим плесам и угодьям
Пристала крытая ладья.
И вышел воин исполин
На материк в шеломе — клювом,
И лопь прозвала гостя — Клюев —
Чудесной шапке на помин! (789)

In early-blue highwater,
To the salmon stretches and grounds
There came a covered vessel.
From it emerged on to the land
A warrior giant in a beak-like [*klyuvom*] helm,
And the Lapps called their guest "Klyuev,"
In memory of his wondrous hat!

This is not the only time that Klyuev's own last name appears in his poetry, and it is far from the only elaboration of a personal myth of antique origins (the direct tie to Avvakum is especially common, and is also present in *Pesn'*). But here there is an evident playfulness in the mythologizing: the story collapses in its very telling, since no local Lapp in the Middle Ages would have been likely to name the newcomer by coining his name from the *Russian* word *klyuv*. In fact, as the poet himself might well have known, the surname may be more reliably identified as a patronymic from the nickname or pagan (that is, non-church) first name Klyui, although one explanation of the meaning of that name does relate it to the Russian word for "beak," albeit in the rather mundane sense of "beak-nosed."[30] This play with the identity and background of the author/narrator's family is especially intriguing against the background of the obvious literary-historical model for the autobiography elaborated here: Mikhail Lomonosov. Klyuev's explicit mythologizing of his own origins runs in parallel (and partly in playful contrast, as in the lines discussed above) to the actual story of the Russian north's greatest son, who is also present in earlier elaborations of the poet's origins, it will be recalled. The great eighteenth-century thinker and writer did indeed come from the White Sea coast, his father was a fisherman and a "free peasant," and the future scholar was reputed, in his youth, to have been associated with Old Believers (which may explain his literacy). Of course, his later career has little in common with Klyuev's, and even the mythologized childhood of the latter presented in *Pesn'* is very different from that of Lomonosov (whose mother, not father, died when the future author was still young), but the famous model—from the people, from the White Sea coast, associated with the Old Belief (later completely rejected by Lomonosov, of course)—certainly haunts Klyuev's displacement of his own birth and childhood northward in his later autobiographical statements.[31]

The section concludes with the narrator, now at home, hearing his grandfather's lamentation for the fate of Russia and receiving a mace with which he is instructed to kill the country's enemies(!). The tenth and last section of the "Second Nest" (which, like the majority of its predecessors, is predominantly in end-stopped iambic tetrameter, although it concludes with a very marked deviation into trochees) describes the death of the narrator's mother. She yearns for ancient Russian pieties, but rejoices that she learned Greek and Arabic. Her repertory of sacred music is equally wide: anticipating her death, she sings "Khristos voskrese" ("Christ Is Risen"; a Church-Slavonic Easter hymn), or else a Latin chorale. Northern nature and Oriental sages accompany her final days with blessings and gifts. Her death is the occasion of universal mysteries, with the description of which the "Second Nest" ends. As elsewhere in *Pesn'*, the mythologizing is not only ecumenical but also slightly playful in its marked improbability, although here the playfulness is rather disorienting, since its context is the description of the last days of the narrator/hero/poet's mother.

The "Third Nest" (the only part to be thus designated in the text, it should be remembered) opens with a section describing the raising of a northern militia intent on defending imperial St. Petersburg. From whom is unclear—the war is with *supostat* (an archaic word for "enemy," often designating "Satan"), nor is the time of action stated, although it seems to be immediately before the Russian Revolutions. However, the narrator, in irregular amphibrachs, catalogues the men and their ancient rituals and then describes their depressing entrance into the capital, where modernity and vulgarity have swept away ancient splendor and purity. The section ends with a chorus of voices, some articulating those negative qualities, while one seems to belong to an officer who is dispatching the narrator and one other to the Cathedral of St. Feodor in Tsarskoe Selo. The second section of this final nest begins with a laudatory address to that cathedral—a lily from the bottom of Lake Svetloyar magically transported to this *chukhonskoe pole* (Finnish field; that is, to the environs of St. Petersburg). The praise for the cathedral, centerpiece of the so-called Feodorovsky Gorodok (Feodor Settlement) where the imperial escort was indeed garrisoned, is intriguing, since the whole architectural ensemble was an early twentieth-century exercise in self-conscious and stylized retrospectivism, creating an Old Russian complex of buildings.[32] In other words, while Akim and his peasant building crew, whose Pokrov church is described at the very beginning of *Pesn'*, represent one artistic analogue and model for *Pesn'* itself, the work of Vladimir Pokrovsky and others in the creation of a highly stylized modern appropriation of ancient forms represents another. Akim and his church come at the beginning of *Pesn'*, and Feodorovsky Gorodok comes near the end. While the former evoke notions of collective and spontaneous creativity, the latter foregrounds that ever-problematic question in Klyuev's oeuvre of stylization. Together they reiterate familiar issues: authenticity, provenance, aesthetic integrity, and artistic meaning. And the equal weight given to each model leaves all the questions open. The syncretic impulse characteristic of Klyuev in general is stated most strongly in the choice of architectural models to represent these literary polarities, while certain cultural markers simultaneously undercut the evident binary oppositions—for example, the revival of ancient Russian architecture is represented by buildings associated with St. Petersburg (the traditional site of all that is opposite to the ancient native idea), while the collective nature of vernacular construction—usually, of course, anonymous—has already been undercut by the identification and elevation of a particular craftsman, Akim.

The cathedral is said to call the tsar, who had been an enthusiastic proponent of its construction, back from *Rasseya* to *solovetskaya belaya Rus'* (that is, the pure, ancient Russia of the Solovetsky Islands), but the narrator is uncertain if Nicholas II will hear this call, and the section ends with further notes of ill omen, here embodied in, among others, a favorite ambiguous figure, Grigorii Rasputin. As with the allusions to Semenov county earlier in *Pesn'*, the description and praise of the cathedral (of which Klyuev had also spoken positively in his earlier "Gagar'ya sud'bina," it will be recalled) may be read as a repentant return to an earlier episode in his life and work. Through the warden of the cathedral, Colonel Dmitrii Loman, a supporter of the arts, Klyuev had, in 1916, been able to protect the young Esenin from more risky military duty by helping to arrange the young poet's assignment to the military hospital based at Feodorovsky Gorodok (*Sd* 240).[33] That hospital was intimately associated, like the settlement itself, with the direct patronage of the imperial family. Loman was a member of the Society for the Rebirth of Artistic Ancient Russia (Obshchestvo vozrozhdeniya khudozhestvennoi Rusi), a group which brought together such leading artists and architects as Vasnetsov, Nesterov, Rerikh, and Shchusev, and which was itself directly associated with the Feodorovsky Gorodok project. Klyuev and Esenin naturally appealed to the artistic program of this group, for whom they performed in October 1916.[34] Around that time, it seems, Loman asked Klyuev and Esenin to produce a book of poems of patriotic nature, including praise for the Cathedral of St. Feodor. Klyuev declined, writing an elegant and clever reply, itself in somewhat stylized form, and citing medieval models.[35] Klyuev's lines on the cathedral in *Pesn'* may thus be seen not only as a fascinating marker of at least one aspect of his aesthetics, but also as a belated return to Loman's request, this time with a positive answer. Tied to this motif, of course, are both the story of Klyuev's relations with Esenin (including the former's ongoing reevaluation of them after the latter's death) and the further exploration of the imperial theme. The Cathedral of St. Feodor was, in a sense, the personal church of the last emperor's family (the Underground Chapel, beneath the main sanctuary, was the project of the empress herself), and its dedication was to the St. Feodor Icon of the Virgin—the patron icon of the Romanov dynasty. Thus, the Feodorovsky Gorodok episode in *Pesn'* is also directly linked to the thematic and symbolic core of the poem—the various manifestations of the work's eponymous image of the Great Mother (pagan "earth mother"; specific mother of the poet/hero/narrator; Mother of God). Its dedication also directs the reader back to Parasha's first beloved, the young Fedor, who perishes defending her from a bear in the "First Nest." It might also be noted that the Feodorovsky Gorodok complex itself was not finished—the First World War interrupted work on it, and the revolutions ensured that the work was not completed. In the Second World War it was badly damaged, and only in the last years of the twentieth century did restoration begin in earnest. At the time of the composition of *Pesn'*, the aesthetic and historical relations between poem and architectural referents were significant, and subsequently the parallels have become quite striking.

The third section of the "Third Nest" opens with a conversation in the *tsarskii sad* (imperial garden) between Rasputin and the narrator—yet another modified reiteration of a story found in one of the "created lives," in this case, "Gagar'ya sud'bina." Rasputin attempts to draw the narrator, in whom he senses a fellow spirit, into his diabolical enchantment of the imperial family. As the narrator attempts to reject Rasputin's invitation, a goat runs out of a nearby grotto and dances with the "mad monk." The goat emerging from the grotto provides another example of the modulation in *Pesn'* between various artistic models and aesthetic programs: the grottoes of Tsarskoe Selo are, of course, artificial, stylized constructions—the product of eighteenth- and nineteenth-century European landscaping ideas; yet out of one of them comes a wild animal, enacting not a theatrical pastoral, but contact between man and nature of a quite different kind. This diabolical scene is followed by the narrator's encounter with the tsar himself, who walks quietly in his garden—presumably this is the garden of the Alexander Palace in Tsarskoe Selo, only a short distance from the cathedral, where the imperial family regularly attended services. However, it is the emperor's bloody fate which is anticipated in the narrator's vision.

In the fourth section the action moves to St. Petersburg, where the narrator makes a nocturnal visit to a *radenie* of a *khlyst* sect, accompanied by a "lad from Ryazan' lands" (that is, Esenin).[36] The *radenie* purges the day's diabolical influences. A conversation between Esenin and the narrator is interrupted as they discover the dying Rasputin, and the section ends with an ambivalent assessment of the last-named.

The Petersburg/Tsarskoe Selo sections are the most compressed parts of *Pesn'* and bring together a series of favorite motifs and stories, here associated in part with the traditional symbolic qualities of the capital city itself—old and new; Russian and foreign; peasant, gentry, proletarian; Orthodoxy, sectarianism, "paganism," and satanism. But the abiding tone is familiar—the coming apocalypse.

The fifth and penultimate section of the "Third Nest" is dated "The Nativity of the Virgin, 1931" (September 21 by the secular calendar, 979). It opens with a lament for the results of the last *twelve* years (again 1919 is the year favored to mark the beginning of the Soviet catastrophe). The Bolsheviks, industrialization, and modernity in general are depicted as satanic, and the speaker calls upon his *posmertnyi drug* (posthumous friend—evidently Esenin) to join him and Russia's—and Klyuev's—favorite saints in flight to an otherworldly haven:

С хоругвями, навстречу нам
Идет Хутынский Варлаам,
С ним Сорский Нил, с Печеньги Трифон.
Борис и Глеб — два борзых грифа.
Зареет утро от попон.
И Анна с кашинских икон —
Смиренное тверское поле.
С пути отведать хлеба-соли
Нас повели в дубовый терем . . .
Святая Русь, мы верим, верим! (811–12)

With banners out to meet us come
Varlam Khutynsky,
With him are Neil of Sora, Trifon from Pechen'ga.
Boris and Gleb, two swift griffins.
The morning shines with horse cloths,
And Anna from the Kashin icons—
The humble fields of Tver'.
To taste hospitality after travel
They took us to a palace of oak wood . . .
Holy Russia, we believe, believe!

The movement of this section is—characteristically—from lamentation to the optimistic assertion in the passage quoted above, but, as ever in such assertions, the grounds for optimism are largely in the millenarian expectations of the speaker himself (stylistically marked by the mixing of narrative tenses—the passage quoted above combines present and past).

The sixth and final section of the "Third Nest" appears to begin the story of Anastasiya (Nastya), the sixteen-year-old daughter of the now long-widowed Arina—presumably the opening of the episode sketched by Klyuev in his notes of October 1930, to which reference was made above. The section seems unfinished, indicating quite clearly that the narrative of *Pesn'* as a whole is incomplete. Nastya is praised in the tradition of the holy maids of Russia, who, although dead and now neglected, will eventually appear again to the world. Poetry may cry, but it will not love concrete. Meanwhile, Nastya continues the line of Parasha in her purity and in her love for Feodor, the son of a bone-carver (she neglects grander suitors). The fragmentary section ends with a description of the divine protection afforded Nastya's abode:

Вдовицын дом хранил Господь
От черной немочи, пожара.
И человеческая свара
Бежала щедрого двора,
Где от ларца до топора
Дышало все ухой да квасом
И осенялось ярым Спасом,
Как льдиной прорубь сельдяная,
Куда лишь зведочка ночная
Роняет изумрудный усик . . . (815–16)

The Lord protected the widow's house
From black ills, and from fire.
And the arguments of men
Passed by the generous home,
Where from chest to axe
All smelt of fish soup and kvass
And was blessed by a fierce-eyed Christ,
As ice floes bless the herring fishing hole,
Where only the nocturnal star
Drops an emerald whisker . . .

Those are the last lines of *Pesn'*, as published, and it is fitting that the poem breaks off with this reiteration of the themes of domestic tranquillity, found in the union of God and nature, with which Parasha's story began early in the "First Nest"—although it may be assumed that this tranquillity was to be severely disrupted in the sections which were to follow.

As can be seen, *Pesn'* is an elaborate, at times even ornamental, work. It is both complex (at times in language, generally in the interweaving of narrative lines, motifs, and themes, and especially in its instability) and also simple—in the evident stylization, in the engagement both with familiar models of narrative verse, including most obviously Pushkin, and with the tradition of the folk tale in verse.[37] These contradictory features of *Pesn'*, and its incomplete status, make it a disorienting work, difficult to classify and, perhaps, difficult to read. Yet it is also an intriguing and even charming work, showing the later Klyuev in a new light. It has a sustained, albeit frequently disrupted, narrative line, which runs in parallel with commentary and with lyric passages relating to the present. The strong mytho-autobiographical element in the story echoes the "created lives" examined in chapter 1, and provides further reasons for resisting any attempt to draw a clear distinction between those creations and the poet's other works—again, the diversity of the poet's artistic efforts and their overall, if contradictory, integrity are striking.

Pesn' also provides a sustained and varied statement of the mother theme, which is prominent in some of the poet's lyrics—especially in the core poems of the various versions of the cycle "Izbyanye pesni." These lyrics, which some commentators see as among Klyuev's best, provide a powerful statement of the spiritual integrity of domestic peasant life and address in part the death of the speaker's mother, treating peasant funeral rituals, the speaker's grief, and the posthumous fate of the mother's soul. They are directly related to the death of Klyuev's mother in 1913, and some versions bear dedications to her. By the time *Pesn'* was written the maternal theme and imagery had been greatly expanded and transformed: not only does Parasha have an elaborate mythic biography, predicated in part upon her role as mother to the erring but clairvoyant poet-son, but she is also symbolically linked to other maternal elements implicit in the title and explicit at times in the work itself—"mother Russia" and the pagan "wet mother earth." All three are, in varying degrees, depicted as victims and even martyrs in *Pesn'*, but all three are equally to be seen as rich and fertile providers of cultural and spiritual nourishment. The personal, domestic elements foregrounded in the story of Parasha guarantee that the grander, mythological aspects of maternity do not descend into cliché.

It is also very significant that the poet's own mythic autobiography is so prominent in *Pesn'*—as with other examples, examined in earlier chapters, the autobiographical stories here function in part to designate cultural and poetic provenance, while also making firm, even polemical, programmatic statements.

Of the purely lyrical themes, the speaker's affection for his young beloved is by far the most evident, echoing the maternal affection so characteristic of Parasha. Here too *Pesn'* gestures both to diversity (from maternal love to homoerotic passion) and to elemental continuity—of the simple category of "love."

In these and other features, *Pesn'* may be argued to belong to a significant and much-debated group of works which seem to form one of the far boundaries of Russian modernism (in range, and, in certain cases, in time). That is to say, it belongs to the group of elaborate and long works which self-consciously combine the lyric and the epic, often using that combination in an ambitious attempt to locate a poetic "I" in a grand historical context. Early exemplars include the *poemy Vozmezdie* (*Retribution*) by Blok and *Mladenchestvo* (*Youth*) by Vyacheslav Ivanov. The most significant late exemplars are Akhmatova's *Poema bez geroya* (*Poem Without a Hero*) and Pasternak's *Doktor Zhivago.* Like the works of Akhmatova (who [mis]quotes Klyuev's address to her in an epigraph to the second part of her *Poema*) and Pasternak, *Pesn'* is strongly marked by a sense of the end of things and, like *Zhivago* in particular, is also much preoccupied with the application of familiar styles and narrative devices to new themes—in its case, aspects of the nineteenth-century *poema-skazka* (the literary folk tale in verse) to a statement of barbaric modernity. Quite unlike the famous, even scandalous works of Akhmatova and Pasternak, *Pesn'* was almost lost and, after its partial recovery, remains in obscurity. It has been an unstated but fundamental position of the discussion in the preceding pages that such obscurity, if easily explained, is unfortunate. Whether Klyuev's hope that the work will sooner or later find a wide and enthusiastic (and even influential) readership is fulfilled remains, of course, to be seen.

Although, as was noted above, Klyuev may have written several *poemy* in Siberia, of them only *Kreml'* is known. Ivanov-Razumnik wrote of it less than flatteringly in his *Pisatel'skie sud'by:*

> Broken by his Narym exile and Tomsk imprisonment, and then again ending up in Narym, Klyuev lost heart and tried to write himself into the ranks of those who had come to an accommodation with the authorities. In 1935 he wrote a large *poema* called *Kremlin,* dedicated to praising Stalin, Molotov, Voroshilov, and other leaders; the *poema* ended with the howl, "Forgive or order me to die!" I don't know if *Kremlin* reached the rulers of the Kremlin, but this attempted accommodation didn't help Klyuev. . . . Incidentally, poetry does not tolerate insincerity and violence. The tortured *Kremlin,* even if it had survived, would not have added laurels to Klyuev's poetic wreath.[38]

In fact, *Kreml'* had survived, among the papers of Yar-Kravchenko, although its release was delayed until 2006, long after other, previously unknown, late works were published. Whether Ivanov-Razumnik's judgement is correct or not is a matter for debate, but it is certainly true that *Kreml'* does praise the Kremlin and its Soviet denizens, and it also ends with the "howl" recalled above (although it was written in 1934, not 1935 as Ivanov-

Razumnik recalled). *Kreml'* explicitly rejects much of Klyuev's familiar aesthetic and philosophical program (repeatedly stating "Ya razlyubil izbu pod el'yu" ["I've ceased to love the peasant house beneath the pine tree"]) and praises an explicitly Soviet Moscow; the poet sends his verse "where Stalin is the helmsman" and offers his heart to the "mighty Kremlin." On many points, the *poema* implicitly rejects the positions taken in "Razrukha" (the last known work before Klyuev's Moscow arrest, and one of the causes of his exile), even praising the White Sea Canal project, which that cycle had described, only a few months earlier, as diabolical. In its turn, the "civic" *Kreml'* is "corrected" by Klyuev's last-known poem, "Est' dve strany: odna — Bol'nitsa," written in Tomsk in 1934, and discussed in chapter 5. Thus, cycle, *poema,* and lyric form a final (and perhaps accidental—other poems may have been written and lost) triptych. *Kreml',* of course, is written to order and, as a work with an intended and explicit worldly *function,* presents considerable problems for the reader attuned to quite different poetry, but in contrast to the "functional" works of many (but by no means all) authors of the period, it is not a work which should be seen as entirely uncharacteristic of the poet's general, late poetics. On the contrary, it is full of features and devices that are very prominent in Klyuev's works, especially in and after the late 1920s: from the almost ubiquitous and usually end-stopped iambic tetrameter to topographical catalogues and occasional obscurity of lexicon, syntax, and grammar. Here lies its paradoxical identity—the poet has denied himself and his poetry, but in his familiar poetic voice (not in a voice imposed or acquired from elsewhere).[39] *Pesn' o Velikoi Materi,* like "Razrukha," might perhaps eventually win Klyuev a wider readership; *Kreml'* certainly will not; "Est' dve strany" surely deserves to. Together, these four last works effectively summarize the fascination of Klyuev's life and work, and express both the beauty and the tragedy of his time and place.

Conclusion

KLYUEV WROTE his last poetry in the year of his death—1937. But almost seventy years later, in 2006, a major late work (*Kreml'*) was published for the first time. It is often said that Russia is a country with an unpredictable past. The same can be said for the biographies and even bibliographies of many of its dead authors. Klyuev, whose self-conscious (but also organic) mutability is so evident in his poetry, prose, and constructed identities, continues to change for reasons quite separate from any literary program.

Klyuev is also, as the preceding pages have attempted to demonstrate, a very paradoxical poet, and the paradoxes of his life and works are nowhere more evident than in his last years. That his last surviving works should be so interrelated and form such contrasts with one another effectively demonstrates many of those paradoxes. At the same time, each of those late works—*Pesn' o Velikoi Materi,* "Razrukha," *Kreml',* and his final lyric, "Est' dve strany: odna — Bol'nitsa"—eloquently testify to the story of Russian culture in the twentieth century (and three of them are entitled to prominent places within the Russian canon), but remain largely ignored by scholars and readers—another characteristic paradox of Klyuev's story.

This study began with claims both of uniqueness and of typicality for Klyuev; it was proposed to look at Klyuev both in "philological" and in "culturological" terms; and a wider readership was called to attend to both poet and poetry, as significant for immanent and historical reasons. The preceding pages have taken the patient reader across many territories within Russian cultural history and through detailed examinations of complex issues of textuality and interpretation within the smaller but by no means easily mapped terrain of Klyuev's poetry and prose. Repeatedly, Klyuev's story has articulated the story of his country in the last century, while his work has often communicated a markedly individual view of that country, that period, and that story.

Of all the authors labeled "new-peasant" or associated with early twentieth-century ruralism, Klyuev is clearly the "most modernist," as is indicated by many of his most striking characteristics: his very wide referential framework bespeaks a "yearning for world culture" from within the Olonian *izba;* his literary self-consciousness, intermittent playfulness, interest in complex, compound formal structures, evident and profound preoccupation with language, and even his presentation of the vatic powers of poet and poetry align him with major figures from Blok to Tsvetaeva, while his sexual orientation and literary treatment of that orientation both seem to be a perfect fit with the Russian "Silver Age." Yet no other modernist figure is close to Klyuev in literary stance—his mythologization of the peasant world has nothing in common with his modernist confrères; his approach to popular religion and his claims to be associated with it are quite different from what is found in Bal'mont, Bely, Kuzmin, and others; his lexicon and his approach to the word evidently have at least something in common with some of the new-peasant poets, and scholarly claims to see in his poetics traces of premodern approaches to discourse should not be dismissed lightly; nor should his "archaism" be relegated to the generally negative category of "stylization," although there are certainly moments of stylization in his work. As for his identity, his created lives, and his presentation of himself, it is entirely characteristic of the problems he poses for readers that it often seems best to see his position as simultaneously self-conscious, acquired, culturally provocative, and also expressive of the most fundamental elements in his poetry and person. Finally, and to put it most bluntly, his martyrdom, the fact that he died both for his literary stance and his homosexuality, and that his final known work reiterates that he is the "singer of the Olonian peasant house," while his penultimate known work had renounced precisely that role, provide a striking summary of the paradoxes and ultimately tragic conjunction of literature, life, and Soviet power that define Klyuev's story.

Given the claims made for Klyuev here, it is appropriate to conclude these discussions by addressing an obvious question: if he is so interesting and so worth reading, why is he not read more widely (after all, other "difficult" poets have many enthusiasts)? The answer, perhaps, lies in a combinantion of circumstances. As has been pointed out, Klyuev had no successors (for that matter, he had no direct ancestors either), and thus no continuing literary context within which to be read. In contrast, most of the great poets of the later decades of Russian modernism were not only, by historical accidents of publishing chronology, contemporaries of the authors of the 1960s, 1970s, and 1980s, but were also their partners in literary endeavors. The late Mandelstam, in particular, was a powerful inspiration for many Russian authors of the neo-avant-garde underground, as were the poets of the OBERIU grouping; Pasternak and Akhmatova held sway over beginning authors; Tsvetaeva attracted a vast readership and many epigones.

Meanwhile, for writers interested in the fate of the countryside, or in the articulation of something "popular," in multiple senses of the word, Esenin was a much more likely model than Klyuev. Moreover, Klyuev's version of Russian archaic, rural, popular culture (the Old Belief, sectarianism, a secret world of global spiritual and artistic associations) may appeal to some in terms of a rather nostalgic neo-Russophile ideology, but as a description or even mythologization of the Russian countryside in the second half of the twentieth century it can hardly have seemed appropriate—after all, the basic paradigms of much Russian literary ruralism in the later Soviet decades assumed acknowledgment of the consequences of loss and destruction already wrought, and represented archaic culture as surviving only in sad fragments, whereas such loss and destruction are, for the most part, anticipated, feared, or witnessed emerging in Klyuev's work, and ancient culture is assumed to live on, however threatened. The modern Russian countryside, for many postwar ideologues or even for less politically engaged observers, was a postapocalyptic cultural and physical landscape; Klyuev's work tends either to describe the preapocalyptic idyll or the apocalypse in progress. And that work most definitely does not give voice to popular, tender, elegiac (and even repentant), but above all accessible lyricism in the manner of some of Esenin's, and thus cannot appeal to a widespread version of popular "Russianness." Nor is there is a "hooligan element" in Klyuev's verse, or a lament for lost youth, with which readers may easily and sentimentally identify.

Klyuev has also been a somewhat unlucky poet in another very important respect: some on the neo-nationalist right have adopted him as a repository of ethnocentric Russian values, although their enthusiasm has sometimes been cautious, and with good reason, for much in Klyuev belongs to those parts of Russian modernism to which, in the late Soviet period, the "liberal intelligentsia" (that is, the polar opposite of the neo-nationalists) felt affinity. But adoption by the right makes Klyuev unpalatable for those with a different politico-cultural agenda (and Klyuev is difficult to read anyway), even if only fairly small parts of his oeuvre can truly fit into a simple political agenda.

Thus, Klyuev's peripheral status in Russian culture today provides a final illustration of the ways in which the poet embodies key paradigms within that culture. The preceding pages have attempted to show the ways in which Klyuev's life and works disrupt familiar polarities and cut across cultural and ideological boundaries, but Russia remains a country with a powerful attraction to binary values and structures. A poet who is always both owned and other, *svoi* and *chuzhoi,* is likely to remain difficult, and without a secure place in the literary canon for the foreseeable future.

It is hoped, however, that the preceding chapters have at least charted a possible passage for Klyuev into the mainstream of Russian literary history, and perhaps even on to the future bookshelves of readers of Russian verse.

The fact that Klyuev's few readers of the 1960s could not have imagined that, within a couple of decades, almost all of his works would be available in print in his homeland is a powerful reminder that it is not only Russia's past but also its future that is highly unpredictable. Perhaps the poet's own faith in a future readership will not be entirely misplaced.

Notes

INTRODUCTION

1. Among the most important collections of scholarly materials, testifying to the growth of a "Klyuev industry," are S. I. Subbotin, ed., *Nikolai Klyuev: Issledovaniya i materialy*, Rossiiskaya Akademiya Nauk, Institut Mirovoi Literatury im. A. M. Gor'kogo (Moscow, 1997); A. P. Kazarkin, ed., *Nikolai Klyuev: Obraz mira i sud'ba: Materialy Vserossiiskoi konferentsii "Nikolai Klyuev: Natsional'nyi obraz mira i sud'ba naslediya"* (Tomsk, 2000); A. Kazarkin and V. Domansky, eds., *Nikolai Klyuev: Obraz mira i sud'ba*, vol. 2 (Tomsk, 2005); E. Markova, ed., *XXI Vek na puti k Klyuevu: Materialy Mezhdunarodnoi konferentsii "Olonetskie stranitsy zhizni i tvorchestva: Nikolai Klyuev i problemy etnopoetiki," posvyashchennoi 120-letiyu so dnya rozhdeniya velikogo russkogo poeta Nikolaya Klyueva 21–25 sentyabrya 2004 g.*, Karel'skii Nauchnyi tsentr, Rossiiskaya Akademiya Nauk (Petrozavodsk, 2006); and the three volumes published to date of *Klyuevskii sbornik*, ed. L. Yatskevich (Vologda, 1999–2002).

2. For a survey of the treatment of Klyuev in the Anglophone world, see Maikl Meikin (Michael Makin), "Nikolai Klyuev v angloyazychnom mire," in *Petryaevskie chteniya '01: Tezisy, doklady*, ed. V. N. Kolupaeva and A. L. Rashkovskii (Kirov-na-Vyatke, 2001), 72–80; full version in *Sever* 4–5–6 (2002): 230–35; revised and expanded version on the website Kluevoslov: http://kluev.org.ua/collegium/m_engl.htm (accessed September 2008).

CHAPTER ONE

1. For a detailed and engaging discussion of these issues, see Svetlana Boym, *Death in Quotation Marks: Cultural Myths of the Modern Poet* (Cambridge, Mass., and London, 1991).

2. Ivanov-Razumnik (Razumnik Vasil'evich Ivanov), *Pisatel'skie sud'by* (New York, 1951), 37. Konstantin Azadovsky traces it to a story told by Anatolii Yar-Kravchenko (K. Azadovsky, *Nikolai Klyuev: Put' poeta* [Leningrad, 1990], 317; K. Azadovsky, *Zhizn' Nikolaya Klyueva: Dokumenta'noe povestvovanie* [St. Petersburg, 2002], 309).

3. Especially significant are the recurrence of the Ivanov-Razumnik story in the two major Western editions of Klyuev, and in the first public commentary on the poet in the Soviet Union since the 1930s: Boris Filippov, "Nikolai Klyuev: Materialy k biografii," in Nikolai Klyuev, *Polnoe sobranie sochinenii,* 2 vols. (New York, 1954), 1:106; the story was repeated in the enlarged version of that essay in Nikolai Klyuev, *Sochineniya,* ed. G. Struve and B. Filippov, introductory articles by B. Filippov, G. McVay, H. Stammler, and E. Rais, 2 vols. (Munich, 1969), 2:151–52; and in V. Orlov, "Nikolai Klyuev," *Literaturnaya Rossiya,* November 25, 1966, 17. Among the story's more recent occurrences was Stanislav Kunyaev, "Zhizn' — okean mnogozvonnyi," preface to Nikolai Klyuev, *Stikhotvoreniya i poemy,* ed. Stanislav Kunyaev (Archangel, 1986), 6.

4. Konstantin Azadovsky, "Lichnost' i sud'ba Nikolaya Klyueva," *Neva* 12 (1988): 182; Nadezhda Khristoforova-Sadomova, "Vospominaniya o poete Klyueve Nikolae Aleskeeviche," in Nikolai Klyuev, "Ot poezii 'izbyanogo kosmosa' k pis'mam iz Sibiri (Pis'ma Nikolaya Klyueva k N. F. Khristoforovoi-Sadomovoi iz Tomska)," ed. with introduction and commentary by Aleksandr Mikhailov, *Nash sovremennik* 5 (1992): 156.

5. Among the many publications dealing with Klyuev's last years are Azadovsky, *Put' poeta,* 292–320; Azadovsky, *Zhizn' Nikolaya Klyueva,* 296–320; Klyuev, "Ot poezii 'izbyanogo kosmosa' k pis'mam iz Sibiri"; Lev Pichurin, *Poslednie dni Nikolaya Klyueva* (Tomsk, 1995); Nikolai Klyuev, "Nikolai Klyuev v poslednie gody zhizni: Pis'ma i dokumenty (Po materialam semeinogo arkhiva)," ed. with introduction and commentary by Georgii Klychkov and Sergei Subbotin, *Novyi mir* 8 (1988): 165–201; Yurii Khardikov, "'Krov' moya svyazuet dve epokhi': Ssylka i gibel' Nikolaya Klyueva," *Nash sovremennik* 12 (1989): 179–89; Vitaly Shentalinsky, *Arrested Voices: Resurrecting the Disappeared Writers of the Soviet Regime,* trans. Robert Crowfoot, ed. Robert Conquest (New York, 1996; published in Britain as *The KGB's Literary Archive* [London, 1996]; first published in French as *La parole ressuscité: Dans les archives littéraires du K.G.B.* [Paris, 1993]; in Russian as *Raby svobody: V literaturnykh arkhivakh KGB* [Moscow, 1995]), 197–209; "Dokumental'nye materialy" (the Tomsk NKVD file), in *Nikolai Klyuev: Obraz mira i sud'ba: Materialy Vserossiiskoi konferentsii "Nikolai Klyuev: Natsional'nyi obraz mira i sud'ba naslediya,"* ed. Kazarkin, 211–23; and Valerii Domansky, *Narym: Klyuev v Sibiri: Poema i ocherk* (Tomsk, 2003).

6. A. Gruntov, "Materialy k biografii N. A. Klyueva," *Russkaya literatura* 1 (1973): 118–19. This article marks the beginning of the scholarly study of Klyuev's biography. Gruntov's work (some of it unpublished) has been used by all subsequent students of the poet.

7. Vasilii Firsov, "Suzhdeniya i fakty (O rannei biografii Nikolaya Klyueva)," *Sever* 5–6 (1996): 147–54. Although most Klyuev scholars do not accept Firsov's questions, he has continued to raise doubts about Klyuev's birth ("'Byt' v trave zelenym, a na kamne serym . . .' [Zametki o zhizni i tvorchestve Nikolaya Klyueva]," *Sever* 11 [2000]: 149–50).

8. Firsov, in his second discussion of the problems of Klyuev's biography, reads this passage as indicating that Klyuev was born in cold weather. I am grateful to Alina Makin for suggesting that the comments attributed by Klyuev to his mother might, however, be read as indicating that she herself was "taken by cold," such as one might feel when getting water from a hole in the ice at what is traditionally the coldest time of the year (Epiphany). Sensations of extreme cold can be encountered during labor and delivery at any time of the year, even if a woman in labor is in very warm conditions—as a peasant woman in the nineteenth century almost certainly would have been, since labor usually took place in the bathhouse or above the stove. Moreover, it would normally be a woman's job to fetch water from holes in the ice (as is still done in Koshtugi, where water comes mostly from the Megra and Kimreka rivers, which, of course, freeze in winter), so women would have the clearest sense of how cold water in an ice hole could be at Epiphany. However, the literary quality of the passage warns the reader to exercise extreme caution, even in these matters of climate and calendar.

9. Nikolai Klyuev, *Pesnoslov,* ed. and intro. S. Subbotin and I. Kostin (Petrozavodsk, 1990), 5–24.

10. The first version is Boris Filippov, "Nikolai Klyuev: Materialy k biografii," in Klyuev, *Polnoe sobranie sochinenii,* 1:7–182.

11. Lev Karokhin, *Sergei Esenin i Nikolai Klyuev* (St. Petersburg, 2002).

12. Some Russians would dispute that notion. Stanislav Kunyaev, for example, remarks that *even now* it is harder to live in the north than in central Russia, *let alone in Klyuev's days* ("Zhizn' — okean mnogozvonnyi," 8). I suggest, however, that it is harder in many ways to live anywhere outside of the major cities of Russia now than it was "in Klyuev's days."

13. Gruntov, "Materialy," 119.

14. Vasilii Firsov has questioned a number of these details in his "Suzhdeniya i fakty," 149–52.

15. Sergei Subbotin, "Nikolai Klyuev — chitatel' L. Trefoleva i P. Yakubovicha," in *Nikolai Klyuev: Issledovaniya i materialy,* ed. Subbotin, 163–82.

16. Gruntov, "Materialy," 119.

17. Azadovsky, *Put' poeta,* 42–43. Azadovsky quotes the entire report, which was found and first cited by Gruntov ("Materialy," 120).

18. Nikolai Klyuev, "Pis'ma N. A. Klyueva k Bloku," ed. with preface and commentary by K. Azadovsky, in *Aleksandr Blok: Novye materialy i issledovaniya, Literaturnoe nasledstvo,* vol. 94, book 4 (Moscow, 1987), 427–523; Nikolai Klyuev, *Pis'ma k Aleksandru Bloku 1907–1915,* ed. with commentary by K. Azadovsky (Moscow, 2003).

19. On Brikhnichev, see V. Bazanov, "Trudnaya biografiya," *Zvezda* 12 (1979): 176–88.

20. *Bratskie pesni* is discussed in some detail in chapter 3.

21. V. Bazanov, *S rodnogo berega: O poezii Nikolaya Klyueva* (Leningrad, 1990), provides particularly critical assessments of these works (112). These re-

marks essentially repeat his comments in the introduction to Nikolai Klyuev, *Stikhotvoreniya i poemy,* ed. L. K. Shevtsova, Biblioteka poeta, small series (Leningrad, 1977), 32–33. Since Bazanov died in 1981, his collection of essays on Klyuev, although published during the period of glasnost, could not exploit the new possibilities for a more considered examination of Klyuev's politics that period would have offered.

22. For example, Gruntov, "Materialy," 123: "The October Revolution was accepted by Klyuev without the slightest hesitation"; Kunyaev, "Zhizn' — okean mnogozvonnyi" (1986), 6: "Klyuev greeted the October Revolution ecstatically."

23. See, among others, Azadovsky, *Put' poeta,* 230–32.

24. The republication of Trotsky's discussion as "Olonetskii poet Nikolai Klyuev," *Karel'skaya kommuna* (Petrozavodsk, October 15, 1922; cited in "Nikolai Alekseevich Klyuev," in *Russkie sovetskie pisateli: Poety: Biobibliograficheskii ukazatel',* ed. O. D. Golubeva et al., vol. 11 [Moscow, 1988], 61), would have been especially damaging. See also Azadovsky, *Put' poeta,* 245–46.

25. The *Slovesnoe drevo* publication is based on "Aleksandr Shiryaevets: Iz perepiski 1912–1917," ed. with preface and commentary by Y. Orlitsky, B. Sokolov, and S. Subbotin, *De visu* 3 (4) (1993): 20. Compare Klyuev's letter to Blok at the end of November 1913, where he notes that he accepted the *laski* (caresses) of white-skinned men and women, but did not go off to the bathhouse with them (Nikolai Klyuev, *Slovesnoe drevo,* ed. V. Garnin, intro. A. Mikhailov [St. Petersburg, 2003], 213).

26. The postcard is not among Klyuev's letters in *Slovesnoe drevo.*

27. The Vyatka dates are from Azadovsky's introduction to Nikolai Klyuev, "Stikhi raznykh let," *Rodnik* 6 (1988): 19. See also Azadovsky's *Zhizn' Nikolaya Klyueva,* 250–51, 264.

28. For details, see Konstantin Azadovsky, "Stikhotvoreniya N. A. Klyueva 30-kh godov: Sbornik 'O chem shumyat sedye kedry,'" *Baikal* 3 (1978): 149–51; and Sergei Subbotin, "Na putyakh k Nikolayu Klyuevu," *Sever* 5 (1988): 111, 112–13.

29. Ivan Gronsky, "O krest'yanskikh pistatelyakh (Vystuplenie v TsGALI 30 sentyabrya 1959 g.)," ed. and intro. M. Niqueux, *Minuvshee: Istoricheskii al'manakh* 8 (1989): 139–74. Gronsky's account has been widely quoted—although this is the only full publication—but there is room to doubt many details, as Niqueux points out.

30. For Klyuev's Moscow arrest and interrogation, see Shentalinsky, *Arrested Voices,* 197–209. For the poet's Siberian period, see Klyuev, "Ot poezii 'izbyanogo kosmosa' k pis'mam iz Sibiri"; Pichurin, *Poslednie dni Nikolaya Klyueva;* Klyuev, "Nikolai Klyuev v poslednie gody zhizni"; and Khardikov, "'Krov' moya svyazuet dve epokhi.'"

31. "Dokumental'nye materialy," 213; Azadovsky, *Zhizn' Nikolaya Klyueva,* 286.

32. Azadovsky, *Zhizn' Nikolaya Klyueva,* 296–97.

33. *Kreml'* was finally published in *Nasledie komet: Neizvestnoe o Nikolae Klyueve i Anatolii Yare,* by Tat'yana Kravchenko and Aleksandr Mikhailov (Moscow and Tomsk, 2006), 203–23.

34. The documents confirming Klyuev's conviction and execution may be found in Pichurin, *Poslednie dni Nikolaya Klyueva,* 92–93, and (more extensively) in "Dokumental'nye materialy," 219–21.

35. Among the many commentaries on his reading, see R. Mensky, "N. A. Klyuev (1887–1937)," *Novyi zhurnal* 32 (1953): 151–52; Ryurik Ivnev, "Vospominaniya o N. A. Klyueve," *Baikal* 4 (1984): 139; Azadovsky, *Put' poeta,* 288–89; and Khardikov, "'Krov' moya svyazuet dve epokhi,'" 189. One of the most striking examples of such testimony is provided by a letter of December 1929 from the conductor Nikolai Golovanov to the singer Antonina Nezhdanova (E. Grosheva and V. Rudenko, eds., *N. S. Golovanov: Literaturnoe nasledie: Perepiska: Vospominaniya sovremennikov* [Moscow, 1982], 98): "He reads so skillfully that I almost burst into tears in one place." However, the most famous portrait of Klyuev the performer is probably to be found in the fictionalized memoir of Ol'ga Forsh, where "Mikula" is transparently the Olonian poet: Ol'ga Forsh, *Sumasshedshii korabl': Povest'* (Washington, D.C., 1964), 208–14.

36. On how Klyuev furnished his rooms, see, for example, Igor' Zapadalov, "Voskreshenie Kitezh-grada: K biografii N. A. Klyueva," *Sibirskie ogni* 2 (1992): 210. Several photographs also depict Klyuev surrounded by village artifacts and Old Russian objects—for example, the portrait of Klyuev and Arkhipov from the Vytegra period, first published in full in *Sergei Esenin v stikhakh i zhizni,* ed. S. P. Mitrofanova-Esenina, S. I. Subbotin, and T. P. Flor-Esenina (Moscow, 1995), between 128 and 129.

37. Viktor Manuilov, "Iz 'Zapisok schastlivogo cheloveka,'" in K. Azadovsky, "'Povest' skorbi' Nikolaya Klyueva," *Iskusstvo Leningrada* 8 (1990): 27, 29.

38. "Mne tridtsat' pyat'. . . ," untitled autobiography recorded by P. Medvedev in 1922, published in *Sovremennye raboche-krest'yanskie poety,* ed. P. Zavolokin (Ivanovo-Vozenesensk, 1925), 218; "Govarival mne moi pokoinyi tyaten'ka . . . ," untitled autobiography, *Krasnaya panorama* 30 (1926): 13. These texts were reproduced in *Sochineniya* (1:211–12). "Praottsy" consists of the first half of the text in *Krasnaya panorama,* plus the text published by Azadovsky in Nikolai Klyuev, "'Ya slavlyu Rossiyu': Iz tvorcheskogo naslediya," *Literaturnoe obozrenie* 8 (1987): 103–4. "Gagar'ya sud'bina" was first published as Nikolai Klyuev, "Gagar'ya sud'bina," ed. with commentary by A. I. Mikhailov, *Sever* 6 (1992): 150–58; and again, in a more reliable version, by Azadovsky in his "O 'narodnom' poete i 'svyatoi Rusi' ('Gagar'ya sud'bina' Nikolaya Klyueva)," *Novoe literaturnoe obozrenie* 5 (1993): 88–121. In 2004 Azadovsky published "Gagar'ya sud'bina," accompanied by an introductory essay, "Nikolai Klyuev — tvorets i mifotvorets," and scholarly commentary, as the book *"Gagar'ya sud'bina" Niko-*

laya Klyuev (St. Petersburg, 2004); and Gordon McVay published the text tentatively dated 1930 in *Sochineniya* (1:185–86).

39. For examples of various sorts of characteristic Soviet autobiographical statements, see Thomas Lahusen, *How Life Writes the Book: Real Socialism and Socialist Realism in Stalin's Russia* (Ithaca, N.Y., and London, 1997), 64–68.

40. Iona Brikhnichev, "Severnoe siyanie (O Nikolae Alekseeviche Klyueve)," *Rul'* 355 (June 18, 1912): 2.

41. Laura Engelstein, *Castration and the Heavenly Kingdom: A Russian Folktale* (Ithaca, N.Y., and London, 1999), 241, endnote 29.

42. P. Sakulin, "Narodnyi zlatotsvet," *Vestnik Evropy* 5 (1916): 193–208. On Sakulin see Karokhin, *Sergei Esenin i Nikolai Klyuev*, 68–69.

43. Azadovsky, "O 'narodnom' poete," 97–98.

44. Nikolai Klyuev, letter to A. A. Izmailov, autumn 1914 (*Sd* 223). The Vytegra region remains, indeed, quite distant from passenger railway lines (although there are a number of narrow-gauge lumber lines in the area)—Lodeinoe Pole, from which the traveler may reach St. Petersburg by a slow train, is some 200 kilometers away to the west; the main line from Moscow to Archangel may be reached at Nyandoma, some 300 kilometers northeast. Both routes require, even today, some patience and willingness to endure discomfort on the part of the traveler.

45. Zapadalov, "Voskreshenie Kitezh-grada," 210; Khristoforova-Sadomova, "Vospominaniya o poete Klyueve Nikolae Alekseeviche," in Klyuev, "Ot poezii 'izbyanogo kosmosa' k pis'mam iz Sibiri," 154.

46. E. V. Ivanova, "Dobrolyubov, Aleksandr Mikhailovich," in *Russkie pisateli 1800–1917: Biograficheskii slovar'*, chief editor P. A. Nikolaev, vol. 2 (Moscow, 1992), 133. See also K. M. Azadovsky, "Put' poeta Aleksandra Dobrolyubova," in *Uchenye zapiski tartuskogo gosudarstvennogo universiteta*, 459; *Tvorchestvo A. A. Bloka i russkaya kul'tura XX veka, Blokovskii sbornik III* (Tartu, 1979), 129. The life of Leonid Semenov (Semenov-Tyan-Shansky) also provides significant parallels, as explored in chapter 3 of the present volume.

47. Vasilii Rozanov, *Apokalipsicheskaya sekta (khlysty i skoptsy)* (St. Petersburg, 1914), 134–52. Selivanov is discussed at length by Engelstein, *Castration and the Holy Kingdom*, 30–40.

48. Azadovsky, "O 'narodnom' poete," 116.

49. Khristoforova-Sadomova, "Vospominaniya o poete Klyueve," 153–54.

50. For example, "Moi krai, moe Pomor'e" of 1926 (660–61, the last part of *Plach o Sergee Esenine*) explicitly makes such associations, not least in its opening line.

51. Shentalinsky, *Arrested Voices*, 199.

52. Pichurin, *Poslednie dni*, 22.

53. See ibid., 38–39.

54. Klyuev, "Nikolai Klyuev v poslednie gody zhizni," 196.

55. Ibid., 167.

56. A useful guide to the different ways in which Klyuev was perceived by those who met him is provided by V. P. Garnin, ed., *Nikolai Klyuev glazami sovremennikov,* seriya Neizvestnyi dvadtsatyi vek (St. Petersburg, 2005). However, some important accounts of Klyuev are missing (for example, Georgii Ivanov's story of his meeting with the poet, discussed in the following pages), while the most hostile voices are somewhat muted.

57. Quoted by Azadovsky from Rozanov's pseudonymous article, in Klyuev, *Pis'ma k Aleksandru Bloku,* 134, note 5. In the same commentary, Azadovsky cites similarly savage commentary on Blok's fascination with Klyuev from a 1907 article by D. Filosofov (134–35, note 6).

58. Georgii Ivanov, "Peterburgskie zimy," in *Iz literaturnogo nasledstva: Stikhotvoreniya; Tretii Rim, roman; Peterburgskie zimy: Memuary; Kitaiskie teni, literaturnye portrety,* ed. N. Bogomolov (Moscow, 1989), 333–34.

59. Vladislav Khodasevich, *Nekropol': Vospominaniya* (Paris, 1976), 186–92.

60. Vasilii Knyazev, *Rzhanye apostoly: Klyuev i klyuevshchina* (Petrograd, 1924), 100, 108.

61. Ibid., 130–31 (emphasis in original).

62. *Literaturnaya entsiklopediya,* chief editor A. V. Lunacharsky (Moscow, 1931), 5:324–25.

63. Gronsky, "O krest'yanskikh pisatelyakh," 149.

64. Ibid., 151, 153, 154.

65. Igor' Bakhterev, "Kogda my byli molodymi (Nevydumannyi rasskaz)," in *Vospominaniya o Zabolotskom,* ed. E. Zabolotskaya and A. Makedonov (Moscow, 1977), 81–82.

66. Editor's note, Ivanov, "Peterburgskie zimy," 550.

67. Examination of the extant recordings made by Sergei Bernshtein, who worked in the 1920s in the Studio for the Study of Artistic Speech (Kabinet po Izucheniyu Khudozhestvennoi Rechi), of Klyuev reading his poetry (1924, 1928; now held in the audio archive of the State Literary Museum, Moscow) suggests that *polyglossia,* rather than diglossia, is the appropriate model for Klyuev's accents and manner of performance. It is hoped that this research, when completed, will provide important insight into Klyuev the performer.

68. Azadovsky, in his *Zhizn' Nikolaya Klyueva,* cites the recollection of I. I. Markov that Daniil Kharms was among the poets who visited Klyuev (205).

69. Nikita Zabolotsky, *The Life of Zabolotsky,* ed. Robin Milner-Gulland (Cardiff, 1994), 78; Russian version: *Zhizn' N. A. Zabolotskogo* (Moscow, 1998).

70. Azadovsky, *Zhizn' Nikolaya Klyueva,* 214–18; Erikh Gollerbakh, *Vstrechi i vpechatleniya* (St. Petersburg, 1998), 298–99.

71. Gollerbakh, *Vstrechi i vpechatleniya,* 299.

72. Azadovsky, "O 'narodnom' poete," 98.

73. V. Orlov, "Nikolai Klyuev," *Literaturnaya Rossiya,* November 25, 1966, 17.

74. Nikolai Nezhenets, "Pevets severnogo kraya," *Russkaya rech'* 1 (1988): 124, 125.

75. Nikolai Nezhenets, *Poeziya narodnykh traditsii* (Moscow, 1988), 49–54.

76. Zapadalov, "Voskreshenie Kitezh-grada," 206, 213. According to Azadovsky, Zapadalov reiterates the same "mythological" elements in verse published in 1992. See "O 'narodnom' poete," 102, note 83.

77. Zapadalov, "Voskreshenie Kitezh-grada," 210, 208, 212, 218–19, 219–20.

78. Ivnev, "Vospominaniya o N. A. Klyueve."

79. S. Volkov [S. Kunyaev], "'Ty, zhguchii otprysk Avvakuma . . . ,'" with text of Nikolai Klyuev, *Kain*, appeared in *Den'*, May 31–June 6, 1992; this article was subsequently republished in *Nash sovremennik* 1 (1993): 92–98. The *Den'* publication was assumed from B. Kravchenko, "Bolee soroka epitetov k slovu 'Oblako,' ili o pol'ze tochnosti," *Voprosy literatury* 5 (1993): 344.

80. Speech by Abramov, as quoted in Kunyaev, "Zhizn' — okean mnogozvonnyi" (1986), 7. Abramov ascribes to Dostoevsky the famous (but never attested) remark that "we have all come out from under 'The Overcoat' of Gogol."

81. Nikolai Klyuev, "'Sei Avvakum dvadtsatogo stolet'ya . . .': Stikhi Nikolaya Klyueva," ed. with preface by Stanislav Kunyaev, *Sibirskie ogni* 1 (1988): 166.

82. Stanislav Kunyaev, "Zhizn' — okean mnogozvonnyi," preface to Nikolai Klyuev, *Stikhotvoreniya i poemy* (Moscow, 1991), 7.

83. Vitalii Shentalinsky, "Vestnik Kitezh-grada," preface to Nikolai Klyuev, *Pesn' o Velikoi Materi: Fragmenty poemy* (Moscow, 1991), 5.

84. Konstantin Azadovsky, "Vokrug Klyueva: spornoe i neosporimoe," *Znamya* 9 (1987): 230–32.

85. Azadovsky, "Vokrug Klyueva," 230, 232.

86. Azadovsky, "Sbornik 'O chem shumyat sedye kedry,'" 151.

87. Subbotin, "Na putyakh k Nikolayu Klyuevu." The brother of the late Anatolii Yar-Kravchenko also has some harsh words for the Kunyaevs: B. Kravchenko, "Bolee soroka epitetov k slovu 'oblako.'"

88. For a more extensive discussion of these issues, see Michael Makin, "Whose Kliuev, Who Is Kliuev? Polemics of Identity and Poetry," *Slavonic and East European Review* 85, no. 2 (2007): 231–70.

89. On Dugin and the National-Bolshevik Party, which he helped to found, see Stephen Shenfield, *Russian Fascism: Traditions, Tendencies, Movements* (Armonk, N.Y., and London, 2001), 190–99; and the prison memoir of Dugin's erstwhile ally Eduard Limonov, *Moya politicheskaya biografiya* (St. Petersburg, 2002), 63–81. Dugin's sixty-minute "radio mystery," "Nikolai Klyuev, prorok sekretnoi Rossii" ("Nikolai Klyuev, Prophet of a Secret Russia"), was broadcast in 1997 on Radio 101. It was subsequently available streamed on the Internet. A cassette of the broadcast can be bought from a website associated with the series of broadcasts (entitled *Finis Mundis*), and the text, as of September 2008, could be found at http://www.arctogaia.com/public/fm/finis15.htm. The notion of Klyuev as a guide to a "hidden" or "secret" Russia is, however, by no means restricted to Dugin.

90. Shentalinsky, "Vestnik Kitezh-grada," 5.

91. Subbotin, "Na putyakh k Nikolayu Klyuevu," 69.

92. "Ochishchenie serdtsa" was first published in A. I. Mikhailov's introduction to extracts from Klyuev's correspondence with Khristoforova-Sadomova: N. A. Klyuev, "'Prostite: Ne zabyvaite . . .' N. Klyuev: Pis'ma k N. F. Khristoforovoi-Sadomovoi," ed. and intro. A. I. Mikhailov, *Sever* 9 (1994): 126–30. Similarly, the editors of the Shiryaevets correspondence, published in 1993, acknowledge that they have cut, in Klyuev's letters, (small) "parts of the text of an intimate character" ("chasti tektsa, nosyashchie intimnyi kharakter"); see Orlitsky, Sokolov, and Subbotin, "Aleksandr Shiryaevets: Iz perepiski," 7.

93. Azadovsky, *Zhizn' Nikolaya Klyueva,* 243, 286. In fact, the first assertion is open to interrogation—see S. Polyakova, "Kolybel'naya v poeme Klyueva 'Pesn' o velikoi materi' [*sic*]," in "Dva etyuda o Klyueve," in her *Oleinikov i ob Oleinikove: Raboty po russkoi literature* (St. Petersburg, 1997), 328.

94. K. K. Rotikov, *Drugoi Peterburg,* 2nd ed. (St. Petersburg, 2001), 188.

95. E. M. Yukhimenko, "Narodnye osnovy tvorchestva N. A. Klyueva," in *Nikolai Klyuev: Issledovaniya i materialy,* ed. Subbotin, 5–15.

96. Ronald Vroon, "The Garden in Russian Modernism: Notes on the Problem of Mentalité in the New Peasant Poetry," *Revue des études slaves* 69, nos. 1–2 (1997): 149. For a survey of Klyuev's relatively limited appearances in the Anglophone world—some of which reiterate the reductive accounts often found in Russian treatments, although others, like Vroon's, shed new light on the poet—see Maikl Meikin (Michael Makin), "Nikolai Klyuev v angloyazychnom mire."

97. A. I. Mikhailov, "Nikolai Klyuev i mir ego poeziya," in Nikolai Klyuev, *Serdtse edinoroga,* ed. V. Garnin, intro. A. Mikhailov (St. Petersburg, 1999), 7–74; A. I Mikhailov, "K istokam poeticheskogo fenomena Nikolaya Klyueva," in *Vytegra: Kraevedcheskii al'manakh,* vol. 1, ed. E. A. Skupinova (Vologda, 1997), 251–77; E. I. Markova, *Tvorchestvo Nikolaya Klyueva v kontekste severnorusskogo slovesnogo iskusstva* (Petrozavodsk, 1997), 59–85.

CHAPTER TWO

1. For a fine summary of these issues, especially in the context of Anglophone scholarship, see the entry on "Textual Criticism" by G. Thomas Tanselle in *The New Princeton Encyclopedia of Poetry and Poetics,* ed. Alex Preminger and T. V. F. Brogan (Princeton, N.J., 1993), 1273–76.

2. For a brief discussion of the problems of the Tikhon chapter, and its role in Dostoevsky mythology, see F. M. Dostoevsky, *Sobranie sochinenii v tridtsati tomakh,* ed. V. G. Bazanov et al., vol. 12 (Leningrad, 1975), 237–46. For a larger account of the issue, see, for example, V. N. Zakharov, "Fakty protiv legendy," in his *Problemy izucheniya Dostoevskogo: Uchebnoe posobie po spetskursu* (Petrozavodsk, 1978), 75–109. Joseph Frank, in volume 4 of his magisterial five-

volume biography of Dostoevsky, gives a survey of the issues, but seems hesitant on the textual problems: *Dostoevsky: The Miraculous Years* (Princeton, N.J., 1995), 431–34.

3. Among many items on this dispute, see John Kidd, "The Scandal of 'Ulysses,'" *New York Review of Books,* June 30, 1988, 32–39, and subsequent discussions in that periodical (for example, August 18, 1988, 63–65, and September 29, 1988, 80–83). For one example among many of the treatment of this dispute in major newspapers of the Anglophone world, see Jan Battles and Eamon Lynch, "Joyce Family Bids to Block $1m 'Corrected' *Ulysses,*" *Sunday Times* (London), January 4, 1998.

4. On Philip Larkin, see Robert Richman, "The 'Collected' Larkin," *New Criterion* 7, no. 8 (1989): 5–14. On Auden, see, for example, Edward Mendelson, "The Two Audens and the Claims of History," in *Representing Modernist Texts: Editing as Interpretation,* ed. George Bornstein (Ann Arbor, Mich., 1991), 157–70. This last-named collection also contains essays on other Anglophone modernists relevant here, including H.D., Marianne Moore, Virginia Woolf, and D. H. Lawrence.

5. Chris L. Nesmith, "'The Law of an Ancient God' and the Editing of Hemingway's *The Garden of Eden:* The Final Corrected Typescript and Galleys," *Hemingway Review* (Spring 2001): 16–36.

6. John Fletcher, "Forster's Self-Erasure: *Maurice* and the Scene of Masculine Love," in *Sexual Sameness: Textual Differences in Lesbian and Gay Writing,* ed. J. Bristow (London, 1992), 64–90.

7. On textological issues in Mandelstam, see, for example, I. M. Semenko, *Poetika pozdnego Mandelstama: Ot chernovykh redaktsii k okonchatel'nouy tekstu* (Rome, 1986); and S. I. Bogatyreva, "Volya poeta i svoevolie ego vdovy," in *"Otdai menia, Voronezh . . . ," Tret'i Mezhdunarodnye Mandestamovskie chteniiya* (Voronezh, 1995), 360–77. On Akhmatova, see, for example, V. V. Perkhin, "K istorii teksta stikhotvoreniya A. A. Akhmatovoi 'A vy, moi druz'ia, poslednego prizyva!'" *Russkaya literatura* 3 (1999): 184–89.

8. An excellent summary in English of the textological problems of the novel is provided by Laura Weeks, "'What I Have Written, I Have Written,'" in *The Master and Margarita: A Critical Companion,* ed. Laura Weeks (Evanston, Ill.: Northwestern University Press, 1996), 4–67. As Weeks points out (55, endnote 22), Marietta Chudakova's "Tvorcheskaya istoriya romana M. Bulgakova *Master i Margarita,*" *Voprosy literatury* 1 (1976): 218–53, is the classic account of the novel's complex composition history. See also M. Chudakova, "Opyt rekonstruktsii teksta M. A. Bulgakova," in *Pamyatniki kul'tury: Novye otkrytiya 1977* (Moscow, 1977), 93–106; M. Bulgakov, *Velikii kantsler: Chernovye redaktsii romana "Master i Margarita,"* ed. with commentary by V. I. Losev (Moscow, 1992); and M. Bulgakov, *Velikii kantsler: Knyaz' t'my,* ed. with commentary by V. I. Losev (Moscow, 2000).

9. The Bakhtin "problem" made it to the cover of *Lingua Franca: The Review of Academic Life* (April 1998) and was the subject of a lengthy article in the same number: Matt Steinglass, "International Man of Mystery," 32–41.

10. Many ordinary Russian readers, for example, probably think of Nekrasov's "Korobeiniki" ("Pedlars") or Sadovnikov's "Iz-za ostrova na strezhen'" ("From behind the island into the channel"; a very popular song about Sten'ka Razin) as "folk songs," although their form clearly indicates that they are literary compositions. Anecdotes are told of amateur singers taking offense at the claim that Yuz Aleshkovsky and not "the Russian people" wrote the "Gulag song" "Tovarishch Stalin, vy bol'shoi uchenyi" ("Comrade Stalin, you are a great scholar"), but he did. Meanwhile, a modern folkloric genre, the *chastushka,* actually does employ literary meters—an example of reverse influence.

11. The verse of Igor' Kholin and some of the prose of Lyudmila Petrushevskaya provide examples.

12. For an excellent, detailed study of some of these issues, see Svetlana Boym, *Common Places: Mythologies of Everyday Life in Russia* (Cambridge, Mass., and London, 1994).

13. The most learned exponent of this approach is Elena Markova, whose *Tvorchestvo Nikolaya Klyueva* explores the Finno-Ugric nexus in detail.

14. On the role of local and national versions of saints, see, among others, L. Kiseleva, "Semanticheskie polya klyuevskoi toponimiki (K postanovke voprosa)," *Vytegorsky vestnik* 1 (1994): 6–11.

15. Oksana Pashko, "Obraz gusya v tvorchestve Nikolaya Klyueva (k analizu ornitologicheskogo koda)," in *Klyuevskii sbornik,* ed. Yatskevich, vol. 3 (Vologda, 2002), 145–61.

16. L. G. Yatskevich, S. B. Vinogradova, and S. K. Golovkina, "Materialy k 'Slovaryu imen sobstvennykh v poezii N. A. Klyueva,'" in *Klyuevskii sbornik,* ed. Yatskevich, vol. 3 (Vologda, 2002), 9. However, *Poeticheskii slovar' Nikolaya Klyueva,* vol. 1, *Chastotnye slovoukazateli,* project director L. G. Yatskevich, ed. M. V. Bogdanova et al. (Vologda, 2007), 174, indicates twenty-one occurrences of the name and its derivatives; L. A. Kiseleva, "Russkaya ikona v tvorchestve Nikolaya Klyueva," *Pravoslavie i kul'tura* 1 (1996): 46–65.

17. Klyuev's "poetics of names" is the subject of an entire book: S. N. Smol'nikov and L. G. Yatskevich, *Na zolotom poroge nemerknuvshikh vremen: Poetika imen sobstvennykh v proizvedeniyakh N. Klyueva* (Vologda, 2006). Among many very useful observations, the authors repeatedly point to Klyuev's tendency to "syncretism" and to an essentially premodern treatment of the noun, and especially the proper noun, as an object.

18. The rivers of this area continue to provide its major transport arteries to this day (but rivers and lakes as integral parts of the northern system of transport are largely absent from Klyuev's poetry, serving quite different purposes in their abundant appearances in his work). Roads remain unreliable, even between

quite large towns, in this area (although the last ten years have seen significant improvements). Today, to reach Vytegra, the center of Klyuev's native region, from Petersburg without private transport, an overnight bus journey is required, part of it on unpaved roads which may be very difficult to pass in spring or autumn. To reach Vytegra from Moscow, the most direct route is overnight by train to Vologda (the first stage of the Archangel railway), and then by bus—an all-day ride—from there to Vytegra. The most easily reached railway station directly from Vytegra (at Lodeinoe Pole, where an *elektrichka* [suburban train] may be taken for a slow journey to St. Petersburg) is, as noted above, more than 200 kilometers away. Of course, there are narrow-gauge railways, built principally to serve the lumber industry in this area, but they do not provide scheduled passenger service.

19. On Klyuev's seasons, see L. P. Pankova, "Zadachi i printsipy opisaniya leksiko-semanticheskoi systemy temporal'noi leksiki v poezii N. A. Klyueva," in *Klyuevskii sbornik,* ed. Yatskevich, vol. 1 (Vologda, 1999), 56–57.

20. For details of the compilation of the collection and its publication, see E. Meksh, "Ot zamysla k voploshcheniyu (tvorcheskaya istoriya sobraniya sochineniya N. A. Klyueva 'Pesnoslov')," in *Traditsii i novatorstvo v sovetskoi literature,* ed. D. Ivlev (Riga, 1986), 65–67.

21. In the apparatus to *Serdtse edinoroga,* Soroga is erroneously described as "Klyuev's [own] hydronym" (878). In fact, the (modest) Soroga River flows into picturesque Lake Seliger north of Ostashkov. There are, it seems, some invented toponyms in Klyuev's work, as will be seen, but this error illustrates the dangers of confidently asserting that a proper noun in Klyuev's work is fictional.

22. Klyuev, *Pis'ma k Aleksandru Bloku,* 144–46, 151–52.

23. *Russkie sovetskie pisateli: Poety,* 11:43.

24. The *Pesnoslov* version of "Pesni iz Zaonezh'ya" is studied in detail, as a "single text," by Markova in her *Tvorchestvo Nikolaya Klyueva,* 112–31.

25. *Russkie sovetskie pisateli: Poety,* 11:33; Azadovsky, *Put' poeta,* 211.

26. On the "Scythians," see Azadovsky, *Put' poeta,* 193–99; Azadovsky, *Zhizn' Nikolaya Klyueva,* 147–50.

27. "Mednyi kit" is analyzed in some detail (a rarity in Klyuev scholarship) by I. Trofimov, "'Smertiyu na smert' nastupi' (Opyt istolkovaniya poemy Nikolaya Klyueva 'Mednyi kit')," in *Russkaya poeziya: God 1917,* ed. E. Meksh, I. Trofimov, and F. Fedorov (Daugavpils, 1998), 89–98.

28. Markova examines the structure of the first volume of *Pesnoslov* in *Tvorchestvo Nikolaya Klyueva,* 88–98.

29. The editors of *Sochineniya* make this suggestion (1:522).

30. E. Meksh, "Ot zamysla," 65–81.

31. Some of the conclusions Meksh reaches are at variance with the commentary in these pages: for example, he sees the grouping of poems as made and broken "freely" (implying, it seems, that they are of little significance ["Ot zamysla," 74]).

32. It might be noted that even details of the contents of "Serdtse edinoroga" are somewhat elusive in the given time and place—the cycle as printed appears to consist of *thirteen* poems, since two have been erroneously printed as one, while the contents page at the end of the volume indicates that "Izbyanye pesni" is the title of the first poem, not of the cycle, which itself appears there to consist of *twelve* lyrics. Among admirers, Mikhailov terms "Izbyanye pesni" "the highest achievement of [Klyuev's] muse in the 1910s" (A. I. Mikhailov, *Puti razvitiya novokrest'yanskoi* poezii [Leningrad, 1990], 13). For Kiseleva it is "without doubt one of the most significant works of Russian poetry in the 1910s" (L. Kiseleva, "Tsikl 'Izbyanye pesni' N. A. Klyueva v tvorcheskoi biografii Sergeya Esenina: K postanovke voprosa," in *O, Rus', vzmakhni krylami*, vol. 1 of *Eseninskii sbornik*, ed. Y. Prokushev [Moscow, 1994], 95).

33. In a chapter on Klyuev's use of female personal names, Smol'nikov notes the collective and folkloric functioning of such names, "indicating not a concrete person, but a peasant woman in general" (Smol'nikov and Yatskevich, *Na zolotom poroge*, 163).

34. Smol'nikov sees the name Paraskov'ya (Paraskeva) and its derivatives, which occur sixty-eight times in Klyuev's work, as the most semantically complex of his female proper nouns (Smol'nikov and Yatskevich, *Na zolotom poroge*, 162).

35. See G. M. Prokhorov, "Povest' o Nilo-sorskom skite," *Pamyatniki kul'tury: Novye otkrytiya: Pis'mennost, Iskusstvo, Arkheologiya* (1977), 12–20. Many of the main buildings of the pre-Soviet monastery are preserved on the banks of the Sora River, at what is now the village of Pustyn' (literally, Hermitage), but they contain a forensic psychiatric hospital, where the inmates appear to be forcibly detained. The site is well off the tourist track but may be reached quite easily; it provides a sobering monument to the more destructive and depressing elements of the Soviet legacy. Klyuev's warnings may be read fruitfully against this background.

36. For a more detailed examination of this work, see Maikl Meikin [Michael Makin], "Nikolai Klyuev i Nil Sorskii," in *XXI Vek na puti k Klyuevu: Materialy Mezhdunarodnoi konferentsii "Olonetskie stranitsy zhizni i tvorchestva: Nikolai Klyuev i problemy etnopoetiki," posvyashchennoi 120-letiyu so dnya rozhdeniya velikogo russkogo poeta Nikolaya Klyueva 21–25 sentyabrya 2004* g., ed. E. Markova, Karel'skii Nauchnyi tsentr, Rossiiskaya Akademiya Nauk (Petrozavodsk, 2006), 87–98.

37. Nikolai Klyuev, *Neuvyadaemyi tsvet: Pesennik* (Chelyabinsk, 1995).

38. For an account of Klyuev's reception in Vytegra in the 1910s and early 1920s, see the memoir of V. Sokolov, "Olonetskii Longfello," as reproduced on the website Klyuevoslov (from the archive of Sergei Subbotin): http://nk-poety.narod.ru/win/klyuev/m002_klyuev.html (accessed September 2008). Sokolov's account suggests that the folkloric stylizations had the widest appeal.

39. One of very few attempts to address this issue in any detail is K.

Azadovsky, "'Plach v roditel'skuyu subbotu' Nikolaya Klyueva," *Russkaya rech'* 6 (1989): 17–24. Here Azadovsky examines Klyuev's reworking of an actual peasant lament (Klyuev's version remained in draft in his notebooks, and is not included in *Serdtse edinoroga*).

40. RGALI, fond 1685, opis' 1, ed. khraneniya 4.

41. Sergei Subbotin, "Nikolai Klyuev 1884–1937," introductory note to publication of three poems in *Den' poezii* (Moscow, 1989), 47.

42. I am extremely grateful to Sergei Subbotin for sharing his knowledge of these materials with me.

43. A. Tarasenkov, *Russkie poety XX veka 1900–1955 bibliografiya* (Moscow, 1966), 176. Tarasenkov's bibliography of Klyuev collections is full and accurate. I am, once again, grateful to Sergei Subbotin for alerting me to this entry. See also Subbotin's commentary to Esenin's letter to Klyuev of May 1922 (Sergei Esenin, *Polnoe sobranie sochinenii v semi tomakh*, ed. Y. L. Prokushev, vol. 6 [Moscow, 1999], 525).

44. As is noted in the commentary to the poem in *Serdtse edinoroga* (930), Klyuev, in a manuscript list of his works, entitled the poem "Pole Iezekiilovo," presumably having in mind the prophet's vision in Ezekiel 37. *Serdtse edinoroga* prefers the text found in the manuscript edition of *L'vinyi khleb* to the version in the published collection. The version quoted here is from the published *L'vinyi khleb*.

45. This interpretation presupposes that the primary model of the poetic collection is a sort of "lyrical diary," albeit far from transparent. While it is beyond the scope of this discussion to prove the primacy of that model, it is surely a very significant one in Russian modernism, as, for example, the poetic collections of Blok, Bely, Pasternak, and Tsvetaeva abundantly demonstrate.

46. Firsov, "'Byt' v trave zelenym, a na kamne serym,'" 152–53. Lyudmila Yatskevich suggests that the church intended is the sixteenth-century Cathedral of St. Sophia in Vologda (Yatskevich and Smol'nikov, *Na zolotom poroge*, 117–18), but this seems especially unlikely given Klyuev's (inaccurate) dating of the Ankhimovo church in his remarks to Shiryaevets. One more curious fact should be added: the Ankhimovo church is now being rebuilt not on its original site, but as part of a large complex on the outskirts of St. Petersburg (the Bogoslovka park complex, on the northern shore of the Neva, within the Neva Forest Park, to the east of the city).

47. The main source of information about late nineteenth-century Koshtugi is an article by a local schoolmaster, published in the *guberniya* newspaper, and quoted by several authors, for example, Azadovsky, *Put' poeta*, 15–16.

48. According to the exemplary research of Lyudmila Yatskevich and her group of students in Vologda, discussed in the following pages (examples have been cited already), Kizhi occurs five times in Klyuev's verse; Palei once; Kargopol' and related qualifiers nine times; Pudozh and related qualifiers eight

times. Some of these places also occur in prose works (the Yatskevich group has worked only with verse). See L. Yatskevich, S. Vinogradova, and S. Golovkina, "Slovar' toponimov i etnonimov N. A. Klyueva: Al'favitnyi chastotnyi slovoukazatel'," in *Klyuevskii sbornik,* ed. Yatskevich, vol. 2 (Vologda, 2000), 37–46.

49. For Kargopol', see, among others, *Arkhangel'skaya oblast': Putevoditel',* Mir vokrug nas, no. 7 (Moscow, 2000), 52–56.

50. Klyuev's letter (from the Vytegra jail) to political exiles in Kargopol' is cited by Azadovsky, *Put' poeta,* 45–46, and discussed by Firsov, "'Byt' v trave zelenym,'" 150–51; for the text, see *Sd* 161–62; for Bryusova's retreat to Kargopol', see Klyuev, *Pis'ma k Aleksandru Bloku,* 315, 329–30 (footnote 16).

51. Kargopol' itself had a monastery and a convent, while the ancient Monastery of St. Cyril Chelmogorsky was nearby; the Muromsky Monastery is on the shore of Lake Onega, not far from Pudozh. See P. Soikin, comp., *Pravoslavnye ruskkie obiteli: Polnoe illyustrirovannoe opisanie vsekh pravoslavnykh monastyrei v rossiiskoi imperii i na Afone,* ed. M. Danilushkin (St. Petersburg, 1995; photo-reprint of edition of the 1910, St. Petersburg, edition), 156–60. The Muromsky Monastery is mentioned in "Gagar'ya sud'bina" and its founder, St. Lazarus, in "Mirskaya duma." See Azadovsky, "O 'Narodnom poete,'" 109, 117–18 (footnotes 73, 74).

52. V. Nikitinsky, "Slovo k chitatelyu," in *Vytegra: Kraevedcheskii al'manakh,* ed. Skupinova, 1:5–6.

53. Tat'yana Ipatova, curator, Vytegra Museum, personal communication, August 25, 2000.

54. Fedor Kostitsyn, personal communication, July 2, 2003.

55. Klyuev, *Pis'ma k Aleksandru Bloku,* 117, endnote 10. This remark has been added to the original apparatus—compare Klyuev, "Pis'ma Klyueva k Bloku," 464, endnote 5. I counted the inhabitants on a visit in August 2000. The village was still inhabited in the autumn of 2005.

56. Tamara Makarova, director of the Vytegra museum, personal communication, October 2002.

57. Representative samples of their work may be seen in A. L. Kazakov, ed., *Olonia: Sbornik tvorcheskikh rabot po fol'kloru i kraevedeniyu uchashchikhsya srednei shkoly no 1 g. Vytegry Vologodskoi oblasti* (Vytegra and Chelyabinsk, 1998); and A. L. Kazakov, ed., *Prionezh'e: Literaturno-kraevedcheskii i etnograficheskii sbornik (Oloniya-2)* (Vytegra-Chelyabinsk, 2002).

58. On time in the prose, see T. A. Ponomareva, *Proza Nikolaya Klyueva 20-kh godov* (Moscow, 1999), 39–40.

59. *Russkie sovetskie pisateli: Poety,* 11:48.

60. On the "cuts" to "Puteshestvie," also see Klyuev, *Sochineniya* (1:554); and Azadovsky, *Put' poeta,* 284–85.

61. Nikolai Klyuev, *Izba i pole* (Murmansk, 2003), with an afterword by S. I. Subbotin, "Poslednyaya prizhiznennaya . . . ," 86–96.

62. *Pogorel'shchina* seems to have been completed in Poltava (695); *Kain* was written in Potrepukhino, which was especially productive for Klyuev, as the following pages illustrate.

63. Yatskevich, Vinogradova, and Golovkina, "Slovar' toponimov," 38. Eighteen references are given, but one appears to be an error.

64. V. Semibratov, "Vyatskii krai v poezii N. A. Klyueva," in *Klyuevskii sbornik,* ed. Yatskevich, vol. 2 (Vologda, 2000), 125–36. This is the longest of a number of publications on this theme by Semibratov and others.

65. L. Yatskevich, "Poeticheskaya geografiya Nikolaya Klyueva," in *Vytegra: Kraevedcheskii al'manakh,* vol. 2, ed. E. Skupinova (Vologda, 2000), 186. Yatskevich's maps, while very enlightening, are of course not intended to present the sort of picture imagined for maps of Klyuev's north in the preceding pages of this chapter.

66. I assume Semibratov to be mistaken in thinking that the poet had been there in the early 1920s; Semibratov, "Vyatskii krai," 125. See Azadovsky, *Zhizn' Nikolaya Klyueva,* 250.

67. Semibratov, "Vyatskii krai," 125, 135, endnote 2.

68. Among their most significant publications are the many articles in the three volumes of *Klyuevskii sbornik* (Vologda, 1999, 2000, and 2003). Smol'nikov and Yatskevich's *Na zolotom poroge nemerknuvshikh vremen* (2006) expands much of their earlier work, while the first issue of the *Poeticheskii slovar' Nikolaya Klyueva* (2007) marks a new stage in the project. Other important articles include Yatskevich, "Poeticheskaya geografiya Klyueva"; S. Smol'nikov, "Metamorfozy krasoty: Zhenskie imena v poezii N. Klyueva," in *Vytegra: Kraevedcheskii al'manakh,* ed. Skupinova, 2:224–39; and L. Yatskevich, "'Sil'ny ne zhelezom . . .' (Otrazhenie natsional'nogo samosoznaniya v poezii N. A. Klyueva)," in *Vologda: Kraevedcheskii al'manakh,* vol. 3, ed. M. A. Beznin (Vologda, 2000), 367–74. A list of early publications and other works may be found in *Klyuevskii sbornik,* ed. Yatskevich, vol. 1 (Vologda, 1999), 115–17.

69. *Poeticheskii slovar' Nikolaya Klyueva,* 1:112.

70. Yatskevich, "Poeticheskaya geografiya," 68; L. Yatskevich, "Poeticheskaya sistema toponimov i etnonimov v tvorchestve N. A. Klyueva," in *Klyuevskii sbornik,* ed. Yatskevich, vol. 2 (Vologda, 2000), 51–65.

71. The first serious treatment of this question was L. Kiseleva, "Semanticheskie polya klyuevskoi toponimiki."

72. Markova, *Tvorchestvo Nikolaya Klyueva,* 141.

73. L. Kiseleva, "Khristianstvo russkoi derevni v poezii Nikolaya Klyueva," *Pravoslavie i kul'tura* 1 (1993): 59–76.

74. On this issue, and on Klyuev's own somewhat contradictory commentaries, see Azadovsky, *Put' poeta,* 143–45.

75. An excellent beginning has been made by B. Gol'din, "Narodno-razgovornoe dialektnoe nachalo v poezii N. Klyueva," in *Istoriya i geografiya russkikh staroobryadchsckikh govorov* (Moscow, 1995), 27–36.

76. On Klyuev and Mel'nikov-Pechersky, see Maikl Meikin (Michael Makin), "Nikolai Klyuev i Mel'nikov-Pecherskii: Zagadki i predpolozheniya," in *In Memoriam: Eduard Bronislavovich Meksh,* ed. F. Fjodorovs and J. Szokalski (Daugavpils, 2007), 166–82.

CHAPTER THREE

1. As A. V. Lavrov writes apropos of Andrei Bely, "The book was the main category in the poetic culture of Russian Symbolism. The reputations of the school's representatives were formed, changed, grew, and were questioned in direct relationship to the fate of the next collection by a particular author, as perceived by contemporaries (and the collection would claim, as a rule, both internal artistic integrity and structural organization)." A. V. Lavrov, "O knige Andreya Belogo 'Stikhotvoreniya' (1923)," in Andrei Bely, *Stikhotvoreniya,* ed. A. V. Lavrov (Moscow, 1988). For an example from the postsymbolist generation, see Michael Makin, *Marina Tsvetaeva: Poetics of Appropriation* (Oxford, 1993), 18–19, 26, 158, 214, 297.

2. Azadovsky's discussion of these issues comes to slightly different conclusions (*Zhizn' Nikolaya Klyueva,* 85). The dating is taken from *Serdtse edinoroga.*

3. This poem has also been omitted from *Serdtse edinoroga.* It is included in *Sochineniya* (2:216–17) and in *Stikhotvoreniya i poemy* (1977), 201–2, however.

4. It is more felicitous because the opening verb of the original first line seems to be a neologism intended to mean "glow with sunset" (*zarya* being "sunset" or "sunrise"), unattested in dictionaries and presumably judged "ugly" by the poet at a later date. Klyuev's changed relations with Iona Brikhnichev and the latter's unwelcome status in the new Soviet state may explain the removal of the original title in *Pesnoslov.*

5. Klyuev was always attentive to the presentation of his work in print, and frequently dissatisfied with the results. When he received his first copy of his very first collection, he was profoundly disappointed with the work of his publisher. He wrote to Blok that he had "received . . . *Sosen perezvon*—my own book—mutilated, with poems muddled up, with titles that are not mine, with many typographical errors, and moreover missing poems that hadn't pleased the publisher" (*Pis'ma k Aleksandru Bloku,* 256–57; letter of November 30, 1911). On the same day he wrote to Bryusov with similar complaints (*Pis'ma k Aleksandru Bloku,* 340). See also his correspondence with the publisher Konstantin Nekrasov, "Knigoizdatel'stvo K. F. Nekrasova i russkie pisateli nachala veka," ed. I. Vaganova, *Rossiiskii arkhiv: Istoriya Otechestva v svidetel'stvakh i dokumentakh XVIII–XX vv.* 5 (1994), 468–74. The point to be made here is not that Klyuev was an exception, but that he was *not* an exception: like most authors, and especially like the poets of the period, he was very concerned with the presentation of his work. He was, perhaps, less able to dictate terms to publishers than most, however, because of his social and financial situation.

6. Nikolai Klyuev, *Mednyi kit: Reprintnoe vosproizvedenie izdaniya 1919 goda* (Moscow, 1990). While the contents are untouched, the front cover, depicting the aged poet with a crown of thorns, adds a new ideological dimension to the text.

7. This edition, too, is not entirely without problems. Some of them are documented by Azadovsky in his review (*Novaya russkaya kniga* 1 [2000]: 27–29) and by Nikita Eliseev in "Krest'yanskii Mayakovsky" ("The Peasant Mayakovsky"), in *Peterburgskii knizhnyi vestnik On-line,* as of September 2008 available at http://bookman.spb.ru/11/Kluev/Kluev.htm.

8. As noted above, reprints have made some of these collections available. In addition to the 1990 reprint of *Mednyi kit,* the following should be noted: a Western reprint of *Sosen perezvon* (Letchworth, Eng., 1979); a reprint of Klyuev's most inaccessible collection, *Neuvyadaemyi tsvet* (Chelyabinsk, 1995); a reprint of Blok's copy of *Sosen perezvon,* with Klyuev's inscription and Blok's notes (Moscow, 2002); and a reprint of *Izba i pole* (Murmansk, 2003).

9. On Sventsitsky, see A. Etkind, *Khlyst: Sekty, literatura i revolyutsiya,* Novoe literaturnoe obozrenie, nauchnoe prilozhenie, vol. 12 (Moscow, 1998), 244–54.

10. V. Sventsitsky, "Vstupitel'naya stat'ya," in Nikolai Klyuev, *Bratskie pesni: Kniga 2* (Moscow, 1912), v, vi, xv.

11. Azadovsky defines "fraternal songs" as "poems stylized in the spirit of religious songs or prayers" (*Zhizn' Nikolaya Klyueva,* 84).

12. *Russkie sovetskie pisateli: Poety,* 11:98. See also Azadovsky's discussion of the reception of *Bratskie pesni* in *Zhizn' Nikolaya Klyueva,* 86–87.

13. Nikolai Gumilev, *Sobranie sochinenii,* 4 vols. (Washington, D.C., 1968), 4:299; Gumilev's review was originally published in *Apollon* 6 (1912).

14. *Strannik* 9 (1912): 428–29; M. Chunosov, "Novye knigi," *Novoe slovo* 9 (1912): 153–54; V. Narbut, "Otzvyvy o knigakh, postupivshikh v redaktsiyu," *Rodnaya strana* 11 (1912): 419.

15. Gumilev, *Sobranie sochinenii,* 4:284.

16. Ibid., 4:299.

17. Klyuev, *Pis'ma k Aleksandru Bloku,* 261–62, 265–66, note 7.

18. Azadovsky, *Zhizn' Nikolaya Klyueva,* 84.

19. Although even here there is confusion: in the brochure "Polunoshchnitsa" appears not only without its title but also without its first fifteen lines, thereby creating the impression of a completely different work, beginning with the line "Rastvoritesya vrata" ("Open, gates").

20. For this reason, among others, readers looking at these poems in posthumous collected works should exercise some caution. While reference is made here within the text to the location of these poems in *Serdtse edinoroga,* the reader should bear in mind that it is the *latest* version of the poem which will be found there, not the version of the 1912 collections; meanwhile, given the atten-

tion paid in these pages to the original *sbornik*, it is the 1912 versions which are quoted here.

21. There is commentary on this ending in John Alexander Ogden, "Nikolai Kliuev and the Construction of the Literary Peasant," Ph.D. dissertation (Stanford University, 1996), 80–82. For Ogden, the cycle enacts the Golgotha Christian principle of literalizing for adherents the experience of Christ on the cross, while the conclusion marks Klyuev's clear distinction between the material and the spiritual worlds.

22. Ogden suggests the influence of Blok's "Pesnya sud'by" ("Song of Fate") here, in "Nikolai Kliuev and the Construction of the Literary Peasant," 87.

23. Bazanov, *S rodnogo berega,* 95.

24. Quoted by Azadovsky, *Put' poeta,* 115. On Izmailov, see Karokhin, *Sergei Esenin i Nikolai Klyuev,* 24–25.

25. Quoted by Azadovsky, *Put' poeta,* 126, from *Novoe vino* 1 (1912): 14.

26. Quoted by Azadovsky, *Put' poeta,* 127.

27. Nikolai Klyuev, letter to Esenin of August 1915, first published in K. M. Azadovsky, "Esenin i Klyuev v 1915 godu (Nachalo znakomstva)," in *Esenin i sovremennost',* ed. M. Bazanov and Y. Prokushev (Moscow, 1975), 240.

28. See Azadovsky, *Zhizn' Nikolaya Klyueva,* 40, 42. On Semenov, see K. Azadovsky, "Rannee tvorchestvo N. A. Klyueva (novye materialy)," *Russkaya literature* 3 (1975): 197–99, and his scholarly apparatus to *Pis'ma k Aleksandru Bloku,* 118–20, note 11.

29. I. M. Dobrotvorsky, *Lyudi bozh'i: Russkaya sekta tak nazyvaemykh dukhovnykh khristian* (Kazan', 1869); N. V. Reutsky, *Lyudi bozh'i i skoptsy: Istoricheskoe issledovanie* (Moscow, 1872).

30. M. Niqueux, "Le mythe des *xlysty* dans la littérature russe," *Revue des études slaves* 69, nos. 1–2 (1997): 207.

31. August Pfizmaier, "Die Gefühlsdichtungen der Chlysten," *Denkschriften der kaiserlichen Akademie der Wissenschaften,* Philosophisch-Historische Classe, vol. 35 (Vienna, 1885), 196–288.

32. Rozanov's essay is included in his *Apokalipsicheskaya sekta,* 43–106.

33. Kuzmin seems to have been from an Old Believer (but not, of course, peasant) background, and during one of his spiritual crises he appears to have spent time in northern monastic communities. See R. Timenchik's entry on him in *Russkie pisateli 1800–1917: Biograficheskii slovar',* chief editor P. A. Nikolaev, vol. 3 (Moscow, 1994), 202–7; and John E. Malmstad, "Mixail Kuzmin: A Chronicle of His Life and Times," in *Sobranie stikhov,* by M. A. Kuzmin, vol. 3 (Munich, 1977), 57–59. Readers attuned to Klyuev's presentation of his Old Believer roots might, however, proceed with caution when approaching Kuzmin, since the latter's early confessional background and later adventures appear to lack documentation.

34. *Pesni russkikh sektantov-mistikov: Sbornik, sostavlennyi T. S. Rozhdest-*

venskim i M. I. Uspenskim (St. Petersburg, 1912). This is the source for all the examples in *Stikhi dukhovnye,* ed. F. M. Selivanov (Moscow, 1991).

35. "Predislovie," in *Pesni russkikh sektanto-mistikov,* vi–ix. Engelstein speaks of "mingling the language of fact and fable" as part of a "typical Skoptsy brew" (*Castration and the Heavenly Kingdom,* 147).

36. K. D. Bal'mont, *Stikhotvoreniya,* Biblioteka poeta, large series (Leningrad, 1969), 364.

37. Mikhail Kuzmin, *Osennie ozera: Vtoraya kniga stikhov* (Moscow, 1912), 212–13.

38. Bazanov, *S rodnogo berega,* 94.

39. Azadovsky, *Put' poeta,* 121; Azadovsky, *Zhizn' Nikolaya Klyueva,* 90–91.

40. Azadovsky, *Put' poeta,* 114; Azadovsky, *Zhizn' Nikolaya Klyueva,* 86.

41. Ogden, "Nikolai Kliuev and the Construction of the Literary Peasant," 74–87.

42. Vroon, "The Garden in Russian Modernism"; Ronald Vroon, "Staroobyradchestvo, sektantstvo i 'sakral'naya rech'' v poezii Nikolaya Klyueva," in *Nikolai Klyuev: Issledovaniya i materialy,* ed. Subbotin, 54–67 (first published in *Skupiska staroobrzedowcow w Europie, Azji i Ameryce: Ich miesce i tradycje we wspolczesnym swiecie,* ed. Iryda Grek-Pabisowa, Irena Maryniakowa, and Richard Morris [Warsaw, 1994], 237–47). See also Vroon's "The Old Belief and Sectarianism as Cultural Models in the Silver Age" in *Christianity and the Eastern Slavs,* vol. 2, *Russian Culture in Modern Times,* ed. Robert Hughes and Irina Paperno (Berkeley, Los Angeles, and London, 1994), 172–90.

43. Ogden, "Nikolai Kliuev and the Construction of the Literary Peasant," 90.

44. Azadovsky, *Zhizn' Nikolaya Klyueva,* 153.

45. E. Soinin, "Pisateli-staroobryadtsy Vygovskoi pustyni," in *Istoriya literatury Karelii,* vol. 3, ed. Y. Dyuzhev (Petrozavodsk, 2000), 21. Soinin also remarks that while they were "local writers" (most were from the region), they created works "by no means local" in significance.

46. See chapter 4 for a discussion of "Gagar'ya sud'bina," and chapter 6 for a discussion of *Pesn' o Velikoi Materi.*

47. Yukhimenko, "Narodnye osnovy tvorchestva N. A. Klyueva."

48. Some indication of these processes is provided by the double edition of the *Revue des études slaves* 69, nos. 1–2 (1997), which is devoted to the Old Belief and to Russian sectarianism. See also A. A. Hansen-Löve, *Allgemeine Häretik, russische Sektierrer und ihre Literarisierung in der Moderne,* Wiener Slawistischer Almanach, supplement 41 (Vienna, 1996). A short version of this was published as "Russkoe sektantstvo i ego otrazhenie v literature russkogo modernizma," in *Russkaya literatura i religiya,* ed. R. Grubel and V. Odinokov (Novosibirsk, 1997), 153–311.

49. Etkind, *Khlyst: Sekty, literatura i revolyutsiya.* The description is taken from the book's colophon.

50. Etkind, *Khlyst: Sekty, literatura i revolyutsiya,* 292. Etkind's opening remarks are very close to those of Hansen-Löve's Klyuev discussion ("Russkoe sektantstvo," 198).

CHAPTER FOUR

1. Azadovsky provided extracts from "Gagar'ya sud'bina" in "'Ya slavlyu Rossiyu,'" 104–5, and quoted from it extensively in *Put' poeta.*

2. V. Bazanov, "Poema o drevnem Vyge," *Russkaya literatura* 1 (1979): 77–96; Nikolai Klyuev, *Pogorel'shchina,* ed. S. Kunyaev and S. Subbotin, introduction and commentary by N. Tolstoy, *Novyi mir* 7 (1987): 78–100.

3. Klyuev, "Gagar'ya sud'bina," 150–58, preceded by Mikhailov's essay "Avtobiograficheskaya proza Nikolaya Klyueva," 146–50; Azadovsky, "O 'narodnom' poete i 'svyatoi Rusi'); Azadovsky's criticism of Mikhailov is on page 99 of the last-named work.

4. The work of Sergei Subbotin on Klyuev's prose—without which much of it would still be almost totally inaccessible—is a notable exception, and will be listed in the following pages. Azadovsky and Mikhailov have worked not only on "Gagar'ya sud'bina" but also, as will be seen, on Klyuev's dream texts. Other exceptions include two significant studies of Klyuev's prose in general: A. P. Kazarkin, "Proza Nikolaya Klyueva: Obosnovanie stilya," in *Problemy metoda i zhanra* (Tomsk, 1997), 175–86; and T. A. Ponomareva, *Proza Klyueva.*

5. K. M. Azadovsky, "Olonetskaya derevnya posle pervoi russkoi revolyutsii (Stat'ya N. A. Klyueva 'S rodnogo berega')," in *Russkii fol'klor,* vol. 15, Sotsial'nyi protest v narodnoi poezii (Leningrad, 1975), 200–209.

6. See S. I. Subbotin, "Proza Nikolaya Klyueva v gazetakh 'Zvezda Vytegry' i 'Trudovoe slovo' (1919–1921 gody): Voprosy stilya i atributsii," *Russkaya literatura* 4 (1984): 136–50; "'Gde chort valyaetsya, tam sherst' ostanetsya': Iz publitsistiki N. Klyueva 1919–1923," ed. S. Subbotin, *Slovo* 4 (1990): 61–66. The night watchman is the subject of "Chelobitnaya" ("Petition") and "'Gde chort valyaetsya,'" 65. *Slovesnoe drevo* does not reproduce this and other short, anonymous pieces attributed to Klyuev (with the exception of the introduction to the selection of verse described in the following pages).

7. "Krasnyi nabat" was first republished in Nikolai Klyuev, "Krasnyi nabat," ed. and intro. S. I. Subbotin, *Moskva* 11 (1987): 26–28; here will also be found "S rodnogo berega" (22–26) and "Porvannyi nevod" (28–32). Six of Klyuev's longer prose pieces ("S rodnogo berega," "V chernye dni: (Iz pis'ma krest'yanina)," "Velikoe zrenie," "Ognennaya gramota," "Krasnyi nabat," and "Porvannyi nevod") were collected in *Poslednii lel': Proza poetov eseninskogo kruga,* ed. and intro. S. Kunyaev (Moscow, 1989), 24–50.

8. "Sorok dva gvozdya" was first republished in "'Gde chort valyaetsya,'" 63–64; "Samotsvetnaya krov'" in 2:364–68.

9. "'Gde chort valyaetsya,'" 62. Ponomareva sees Klyuev's postrevolutionary prose as continuous both with his poetry of the period and with his earlier prose, and also speaks of a "red cycle" of works from 1919 (*Proza Klyueva,* 17–18, 19).

10. Subbotin, "Proza Nikolaya Klyueva v gazetakh," 141; Azadovsky, *Put' poeta,* 248–49.

11. The flour-cutting is described in the title piece in "'Gde chort valyaetsya,'" 65.

12. "Poety Velikoi Russkoi revolyutsii" was first republished in Subbotin's "Proza Nikolaya Klyueva v gazetakh," 145. It appears to have been included in *Slovesnoe drevo,* despite being an anonymous publication, because a manuscript of Klyuev's characterization of all the other poets except himself exists (*Sd* 510–11).

13. Ponomareva, in her chapter on Klyuev's Vytegra prose, analyzes at some length the author's eclectic style, and places great emphasis on his utopian and apocalyptic thematics (*Proza Klyueva,* 9–81).

14. Subbotin, "Proza Nikolaya Klyueva v gazetakh," 138–41; on Old Russian literature as a model, see also Ponomareva, *Proza Klyueva,* 18; Kazarkin, "Proza Nikolaya Klyueva," 181; and Y. B. Orlitsky, "O stikhoslozhenii novokrest'yanskikh poetov," in *Nikolai Klyuev: Issledovaniya i materialy,* ed. Subbotin, 161.

15. Subbotin, "Proza Nikolaya Klyueva v gazetakh," 141.

16. For this reason, Bakhtin's reading of Rabelais resonated so strongly with the *Soviet period* in which his study was composed, and D. S. Likhachev, A. M. Panchenko, and N. V. Ponyrko, while writing about *medieval* Russia in their famous *Smekh v drevnei Rusi* (*Laughter in Old Russia* [Leningrad, 1984]), provide, perhaps self-consciously, important models and tools for understanding Russian culture in the second half of the *twentieth century.* The last volume of the ongoing series Biblioteka literatury drevnei Rusi (Library of the Literature of Ancient Russia; St. Petersburg, 1997–) is announced as covering the eighteenth to the twentieth centuries, while recent volumes of the exemplary *Trudy otdela drevenerusskoi literatury* (*Works of the Department of Old Russian Literature*) have included studies of "modern" texts.

17. See Mikhailov's comments, "'Prostite ne zabyvaite . . . ,'" 120.

18. Azadovsky, *Put' poeta,* 288–90.

19. A. I. Mikhailov, "Klyuev o Esenine," *Annales instituti philologiae slavicae Universitatis Debreceniensis de Ludovico Kossuth nominatae,* Slavica 27 (1995): 142–44.

20. Nikolai Klyuev, "'Snovideniya' Nikolaya Klyueva," ed. with a preface by Konstantin Azadovsky, *Russkaya mysl',* January 18 and January 25, 1991 (nos. 3862 and 3863); Nikolai Klyuev, "Sny Nikolaya Klyueva," ed. and intro. Aleksandr Mikhailov, *Novyi zhurnal* 4 (Leningrad, 1991): 3–26; Aleksandr Mikhailov, "O snovideniyakh v tvorchestve Alekseya Remizova i Nikolaya Klyueva," in *Aleksei Remizov: Issledovaniya i materialy,* ed. A. Gracheva (St. Petersburg, 1994),

89–103. See also Kazarkin's remarks in "Proza Nikolaya Klyueva," 181–84; and Ponomareva's discussion of them in *Proza Klyueva,* 108–22.

21. Subbotin, "Proza Nikolaya Klyueva v gazetakh," 138, 139, footnote 22.

22. Mikhailov, "Avtobiograficheskaya proza," 150.

23. Azadovsky, "O 'narodnom' poete," 99 (emphasis added).

24. Azadovsky, "O 'narodnom' poete," 103, 111, endnote 1.

25. Mikhailov, "Avtobiograficheskaya proza," 141.

26. Azadovsky, "O 'narodnom' poete," 99.

27. Ibid., 95, 101, endnote 49.

28. See also his comments in *Put' poeta,* 129, 244.

29. Ponamareva, *Proza Klyueva,* 92–106.

30. Ibid., 106–8. Indeed, Ponomareva uses the term "spiral" herself in describing the architectonics of the autobiographical prose (106).

31. V. E. Flint et al., eds., *A Field Guide to Birds of Russia and Adjacent Territories,* trans. Natalia Bourso-Leland (Princeton, N.J., 1991), 3.

32. E. Armstrong, *The Folklore of Birds,* 2nd rev. ed. (New York, 1970), 68.

33. I am grateful to Alina Makin for this observation.

34. The number comes, it will be recalled, from Oksana Pashko's list of birds in "Obraz gusya v tvorchestve Nikolaya Klyueva," 161. In *Plach o Sergee Esenine,* Esenin's fate is identified with the loon ("Tvoya sud'ba-gagar'ya" ["Your loon-fate"], 661); in "Na sivom plese gagarii zyk" of 1914 ("On the gray river stretch, a loon cry," 208–9), the bird's cry heralds rain; in "Poskonnym portam ne byvaet iznosu" of 1914 ("Hempen trousers do not wear out," 225–26), the addressee is told to build a (hermit's) cell where loons fly, while Andrei Rublev is said to have known the loon's plumage; in "Ot sutemok do zvezd i ot zvezd do zari" of 1914 ("From twilight to the stars, from the stars to dawn," 239–40), loons calling to one another are part of the natural order into which the peasant house fits; in "Zadvorki Rusi — matyugi na zabore" of 1921 (492–93), the "loon's baptism" is one of a series of images of the purity of the north; in the final lines of "Nasha russkaya pravda zagibla" of 1928 (543–45), loon nests on water lilies seem to presage peace and redemption; and in "Ya leto zoril na Vyatke" of 1932–33 (593–94), the loon seems to be a metaphor for the natural order of the countryside. As Elena Markova points out, the Shaman calls Parasha a *gagara* (loon) in *Pesn' o Velikoi Materi* (732); for Markova, this is a sign of the poem's orientation not only toward Russian but also toward Finno-Ugric culture, since for the Saams the first bird was a loon (Markova, *Tvorchestvo Nikolaya Klyueva,* 39).

35. Azadovsky, "O 'narodnom' poete," 121, note 115.

36. In a letter of December 1929 to Anatolii Yar-Kravchenko, Klyuev remarks that he read his *poema Pogorel'shchina* to Nesterov at the latter's home, and that Nesterov was greatly moved by the poem (*Sd* 264).

37. Azadovsky, "O 'narodnom' poete," 97.

38. Karokhin, *Sergei Esenin i Nikolai Klyuev,* 79–80. "At the invitation of

the Empress Aleksandra Fedorovna they once visited the Aleksandr Palace together." Karokhin's assertion, however, is not entirely supported by the memoir which he cites (Yurii Morfessi, *Zhizn', Lyubov', Stsena: Vospominaniya russkogo bayana* [Paris, 1937], 179). In that memoir the singer Morfessi seems to suggest that he recommended that Esenin alone read to the empress, after hearing the two poets read in Feodorovsky Gorodok. Moreover, he calls the second poet "Kusikov" (presumably in error, since, as Karokhin states, it could not have been the poet Aleksandr Kusikov, but nonetheless a warning that the memoir should be treated with caution).

CHAPTER FIVE

1. *Russkie sovetskie pisateli: Poety,* 11:49.
2. Gregory Freidin, "Mandel'shtam's 'Ode to Stalin': History and Myth," *Russian Review* 4 (1982): 400–426.
3. For a reading of *Kreml'* and a discussion of its problematic status, see Maikl Meikin (Michael Makin), "Paradoksy *Kremlya,*" in *Narymskaya poema N. Klyueva "Kreml'": Interpretatsiya i kontekst,* ed. V. A. Domansky (St. Petersburg, 2008): 147–89.
4. Azadovsky, *Put' poeta,* 259.
5. See also A. I. Mikhailov, "K biografii N. A. Klyueva poslednego perioda ego zhizni i tvorchestva (Po materialam semeinogo arkhiva B. N. Kravchenko)," in *Ezhegodnik rukopisnogo otdela Pushkinskogo doma za 1990 god* (St. Petersburg, 1993), 172–73; and Azadovsky, *Zhizn' Nikolaya Klyueva,* 288–89. On the poet's anxiety to keep other works secret, see his letter to Yar-Kravchenko of May 18, 1933 (*Sd* 298–99).
6. Gronsky, "O krest'yanskikh pisatelyakh," 150–51.
7. It was first published in Azadovsky, "'Povest' skorbi,'" 24–27; and again by A. I. Mikhailov in "Nikolai Klyuev 'Odinochestvo—strashnoe slovo,'" *Nashe nasledie* 1 (1991): 116–17.
8. On McVay, see Maikl Meikin (Michael Makin), "Britanskii pervootkryvatel' Nikolaya Klyueva," *Krasnoe znamya* (Vytegra), October 18, 2001; full version "Britanskii pervootkryvatel' pozdnego Klyueva," *Nauka i biznes na Murmane: Nauchnoprakticheskii zhurnal,* Dukhovnaya praktika series, 4 (2002): 11–13.
9. See Subbotin's apparatus to "O chem shumyat sedye kedry" in *Pesnoslov* (1990), 237; his argument is drawn from Klyuev's designation of the work in his letter to Mikhail Zenkevich of December 21, 1932 (*Sd* 286), first published by Subbotin himself—Nikolai Klyuev, "Pis'ma Nikolaya Klyueva raznykh let," ed. S. I. Subbotin, in *Nikolai Klyuev: Issledovaniya i materialy,* ed. Subbotin, 228–29.
10. Azadovsky, "Sbornik 'O chem shumyat sedye kedry,'" 149–53.

11. Subbotin, "Na putyakh k Nikolayu Klyuevu," 108–13.

12. It will be recalled that, according to Gronsky's memoir, only when Klyuev sent him what may be taken to be "O chem shumyat sedye kedry" (Gronsky speaks simply of a *poema*) did he realize, with the help of Pavel Vasil'ev, that Klyuev was a homosexual. This realization contributed to his persecution of the poet (Gronsky, "O krest'yanskikh pisatelyakh," 150).

13. Nikolai Klyuev, "Iz neopublikovannogo," ed. Stanislav Kunyaev and L. Shevtsova, intro. L. Shevtsova, *Druzhba narodov* 12 (1987): 139.

14. Klyuev, "Stikhi raznykh let," 20; Klyuev, *Pesnoslov* (1990), 221–22.

15. The first part of "Mne revolyutsiya ne mat'" appears in 2:261–62. The second part was first published by Gordon McVay in "Nikolay Klyuev and Sergey Klychkov: Unpublished Texts," *Oxford Slavonic Papers*, new series, vol. 17 (1984): 93. It appeared in full first in *Den' poezii* (Moscow, 1987), and again in Subbotin's *Pesnoslov* (1990), 220–21. The first part of the poem, beginning "Prodrogli lipy do kostei," was published in 2:269–71, and again in *Stikhotvoreniya i poemy* (1986), 205–6, in both cases without a title. Subbotin published the final seventeen lines in his review of the last-named work (*Sever* 5 [1988]: 111), and published the entire poem, with title, in *Pesnoslov* (1990), 166–68. The other poem, entitled "Moemu drugu Anatoliyu Yaru," was published by Azadovsky in *Zvezda* 3 (1991): 163–64, and by Mikhailov in *Nashe nasledie* 1 (1991): 115–16.

16. It was first published in Nikolai Klyuev, "Gamayun — Ptitsa Veshchaya," ed. Vitalii Shentalinsky, *Ogonek* 43 (1989): 10. See also Shentalinsky, *Arrested Voices*, 200.

17. Klyuev, "Gamayun," 10. See also Gronsky, "O krest'yanskikh pisatelyakh," 150–51; and Klyuev's letter to Gorbacheva of October 25, 1935, mentioned above (*Sd* 371).

18. Klyuev, *Pesnoslov* (1990), 241.

19. Ibid., 241.

20. For a more extended treatment of Klyuev and prophecy, see Michael Makin, "Nikolai Kliuev—Prophet of Loss," *Slavic and East European Journal* 49, no. 4 (2005): 591–611.

21. Shentalinsky, *Arrested Voices*, 202.

22. Lyudmila Kalinina, "'Gremel moi praded Avvakum,'" *Nizhnii Novgorod* 2 (1997): 211.

23. Shentalinsky, *Arrested Voices*, 202; Eduard Meksh, "'Nispala polynnaya zvezda' (prorochestvo Nikolaya Klyueva)," in *Nikolai Klyuev: Issledovaniya i materialy*, ed. Subbotin, 75.

24. Klyuev, "Gamayun," 9–10; Shentalinsky, *Arrested Voices*, 199–200. The translation of the passage which follows is my own, not that of *Arrested Voices*.

25. Klyuev, *Pis'ma k Aleksandru Bloku*, 273–75, letter of September 9, 1912.

26. Klyuev, *Pesnoslov* (1990), 241–42.

27. Elena Markova, in her *Elementy finno-ugorskoi kul'tury v khudozhestvennoi sisteme Nikolaya Klyueva: Reprint doklada na zasedanii Uchenogo soveta Instituta yazyka, literatury i istorii* (Petrozavodsk, 1991), 15–16, sees this episode as the inversion of a Finno-Ugric myth about the whitefish as a totem.

28. For more details of Klyuev's treatment of the Kitezh motif, see S. N. Smol'nikov, "Mifologema-toponim 'Kitezh' v poeticheskoi sisteme Klyueva," in *Klyuevskii sbornik*, ed. Yatskevich, vol. 1 (Vologda, 1999), 88–107.

29. Karokhin, *Sergei Esenin i Nikolai Klyuev*, 56–58.

30. On the White Sea Canal and its treatment in Russian literature, see Cynthia Ruder, *Making History for Stalin: The Story of the Belomor Canal* (Gainesville, 1998); Klyuev's treatment of the canal is discussed on 181–85.

31. Klyuev, *Pesnoslov* (1990), 242–43.

32. Eduard Meksh, *Obraz Velikoi Materi (religiozno-mifologicheskie traditsii v epicheskom tvorchestve Nikolaya Klyueva)* (Daugavpils, 1995), 116.

33. See Meksh, *Obraz Velikoi Materi*, 122; Nikolai Pereyaslov, "Ot obshchego istoka (Motivy i obrazy 'Slova o polku Igoreve')," *Sever* 8 (1993): 155–57; Nikolai Pereyaslov, *Nerasshifrovannye poslaniya (Zagadki russkoi literatury ot "Slova o polku Igoreve" do nashikh dnei* (Moscow, 2001), 131–36; and G. N. Shershneva, "Tema 'Svyatoi Rusi' v tvorchestve N. Klyueva kontsa 20- nachala 30-kh godov," in *Religiya i tserkov' v kul'turno-istoricheskom razvitii Russkogo Severa (K 450-letiyu Prepodobnogo Trifona, Vyatskogo Chudotvortsa): Materialy Mezhdunarodnoi nauchnoi konferentsii*, vol. 2, ed. V. V. Nizov (Kirov, 1996), 88.

34. Klyuev, *Pesnoslov* (1990), 242.

35. For the aspen and Judas, see, for example, A. Afanas'ev, *Poeticheskie vozzreniya slavyan na prirodu v trekh tomakh* (Moscow, 1994; photo-reprint of the Moscow, 1868, edition), 2:307.

36. Nancy Pollack, *Mandelstam the Reader* (Baltimore, 1995), 84–85. On "Est' dve strany . . . ," see Maikl Meikin (Michael Makin), "Iz Sibiri v kushchi raya: poslednee stikhotvorenie Nikolaya Klyueva," in *Nikolai Klyuev: Obraz mira i sud'ba*, ed. Kazarkin and Domansky, vol. 2 (2005), 46–62.

37. See the editor's comments, and his quotation of Filippov's commentary, in the first publication of this poem—Gordon McVay, "Nikolai Klyuev and Sergeiy Klychkov: Unpublished Texts," *Oxford Slavonic Papers*, new series, vol. 17 (1984): 92–93. The source of the text was the archive of Yar-Kravchenko, to whom it seems to have been sent in 1937. For the same reason, *Kreml'* has been preserved, while any other poems Klyuev may have written in Siberia seem to have been lost, if they existed at all.

38. Pichurin, *Poslednie dni*, 33. Valerii Domansky, in his essay "Tomskii tekst Nikolaya Klyueva" (*Narym*, 44–45), expands this point by noting that there was a "country of cemeteries," consisting of a territory comprising the Orthodox, Old Believer, Jewish, and Polish burial grounds.

CHAPTER SIX

1. Viktor Garnin, in his apparatus to *Slovesnoe drevo* (593–94), expresses the opposite opinion—that Klyuev "never turned to the mixing and substitution of genres."

2. Mensky, "N. A. Klyuev," 153.

3. Esenin, *Polnoe sobranie sochinenii,* 2:86.

4. Ibid., 2:183–84.

5. Meksh, *Obraz Velikoi Materi,* 66–67.

6. According to *Russkie sovetskie pisateli: Poety,* 11:64–65, 105, there were no reactions in print to the work, whereas the other two *poemy* of the period, *Plach o Sergee Esenine* and *Derevnya,* drew considerable, and often hostile, comment.

7. Esenin, *Polnoe sobranie sochinenii,* 1:170. These, the final lines of "Snova p'yut zdes', derutsya i plachut," were, according to Ol'ga Forsh, dramatically declaimed by Klyuev himself at the memorial evening for Esenin, when Klyuev gripped his audience first by reading his own poetry and then by slipping seamlessly into a reading of Esenin's verse (*Sumasshedshii korabl',* 212–13).

8. Nikolai Klyuev, *Solovki,* ed. and intro. ("K istorii publikuemogo teksta") Sergei Subbotin, *Novyi mir* 3 (1989): 229–32.

9. It will be recalled that fragments of *Kain* seem to have appeared in *Den',* no. 22 (May 31–June 6, 1992), within Kunyaev's "'Ty, zhguchii otprysk Avvakuma,'" then, under the same in *Nash sovremennik,* and finally in S. Kunyaev and S. Kunyaev, *Rasterzannye teni* (Moscow, 1995), 204–28.

10. Meksh, *Obraz Velikoi Materi,* 111.

11. On Klyuev reading *Pogorel'shchina* see, among other sources, Mensky, "N. A. Klyuev," 132–33; Boris Filippov, "*Pogorel'shchina* Nikolaya Klyueva," in *Studi in onore di Ettore lo Gatto e Giovanni Maver* (Florence, 1962), 236–37; and Azadovsky, *Zhizn' Nikolaya Klyueva,* 235–37. Among the famous to whom he read the poem was the artist Nesterov (see Klyuev's letter of December 18, 1929, to Yar-Kravchenko [*Sd* 264]). Klyuev hoped at one time that the work would be published, as that letter indicates; his letter of May 18, 1933, to the same addressee gives details of the nonpublication (*Sd* 298). In his letter from Kolpashevo of June 12, 1934 (to Sergei Klychkov), he writes: "I have been burned on my own "Burnt Ruins," as once my ancestor the Archpriest Avvakum was burnt on the fire at Pustozersk" (where Avvakum was executed; *Sd* 313).

12. See Subbotin's apparatus to Klyuev, *Pesnoslov* (1990), 239.

13. Ettore lo Gatto, "Vospominaniya o N. A. Klyueve," *Novyi zhurnal* 35 (1953): 125.

14. Klyuev, *Polnoe sobranie sochinenii,* 2:117–41.

15. See Filippov's comments in "*Pogorel'shchina* Nikolaya Klyueva," 235.

The English translation is by John Glad, *Nikolai Klyuev: Poems* (Ann Arbor, Mich., 1977), 46–68.

16. Klyuev, *Stikhotvoreniya i poemy* (1986), 235–38; Klyuev, *Pogorel'shchina,* 78–100.

17. O. Mramornov, "Eshche odin spisok *Pogerel'shchiny," Novyi mir* 12 (1987): 258–59; Klyuev, *Pesnoslov* (1990), 239.

18. Mikhailov, *Puti razvitiya,* 208.

19. See discussions of the opening lines by Mikhailov (*Puti razvitiya,* 207) and Meksh (*Obraz Velikoi Materi,* 82). Both see this opening as echoing polemically the beginning of Esenin's *Anna Snegina.*

20. See Tolstoy's commentary to the poem, Klyuev, *Pogorel'shchina,* 98; this is disputed by Lyudmila Kiseleva, "Poema *Pogorel'shchina* v kontekste obraznogo myshleniya N. A. Klyueva," *Voprosy russkoi literatury,* vol. 57 (L'vov, 1991), 38.

21. Mikhailov clearly views Klyuev's *poemy* as sui generis: "Klyuev's epic works run their own particular course through the 1920s" (*Puti razvitiya,* 202).

22. Ivanov-Razumnik, *Pisatel'skie sud'by,* 37.

23. Meksh summarizes these accounts, *Obraz Velikoi Materi,* 124–25.

24. The entire work was first published in *Znamya* 11 (1991): 4–44.

25. The most extensive study of the work is in Meksh, *Obraz Velikoi Materi,* 124–86. Among other studies are Markova, *Tvorchestvo Nikolaya Klyueva,* 267–304; A. P. Kazarkin, "Apokaliptika Nikolaya Klyueva (k istolkovaniyu poemy *Pesn' o Velikoi Materi*)," *Vestnik Tomskogo gosudarstvennogo universiteta,* vol. 266, Gumanitarnyi spetsial'nyi vypusk (Tomsk, 1998), accessed at http://www.tsu.ru/webdesign/tsu/Library.nsf/designobjects/vestnik267/$file/kluev.html, September 2008; and L. Kiseleva, "Mif i real'nost' staroobryadchestva v *Pesni o Velikoi Materi* Nikolaya Klyueva," in *Vytegra: Kraevedcheskii al'manakh,* ed. Skupinova, 2:210–23.

26. Azadovsky, *Put' poeta,* 277; Azadovsky, *Zhizn' Nikolaya Klyueva,* 238. To his interrogator in 1934 Klyuev "confessed" to reading *Pogorel'shchina* at the homes of Esenin's widow, of Klychkov, Vsevolod Ivanov, Elena Tager, and, as noted earlier, Nesterov (Shentalinsky, *Arrested Voices,* 200).

27. *Russkie pisateli, 1800–1917: Biograficheskii slovar',* chief editor P. A. Nikolaev, 2:555–59.

28. Azadovsky, *Zhizn' Nikolaya Klyueva,* 259.

29. Meksh, *Obraz Velikoi Materi,* 129.

30. V. A. Nikonov, *Slovar' russkikh familii* (Moscow, 1993), 53.

31. On Lomonosov's possible ties to the Old Belief in his youth, see Ilya Z. Serman, *Mikhail Lomonosov: Life and Poetry* (Jerusalem, 1988), 13; and G. E. Pavlova, ed., *M. V. Lomonosov v vospominaniyakh i kharkteristikakh sovremennikov* (Moscow and Leningrad, 1962), 50.

32. William Craft Brumfield, *A History of Russian Architecture* (Cam-

bridge, Eng., 1993), 464; A. N. Petrov et al., eds., *Pamyatniki arkhitektury prigorodov Leningrada* (Leningrad, 1985), 126–27; Meksh, *Obraz Velikoi Materi,* 176–77.

33. Y. D. Loman, "Feodorovsky gorodok," in *Vospominaniya o Sergee Esenine,* ed. Y. L. Prokushev (Moscow, 1965), 161–66; Karokhin, *Sergei Esenin i Nikolai Klyuev,* 76–85.

34. Karokhin, *Sergei Esenin i Nikolai Klyuev,* 83.

35. V. A. Vdovin, "Sergei Esenin na voennoi sluzhbe," *Filologicheskie nauki* 1 (1964): 144; Azadovsky, *Put' poeta,* 180–81; N. I. Shubnikova-Guseva et al., eds., *Sergei Esenin v stikhakh i zhizni: Pis'ma dokumenty* (Moscow, 1995), 312–13. Vdovin does not provide the source of Klyuev's letter, and it is not included in *Slovesnoe drevo.* The editors of *Sergei Esenin v stikhakh i zhizni* state that they have not been able to find the original.

36. Shentalinsky's original publication of *Pesn'* in *Znamya* divides the "Third Nest" into only five sections, and this Petersburg episode, which forms a separate section in *Serdtse edinoroga* (804–8), is a continuation of the Tsarskoe Selo section.

37. On the folk tale in verse see Makin, *Marina Tsvetaeva: Poetics of Appropriation,* 100–106. Parts of Klyuev's *Pesn'* are quite close in manner to Tsvetaeva's *poemy-skazki.* A comparison of her *Egorushka,* also incomplete, with *Pesn'* might, for example, be quite revealing.

38. Ivanov-Razumnik, *Pisatel'skie sud'by,* 37.

39. The paradoxical character of *Kreml'* is explored in some detail in Meikin (Makin), "Paradoksy *Kremlya.*"

Selected Bibliography

WORKS BY NIKOLAI KLYUEV

Bratskie pesni: Kniga 2, with a preface by V. Sventsitsky (Moscow, 1912).
Bratskie pesni: Pesni golgofskikh khristian (Moscow, 1912).
Chetvertyi Rim (Petrograd, 1922).
"Gagar'ya sud'bina," ed. with commentary by A. I. Mikhailov, *Sever* 6 (1992): 150–58.
"Gamayun — Ptitsa Veshchaya," ed. Vitalii Shentalinsky, *Ogonek* 43 (1989): 9–12.
"'Gde chort valyaetsya, tam sherst' ostanetsya': Iz publitsistiki N. Klyueva 1919–1923," ed. S. Subbotin, *Slovo* 4 (1990): 61–66.
Izba i pole, afterword by S. I. Subbotin (Murmansk, 2003).
Izba i pole: Izbrannye stikhotvoreniya (Leningrad, 1928).
Izbrannoe, ed. and intro. V. G. Bazanov, with L. K. Shevtsova (Moscow, 1981).
Izbyanye pesni (Berlin, 1920).
"Iz neopublikovannogo," ed. Stanislav Kunyaev and L. Shevtsova, intro. L. Shevtsova, *Druzhba narodov* 12 (1987): 136–41.
"Krasnyi nabat," ed. and intro. S. I. Subbotin, *Moskva* 11 (1987): 20–32.
Lenin (Petrograd, 1924 [actually 1923]; 2nd edition, Leningrad, 1924; 3rd edition, Leningrad, 1924).
Lesnye byli (Moscow, 1912).
Lesnye byli: Kniga 3 (Moscow, 1913).
L'vinyi khleb (Moscow, 1922).
Mat'-Subbota (Petrograd, 1922).
Mednyi kit (Petrograd, 1919 [actually 1918]).
Mednyi kit: Reprintnoe vosproizvedenie izdaniya 1919 goda (Moscow, 1990).
Mirskye dumy (Petrograd, 1916).
Neuvyadaemyi tsvet (Vytegra, 1920).
Neuvyadaemyi tsvet: Pesennik (Chelyabinsk, 1995; photo-reprint of the 1920, Vytegra, edition).
Nikolai Klyuev: Poems, trans. John Glad (Ann Arbor, Mich., 1977).
"Nikolai Klyuev v poslednie gody zhizni: Pis'ma i dokumenty (Po materialam

semeinogo arkhiva)," ed. with introduction and commentary by Georgii Klychkov and Sergei Subbotin, *Novyi mir* 8 (1988): 165–201.

"Ot poezii 'izbyanogo kosmosa' k pis'mam iz Sibiri (Pis'ma Nikolaya Klyueva k N. F. Khristoforovoi-Sadomovoi iz Tomska)," ed. with introduction and commentary by Aleksandr Mikhailov, *Nash sovremennik* 5 (1992): 141–56.

"Pesn' o Velikoi Materi," *Znamya* 11 (1991): 4–44.

Pesn' o Velikoi Materi: Fragmenty poemy (Moscow, 1991).

Pesn' Solntsenostsa: Zemlya i zhelezo (Berlin, 1920).

Pesnoslov, 2 vols. (Petrograd, 1919).

Pesnoslov, ed. and intro. S. I. Subbotin and I. A. Kostin (Petrozavodsk, 1990).

Pis'ma k Aleksandru Bloku 1907–1915, ed. with commentary by K. Azadovsky (Moscow, 2003).

"Pis'ma N. A. Klyueva k Bloku," ed. with preface and commentary by K. Azadovsky, in *Aleksandr Blok: Novye materialy i issledovaniya, Literaturnoe nasledstvo,* vol. 94, book 4 (Moscow, 1987), 427–523.

"Pis'ma Nikolaya Klyueva raznykh let," ed. S. I. Subbotin, in *Nikolai Klyuev: Issledovaniya i materialy,* ed. S. I. Subbotin (Moscow, 1997), 199–230.

Pogorel'shchina, ed. S. Kunyaev and S. Subbotin, introduction and commentary by N. Tolstoy, *Novyi mir* 7 (1987): 78–100.

Polnoe sobranie sochinenii, ed. B. Filippov, 2 vols. (New York, 1954).

"'Prostite: Ne zabyvaite . . .' N. Klyuev: Pis'ma k N. F. Khristoforovoi-Sadomovoi," ed. and intro. A. I. Mikhailov, *Sever* 9 (1994): 117–31.

"'Sei Avvakum dvadtsatogo stolet'ya . . .': Stikhi Nikolaya Klyueva," ed. with preface by Stanislav Kunyaev, *Sibirskie ogni* 1 (1988): 166–71.

Serdtse edinoroga, ed. V. Garnin, intro. A. Mikhailov (St. Petersburg, 1999).

Slovesnoe drevo, ed. V. Garnin, intro. A. Mikhailov (St. Petersburg, 2003).

"'Snovideniya' Nikolaya Klyueva," ed. with a preface by K. Azadovsky, *Russkaya mysl',* January 18 and January 25, 1991 (nos. 3862 and 3863).

"Sny Nikolaya Klyueva," ed. and intro. Aleksandr Mikhailov, *Novyi zhurnal* 4 (Leningrad, 1991): 3–26.

Sochineniya, ed. G. Struve and B. Filippov, introductory articles by B. Filippov, G. McVay, H. Stammler, and E. Rais, 2 vols. (Munich, 1969).

Solovki, ed. and intro. ("K istorii publikuemogo teksta") Sergei Subbotin, *Novyi mir* 3 (1989): 229–32.

Sosen perezvon (Moscow, 1912 [actually 1911]).

Sosen perezvon, photo-reprint of Aleksandr Blok's copy of the 1911 edition, with Klyuev's dedication, Blok's marginalia, and Gumilev's 1912 review (Moscow, 2002).

Sosen perezvon, 2nd edition (Moscow, 1913).

Sosen perezvon (Letchworth, Eng., 1979).

"Stikhi raznykh let," intro. K. Azadovsky, *Rodnik* 6 (1988): 18–20.

Stikhotvoreniya i poemy, ed. L. K. Shevtsova, intro. V. G. Bazanov, Biblioteka poeta, little series (Leningrad, 1977; reprinted 1982).

Stikhotvoreniya i poemy, ed. Stanislav Kunyaev (Archangel, 1986).
Stikhotvoreniya i poemy, ed. and intro. Stanislav Kunyaev, Biblioteka 20-go veka: Poet i vremya, vol. 14 (Moscow, 1991).
Stikhotvoreniya i poemy, ed. and intro. A. I. Mikhailov (Stavropol', 1992).
Stikhotvoreniya: Poemy, ed. and intro. K. Azadovsky (Moscow, 1991).
"'Ya slavlyu Rossiyu': Iz tvorcheskogo naslediya," ed. and intro. K. Azadovsky, *Literaturnoe obozrenie* 8 (1987): 101–10.

OTHER SOURCES

Afanas'ev, Aleksandr, *Poeticheskie vozzreniya slavyan na prirodu v trekh tomakh,* (Moscow, 1994; photo-reprint of the Moscow, 1868, edition).
Arkhangel'skaya oblast': Putevoditel', Mir vokrug nas, no. 7 (Moscow, 2000).
Armstrong, Edward, *The Folklore of Birds,* 2nd revised edition (New York, 1970).
Azadovsky, Konstantin, "Esenin i Klyuev v 1915 godu (Nachalo znakomstva)," in *Esenin i sovremennost',* ed. M. Bazanov and Y. Prokushev (Moscow, 1975), 233–44.
———, *"Gagar'ya sud'bina" Nikolaya Klyueva,* intro. ("Nikolai Klyuev—tvorets i mifotvorets") and commentary by Konstantin Azadovsky (St. Petersburg, 2004).
———, "Lichnost' i sud'ba Nikolaya Klyueva," *Neva* 12 (1988): 177–89.
———, *Nikolai Klyuev: Put' poeta* (Leningrad, 1990).
———, "O 'narodnom' poete i 'svyatoi Rusi' ('Gagar'ya sud'bina Nikolaya Klyueva)," *Novoe literaturnoe obozrenie* 5 (1993): 88–121.
———, "Olonetskaya derevnya posle pervoi russkoi revolyutsii (Stat'ya N. A. Klyueva 'S rodnogo berega')," *Russkii fol'klor,* vol. 15, Sotsial'nyi protest v narodnoi poezii (Leningrad, 1975), 200–209.
———, "'Plach v roditel'skuyu subbotu' Nikolaya Klyueva," *Russkaya rech'* 6 (1989): 17–24.
———, "'Povest' skorbi' Nikolaya Klyueva," *Iskusstvo Leningrada* 8 (1990): 21–26.
———, "Put' poeta Aleksandra Dobrolyubova," *Uchenye zapiski tartuskogo gosudarstvennogo universiteta,* 459, *Tvorchestvo A. A. Bloka i russkaya kul'tura XX veka, Blokovskii sbornik III* (Tartu, 1979), 121–46.
———, "Rannee tvorchestvo N. A. Klyueva (novye materialy)," *Russkaya literature* 3 (1975): 191–212.
———, review of Nikolai Klyuev, *Serdtse Edinoroga,* in *Novaya russkaya kniga* 1 (2000): 27–29.
———, "Stikhotvoreniya N. A. Klyueva 30-kh godov. Sbornik 'O chem shumyat sedye kedry,'" *Baikal* 3 (1978): 149–53.
———, "Vokrug Klyueva: spornoe i neosporimoe," *Znamya* 9 (1987): 230–32.
———, *Zhizn' Nikolaya Klyueva: Dokumental'noe povestvovanie* (St. Petersburg, 2002).

Bal'mont, K. D., *Stikhotvoreniya,* ed. and intro. V. Orlov, Biblioteka poeta, large series (Leningrad, 1969).

Battles, Jan, and Eamon Lynch, "Joyce Family Bids to Block $1m 'Corrected' *Ulysses,*" *Sunday Times* (London), January 4, 1998.

Bazanov, Valerii, "Poema o drevnem Vyge," *Russkaya literatura* 1 (1979): 77–96.

———, *S rodnogo berega: o poezii Nikolaya Klyueva* (Leningrad, 1990).

———, "Trudnaya biografiya," *Zvezda* 12 (1979): 176–18.

Bogatyreva, Svetlana, "Volya poeta i svoevolie ego vdovy," in *"Otdai menia, Voronezh . . . . ," Tret'i Mezhdunarodnye Mandelstamovskie chteniiya* (Voronezh, 1995), 360–77.

Bogdanova, M. V., et al., eds., *Poeticheskii slovar' Nikolaya Klyueva,* vol. 1, *Chastotnye slovoukazateli,* project director L. G. Yatskevich (Vologda, 2007).

Boym, Svetlana, *Common Places: Mythologies of Everyday Life in Russia* (Cambridge, Mass., and London, 1994).

———, *Death in Quotation Marks: Cultural Myths of the Modern Poet* (Cambridge, Mass., and London, 1991).

Brikhnichev, Iona, "Severnoe siyanie (O Nikolae Alekseeviche Klyueve)," *Rul'* 355 (June 18, 1912): 2.

Brumfield, William Craft, *A History of Russian Architecture* (Cambridge, Eng., 1993), 464.

Bulgakov, Mikhail, *Velikii kantsler: Chernovye redaktsii romana "Master i Margarita,"* ed. with commentary by V. I. Losev (Moscow, 1992).

———, *Velikii kantsler: Knyaz' t'my,* ed. with commentary by V. I. Losev (Moscow, 2000).

Chudakova, Marietta, "Opyt rekonstruktsii teksta M. A. Bulgakova," *Pamyatniki kul'tury: Novye otkrytiya 1977* (Moscow, 1977), 93–106.

———, "Tvorcheskaya istoriya romana M. Bulgakova *Master i Margarita,*" *Voprosy literatury* 1 (1976): 218–53.

Chunosov, M. [pseudonym of Ieronim Yasinskii], "Novye knigi," *Novoe slovo* 9 (1912): 153–54.

Dobrotvorsky, Ivan, *Lyudi bozh'i: Russkaya sekta tak nazyvaemykh dukhovnykh khristian* (Kazan', 1869).

"Documental'nye materialy" (the Tomsk NKVD file), in *Nikolai Klyuev: Obraz mira i sud'ba: Materialy Vserossiiskoi konferentsii "Nikolai Klyuev: Natsional'nyi obraz mira i sud'ba pisatelya,"* ed. A. P. Kazarkin (Tomsk, 2000), 211–23.

Domansky, Valerii, *Narym: Klyuev v Sibiri: Poema i ocherk* (Tomsk, 2003).

Dostoevsky, Fedor, *Sobranie sochinenii v tridtsati tomakh,* ed. V. G. Bazanov, et al. (Leningrad, 1975–90).

Dugin, Pavel, "Nikolai Klyuev, prorok sekretnoi Rossii," radio broadcast, available online (October 2008) at http://www.arctogaia.com/public/fm/finis15.htm.

Eliseev, Nikita, "Krest'yanskii Mayakovsky," *Peterburgskii knizhnyi vestnik Online,* available online (October 2008) at http://bookman.spb.ru/11/Kluev/Kluev.htm.
Engelstein, Laura, *Castration and the Heavenly Kingdom: A Russian Folktale* (Ithaca, N.Y., and London, 1999).
Esenin, Sergei, *Polnoe sobranie sochinenii v semi tomakh,* ed. Yurii Prokushev (Moscow, 1995–2000).
Etkind, Aleksandr, *Khlyst: Sekty, literatura i revolyutsiya,* Novoe literaturnoe obozrenie, nauchnoe prilozhenie, vol. 12 (Moscow, 1998).
Filippov, Boris, "Nikolai Klyuev: Materialy k biografii," in Nikolai Klyuev, *Sochineniya,* 1:5–182 (revised and expanded version of "Nikolai Klyuev: Materialy k biografii," in Nikolai Klyuev, *Polnoe sobranie sochinenii,* 8–114).
———, "*Pogorel'shchina* Nikolaya Klyueva," *Studi in onore di Ettore lo Gatto e Giovanni Maver* (Florence, 1962), 235–42.
Firsov, Vasilii, "'Byt' v trave zelenym, a na kamne serym . . .' (Zametki o zhizni i tvorchestve Nikolaya Klyueva)," *Sever* 11 (2000): 149–60.
———, "Suzhdeniya i fakty (O rannei biografii Nikolaya Klyueva)," *Sever* 5–6 (1996): 147–54.
Fletcher, John, "Forster's Self-Erasure: *Maurice* and the Scene of Masculine Love," in *Sexual Sameness: Textual Differences in Lesbian and Gay Writing,* ed. J. Bristow (London, 1992), 64–90.
Flint, V. E., et al., eds., *Field Guide to Birds of Russia and Adjacent Territories,* trans. Natalia Bourso-Leland (Princeton, N.J., 1991).
Forsh, Ol'ga, *Sumasshedshii korabl': Povest'* (Washington, D.C., 1964).
Freidin, Gregory, "Mandel'shtam's 'Ode to Stalin': History and Myth," *Russian Review* 4 (1982): 400–426.
Garnin, V. P., ed., *Nikolai Klyuev glazami sovremennikov,* seriya Neizvestny dvadtsatyi vek (St. Petersburg, 2005).
Gol'din, Boris, "Narodno-razgovornoe dialektnoe nachalo v poezii N. Klyueva," in *Istoriya i geografiya russkikh statoobryadcheskikh govorov* (Moscow, 1995), 27–36.
Gollerbakh, Erik, *Vstrechi i vpechatleniya* (St. Petersburg, 1998).
Golubeva, O. D., et al., eds., *Russkie sovetskie pisateli: Poety: Biobibliograficheskii ukazatel',* vol. 11 (Moscow, 1988).
Gronsky, Ivan, "O krest'yanskikh pistatelyakh (Vystuplenie v TsGALI 30 sentyabrya 1959 g.)," ed. and intro. M. Niqueux, *Minuvshee: Istoricheskii al'manakh* 8 (1989): 139–74.
Grosheva, E., and V. Rudenko, eds., *N. S. Golovanov: Literaturnoe nasledie: Perepiska: Vospominaniya sovremennikov* (Moscow, 1982).
Gruntov, Aleksandr, "Materialy k biografii N. A. Klyueva," *Russkaya literatura* 1 (1973): 118–25.
Gumilev, Nikolai, *Sobranie sochinenii,* 4 vols. (Washington, D.C., 1968).

Hansen-Löve, Aage, *Allgemeine Häretik, russische Sektierrer und ihre Literarisierung in der Moderne,* Wiener Slawistischer Almanach, supplement 41 (Vienna, 1996).

——— [as Khanzen-Leve, A. A.], "Russkoe sektantstvo i ego otrazhenie v literature russkogo modernizma," in *Russkaya literatura i religiya,* ed. R. Grubel and V. Odinokov (Novosibirsk, 1997), 153–311.

Ivanova, Evgeniya, "Dobrolyubov Aleksandr Mikhailovich," in *Russkie pisateli 1800–1917: Biograficheskii slovar',* chief editor P. A. Nikolaev, vol. 2 (Moscow, 1992), 133–34.

Ivanov-Razumnik (Razumnik Vasil'evich Ivanov), *Pisatel'skie sud'by* (New York, 1951).

Ivnev, Ryurik, "Vospominaniya o N. A. Klyueve," *Baikal* 4 (1984): 132–39.

Kalinina, Lyudmila, "'Gremel moi praded Avvakum,'" *Nizhnii Novgorod* 2 (1997): 207–15.

Karokhin, Lev, *Sergei Esenin i Nikolai Klyuev* (St. Petersburg, 2002).

Kazakov, A. L., ed., *Olonia: Sbornik tvorcheskikh rabot po fol'kloru i kraevedeniyu uchashchikhsya srednei shkoly no 1 g. Vytegry Vologodskoi oblasti* (Vytegra and Chelyabinsk, 1998).

———, ed., *Prionezh'e: Literaturno-kraevedcheskii i etnograficheskii sbornik (Oloniya-2)* (Vytegra and Chelyabinsk, 2002).

Kazarkin, Aleksandr, "Apokaliptika Nikolaya Klyueva (k istolkovaniyu poemy *Pesn' o Velikoi Materi*)," *Vestnik Tomskogo gosudarstvennogo universiteta,* vol. 266, Gumanitarnyi spetsial'nyi vypusk (Tomsk, 1998), available online (October 2008), at http://www.tsu.ru/webdesign/tsu/Library.nsf/designobjects/vestnik267/$file/kluev.html.

———, ed., *Nikolai Klyuev: Obraz mira i sud'ba: Materialy Vserossiiskoi konferentsii "Nikolai Klyuev: Natsional'nyi obraz mira i sud'ba nslediya"* (Tomsk, 2000).

———, "Proza Nikolaya Klyueva: Obosnovanie stilya," *Problemy metoda i zhanra* 19 (Tomsk, 1997): 175–86.

Kazarkin, A., and V. Domansky, eds., *Nikolai Klyuev: Obraz mira i sud'ba,* vol. 2 (Tomsk, 2005).

Khardikov, Yurii, "'Krov' moya svyazuet dve epokhi': Ssylka i gibel' Nikolaya Klyueva," *Nash sovremennik* 12 (1989): 179–89.

Khodasevich, Vladislav, *Nekropol': Vospominaniya* (Paris, 1976).

Khristoforova-Sadomova, Nadezhda, "Vospominaniya o poete Klyueve Nikolae Aleskeeviche," in Nikolai Klyuev, "Ot poezii 'izbyanogo kosmosa' k pis'mam iz Sibiri (Pis'ma Nikolaya Klyueva k N. F. Khristoforovoi-Sadomovoi iz Tomska)," ed. with introduction and commentary by Aleksander Mikhailov, *Nash sovremennik* 5 (1992): 153–56.

Kidd, John, "The Scandal of 'Ulysses,'" *New York Review of Books,* June 30, 1988, 32–39.

Kiseleva, Lyudmila, "Khristianstvo russkoi derevni v poezii Nikolaya Klyueva," *Pravoslavie i kul'tura* 1 (1993): 59–76.

———, "Mif i real'nost' staroobryadchestva v *Pesni o Velikoi Materi* Nikolaya Klyueva," in *Vytegra: Kraevedcheskii al'manakh,* vol. 2, ed. E. A. Skupinova (Vologda, 2000), 210–23.

———, "Poema *Pogorel'shchina* v kontekste obraznogo myshleniya N. A. Klyueva," *Voprosy russkoi literatury,* vol. 57 (L'vov, 1991), 31–42.

———, "Russkaya ikona v tvorchestve Nikolaya Klyueva," *Pravoslavie i kul'tura* 1 (1996): 46–65.

———, "Semanticheskie polya klyuevskoi toponimiki (K postanovke voprosa)," *Vytegorskii vestnik* 1 (Vytegra, 1994): 6–11.

———, "Tsikl 'Izbyanye pesni' N. A. Klyueva v tvorcheskoi biografii Sergeya Esenina: K postanovke voprosa," in *O, Rus', vzmakhni krylami,* vol. 1 of *Eseninskii sbornik,* ed. Y. Prokushev (Moscow, 1994), 95–103.

Knyazev, Vasilii, *Rzhanye apostoly: Klyuev i klyuevshchina* (Petrograd, 1924).

Kravchenko, Boris, "Bolee soroka epitetov k slovu 'Oblako', ili o pol'ze tochnosti," *Voprosy literatury* 5 (1993): 343–46.

Kravchenko, Tat'yana, and Aleksandr Mikhailov, *Nasledie komet: Neizvestnoe o Nikolae Klyueve i Anatolii Yare* (Moscow and Tomsk, 2006).

Kunyaev, Sergei, ed., *Poslednii lel': proza poetov eseninskogo kruga* (Moscow, 1989).

Kunyaev, Stanislav, and Sergei Kunyaev, *Rasterzannye teni* (Moscow, 1995).

Kuzmin, Mikhail, *Osennie ozera: Vtoraya kniga stikhov* (Moscow, 1912).

Lahusen, Thomas, *How Life Writes the Book: Real Socialism and Socialist Realism in Stalin's Russia* (Ithaca, N.Y., and London, 1997).

Lavrov, Alesksandr, "O knige Andreya Belogo 'Stikhotvoreniya' (1923)," in Andrei Bely, *Stikhotvoreniya,* ed. A. V. Lavrov (Moscow, 1988), 531–44.

Likhachev, Dmitrii, Aleksandr Panchenko, and Natal'ya Ponyrko, *Smekh v drevnei Rusi* (Leningrad, 1984).

Limonov, Eduard, *Moya politicheskaya biografiya* (St. Petersburg, 2002).

Literaturnaya entsiklopediya, chief editor A. V. Lunacharsky, 11 vols. (Moscow, 1929–39).

Lo Gatto, Ettore, "Vospominaniya o N. A. Klyueve," *Novyi zhurnal* 35 (1953): 123–29.

Loman, Yurii, "Feodorovskii gorodok," in *Vospominaniya o Sergee Esenine,* ed. Y. L. Prokushev (Moscow, 1965), 161–66.

Makin, Michael [as Maikl Meikin], "Britanskii pervootkryvatel' pozdnego Klyueva," *Nauka i biznes na Murmane: Nauchnoprakticheskii zhurnal,* Dukhovnaya praktika series, 4 (2002): 11–13; first published in in *Krasnoe znamya* (Vytegra), October 18, 2001.

——— [as Maikl Meikin], "Iz Sibiri v kushchi raya: Poslednee stikhotvorenie

Nikolaya Klyueva," in *Literaturnoe nasledie N. Klyueva: Kartina mira i obraz cheloveka*, vol. 2, ed. V. Domansky (Tomsk, 2005), 46–62.

———, *Marina Tsvetaeva: Poetics of Appropriation* (Oxford, 1993).

——— [as Maikl Meikin], "Nikolai Klyuev i Mel'nikov-Pecherskii: Zagadki i predpolozheniya," in *In Memoriam: Eduard Bronislavovich Meksh*, ed. F. Fjodorovs and J. Szokalski (Daugavpils, 2007), 166–82.

——— [as Maikl Meikin], "Nikolai Klyuev i Nil Sorskii," in *XXI Vek na puti k Klyuevu: Materialy Mezhdunarodnoi konferentsii "Olonetskie stranitsy zhizni i tvorchestva: Nikolai Klyuev i problemy etnopoetiki," posvyashchennoi 120-letiyu so dnya rozhdeniya velikogo russkogo poeta Nikolaya Klyueva 21–25 sentyabrya 2004 g.*, ed. E. Markova, Karel'skii Nauchnyi tsentr, Rossiiskaya Akademiya Nauk (Petrozavodsk, 2006), 87–98.

———, "Nikolai Kliuev—Prophet of Loss," *Slavic and East European Journal* 49, no. 4 (2005): 591–611.

——— [as Maikl Meikin], "Nikolai Klyuev v angloyazychnom mire," *Petryaevskie chteniya '01: Tezisy, doklady*, ed. V. N. Kolupaeva and A. L. Rashkovskii (Kirov-na-Vyatke, 2001), 72–80; full version in *Sever* 4–5–6 (2002): 230–35; revised and expanded version on the website Kluevoslov, 2005: http://kluev.org.ua/collegium/m_engl.htm (accessed September 2008).

——— [as Maikl Meikin] "Paradoksy *Kremlya*," in *Narymskaya poema N. Klyueva "Kreml': Interpretatsiya i kontekst*, ed. V. A. Domansky (St. Petersburg, 2008).

———, "Whose Kliuev, Who Is Kliuev? Polemics of Identity and Poetry," *Slavonic and East European Review* 85, no. 2 (2007): 231–70.

Malmstad, John E., "Mixail Kuzmin: A Chronicle of His Life and Times," in M. A. Kuzmin, *Sobranie stikhov*, ed. J. Malmstad and V. Markov, 3 vols. (Munich, 1977), 3:7–319.

Manuilov, Viktor, "Iz 'Zapisok schastlivogo cheloveka,'" in "'Povest' skorbi' Nikolaya Klyueva," by K. Azadovsky, *Iskusstvo Leningrada* 8 (1990): 26–29.

Markova, Elena, *Elementy finno-ugorskoi kul'tury v khudozhestvennoi sisteme Nikolaya Klyueva: Reprint doklada na zasedanii Uchenogo soveta Instituta yazyka, literatury i istorii* (Petrozavodsk, 1991).

———, *Tvorchestvo Nikolaya Klyueva v kontekste severnorusskogo slovesnogo iskusstva* (Petrozavodsk, 1997).

———, ed., *XXI Vek na puti k Klyuevu: Materialy Mezhdunarodnoi konferentsii "Olonetskie stranitsy zhizni i tvorchestva: Nikolai Klyuev i problemy etnopoetiki," posvyashchennoi 120-letiyu so dnya rozhdeniya velikogo russkogo poeta Nikolaya Klyueva 21–25 sentyabrya 2004 g.*, Karel'skii Nauchnyi tsentr, Rossiiskaya Akademiya Nauk (Petrozavodsk, 2006).

McVay, Gordon, "Nikolay Klyuev and Sergey Klychkov: Unpublished Texts," *Oxford Slavonic Papers*, new series, vol. 17 (1984): 90–108.

Meksh, Eduard, "'Nispala polynnaya zvezda' (prorochestvo Nikolaya Klyueva)," in *Nikolai Klyuev: Issledovaniya i materialy,* ed. S. I. Subbotin (Moscow, 1997), 68–77.

———, *Obraz Velikoi Materi (religiozno-mifologicheskie traditsii v epicheskom tvorchestve Nikolaya Klyueva)* (Daugavpils, 1995).

———, "Ot zamysla k voploshcheniyu (tvorcheskaya istoriya sobraniya sochinenii N. A. Klyueva 'Pesnoslov'), in *Traditsii i novatorstvo v sovetskoi literature,* ed. D. Ivlev (Riga, 1986), 65–81.

Mendelson, Edward, "The Two Audens and the Claims of History," in *Representing Modernist Texts: Editing as Interpretation,* ed. George Bornstein (Ann Arbor, Mich., 1991), 157–70.

Mensky, Roman, "N. A. Klyuev (1887–1937)," *Novyi zhurnal* 32 (1953): 149–57.

Mikhailov, Aleksandr, "K biografii N. A. Klyueva poslednego perioda ego zhizni i tvorchestva (Po materialam semeinogo arkhiva B. N. Kravchenko)," in *Ezhegodnik rukopisnogo otdela Pushkinskogo doma za 1990 god* (St. Petersburg, 1993), 160–83.

———, "K istokam poeticheskogo fenomena Nikolaya Klyueva," in *Vytegra: Kraevedcheskii al'manakh,* vol. 1, ed. E. A. Skupinova (Vologda, 1997), 251–77.

———, "Klyuev o Esenine," *Annales instituti philologiae slavicae Universitatis Debreceniensis de Ludovico Kossuth nominatae,* Slavica 27 (1995): 129–47.

———, "Nikolai Klyuev i mir ego poeziya," in Klyuev, *Serdtse edinoroga,* 7–74.

———, "Nikolai Klyuev 'Odinochestvo — strashnoe slovo,'" *Nashe nasledie* 1 (1991): 113–17.

———, "O snovideniyakh v tvorchestve Alekseya Remizova i Nikolaya Klyueva," in *Aleksei Remizov: Issledovaniya i materialy,* ed. A. Gracheva (Saint Petersburg, 1994), 89–103.

———, *Puti razvitiya novokrest'yanskoi* poezii (Leningrad, 1990).

Mitrofanova-Esenina, S. P., S. I. Subbotin, and T. P. Flor-Esenina, eds., *Sergei Esenin v stikhakh i zhizni* (Moscow, 1995).

Morfessi, Yurii, *Zhizn', Lyubov', Stsena: Vospominaniya russkogo bayana* (Paris, 1937).

Mramornov, Oleg, "Eshche odin spisok *Pogerel'shchiny,*" *Novyi mir* 12 (1987): 258–59.

Narbut, Vladimir, "Otzvyvy o knigakh, postupivshikh v redaktsiyu," *Rodnaya strana* 11 (1912): 419.

Nesmith, Chris, "'The Law of an Ancient God' and the Editing of Hemingway's *The Garden of Eden:* The Final Corrected Typescript and Galleys," *Hemingway Review* (Spring 2001): 16–36.

Nezhenets, Nikolai, "Pevets Severnogo kraya," *Russkaya rech'* 1 (1988): 121–31.

Nikitinsky, V., "Slovo k chitatelyu," in *Vytegra: Kraevedcheskii al'manakh,* vol. 1, ed. E. Skupinova (Vologda, 1997), 5–6.

Nikolaev, P. A., chief editor, *Russkie pisateli 1800–1917: Biograficheskii slovar'* (Moscow, 1989–).

Nikonov, Vladimir, *Slovar' russkikh familii* (Moscow, 1993).

Niqueux, Michel, "Le mythe des *xlysty* dans la littérature russe," *Revue des études slaves* 69, nos. 1–2 (1997): 201–22.

Ogden, John Alexander, "Nikolai Kliuev and the Construction of the Literary Peasant," unpublished Ph.D. dissertation (Stanford University, 1996).

Orlitsky, Yurii, "O stikhoslozheni novokrest'yanskikh poetov," in *Nikolai Klyuev: Issledovaniya i materialy,* ed. S. I. Subbotin (Moscow, 1997), 150–62.

Orlitsky, Y., B. Sokolov, and S. Subbotin, eds., "Aleksandr Shiryaevets: Iz perepiski 1912–1917," *De visu* 3 (4) (1993): 5–42.

Orlov, Vladimir, "Nikolai Klyuev," *Literaturnaya Rossiya,* November 25, 1966, 17.

Pankova, Lyudmila, "Zadachi i printsipy opisaniya leksiko-semanticheskoi systemy temporal'noi leksiki v poezii N. A. Klyueva," in *Klyuevskii sbornik,* ed. L. Yatskevich, vol. 1 (Vologda, 1999), 56–57.

Pashko, Oksana,"Obraz gusya v tvorchestve Nikolaya Klyueva (k analizu ornitologicheskogo koda)," in *Klyuevskii sbornik,* ed. L. Yatskevich, vol. 3 (Vologda, 2002), 145–61.

Pavlova, G. E., ed., *M. V. Lomonosov v vospominaniyakh i kharakteristikakh sovremennikov* (Moscow and Leningrad, 1962).

Pereyaslov, Nikolai, *Nerasshifrovannye poslaniya (Zagadki russkoi literatury ot "Slova o polku Igoreve" do nashikh dnei* (Moscow, 2001).

———, "Ot obshchego istoka (Motivy i obrazy 'Slova o polku Igoreve')," *Sever* 8 (1993): 155–60.

Perkhin, Vladmir, "K istorii teksta stikhotvoreniya A.A. Akhmatovoi 'A vy, moi druz'ia, poslednego prizyva!' " *Russkaya literatura* 3 (1999): 184–89.

Pesni russkikh sektantov-mistikov: Sbornik, sostavlennyi T. S. Rozhdestvenskim i M. I . Uspenskim (St. Petersburg, 1912).

Petrov, A. N., et al., eds., *Pamyatniki arkhitektury prigorodov Leningrada* (Leningrad, 1985).

Pfizmaier, August, "Die Gefühlidschtungen der Chlysten," *Denkschriften der kaiserlichen Akademie der Wissenschaften,* Philosophisch-Historische Classe, vol. 35 (Vienna, 1885), 196–288.

Pichurin, Lev, *Poslednie dni Nikolaya Klyueva* (Tomsk, 1995).

Pollack, Nancy, *Mandelstam the Reader* (Baltimore, 1995).

Polyakova, S., "Kolybel'naya v poeme Klyueva 'Pesn' o velikoi materi' [*sic*]," in "Dva etyuda o Klyueve," in *Oleinikov i ob Oleinikove: raboty po russkoi literature* (St. Petersburg, 1997), 323–33.

Ponomareva, Tat'yana, *Proza Nikolaya Klyueva 20-kh godov* (Moscow, 1999).

Prokhorov, Gelian, "Povest' o Nilo-Sorskom skite," *Pamyatniki kul'tury: Novye otkrytiya: Pis'mennost, Iskusstvo, Arkheologiya* (1977), 12–20.

Reutsky, Nikolai, *Lyudi bozh'i i skoptsy: Istoricheskoe issledovanie* (Moscow, 1872).

RGALI, fond 1685, opis' 1, ed. khraneniya 4 (manuscript version of Klyuev's *L'vinyi khleb*).

Richman, Robert, "The 'Collected' Larkin," *New Criterion* 7, no. 8 (1989): 5–14.

Rotikov, K. K. [pseudonym of Yurii Piryutko], *Drugoi Peterburg*, 2nd edition (St. Petersburg, 2001).

Rozanov, Vasilii, *Apokalipsicheskaya sekta (khlysty i skoptsy)* (St. Petersburg, 1914).

Ruder, Cynthia, *Making History for Stalin: The Story of the Belomor Canal* (Gainesville, 1998).

Sakulin, Pavel, "Narodnyi zlatotsvet," *Vestnik Evropy* 5 (1916): 193–208.

Selivanov, F. M., ed., *Stikhi dukhovnye* (Moscow, 1991).

Semenko, Irina, *Poetika pozdnego Mandelstama: Ot chernovykh redaktsii k okonchatel'nomu tekstu* (Rome, 1986).

Semibratov, Vladimir, "Vyatskii krai v poezii N. A. Klyueva," in *Klyuevskii sbornik*, ed. L. Yatskevich, vol. 2 (Vologda, 2000), 125–36.

Serman, Il'ya, *Mikhail Lomonosov: Life and Poetry* (Jerusalem, 1988).

Shenfield, Stephen, *Russian Fascism: Traditions, Tendencies, Movements* (Armonk, N.Y., and London, 2001).

Shentalinsky, Vitalii, *Raby svobody: V literaturnykh arkhivakh KGB* (Moscow, 1995); translated into English as Vitaly Shentalinsky, *Arrested Voices: Resurrecting the Disappeared Writers of the Soviet Regime*, trans. Robert Crowfoot, ed. Robert Conquest (New York, 1996); British edition, *The KGB's Literary Archive* (London, 1996); translated into French as Vitaly Shentalinsky, *La parole ressuscité: Dans les archives littéraires du K.G.B.* (Paris, 1993).

———, "Vestnik Kitezh-grada," preface to Nikolai Klyuev, *Pesn' o Velikoi Materi: Fragmenty poemy* (Moscow, 1991), 5.

Shershneva, Galina, "Tema 'Svyatoi Rusi' v tvorchestve N. Klyueva kontsa 20-nachala 30-kh godov," in *Religiya i tserkov' v kul'turno-istoricheskom razvitii Russkogo Severa (K 450-letiyu Prepodobnogo Trifona, Vyatskogo Chudotvortsa): Materialy Mezhdunarodnoi nauchnoi konferentsii*, vol. 2, ed. V. V. Nizov (Kirov, 1996), 87–90.

Shubnikova-Guseva, N. I., et al., eds., *Sergei Esenin v stikhakh i zhizni: Pis'ma dokumenty* (Moscow, 1995).

Smol'nikov, Sergei, "Metamorfozy krasoty: Zhenskie imena v poezii N. Klyueva," in *Vytegra: Kraevedcheskii al'manakh*, vol. 2, ed. E. A. Skupinova (Vologda, 2000), 224–39.

———, "Mifologema-toponim 'Kitezh' v poeticheskoi sisteme Klyueva," in *Klyuevskii sbornik*, ed. L. Yatskevich, vol. 1 (Vologda, 1999), 88–107.

Smol'nikov, Sergei, and Lyudmila Yatskevich, *Na zolotom poroge nemerknuv-*

shikh vremen: Poetika imen sobstvennikh v proizvedeniyakh N. Klyueva (Vologda, 2006).

Soikin, P., comp., *Pravoslavnye ruskkie obiteli: Polnoe illyustrirovannoe opisanie vsekh pravoslavnykh monastyrei v rossiiskoi imperii i na Afone,* ed. M. Danilushkin (St. Petersburg, 1995; photo-reprint of the 1910, St. Petersburg, edition).

Soinin, E., "Pisateli-staroobryadtsy Vygovskoi pustyni," in *Istoriya literatury Karelii,* vol. 3, ed. Y. Dyuzhev (Petrozavodsk, 2000), 19–25.

Sokolov, Vasilii, "Olonetskii Longfello," available online (September 2008) at http://nk-poety.narod.ru/win/klyuev/m002_klyuev.html.

Solntseva, Natal'ya, *Strannyi eros: Intimnye motivy poezii Nikolaya Klyueva* (Moscow, 2000).

Steinglass, Matt, "International Man of Mystery," *Lingua Franca: The Review of Academic Life* (April 1998): 32–41.

Subbotin, Sergei, "Na putyakh k Nikolayu Klyuevu," *Sever* 5 (1988): 108–13.

———, "Nikolai Klyuev—chitatel' L. Trefoleva i P. Yakubovicha," in *Nikolai Klyuev: Issledovaniya i materialy,* ed. S. Subbotin (Moscow, 1997), 163–82.

———, ed., *Nikolai Klyuev: Issledovaniya i materialy,* Rossiiskaya Akademiya Nauk. Institut Mirovoi Literatury im. A. M. Gor'kogo (Moscow, 1997).

———, "Nikolai Klyuev 1884–1937," in *Den' poezii* (Moscow, 1989), 47.

———, "Poslednyaya prizhiznennaya . . . ," afterword to Nikolai Klyuev, *Izba i pole* (Murmansk, 2003), 86–96.

———, "Proza Nikolaya Klyueva v gazetakh 'Zvezda Vytegry' i 'Trudovoe slovo' (1919–1921 gody): Voprosy stilya i atributsii," *Russkaya literatura* 4 (1984): 136–50.

Tanselle, G. Thomas, "Textual Criticism," *The New Princeton Encyclopedia of Poetry and Poetics,* ed. Alex Preminger and T. V. F. Brogan (Princeton, N.J., 1993), 1273–76.

Tarasenkov, Anatolii, *Russkie poety XX veka 1900–1955 bibliografiya* (Moscow, 1966).

Trofimov, Iosif, "'Smertiyu na smert' nastupi' (Opyt istolkovaniya poemy Nikolaya Klyueva 'Mednyi kit')," *Russkaya poeziya: God 1917,* ed. E. Meksh, I. Trofimov, and F. Fedorov (Daugavpils, 1998), 89–98.

Trotsky, Lev, "Olonetskii poet Nikolai Klyuev," *Karel'skaya kommuna* (Petrozavodsk, October 15, 1922).

Vaganova, I., ed., "Knigoizdatel'stvo K. F. Nekrasova i russkie pisateli nachala veka," *Rossiiskii arkhiv: Istoriya Otechestva v svidetel'stvakh i dokumentakh XVIII–XX vv.* 5 (1994), 468–74.

Vdovin, Vitalii, "Sergei Esenin na voennoi sluzhbe," *Filologicheskie nauki* 1 (1964): 135–50.

Volkov S. [S. Kunyaev], "'Ty, zhguchii otprysk Avvakuma,'" *Nash sovremennik* 1 (1993): 91–98.

Vroon, Ronald, "The Garden in Russian Modernism: Notes on the Problem of Mentalité in the New Peasant Poetry," *Revue des études slaves* 69, nos. 1–2 (1997): 135–50.

———, "The Old Belief and Sectarianism as Cultural Models in the Silver Age," in *Christianity and the Eastern Slavs,* vol. 2, *Russian Culture in Modern Times,* ed. Robert Hughes and Irina Paperno (Berkeley, Los Angeles, and London, 1994), 172–90.

———, "Staroobyradchestvo, sektantstvo i 'sakral'naya rech'' v poezii Nikolaya Klyueva," in *Nikolai Klyuev: Issledovaniya i materialy,* ed. S. I. Subbotin (Moscow, 1997), 54–67 (first published in *Skupiska staroobrzedowcow w Europie, Azji i Ameryce: Ich miesce i tradycje we wspolczesnym swiecie,* ed. Iryda Grek-Pabisowa, Irena Maryniakowa, and Richard Morris [Warsaw, 1994], 237–47).

Weeks, Laura, "'What I Have Written, I Have Written,'" in *The Master and Margarita: A Critical Companion,* ed. Laura Weeks (Evanston, Ill.: Northwestern University Press, 1996), 4–67.

Yatskevich, Lyudmila, ed., *Klyuevskii sbornik,* numbers 1, 2, and 3 (Vologda, 1999–2002).

———, "Poeticheskaya geografiya Nikolaya Klyueva," in *Vytegra: Kraevedcheskii al'manakh,* vol. 2, ed. E. Skupinova (Vologda, 2000), 186.

———, "Poeticheskaya sistema toponimov i etnonimov v tvorchestve N. A. Klyueva,'" in *Klyuevskii sbornik,* ed. L. Yatskevich, vol. 2 (Vologda, 2000), 51–65.

———, "'Sil'ny ne zhelezom . . .' (Otrazhenie natsional'nogo samosoznaniya v poezii N. A. Klyueva)," in *Vologda: Kraevedcheskii al'manakh,* vol. 3, ed. M. A. Beznin (Vologda, 2000), 367–74.

Yatskevich, L. G., S. B. Vinogradova, and S. K. Golovkina, "Materialy k 'Slovaryu imen sobstvennykh v poezii N. A. Klyueva,'" in *Klyuevskii sbornik,* ed. L. Yatskevich, vol. 3 (Vologda, 2002), 9–137.

———, "Slovar' toponimov i etnonimov N. A. Klyueva: Al'favitnyi chastotnyi slovoukazatel'," in *Klyuevskii sbornik,* ed. L. Yatskevich, vol. 2 (Vologda, 2000), 37–46.

Yukhimenko, Elena, "Narodnye osnovy tvorchestva N. A. Klyueva," in *Nikolai Klyuev: Issledovaniya i materialy,* ed. S. I. Subbotin (Moscow, 1997), 5–15.

Zabolotsky, Nikita, *The Life of Zabolotsky,* ed. Robin Milner-Gulland (Cardiff, 1994).

———, *Zhizn' N. A. Zabolotskogo* (Moscow, 1998).

Zakharov, Vladimir, *Problemy izucheniya Dostoevskogo: Uchebnoe posobie po spetskursu* (Petrozavodsk, 1978).

Zapadalov, Igor', "Voskreshenie Kitezh-grada: k biografii N. A. Klyueva," *Sibirskie ogni* 2 (1992): 205–25.

Index of Works by Nikolai Klyuev

Works here are listed by title or first line. (If a work's title and first line are both cited in the text, both are listed, with the first line cross-referenced to the title.) Translations are provided after Russian titles, and translated titles and first lines are cross-referenced to the Russian originals. Klyuev had a tendency to retitle his works repeatedly, to change the first line (only) of poems, and even to use the same title for different works. Where multiple titles or first lines are discussed in the text, all variants are referenced.

Index of Works by Nikolai Klyuev

Index of Works by Nikolai Klyuev

Index of Works by Nikolai Klyuev

Subject Index